Criminal Justice
and the
Treatment of Offenders

AUSTRALIA
The Law Book Company Ltd.
Sydney : Melbourne : Brisbane

CANADA AND U.S.A.
The Carswell Company Ltd.
Toronto

INDIA
N. M. Tripathi Private Ltd.
Bombay

ISRAEL
Steimatzky's Agency Ltd.
Jerusalem : Tel Aviv : Haifa

NEW ZEALAND
Sweet & Maxwell (N.Z.) Ltd.
Wellington

PAKISTAN
Pakistan Law House
Karachi

CRIMINAL JUSTICE AND THE TREATMENT OF OFFENDERS

by

J. D. McCLEAN, B.C.L., M.A.
of Gray's Inn, Barrister-at-Law, of the Faculty of Law, University of Sheffield

and

J. C. WOOD, LL.M.
of Gray's Inn, Barrister-at-Law, of the Faculty of Law, University of Sheffield

LONDON
SWEET & MAXWELL
1969

Published in 1969 by
Sweet & Maxwell Limited of
11 New Fetter Lane London
and printed in Great Britain
by The Eastern Press Limited
of London and Reading

SBN 421 10170 9

PREFACE

It is to be hoped that the aim of this book will be obvious. It is intended as an introduction to the process of criminal trial and the treatment of offenders. Both the authors have met the need for such a book in the course of teaching university students of criminology, as well as magistrates and police. There is a growing number of good books on several aspects of the subject but it was felt that there was room for a general introduction.

Not long ago the study of criminal law, of methods of trial, of the problems of treatment were all neglected at an academic level. This has markedly changed and scholars are turning to the study of criminology from many disciplines. The result is a great increase of research and writing. At the same time the reform of legal and penal institutions is being pressed forward. Many of the methods considered in this book are the subject of current social and political debate—indeed the reader will find it hard to discover a section of which this is not true. A multiplicity of organisations, government bodies and commentators are putting forward their views as to what is wrong and what ought to be done.

Just at the time when the subject is at its liveliest, more and more are turning to its study. It is now commonplace that those concerned in the workings of the system are encouraged to study it critically. Thus, for example, most policemen have the opportunity of attending voluntary courses. The Lord Chancellor is insisting upon training courses for lay magistrates.

It is the coming together of an effervescent subject and a growing number of students that made us feel that an introduction to the subject would prove useful. We have tried to delineate the present system as clearly as possible; we have tried to indicate the areas of controversy and concern. We have been particularly keen to indicate where the reader can pursue further study on such aspects of the area we cover which particularly concern or interest him. In all this we are mindful that our subject is an amalgam of several disciplines. Psychology, sociology and law have each an important contribution to make and we are conscious of the fact that we approach the subject from the last of these disciplines.

We have been helped by reactions of students over a number of years. We are indebted to our colleagues in the Faculty of

Law, University of Sheffield, and in particular to Mr. P. Johnson, who kindly helped with the proofs. We have tried to describe the system as it is on October 1, 1968, but we sadly realise that events will have overtaken several points before the book reaches the hands of the reader.

J. D. McC.
J. C. W.

CONTENTS

Chapter 5

YOUNG OFFENDERS

Chapter 6

SPECIAL GROUPS

Chapter 7

OBSOLETE PENALTIES

Chapter 8

FINANCIAL ASPECTS

Chapter 9

THE FUTURE

TABLE OF CASES

[*NOTE*: *Cases in which the Crown appeared as prosecutor or plaintiff are listed under the name of the defendant.*]

TABLE OF STATUTES

TABLE OF STATUTORY INSTRUMENTS

Chapter 1

CRIME AND THE CRIMINAL COURTS

The Framework of the Criminal Law

The problems of criminology and penology, although in many of their aspects psychological and sociological, are created within the framework provided by the criminal law. It is this body of legal rules, along with the procedural law and the institutional framework, which determine who shall be classed as offenders and thus become the subject of the processes and problems discussed in this book. The shape of the criminal law is then of importance not merely because it mirrors the types of behaviour society feels it should check but also because it predetermines the general types of offender who will emerge.

There are two problems of fundamental importance which require consideration. The first, which is common to every area of law, concerns the determination of the bounds of crime. Although there is a large area of general consensus (few would argue that murder, rape or arson should not be criminal, or adultery or lying should be) there is a wide cleavage of general approach as well as a number of areas of current controversy. The second concerns the mental element of crime. The traditional lawyer's view is that as far as possible only those with guilty minds should be held responsible for their acts. Again this is a doctrine which has attracted considerable theoretical opposition. It has also given rise to an apparently insoluble problem, its application to the great body of regulatory offences which have become within the last hundred years the most notable feature of our criminal law.

Bounds of crime

It has already been noted that this problem exists at two levels. The general approach was given fairly recent prominence in a case concerning a relatively trivial crime. In *Shaw* v. *Director of Public Prosecutions* [1] the appellant published a booklet giving the names and addresses of prostitutes—the *Ladies Directory*. He was charged with conspiracy to corrupt public morals and a legal dispute arose as to whether this was in fact a

[1] [1962] A.C. 220 (H.L.).

crime known to the common law. It was a point of some substance but the attitude of the House of Lords in considering it is of real interest. Viscount Simonds said:

> "In the sphere of criminal law I entertain no doubt that there remains in the courts of law a residual power to enforce the supreme and fundamental purpose of the law, to conserve not only the safety and order but also the moral welfare of the State, and that it is their duty to guard it against attacks which may be the more insidious because they are novel and unprepared for."

Although there was some dissent to this view Shaw's conviction was upheld. Lord Simonds indicates in a later sentence the possible sociological justification for his approach when he says:

> "The law must be related to the changing standards of life, not yielding to every shifting impulse of the popular will but having regard to fundamental assessments of human values and the purposes of society."

The same approach has been given a more ethical justification by Lord Devlin in his lecture on morals and the criminal law.[2]

These views are contrary to the more usual attitude adopted by the courts and strongly upheld by academic comment. The opposite standpoint starts from the basic freedom of the individual and finds any process which threatens this objectionable unless it is the result of clear, unambiguous legal regulation. It follows that judicial lawmaking in modern times cannot be acceptable and even the legislation of Parliament must be subject to careful scrutiny and restrictive interpretation. This attitude has been expressed most forcibly and attractively by Professor Seaborne Davies.[3] A few sentences of quotation will illustrate both his point and the fervour with which it is held. He is speaking of the *Shaw* case and says:

> "What damns their Lordships in this case is the assertion by at least two of them, and the failure of the rest of them to deny (excluding the superb dissent of Lord Reid) that the criminal law is an indefinitely expansible creature of the judges. . . . The penal provisions of the law should be certain and clear, not couched in such vague terms that they constitute a dragnet to catch anyone whom a particular court and jury can be persuaded to envelop in it."

[2] *The Enforcement of Morals*, Lord Devlin, 1965. This is the 1959 Maccabaean Lecture in Jurisprudence printed as Chap. 1.

[3] (1961) 6 J.S.P.T.L. 104.

Apart from this general difference, arguments rage from time to time about the propriety of including or not including certain conduct in the calendar of crime. Most recently the argument has centred around abortion. The general principles and considerations were discussed in the Report of the Committee on Homosexual Offences and Prostitution.[4] That Committee took what many would regard as a liberal line. Its general approach was based on two propositions, one positive, the other negative.

> " In this field, its (the criminal law's) function, as we see it, is to preserve public order and decency, to protect the citizen from what is offensive or injurious, and to provide sufficient safeguards against exploitation and corruption of others, particularly those who are specially vulnerable because they are young, weak in body or mind, inexperienced, or in a state of special physical, official or economic dependence.
>
> " It is not, in our view, the function of the law to intervene in the private lives of citizens, or to seek to enforce any particular pattern of behaviour, further than is necessary to carry out the purposes we have outlined."

It is obvious that the application of principles of this sort depends very much on the intensity of moral and ethical precepts. The puritan could justify under the term public decency rules which would be to a liberal a gross invasion of the private domain. In the result the growth of the criminal law reflects the social dialogue that is continually being held in society between the opposing viewpoints.

Mens rea

It is impossible to understand fully the shape of the criminal law without an understanding of the law's insistence upon a guilty mind. The maxim *actus non facit reus nisi mens sit rea* is regarded by lawyers as a liberal and sophisticated requirement which differentiates between the man who has achieved anti-social consequences through no fault of his own and the man who can be said to be blameworthy. Thus the guilty mind is an essential element of all serious crime [5] and in the area of regulatory offences, where it is not soundly established, there are those who would afford it greater importance.

At its most obvious *mens rea* is the intention to achieve the consequences which are the subject of the criminal charge. The

[4] Cmnd. 247.
[5] Except for criminal libel and public nuisance.

vast majority of crimes which are committed outside the regulatory offences are indeed the result of such intentional conduct and present no difficulty for the intention, if not admitted, will be obvious. Greater difficulty arises where the conduct is not intentional but reckless. This occurs where the consequence which is criminal has been foreseen but the accused cannot be said to have intended it. Rather his attitude has been one of indifference as to whether it occurred or not. It is hard to formulate a satisfactory test to identify reckless conduct but there are a large number of very obvious cases where the accused has plainly anticipated the harm and proceeded regardless of its likely occurrence. This most often arises in relation to offences against the person where the accused has selfishly disregarded the possible personal injury to others by his actions. In strict theory the third state of mind, that of negligence, should not be classified as *mens rea* for it involves an unawareness of the possibility of forbidden consequences of conduct. Some academic commentators have attempted to maintain this classification but only by a somewhat unnatural extension of recklessness to cover "knew or *ought to have known*." Such implied recklessness cannot be a satisfactory basis for classification. The alternative, which is more usually adopted, is to accept that certain instances of negligent mental states accompanying criminal conduct will be sufficient to constitute *mens rea*. These instances are usually called gross or culpable or criminal negligence.

It is from these general rules that the criminal law proceeds to evaluate individual cases. It would be wrong to pretend that the task is always easy in a crime such as manslaughter, which may vary on its facts from a simple act causing death—such as pulling a ladder away from a man, to a quite obviously criminal act such as throwing a brick from a tall building into a busy street. Despite this the common law has been firm on its insistence on *mens rea*. We must examine criticisms of this attitude in a moment.

Mens rea in statutory offences

The movement from a criminal law consisting of a few relatively serious crimes to a very large body of regulatory offences far outweighing the traditional body of crime has led to a serious inability to achieve a consistent policy with regard to *mens rea*. Regulatory offences are the creation of modern statutes and the judicial handling of these new offences is exceeded in complexity only by the vagaries of the parliamentary draftsmen who have used a multiplicity of forms.

The problem to be faced is easily illustrated. A man is trying very hard to avoid breaking the speed limit but due to a faulty speedometer he still breaks the limit. He is in no way to blame for the speedometer's failure nor is he aware of it. Is he to be acquitted for lack of guilty mind, or convicted for doing a forbidden act?

English judicial tradition is largely against general speculation and the judge normally turns his attention to the source of the crime—the statutory provision. In some cases he will find clear direction as to the need or otherwise for *mens rea* as a constituent part of the crime. More usually the statute will merely provide punishment for certain conduct:

> " It shall not be lawful for a person to drive a motor vehicle on a restricted road at a speed exceeding thirty miles per hour " [6]

The courts are left to decide the *mens rea* question and in general they have adopted two lines of approach. It is possible to rely upon the rule of statutory interpretation that a statute is to be taken as being in conformity with existing law if the reverse is not clearly laid down. This approach can also be justified by the rule that criminal statutes must be construed strictly in favour of the accused.

The illustration chosen, speeding, is an example of the other, more generally used approach. The judge concentrates upon the fact that Parliament is seeking to outlaw certain conduct, the accused has committed it and no more is required. It is possible to rationalise this approach by various, somewhat suspect, arguments. It is sometimes said that the existence of the need for proof of *mens rea* would seriously complicate the prosecution's task. More persuasively it is argued that the consequences of conviction are so trivial as to make the somewhat harsh rule justifiable. Some even urge that to include *mens rea* as an element of crimes of this sort would be to encourage defended cases.

The resulting law after many decades of crimes of this regulatory sort is a jungle in which academic review flourishes. It is impossible to isolate general rules or even major trends and the careful lawyer must advise study of the individual crime as of individual character. Indeed the key to the attitudes of the courts is probably to be found in the personality of individual judges and the general atmosphere of the time rather than in any strictly legal factors or canons of statutory interpretation.

6 Road Traffic Act 1960, s. 19 (1). This provision has recently been replaced by the similarly worded Road Traffic Regulation Act 1967, s. 71.

Three strands appear to be entwined here. The common law training of lawyers with emphasis on *mens rea* establishes a background of blameworthiness; the sociological approach seems to emphasise the necessary regulation of the complexity of everyday modern life and, if it considers the effect of conviction for this type of offence, tends to minimise it. Finally there is a considerable element of expediency—only without *mens rea* can the vast bulk of offences be quickly dealt with. The problem has been interestingly considered by Baroness Wootton who seems ready to see an extension of the strict, no *mens rea*, basis of liability. She attacks the ethical concern of the traditional legal approach with its central idea of blameworthiness.

Whereas several legal commentators attempt to make order out of the present chaos—Lord Devlin leads here—by distinguishing between real crime where *mens rea* is important, usually called *mala in se*, and regulatory offences where it is not, called *mala prohibita*, Baroness Wootton has attacked this basic idea:

> " If the law says that certain things are not to be done, it is illogical to confine this prohibition to occasions on which they are done from malice aforethought; for at least the material consequences of an action, and the reasons for prohibiting it, are the same whether it is the result of sinister malicious plotting, of negligence or of sheer accident."

Although her arguments mis-state the notion of *mens rea* they indicate most clearly that an approach based on social disturbance is a sensible alternative to one based primarily upon ethical considerations. It is easy to illustrate the uncertainty of ethical standards as a basis of an important legal distinction and the failure of the law to evolve a satisfactory and consistent pattern on this itself shows weakness.

The approach based on social disturbance has itself two major weaknesses. It is hard to see a rational basis for determining which conduct is to be followed by criminal review. It is plain, as Baroness Wootton recognises, that many purely civil wrongs cause a great deal of social upheaval—the so-called matrimonial offences are a good example. The great difference at present between criminal and civil matters is the theoretical inevitability of legal process following upon crime as opposed to the permissive right of a person injured bringing a civil action. To move all serious social disturbance into the criminal area would increase alarmingly, and often unnecessarily, the work of the courts.

The second problem of a social approach is easier to state

than to prove. It cannot, however, be doubted that everyone has his own conception of the bounds of "real crime." The fact that the exact boundary is far from clear does not destroy the basic idea of crime on the one hand and offence on the other.

Finally in this brief discussion of what is a most complicated disagreement it must be emphasised that personal responsibility plays an important part in a man's assessment of his own guilt. This is never illustrated more clearly than in the common crime of careless driving which has developed so that it is the result achieved which brings responsibility, not the manner of achieving it. Thus a fairly competent driver, doing his best in a particularly awkward situation, may still be driving carelessly. He will rarely *feel* that his conviction is justified. The law at present goes quite a long way to recognise this in insisting that the conduct must be voluntary. In this way it excuses from responsibility the man whose action flows from illness, involuntary conduct of various types,[7] sleep, insanity and so on and there is a similar permissive attitude to children on the ground that they have not reached the years of responsibility.

Responsibility and punishment

These matters have been considered at some length because they have a direct bearing upon the approach to punishment—indeed it can be argued that the basic idea of responsibility is present whichever approach is adopted. In the *mens rea* approach it has to be established to secure a conviction. Once this conviction is secured the person convicted is in one sense deserving of punishment. The court can then go on to assess the appropriate type of punishment. Where the offence is a strict one and can be established irrespective of the state of mind of the accused then before punishment can be fairly considered the mental state of the offender at the time he committed the crime should be investigated. Thus the careless driver mentioned in the last section has a strong claim, because of his lack of *mens rea*, for a different scale of punishment to the man whose driving was more representative of the effort he was putting into it.

It is unfortunate in practice that these matters, raised on conviction for regulatory offences, tend to receive less attention than they should. The present trend indeed is towards bringing sentences closer into line. This accentuates the harshness of treating offenders who have committed the same crime as automatically qualified for the same sort of punishment. In practice

[7] The leading case is *Hill* v. *Baxter* [1958] 1 Q.B. 277.

it would appear to lead to the under-use by the lower courts of "lenient" sentences, particularly the discharge. The difference in level of consideration of the personal factors surrounding the commission of the crime in say a driving offence and larceny or a moderately serious offence of violence is quite remarkable. The trouble probably springs from the routine nature of much regulatory crime seen through the eyes of a court. The tendency is to spend too little time considering the individual position of the particular offender in relation to the offence.

The Legal System

Introduction

It is a matter of speculation as to how far the organisation of the legal system affects sentencing. It cannot, however, be denied that it has considerable influence. The law itself lays down maximum penalties, both in relation to offences and in relation to the powers of particular courts. These maxima are limits within which the courts must work and they may at times fetter the court and prevent it dealing with an offender as it wishes. There is little rationality in such maxima.[8] The Criminal Justice Act 1967 has, at least temporarily, improved the position of maximum fines by laying down a new set of amounts aimed at curing the erosion brought on by inflation.[9] On the other hand, the same statute has itself considerably decreased the powers of courts to deal as they wish with offenders by its provision for mandatory suspension of certain short sentences of imprisonment.[10]

In the same way the details of the legal process will often affect the powers of a court. Certain facts may have to be proved, or inquiries made before the court can proceed to a certain course of action. The date from which sentences run, their relation to each other and the effect of appeals are examples of matters which have an indirect bearing upon sentencing. Many of these rules are of necessity detailed and complex; they are very much lawyers' law. Nonetheless they are of great importance.

There are in addition many imponderable factors which arise from the shape of the legal process. The composition of the court is plainly of paramount importance but a full study of matters of this sort lies within the field of sociology. In the same way the differing effects upon sentencing of pleas of guilty and

[8] Those relating to imprisonment were the subject of a study by a committee of "Justice." See [1959] Crim.L.R. 393.

[9] Sched. 3.

[10] s. 39 (3). This provision was strongly opposed by the Magistrates' Association.

not guilty are frequently in the minds of those accused. There is no doubt that a sympathetic summary of a case by a prosecutor can give an entirely different impression from the testimony in a lengthy trial but this cannot be evaluated without lengthy and expert observation and analysis.

The purpose of this introductory sketch of the legal system is to provide a background against which the problems of sentencing will be tackled. Detailed rules which have a bearing upon powers of sentencing will be considered and a more general indication given of other factors which may, more arguably and uncertainly, have a bearing upon the choice of sentence.

Criminal Courts

There are fundamentally three courts where an offender may be sentenced—courts of summary jurisdiction, quarter sessions and assizes. Each of these will be considered in this section. Each has its variants and other courts and tribunals have powers of punishment which can be ignored for the purposes of this book. The hierarchy of the criminal courts, including the provisions for appeals, is set out on the following page.

There is ample scope for confusion and certain basic complexities arise when the jurisdiction and functions of the courts are considered. Terminology must carry some share of the blame but the real culprit is the steady shift of emphasis towards the summary method of trial.[11] The higher courts, quarter sessions and assizes, provide the venue for trial by jury, the method which is invariably used for the most serious offences. It is also the method available for all crimes which are designated as indictable—a word which indicates that trial must be on indictment before judge and jury. There are also a large number of offences, called summary offences, which cannot be tried by jury. The appropriate court for dealing with these offences is the magistrates' court sitting as a trial court with the magistrates performing a rather subtle function as judges of both law and fact.[12]

There are, however, a large number of offences which do not fall neatly into either of these two heads. Some offences are given dual personality by the statute creating them.[13] They can be proceeded with under either method of trial. In addition there is a growing tendency for provision that indictable offences

11 For a brief discussion of the method of trial, see *infra* p. 42.

12 The court of summary jurisdiction. The term "magistrates' court" is often used but summary trial is only one function of the magistrates' court. It is a term much to be preferred to the once popular "police court."

13 *e.g.*, dangerous driving—Road Traffic Act 1960, s. 2.

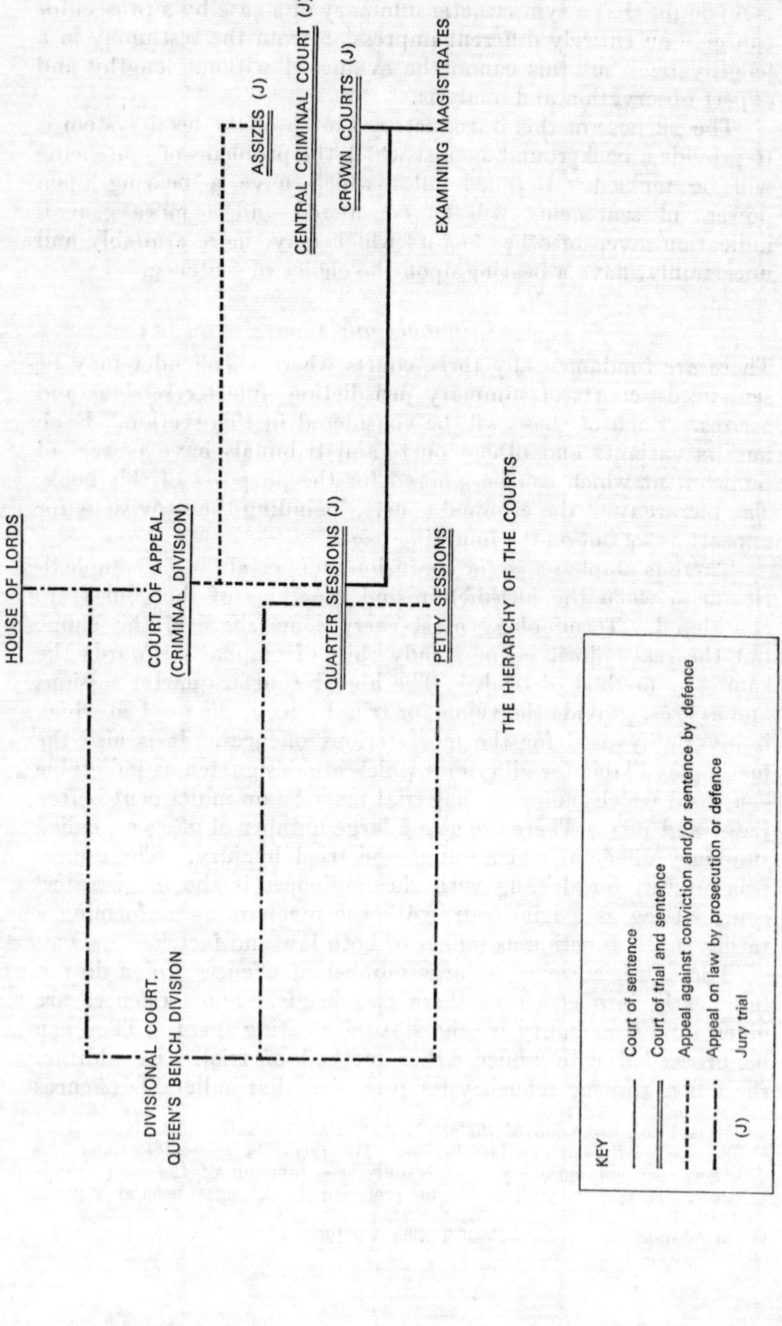

THE HIERARCHY OF THE COURTS

can be dealt with summarily.[14] Indeed most pressures point in this direction. Summary trial is cheaper, it usually saves the accused a considerable period of waiting time and it has a less serious atmosphere for the offender who wishes to expiate his guilt as painlessly as possible. The statistics show the position clearly:

Indictable offences—Findings of Guilt

Magistrates' courts	1938	69,851
	1965	207,823
	1966	220,870
	1967	230,664
Higher courts	1938	6,367
	1965	26,864
	1966	28,838
	1967	30,265

The organisation of the courts of criminal trial is at present under review. A Royal Commission has been set up to consider courts of assize and quarter sessions under Lord Beeching.[15] It is expected to report late in 1968 and will in all probability be followed by a review of magistrates' courts. The area has been recently considered as a result of the concern felt at the time spent awaiting trial. An Interdepartmental Committee on the Business of the Criminal Courts was formed under the chairmanship of Mr. Justice Streatfeild. The Committee's Report is an excellent source of information. It has some particularly interesting figures illustrating the growth in the weight of work undertaken by the courts.[16]

Court	*Persons for trial*		*Cases for trial*	
	1938	1959	1938	1959
Assizes	1,992	3,919	1,615	3,005
Quarter sessions	6,222	21,494	4,336	14,694
Crown Courts *	690	2,599	482	1,790

* the Crown Courts figures for 1938 are for cases at Liverpool and Manchester sessions and assizes. The Crown Court jurisdiction is slightly wider.

There is then a double standard of importance. The magistrates' courts and summary trial account for a large majority of criminal cases: the higher courts deal with the more serious crimes and so have more extensive powers of punishment. Each of these courts will be considered, followed by a consideration of the system of appeals.

14 The basic list is in the Magistrates' Courts Act 1952, Sched. 1. The Criminal Justice Administration Act 1962 added many important crimes including the breaking offences other than housebreaking.

15 Set up on December 7, 1966.

16 Cmnd. 1289, Table 6.

Petty sessions

A. Courts of summary jurisdiction

Composition. A court of summary jurisdiction is composed of justices of the peace, a stipendiary magistrate or a metropolitan magistrate. This is not the place to discuss the merits of the use of laymen as magistrates or the sparse use that is made of the power to appoint stipendiaries.[17] The present legal position is regulated largely by the Justices of the Peace Act 1949.

The rules of more immediate concern to this work are to be found in the Magistrates' Courts Act 1952. It is here provided that a magistrates' court must not try an information summarily [18] unless there are at least two justices sitting.[19] Stipendiary and metropolitan magistrates are not only paid, for the purpose of this provision they equal two magistrates.[20]

There are certain statutory powers enabling one magistrate to try particular offences. These include simple drunkenness,[21] offences relating to poaching,[22] and offences under the vagrancy laws.[23] Sittings of this sort are very exceptional and this point is underlined by the very restricted powers of the single magistrate. He may not impose a term of imprisonment of more than fourteen days, nor a monetary payment [24] of more than twenty shillings.[25] These are all relics from the last century and there seems little practical reason for continuing these exceptional powers.

Perhaps the most important exceptional rule on composition is that which allows the bench which sentences an offender to be different from that which convicted him. Where there is an adjournment after conviction, and this is by no means unusual, it may be difficult to reassemble the same bench. It is provided that the bench that sentences need not be composed of the same justices.[26] Where there is a difference the necessary facts and circumstances must be given so that the newcomers are fully

[17] In *The Law List*, 1967, there appear only 14 stipendiary magistrates in England and Wales (there were even two of these posts vacant). There are 36 metropolitan magistrates listed.
[18] It must be emphasised here that this rule does not apply to committal proceedings.
[19] Magistrates' Courts Act 1952, s. 98 (1).
[20] *Ibid.* s. 121.
[21] Licensing Act 1872, s. 12.
[22] Larceny Act 1861, *e.g.*, s. 17, killing rabbits in a warren. The rump of this Act, left behind in the 1916 revision, is a strange anomaly. The entire 1861 Act has been repealed by the Theft Act 1968.
[23] Vagrancy Act 1824, s. 3, "idle and disorderly persons" and s. 4, "rogues and vagabonds."
[24] Of all forms—fines, compensation or costs.
[25] Magistrates' Courts Act 1952, s. 98 (5).
[26] Magistrates' Courts Act 1952, s. 98 (7).

acquainted with the position. This subsection is a welcome recognition of organisational difficulties which can occur. It says nothing to indicate that changes in benches should be avoided wherever possible, but common sense would indicate this. Apart from this provision it is essential that justices should be present during the whole of the proceedings in which they are acting as the court. A magistrate may retire from a case provided that two magistrates are left to continue the case.[27]

It is of the greatest importance to recognise that the magistrates who comprise the court are the sole judges of all issues, whether of guilt or subsequently of punishment. The reports contain some salutary examples of instances where this fundamental precept has been broken. It is appropriate here to mention the position and function of the clerk of the court. The statutes regulate the appointment of clerks which must now be made from the ranks of the legal profession,[28] they regulate the administrative duties and responsibilities of the clerk but they say little about his position and function during the course of trial and sentencing. It would be unrealistic not to admit that magistrates' courts take a considerable part of their individual characters from the attitude and personality of their clerk. This is inevitable and in no way improper for the most important of the clerk's functions is to supervise the conduct of the proceedings and to ensure that the myriad of legal and evidential rules are obeyed. He is also there to advise the magistrates on the law, and again this phrase, interpreted liberally, includes maximum sentences appropriate to the offences in question, if not usual sentences.

In 1952–53 there was a spate of three cases which led to consideration of some of the problems involved. In the first [29] the clerk came from the magistrates' room to which he had retired, obtained a piece of paper—it subsequently transpired that it contained details of the accused's record [30]—from the police and returned. In the second,[31] the clerk spent virtually the whole period of the retirement with the magistrates and at one stage sent for a shorthand writer who had been in court so

27 *Ibid.* s. 98 (6).

28 The qualification is that of barrister or solicitor of at least five years' standing. There were savings for those already embarked on the career without such qualifications. A weakness of the provisions is that they only apply to *the* clerk. His deputies need not be qualified. While several courts sit regularly only one may have the services of a qualified clerk.

29 *R.* v. *East Kerrier Justices, ex p. Mundy* [1952] 2 Q.B. 719.

30 For a discussion of the inter-related point of the use of an accused person's record see *infra*, at p. 46.

31 *R.* v. *Welshpool Justices, ex p. Holley* [1953] 2 Q.B. 403.

that the magistrates' impression of part of the evidence could be confirmed.[32] In the third,[33] the point was merely that the clerk had retired immediately with the magistrates. These cases led to the Lord Chief Justice issuing a Practice Direction in November 1953. This can be usefully set out almost in full:

> " There are two questions which arise in this connection. The first is: On what matters may magistrates consult their clerk? The second, and one of equal importance, is: In what manner should they consult him?
>
> On the first question, it is clear that they may seek his advice on questions of law, or of mixed law and fact, and also on questions regarding the practice and procedure of the court. The latter are, indeed, questions of law. There are other matters on which justices may require the assistance of their clerk and on which they are entitled to ask his advice. They may, for instance, ask him for information of the sentences which have been imposed by their bench, or by neighbouring benches, in respect of similar offences to that which they are trying. It is, indeed, most desirable that penalties for such matters as obstruction . . . should have some degree of uniformity. Moreover, it would be proper for the clerk himself to call the justices' attention to the fact that a question of law does, or may, arise if they do not appear to be already aware of it. It would then be for them to consider whether they wanted his further advice on that question. In no circumstances, however, may justices consult their clerk as to the guilt or innocence of the accused, so far as it is simply a question of fact, but, if a question arises as to the construction of a statute or regulation, they may consult him on whether the facts found by them constitute an offence, because that would be a question of mixed law and fact. They may also properly ask the clerk to refresh their memory as to any matter of evidence which has been given. They can take with them, or send for, any note the clerk may have taken, and if there is anything in the note which needs elucidation, or if they think something has been omitted or wrongly taken down, it would be perfectly proper for them to consult him. They must not ask his opinion as to the sentence which they ought to impose, but they may, as I have said, ask for information as

[32] This use of the shorthand writer was approved but it was said that it would have been better to ask for the note to have been read back in open court.

[33] *R.* v. *Barry (Glamorgan) Justices, ex p. Nagi Kashim* [1953] 1 W.L.R. 1320.

to the sentences imposed for comparable offences, and they most certainly may consult him on what penalties the law allows in any particular case if they already do not know it, and on any consequential matters that may follow on conviction. . . .

As regards the manner in which justices may consult their clerk, the court, I think, made it clear in the *East Kerrier* case that the decision of the court must be the decision of the justices, and not that of the justices and their clerk, and that, if the clerk retires with the justices as a matter of course, it is inevitable that the impression will be given that he may influence the justices as to the decision, or sentence, or both. A clerk should not retire with his justices as a matter of course, nor should they attempt to get round the decisions to which I have referred merely by asking him in every case to retire with them, or by pretending that they require his advice on a point of law. Subject to this, it is in the discretion of the justices to ask their clerk to retire with them if, in any particular case, it has become clear that they will need his advice. If, in the course of their deliberations, they find that they need him, they can send for him. On this matter I would stress one further point, and that is, that if the clerk does retire with the justices, or is sent for by them, he should return to his place in court as soon as he is released by the justices, leaving them to complete their deliberations in his absence and come back into court in their turn. I wish to add that the rulings this court has given on the subject derive from, and are really part of, the rule so often emphasised that justice must not only be done but must manifestly appear to be done, and, if justices bear that in mind, I feel sure they will have no difficulty in loyally following the decisions of this court." [34]

The Probate, Divorce and Admiralty Divisional Court approved these rules in relation to matrimonial cases in the magistrates' courts.[35] Cases are still occasionally reported of transgression. For instance in *R.* v. *Stafford Justices, ex p. Ross* [36] the clerk handed a note to the magistrates which sought to influence them on the facts of the case. On appeal conviction

[34] [1953] 2 All E.R. 1306.
[35] Practice Direction [1954] 1 All E.R. 230. For a recent case in this area raising these problems see *Hudson* v. *Hudson* [1965] 1 W.L.R. 567.
[36] [1962] 1 W.L.R. 456; and see *R.* v. *Consett JJ., ex p. Postal Bingo* [1967] 2 Q.B. 9.

was quashed and it was again emphasised that the magistrates should have had nothing to do with the note once they realised it related to a matter of fact.

The relationship between bench and clerk is a fairly delicately poised matter. Other transgressions that have been reported are more clearly wrong and need only be instanced. In one case the magistrates interviewed a police superintendent in their private room,[37] and in another they did likewise with a witness as to the accused person's character.[38] Both convictions were not allowed to stand on appeal.

Place. To prevent hole-in-the-corner justice which nowadays seems a remote possibility it is provided that the court must sit in a petty sessional court house or in an occasional court house.[39] Any other venue is illegal and the powers of the court are cut to that of a single magistrate where it is sitting in an occasional court house—that is to say to a maximum of fourteen days' imprisonment or a monetary payment of twenty shillings.

Jurisdiction. It will suffice for the purposes of this book to say that a court of summary jurisdiction has now jurisdiction over crimes committed in its own or any other area.[40] Of far greater importance is a consideration of the types of crime which can be dealt with summarily. The first distinction is easy to formulate but it is unfortunately only a beginning of a very complicated pattern. There is a basic distinction into summary and indictable offences. The Magistrates' Courts Act 1952 offers a definition of a summary offence, unbeatable in its unhelpfulness:

> " an offence which, if committed by an adult, is triable by a magistrates' court (whether or not it is also triable on indictment). . . ." [41]

There is a parallel definition of an indictable offence which merely begs the converse question. The truth of the matter is that no general definition is possible because each offence must be considered separately. When this is done there will be seen to be three groups of offences. Those triable only on indictment. Here is to be found each of the serious common law crimes such as

37 *R.* v. *Bucks Justices* (1922) 86 J.P.N. 636.

38 *R.* v. *Bodmin Justices, ex p. McEwen* [1947] K.B. 321.

39 Magistrates' Courts Act 1952, ss. 98 (3) and 123. There is no restriction on other uses the court house may be put to and there are many interesting variants on the court house/chapel, court house/dance hall theme.

40 Criminal Justice Act 1967, s. 28. It is not always easy to determine where a crime was committed, *e.g.*, blackmail, and there are problems of crimes committed on national boundaries, on journeys and at sea. Magistrates' Courts Act 1952, s. 3, deals with some of these problems.

41 Magistrates' Courts Act 1952, s. 125.

murder and manslaughter. At the opposite end of the scale are offences only triable summarily and here is to be found any offence of a trivial nature such as obstruction, no lights and so on. In between are a substantial number of offences which may be dealt with in either way. Finally there is a right vested in an offender in certain circumstances to claim trial on indictment.

(i) *Indictable offences.* The court of summary jurisdiction has, of course, no jurisdiction over purely indictable offences. It should be mentioned, however, in passing that the same magistrates who sit as a court of summary jurisdiction will see the indictable offences at the committal stage. They will, in exercising their power not to commit, have some influence on the type and number of cases going forward and their decisions on questions such as remand, bail and legal aid will have considerable effect on the accused.

(ii) *Summary offences.* The power to try summary offences is to be found in the Magistrates' Courts Act 1952, s. 13, and the procedure to be followed at trial in the Magistrates' Courts Rules 1952, as amended, notably by the 1967 Rules.

(iii) *Offences triable on indictment or summarily.*[42] Where an offence is hybrid the assumption is that it will be tried on indictment when the accused person is fourteen years old or over. It is open, however, to the prosecutor to ask that the court try the matter summarily. The court must then decide whether or not to accede to this request. The application must be made at the outset, before evidence has been called. It will not be fatal to the case if the prosecutor has forgotten to ask the formal question. In *James* v. *Bowkett*[43] the accused had elected for summary trial, he could have asked for trial on indictment under the rules to be discussed shortly, and the prosecutor proceeded without asking for summary trial. On appeal the divisional court made it quite clear that a request could be inferred from the manner in which he had proceeded. It was felt, however, that the clerk should ask in each appropriate case so that the position is made clear at the outset.

There is built into the procedure here the power of the court, whichever way it has begun to proceed, to change its procedure to the other method. Thus where an offender is being committed for trial by examining magistrates, they may, having regard to

[42] Magistrates' Courts Act 1952, s. 18.

[43] [1952] 2 All E.R. 320—a case of drunken driving, then under s. 15 (1) of the Road Traffic Act 1930. There is a similar later case reported: *Ex p. Rigby* [1958] 1 W.L.R. 843—taking and driving away, then under s. 28 of the Road Traffic Act 1930.

the views of both the prosecutor and the accused and to the nature of the case, decide to proceed with it summarily.[44] In the same way the court, hearing a matter as summary trial, may at any time before the conclusion of the prosecution evidence proceed as examining justices with a view to possible committal for trial.[45] The theoretical reasons for these rules are obvious. Cases often turn out to be not what they were at first sight. In particular their seriousness may, when evidence has been heard, be considerably increased or diminished. If this occurs the course decided upon may subsequently appear inappropriate and the power to revert to the alternative form is then useful. Unfortunately in practice this rarely occurs and the different usual composition of the court—three magistrates for summary trial, one for committal proceedings, and the paraphernalia usual for committal—a shorthand writer or typist may be in part to blame for this. It may also be that the prosecution is rarely very far wrong in its assessment of the type of case it has to present.

(iv) *Indictable offences triable summarily.* There can be no doubt that this head of hybrid offence is of greatest practical importance. The rules, on the grounds of convenience, allow the quicker and simpler summary method of trial on the application of the prosecution. The rules for those above and below seventeen differ.[46]

A very large number of indictable offences are each year tried summarily.[47] They comprise offences contained in a list in the First Schedule to the Magistrates' Courts Act 1952. It would be inappropriate to reproduce the list of offences here but some idea of its scope can perhaps be given by consideration of recent extensions secured by the Criminal Justice Administration Act 1962.[48] This statute added concealing the birth of a child,[49] uttering forged documents [50] with a monetary value ceiling of £100—sacrilege,[51] housebreaking [52]—but not where the premises are a dwelling-house [53]—and various night offences such as being

44 Magistrates' Courts Act 1952, s. 18 (3).
45 *Ibid.* s. 18 (5).
46 For those between 14 and 17 see *infra.*
47 See Tables, *supra*, p. 11.
48 s. 12 and Sched. 2.
49 Offences against the Person Act 1861, s. 60. Also abandoning or exposing a child, *ibid.* s. 27.
50 Forgery Act 1911, s. 6.
51 Larceny Act 1916, s. 24 with technical limitations. This Act is to be replaced in 1969 by the Theft Act 1968.
52 *Ibid.* ss. 26, 27. Housebreaking, rather inappropriately, is the permissible generic term for offences under these sections which include warehouse-breaking, shopbreaking, officebreaking and so on. See n. 51, above.
53 The term " dwelling-house " is well delineated in case-law.

found with housebreaking instruments.[54] The limitation on the inclusion of housebreaking is a good illustration of the rationale. It was felt that a large amount of the work of quarter sessions relating to breaking offences could be properly transferred to the summary court. On the other hand the implications of breaking into a dwelling-house are quite far-reaching, for this type of crime, it is well known, causes a great deal of fear and worry to householders who have been victims. It cannot be denied that the atmosphere of the summary court often lacks a sense of gravity—a factor increased by the large number of respectable and respected people who find themselves there on motoring summonses. When this type of consideration was balanced against the speed, convenience and economy of summary trial the line was drawn so as to maintain dwelling-house breaking as an indictable offence. There are aspects relating to the selection of punishment which arise here. If the magistrates feel their power inadequate they can, as we shall see,[55] commit for sentence to quarter sessions. But this will split the proceedings into two very distinct parts with certain disadvantages, a point to which it will be worth while returning when commitals for sentence are considered.

The power to try indictable offences summarily is subject to agreement by the accused.[56] The Act is very specific about this point.[57] It lays down that the charge against the accused must be written down, if this has not already been done, it must be read to him and he must be told that he has the option of being tried summarily if he consents, or of being tried by a jury. If the court thinks it necessary, it must explain what is meant so that he clearly understands the choice before him. At the same time, if the offence is triable at quarter sessions the accused must be told of the magistrates' power of committing him to that court for sentence if they feel on hearing his character and antecedents that their own powers are too limited.[58]

The ease and advantages of this procedure of summary trial of indictable offences have led to the practice of reducing charges against an accused so as to allow summary trial. Both parties, prosecution and accused, might desire summary trial but appellate courts have disapproved, most strongly, this practice. This point arose in *R.* v. *Bodmin Justices, ex p. McEwen* [59] where a barrack room fight led to a charge of wounding with intent to do

[54] The others are found by night, armed or with intent to commit a felony.
[55] *Infra*, p. 27.
[56] Magistrates' Courts Act 1952, s. 19.
[57] *Ibid.* s. 19 (3).
[58] *Ibid.* s. 19 (4).
[59] [1947] K.B. 321.

grievous bodily harm. The soldier who had been wounded was, in fact, not expected to recover but did so. The magistrates allowed the charge, over which they had no jurisdiction, to be reduced to unlawful wounding, over which they had.[60] In the King's Bench Divisional Court Lord Goddard C.J. said:

> "Here is a case in which a man's life has been seriously imperilled and if he had died, this applicant . . . would have been charged with murder. It was never intended that where a man, whether under the influence of drink or not, takes a bayonet and stabs a fellow soldier in the back, with the consequences which are disclosed in this case, justices should deal with such a case by reason of that section. For justices to exercise jurisdiction under that section by treating a case of this sort as nothing much more than common assault is a most extraordinary state of affairs. Justices should remember that they have to deal with matters of this sort judicially, and, although they must take into account what the prosecution and defence say with regard to whether or not it is a proper case for the charge to be reduced, they are not bound to assent to dealing with the case summarily because the prosecution want to get the matter dealt with there and then, without the necessity of going to the assizes, where this case undoubtedly should have been sent." [61]

Cases then fall into these four categories—indictable offences, summary offences, offences both indictable and summary, and indictable offences which can be tried summarily. The categories depend upon the offence in question. There is a further variant which arises not so much from the offence as from the punishment possible. The accused is given the right to elect for jury trial.

(v) *Election for jury trial.* Where a person over fourteen is charged with a summary offence on conviction for which he is liable [62] to be sentenced to three months' imprisonment he may, with minor exceptions, elect to be tried by jury, that is to say at quarter sessions.[63] Again the statute is quite specific about this option being put to the accused by the court before his plea is taken.[64] There is one small point of difficulty which arises

60 Wounding with intent is the most serious felonious wounding and requires proof of a specific intent on the part of the accused to do a certain type of harm to the victim. Unlawful wounding merely requires proof of the general intent to assault resulting in a wounding.

61 [1947] K.B. 321 at p. 324.

62 Or would be if he is not yet adult.

63 Magistrates' Courts Act 1952, s. 25 (1). The exceptions are under the Sexual Offences Act 1956, *e.g.*, living on earnings of prostitution.

64 Magistrates' Courts Act 1952, s. 25 (3).

here. Some offences qualify for election only where the accused has already had one conviction for the same offence. It is not basically proper for the magistrates at this early stage to be in possession of an accused's antecedents, so the position must be explained to every accused in this type of offence so that, if he has the requisite previous conviction, he can elect for jury trial if he so wishes.[65]

The use, or non-use, of this power could well be the subject of a factual study. In general it is fairly safe to say that the normal reaction is to accept summary trial since it ensures that the matter is dealt with straightaway in a fairly simple way. In some situations however, the matter is more complex. In charges involving drink and cars it is fairly common to elect for jury trial for it is fairly well known that juries seem somewhat reluctant to convict in these cases, certainly more so than magistrates. This tendency is sometimes reversed in a particular area where the sentence on conviction at quarter sessions appears unduly harsh. The accused has then to weigh the chance of acquittal against the chance, if convicted, of a severe sentence. It will be readily appreciated that situations and considerations such as this are important to the individual accused but they do not bring a great deal of credit upon the legal system.

POWERS. One of the boundaries within which the selection of the appropriate punishment is made is that which limits a particular court to certain powers. In general it is true to say that whilst higher courts are limited only by the maximum punishment attached to particular offences courts of summary jurisdiction are specifically limited in power, largely because they are seen as non-specialist courts dealing with relatively minor offences. Any difficulties which this might lead to are obviated by the power to commit to a higher court for sentence in appropriate cases. We must consider the powers of magistrates and their limitations. These can be dealt with under two heads—those powers involving interference with liberty and those involving financial penalties.

Interference with liberty. The upper limits of the power to sentence to imprisonment are as follows. Where an indictable offence has been dealt with summarily the maximum term of imprisonment which can be awarded is six months.[66] To this may be added a period of imprisonment in default of payment of any fine which is awarded concurrently.[67] Where an accused is

65 Magistrates' Courts Act 1952, s. 25 (4).
66 Magistrates' Courts Act 1952, s. 19 (6).
67 *Ibid.* s. 108 (4).

tried on more than one offence the magistrates cannot, by making the sentences run consecutively, exceed an aggregate term of imprisonment of six months, or, in the case of summary trial of indictable offences, twelve months.[68]

There is also a lower limit of five days.[69] Below this period there is power to award detention.

There are two age limits. No one under the age of seventeen years may be imprisoned [70] and a convicted person between seventeen and twenty-one must only be imprisoned if there is no other appropriate method of punishment. The reasons for the choice of imprisonment must be recorded.[71]

Detention for up to four days may be ordered.[72] It involves being kept in custody in a place other than a prison, usually cells under the control of the police. There is power to impose a nominal detention for one day.[73] This involves detention within the precincts of the court house or at any police station for a period not longer than until 8 p.m. of the day in question. This power must not be exercised so as to prevent the detainee returning to his home on that day.

The Criminal Justice Act 1967 which has introduced the concept of a suspended sentence of imprisonment has also severely restricted the powers of magistrates' courts to imprison. It has provided for mandatory suspension of sentences of imprisonment of six months or less unless certain conditions are present.[74] These are conditions relating either to the offence in question—for example, it is an assault or threat of violence or it involves indecent conduct towards a person under sixteen; or to the offender—he has already served a term of imprisonment, or been subject to a suspended sentence. The rules virtually reduce the powers of a court to pass a sentence of immediately effective imprisonment of six months or less on anyone who has not previously been sentenced to custodial treatment. The exceptions relate to a few offences basically involving violence or danger to others. This provision is not limited to magistrates' courts but it obviously affects them most. It was resisted by the Magistrates' Association as being an unwelcome fetter upon their judicial discretion. It is nonetheless firmly in line with government policy of avoiding short sentences and represents perhaps only the first step in this direction, for the Home Secretary is

[68] Magistrates' Courts Act, 1952, s. 108 (1) (2).
[69] *Ibid.* s. 107 (1).
[70] *Ibid.* s. 107 (2).
[71] *Ibid.* s. 107 (3).
[72] *Ibid.* s. 109.
[73] *Ibid.* s. 110.
[74] Criminal Justice Act 1967, s. 39 (3). See further, *infra*, pp. 125–128.

empowered to increase the sentence period to twelve months instead of six.[75]

Fines. Limitations upon the power to fine arise in two ways. Each offence will, normally speaking, carry a maximum fine. There is also a special limitation upon magistrates' courts. The limitation upon magistrates' courts has been raised by the Criminal Justice Act 1967 from £100 to £400.[76] This applies to all convictions for indictable offences tried summarily. Where an offence only carries an expressed punishment of imprisonment the magistrates have power now to fine up to £100.[77]

There is a special limitation relating to those under fourteen years of age when the maximum fine is laid down as £10.[78]

Although the maximum fine for an individual offence is normally to be found in the statute laying down that offence, the fall in the value of money has meant that the original amounts have not been realistic. The Criminal Justice Act 1967 has raised a large number of amounts—the increases are set out in Schedule 3. Amendment of this sort makes for a rather complicated state of law—with the offence in one statute and the amended maximum fine in another.[79]

One of the important tasks of a court imposing a fine is assessing ability to pay. This becomes of paramount importance when the court is considering imprisonment for non-payment. The rather haphazard system of fixing an alternative period of imprisonment to be served in the event of default in payment has now been replaced by a more sophisticated system aimed at avoiding the necessity of imprisonment if at all possible. The methods of enforcing fines have also been restated and improved.[80] Although these are matters which concern magistrates' courts a great deal they are problems general to all courts and will be considered when fining is dealt with as a punishment.[81]

The courts have also the power to award compensation under the Forfeiture Act 1870.[82] This enactment relates to convictions

[75] A draft order must be laid before and approved by both Houses of Parliament: *ibid.* s. 39 (5) (6).
[76] s. 43 (1)—increasing the amount laid down in the Magistrates' Courts Act 1952, s. 19 (6).
[77] s. 43 (2)—similarly altering the amount in s. 27 (3).
[78] Magistrates' Courts Act 1952, s. 32; Criminal Justice Act 1961, s. 8.
[79] This could only be avoided by tying penalties to some "cost of living" type index, or basing it upon the offender's means—say, in terms of days' pay.
[80] Criminal Justice Act 1967, ss. 44–50.
[81] See *infra*, pp. 152–157.
[82] Magistrates' Courts Act 1952, s. 34.

for what was then a felony—now arrestable offences.[83] It is a somewhat limited power and is surprisingly little used.

B. Committal proceedings

The second important function of magistrates' courts in relation to the criminal law, committal proceedings, has no direct importance to the problems of conviction and punishment. Committal proceedings are merely a device for preliminary consideration of serious charges to ensure that no person is required to undergo jury trial without the charge having some substance. We have already considered in outline the somewhat complicated powers of the court to switch from one function, say committal, to summary trial, and if need be back again. In practice, since only one magistrate is normally used for committal proceeding and at least two are required for summary trial such switching is not as easy as in theory.

It is interesting to note that the historical reasons for a preliminary hearing of this sort—it used to be before a grand jury who were invited to find " a true bill "—have largely disappeared with the growth of professional and responsible police forces. There has followed a weight of opinion that feels that committal proceedings, with their basic task of finding " a case to answer," are no longer necessary. This view has been strengthened by the difficulty that often follows committal in well-publicised cases in empanelling a jury which is not to some extent prejudiced with what it has read of the early proceedings.[84] This is made doubly unfortunate because it is rare for the defence to show its hand at committal proceeedings, most of those accused plead not guilty and " reserve their defences."

The Criminal Justice Act 1967 has taken what is probably the first step in making committal proceedings optional and relatively rare. It has provided two important innovations. The first allows wide use of written statements rather than oral evidence.[85] The Act provides several safeguards, including the ultimate one that other parties to the case may object and so prevent the use of written statements. This important relaxation in the strict rules of proof allows for a formal type of committal proceeding. It is provided that where all the evidence, with the exception of exhibits, consists of signed statements of this type then the committal court may commit the accused for trial without considering those statements.[86] This makes the committal court an

83 Criminal Law Act 1967, s. 2.
84 A notable example was the trial of Dr. Bodkin Adams.
85 s. 2.
86 s. 1.

administrative agent only with no judicial discretion if it wishes so to act. Again there are safeguards. This "conduit pipe" procedure cannot be used unless each defendant is legally represented nor can it be used if the court is invited to consider a submission that the statements do not disclose sufficient evidence to put the defendant before a jury.

The Criminal Justice Act 1967 has also severely restricted the publication and broadcasting of details of committals.[87] The basic facts only can be published—these include the names of the defendants, their addresses, occupations and ages; similar information about witnesses; the offences or a summary of the offences charged; the decision of the committal court and so on. It prevents a detailed account of the evidence which will probably be given at the trial.

Many feel that committal proceedings could be dispensed with entirely except where those accused ask for them. This stage cannot be reached, even if it is thought wise in principle, until arrangements can be made for ancillary matters such as grant of bail and legal aid. If the criminal equivalent of the civil summons for directions under which the parties approach an official of the court for a decision on preliminary and ancillary matters can be established there seems a strong probability that further restrictions in the use of committal proceedings will occur.

Quarter sessions

The lesser of the courts in which an accused person can be tried by jury is the court of quarter sessions. It, like the assizes, is of great antiquity and it now takes two forms, the county and the borough quarter sessions. The principal difference between the two forms is in the composition of the court, the county quarter sessions being still a court of magistrates whereas the borough quarter sessions is presided over by a recorder and the local magistrates have lost their judicial powers.[88]

Composition

(a) COUNTY. All the magistrates of the county are entitled to sit at quarter sessions. The minimum number for a trial court is two,[89] and no bench must consist of more than nine magistrates. Although proceedings are controlled by the chairman each magistrate sitting has an equal vote.

87 s. 3. The accused can ask for publicity; *ibid.*, s. 3 (2).

88 They now sit as assessors on appeals from juvenile courts, see below, pp. 188–189.

89 The principal regulatory statute is the Justice of the Peace Act 1949.

There is provision for the appointment of legally qualified chairmen and deputy chairmen.[90] Appointment is by the Crown on the recommendation of the Lord Chancellor but in making his recommendation the Lord Chancellor must where practicable consider the appointment of a person with residence or other connection with the area.[91] In three areas, Hertfordshire, Middlesex and Lancashire, special statutory provisions have led to the appointment of full-time salaried chairmen and deputies.

The principal effect of the appointment of a legally qualified chairman is the extension of jurisdiction which follows.[92]

(b) London. There is a special quarter sessions for London.[93] This court covers the London Commission area but does not extend to the City of London.[94] The trial of indictable offences in the City of London is undertaken by the Central Criminal Court and the quarter sessions, called the Court of the Lord Mayor and Alderman of London, merely exercises its appellate jurisdiction.

(c) Borough. All county boroughs have separate commissions of the peace and therefore hold their own quarter sessions. Non-county boroughs which had separate commissions before the Justices of the Peace Act 1949 were allowed, upon certain conditions, to retain them. This statute provided some administrative tidying up but there cannot now be said to be a logical pattern of quarter sessions. Amongst the 103 listed [95] in the 1966 *Law List* are places as different in size as say Leeds [96] and Pontefract.[97]

A court of borough quarter sessions has as its judge a recorder. His appointment is part-time and he must be a barrister of at least five years' standing. Appointment is by the Crown on the recommendation of the Lord Chancellor.

Powers

It is easy to express the powers of quarter sessions in general terms but the actual details of jurisdiction are very complicated. Generally it can be said that quarter sessions deal with all indictable offences except the most serious which are reserved to the assize court jurisdiction. Historically, indeed, this exactly

90 Administration of Justice (Miscellaneous Provisions) Act 1938.
91 *Ibid.* s. 1 (1).
92 See *infra*, p. 27; List A, Division II.
93 Now called Greater London Sessions, Administration of Justice Act 1964.
94 For a definition see Administration of Justice Act 1964, s. 2.
95 Of these about six do not have independent sessions but have merged them, *e.g.*, Manchester and Liverpool in the Crown Courts, Preston in Lancashire county sessions.
96 Population—over half-a-million.
97 Population—under 25,000.

expresses the position; quarter sessions had complete jurisdiction but in practice reserved the serious cases for a judge of assize. The jurisdiction is now regulated by statute of which the latest is the Criminal Law Act 1967. It will be recalled that magistrates' courts, the courts of summary jurisdiction, have been given increasing power to deal with indictable offences thus eroding the work of quarter sessions.[98]

The 1967 Act provides three lists of offences.[99] List A, Division I, is of offences which are triable by all courts of quarter sessions. This lists burglary, certain special offences of arson, larceny, perjury and forgery. The second list, List A, Division II, is of offences triable by courts of quarter sessions whose jurisdiction is not restricted. This adds bigamy and certain other offences of perjury, forgery and sexual offences. The final list, List B, lists those offences which, subject to List A, are excluded from the jurisdiction of courts of quarter sessions. These are the nineteen heads of crime reserved to the assizes. They include offences carrying a maximum penalty of life imprisonment, or carrying the death penalty, causing death by dangerous driving, attempted murder, misprision of treason, offences under the Official Secrets Acts 1911 to 1939 and bribery and corruption.

From this welter of detail a fairly clear pattern emerges. Individual sessions obviously vary enormously depending upon the opportunities in and specialities of different districts and different times. Nonetheless the staple crimes are fairly constant —housebreaking, forgery, indecency, embezzlement, fraudulent conversion, receiving, drunk in charge of a car—some are exclusively within the jurisdiction of quarter session, others could have been tried in the lower court but for one reason or another have not been.[1]

Apart from dealing with indictable crime which falls within its jurisdiction a court of quarter sessions also has the function of sentencing accused persons who have been found guilty, or pleaded guilty, in a court of summary jurisdiction and have been sent for sentence under sections 28–29 of the Criminal Justice Act 1948. This can arise where the offender has been before the summary court on an indictable offence,[2] where the lower court felt that a Borstal sentence was appropriate or under the somewhat archaic rules relating to incorrigible rogues.[3]

98 See *supra*, at p. 18.
99 s. 8 and Sched. 1.
1 For a discussion of this point see p. 19.
2 Magistrates' Courts Act 1952, s. 29.
3 Vagrancy Act 1824, ss. 5, 10.

The procedure in these instances follows closely the normal procedure after a plea of guilty. The Crown outlines the case against the offender and he then proceeds to mitigate his offence. In practice the court often finds it harder to obtain collateral information, for instance from the arresting officer, without the trouble of adjournment.

Sittings

The name suggests that quarter sessions sit four times each year and this indeed was the historical pattern which lingered until recently in those sessions without a great deal of work. This gave rise to problems of the time spent awaiting trial and the whole matter was considered by the Streatfeild Committee.[4] Proposals were made to improve the position, notably that quarter sessions should be regarded as a legally continuous court able to sit as often as necessary. Previously courts which had sat more often than quarterly had done so by holding "adjourned sessions." The Streatfeild Committee thought that the aim should be to avoid an accused person awaiting trial for over eight weeks and that this should be achieved by more frequent sittings and by co-ordination between neighbouring sessions with power to commit to the next convenient sessions. These suggestions have been given legislative form by the Criminal Justice Administration Act 1962.

Thus a greater degree of flexibility has been achieved but it seems inevitable that the Royal Commission at present sitting will have far-reaching recommendations for further rationalisation.

Assizes

The serious indictable offences are tried by judge and jury at assizes. The judge is a judge of the Queen's Bench Division sitting by virtue of his receipt of the Royal Commissions of Oyer and Terminer and Gaol Delivery.[5] The country is divided into seven circuits and each circuit has assize towns which are visited in turn by the assize judges.

This is an age-old system, dating from the twelfth century, which has had only slight modifications. Most notable of these are the establishment of three permanent courts—the Central Criminal Court in London (the famous Old Bailey), and the

[4] February 1961; Cmnd. 1289.

[5] Occasionally others, retired colonial judges or eminent practitioners are given these commissions at a particular assize and they sit as Commissioners.

Crown Courts at Liverpool and Manchester. The Central Criminal Court was set up in 1834.[6] The two Crown Courts in 1956.[7] The courts are permanent in that they sit virtually continuously.[8] They each have their own special judges, the recorder and Common Serjeant at the Central Criminal Court and the recorders at the Crown Courts. Judges of the Queen's Bench Division also sit in these courts.

There seems to be a great deal to be said in favour of these centralised, continuous courts and the most recent creations of Crown Courts at Liverpool and Manchester seemed to be setting the future pattern. Rather surprisingly the Streatfeild Committee came out against any immediate extension of these types of courts. The reasons for this decision are not very convincing and it would still seem that future changes will be along these lines.

Appeals

Historical note

Most of the precedents to which students of criminology are referred are reports of appeals. Strangely, a regular system of criminal appeals was slow to emerge and full integration has only just occurred.[9] Important courts have been superseded.

Crown Cases Reserved

> "The solemnity of jury trial was so great that it was hardly thinkable that a verdict could be set aside for any reason. . . ."[10]

The only method available, the Writ of Error, was issued by the Crown and so an appeal was only possible where the Crown accepted that a trial should be reviewed. The judges found this lack of a court of appeal inconvenient and they began the practice of informally discussing cases in which they had reserved judgment. These discussions took place with colleagues in the Inn—Serjeants' Inn. The procedure was formalised by the Crown Cases Reserved Act 1848.[11] It will be appreciated that the initiative for review was that of the judge. He would reserve a case where he felt uncertain in his own mind. This would arise on points of legal difficulty and indeed the deliberations of the

6 Central Criminal Court Act 1834.
7 Criminal Justice Administration Act 1956.
8 The Crown Courts, for example, sit each month except August.
9 Criminal Appeal Act 1966, effective October 1, 1966.
10 T. F. T. Plucknett, *A Concise History of the Common Law*, p. 213.
11 Cases were reserved both from assizes and quarter sessions.

judges in reserved cases has produced some notable differences of opinion.[12]

There was still no provision for a review of a trial on the grounds that it had been unsatisfactory. This had to wait until the Criminal Appeal Act 1907.

Court of Criminal Appeal

The Court of Criminal Appeal consisted of the Lord Chief Justice and all the judges of the Queen's Bench Division of the High Court.[13] It sat in divisions. The Act provided that there must be an uneven number with a quorum of three and this was the usual number. The Lord Chief Justice presided over one division. The others were presided over by the senior judge. On occasion more judges sat.[14] Indeed if there was a strong dissentient judge a case could be reargued before a fuller court, usually of five judges.[15]

Perhaps the most important procedural rule was that only one judgment be delivered unless there were exceptional circumstances. The aim of this provision was to secure greater certainty, always regarded as essential in the field of criminal law.

The jurisdiction of the court was to hear appeals from convictions on indictment and from sentences passed after such convictions. Appeal on a point of law was of right, on a point of fact, or mixed law and fact with the leave of the trial judge or the court itself. The court's leave was also needed for appeals against sentence. In practice the court would run together the applications and treat an application for leave to appeal as an appeal itself. The grounds on which the court could allow an appeal against conviction were set out in the Act.[16]

An appeal must be allowed where the verdict of the jury was thought to be unreasonable or not supported by the evidence. It must be allowed where the trial court had made a wrong decision on a question of law or where there is any ground for saying there had been a miscarriage of justice. Where the appeal was against sentence the power was to quash the original sentence and replace it with a fresh sentence, whether greater or

[12] *e.g.*, *Ashwell* (1885) 16 Q.B.D. 190, a case of larceny by mistake had seven judges in favour of conviction and seven against. The conviction stood.
[13] These are the judges who try criminal cases on assize. The 1907 Act provided for eight judges to be nominated but this was changed by the Criminal Appeal Amendment Act 1908.
[14] Kenny cites *Norman* [1924] 2 K.B. 315 where 13 judges sat!
[15] *e.g.*, for an adjournment see *R.* v. *Patterson* [1962] 2 Q.B. 429.
[16] s. 4 (1).

lesser than the one originally passed. The convicted prisoner had ten days in which to lodge his appeal and in addition the court had power to extend this period.

It is from this court that the weight of precedents on criminal law, evidence, sentencing policy and so on has come.[17] The Lord Chief Justice and this court have been at the centre of the development of judicial attitudes since 1907. As we shall see the new Criminal Division of the Court of Appeal which has superseded this court has taken over most of its character. The Court of Criminal Appeal has not yet been the subject of a full study.[18] It was the subject of considerable criticisms on fairly minor points and an Interdepartmental Committee was set up in 1964 under Lord Donovan to consider its future. The Committee's report is a valuable résumé of all aspects of the court which had attracted critical attention.[19] It is as a result of the report that the present system was set up.

Divisional Court of the Queen's Bench Division

This is the court of appeal from a court of summary jurisdiction and quarter sessions upon points of law. It is of interest as the court which moulds the judicial attitude to crimes solely within the jurisdiction of magistrates' courts. These are usually crimes of a relatively trivial nature but of great quantitative importance since they include a large number of the regulatory offences which now govern a wide part of everyday life. Occasionally reference to the court will involve a point of law concerning procedure which has a direct bearing on sentencing. The aim of these courts is to ensure a degree of uniformity in legal interpretation between the large number of lower courts.

A Divisional Court consists of two or three judges of the Queen's Bench Division. They hear appeals by way of case stated. That is to say the appellant asks the court to state why it has reached a particular decision. Courts of summary jurisdiction do not deliver reasoned judgments and this is the only certain way of knowing upon what principles a decision has been reached.

An appeal by way of case stated is unusual in that it may be made either by a convicted person or, where there has been an acquittal, by the prosecutor. The Divisional Court has no final

17 There is a set of law reports devoted solely to criminal appeals—the *Criminal Appeal Reports* (Cr.App.R.).

18 But see D. Seaborne Davies, "The Court of Criminal Appeal: The First Forty Years" [1947] J.S.P.T.L. 425.

19 Cmnd. 2755, August 1965.

function. It merely considers the legal problems involved and remits the case to the original court with the appropriate direction, if it feels there has been an error. One of the most important effects is to keep the law untainted by considerations of sympathy aroused by a particular case. Where, for example, justices thought that a driver who had failed to stop to give precedence to pedestrians on a crossing had not been proved negligent and so they dismissed the charge. The Divisional Court sent back the case with directions to convict.[20] If the magistrates still feel that the convicted person is relatively blameless they can express this with a nominal sentence—a very small fine or a discharge.

Quarter sessions

These courts, which have already been described as trial courts,[21] also hear appeals by persons convicted and sentenced in the courts of summary jurisdiction. They hear appeals both against conviction and against sentence.

The usual pattern is that appeals against magistrates' decisions are heard by the local borough or county quarter sessions. The recorder sits alone, that is to say, without a jury, to hear appeals in boroughs. In the counties, strangely, the court is made up of the same magistrates, though not of course the same personnel as adjudicated at the original hearing.[22] An important innovation has been made where the appeal is from a juvenile court. Where practicable the recorder must be joined by two assessors from the panel of juvenile court magistrates.[23] In the county areas in such circumstances at least half the magistrates sitting on such appeals must be qualified to sit as members of a juvenile court and of those so qualified at least one must be of each sex.

The different pattern of criminal courts requires rather special provisions for London, Liverpool and Manchester. The position in the last two is relatively simple. The statute setting up the Crown Courts provides that these courts shall act as quarter sessions for the respective cities and when doing so shall be subject to the general rules.[24]

20 *Gibbons* v. *Kahl* [1956] 1 Q.B. 59.
21 See *supra*, p. 25.
22 The appeals committee system was ended recently by the Criminal Justice Administration Act 1962, s. 4 (5).
23 Children and Young Persons Act 1963, s. 19 (1).
24 Criminal Justice Administration Act 1956, s. 3.

The position in London is more complicated. The Greater London Sessions covers the whole of the London Commission Area and acts as a normal county quarter sessions.[25] The City of London, however, had its own quarter sessions—the Court of the Lord Mayor and Aldermen of London. This court deals only with appeals, for although it has the usual quarter sessions' jurisdiction, that relating to indictable offences is exercised by the Central Criminal Court, the Old Bailey.

A convicted person may appeal:

(a) if he pleaded guilty, against sentence;
(b) if he did not, against conviction or sentence.[26]

There are two special points of note. A plea of guilty is a bar to an appeal against conviction. This is a general rule applying to all appeals, not just those from courts of summary jurisdiction, and it has, not surprisingly, been the subject of a fair amount of case-law. The first point to note is that the plea of guilty must be clear and unambiguous.

> "Every judge and most magistrates know that it is quite a common thing for a prisoner arraigned at assizes or quarter sessions, when the charge is put to him, to say he is Guilty, but so-and-so, and the clerk of assize always says: 'That is a plea of Not Guilty. Enter a plea of Not Guilty.'" [27]

In the case in which the Lord Chief Justice said this the accused had pleaded guilty before the magistrates to a charge of larceny. After a statement by the prosecution he had made a statement which was in effect a claim of right, which, if accepted, would be a complete defence. The Divisional Court said that this was an appropriate case in which an appeal could be entertained. Where an appeal is lodged by a person who had pleaded guilty it is usual to call the court clerk to explain the circumstances. Misunderstanding may arise between client and lawyer but the rule is that the prisoner himself must plead.[28]

A probation order or a discharge is not a sentence.[29] There is therefore no appeal against these although if subsequently upon breach of the probation order or condition of the discharge a

25 Administration of Justice Act 1964, s. 2.
26 Magistrates' Courts Act 1952, s. 83 (1).
27 *Durham Quarter Sessions, ex p. Virgo* [1952] 2 Q.B. 1, *per* Lord Goddard C.J. at p. 3. Special care must be taken where the accused is a child that the plea is clearly understood: *Blandford Justices, ex p. G. (an Infant)* [1967] 1 Q.B. 82.
28 *Heyes* [1951] 1 K.B. 29.
29 Magistrates' Courts Act 1952, s. 83 (3).

sentence is passed in respect of the original offence, then the right to appeal against this sentence is expressly reserved by statute.[30]

Notice of appeal must be given within fourteen days of the day on which the decision was given which may usually be taken as the day on which sentence is passed. There is provision for the court to hear appeals that are out of time.

Appeal against conviction means a new trial before quarter sessions—without in the case of county quarter sessions a jury. The case proceeds *de novo* and the prosecution has to prove its case. In only one sense is the time of the original trial important. This was illustrated by a case where the accused was sentenced to approved school, appealed, was found guilty again and the same sentence was applied. In the meantime the accused had passed the age when such a sentence was appropriate but it was held that the sentence was proper.[31] Where the appeal is solely against conviction the respondent, usually the Crown, opens the case which proceeds very much as a case at first instance with a guilty plea. The court can impose any sentence which it deems appropriate (within the legal maxima) and its decision may be more or less severe than that of the original court. There is no further appeal against either conviction or sentence of a general nature. It is possible, however, to ask the quarter sessions to state a case to the Divisional Court on a point of law.

Court of Appeal—Criminal Division

From October 1966 this court has taken the place of the Court of Criminal Appeal. It hears appeals against both conviction and sentence from courts of quarter sessions and assizes. The Act bringing about the change, the Criminal Appeal Act 1966, has also made several improvements in the system of appeals.[32] These will be considered in the appropriate paragraphs.

The basic change may be said to be an increase in the apparent status of criminal appeals. They are now dealt with in the same way as civil appeals by a court of a higher status than the court of trial. It was felt, however, that the court should include judges with recent trial experience so the Division is not exclusively staffed by appeal court judges—Lords Justices of Appeal. Any member of the Queen's Bench Division may be invited by the Lord Chief Justice to sit.[33] The statute does not give detailed rules as to the composition of each Division in which the court

30 Magistrates' Courts Act 1952, s. 83 (2).
31 *Drover* v. *Rugman* [1951] 1 K.B. 380.
32 For an interesting review of this statute see M. Dean [1966] Crim.L.R. 535.
33 Criminal Appeal Act 1966, s. 1.

may sit. It follows from the continued practice of using puisne judges that a trial judge might conceivably find himself reviewing his own case. This possibility is now barred by statute.[34]

The Donovan Committee gave considerable attention to the statutory powers of the Court of Criminal Appeal to set aside jury verdicts and recommended changes. As a result an amended formula is now laid down. A verdict may be set aside where the court is satisfied that " under all the circumstances of the case it is unsafe or unsatisfactory." [35] The judgment of a court may be set aside " on the ground of a wrong decision of any question of law " [36] or on the ground that " there was a material irregularity in the course of the trial." [37]

Even though the court may feel that the point argued by the appellant is a good one under a general proviso they do not necessarily allow the appeal if they feel that no miscarriage of justice has occurred.[38] This proviso raises the whole question of the purpose of an appeal by way of review of a trial. Clearly modern opinion could not justify the medieval insistence on complete detailed compliance with due form. Once this is accepted the court's subjective assessment of the requirements of justice becomes of paramount importance. It varies very much with the type of ground upon which the appeal is based but three very different grounds can be used to illustrate the approach.

Where the point involves the question whether evidence should or should not have been put before a jury or whether they should have been directed differently on the cogency of evidence before them the rule seems to be that the court will not upset the result if the conduct it regards as correct would still have led the jury to come to the same conclusion. The test seems to be whether a jury " properly directed would have returned the same verdict." [39]

Where the misdirection as to law is the point of appeal the court seems to feel able to exercise its discretion under the proviso fairly freely. Lord Goddard C.J. put the attitude succinctly in *R.* v. *Whybrow*, saying " . . . we see how far the case is affected by the wrong direction given by the presiding Judge, and we must take the whole of the facts into account and regard the

34 *Ibid.* s. 2.
35 *Ibid.* s. 4 (1) (*a*), replacing the old formula "unreasonable or cannot be supported having regard to the evidence."
36 This provision of the Criminal Appeal Act 1907, s. 4 (1), remains unaltered.
37 Criminal Appeal Act 1966, s. 4 (1) (*b*), replacing the old formula "there was a miscarriage of justice."
38 Criminal Appeal Act 1907, s. 4 (1). Now Criminal Appeal Act 1968, s. 2 (1) (*a*). The need for the miscarriage to be " substantial " was removed. See Criminal Appeal Act 1968, s. 2 (1).
39 *Haddy* [1944] K.B. 442 at p. 445.

whole of the circumstances." [40] In that case, despite a serious misdirection of law, the proviso was used.

The approach of the court is somewhat different where the appellant's claim is that he has been denied a properly conducted trial. In this "justice must be seen to be done" area the Court of Criminal Appeal has taken a fairly firm line and quashed convictions. There are two fairly recent cases involving the handling of a jury. In one they were allowed out to lunch whilst considering their verdict,[41] in the other they were virtually set a time limit by the judge to reach a verdict.[42] In both cases the conviction was quashed and the proviso was not used.

One factor of appeals which bothered the Court of Criminal Appeal for many years was their inability to order a new trial. This lack of power was felt particularly in cases of murder where the murder verdict could not be allowed to stand but where a conviction for manslaughter of a serious kind was obviously the proper result.[43] The matter has been rectified by the Criminal Appeal Act 1964. Where an appeal is allowed on the grounds of the use of evidence at the earlier trial the appellate court can, if it thinks the interests of justice demand, order a new trial. This new trial is restricted to offences contained in the original indictment, either directly or as alternative counts or as alternative offences of which he could have been found guilty under the original indictment.[44]

A convicted person has twenty-eight days in which to appeal.[45] An appeal, in contrast to one to quarter sessions, takes the form of a review of the original trial rather than a rehearing. Indeed most appeals against conviction turn upon the conduct of the trial. Most frequently challenged are the admissibility of evidence and the correctness of the judge's directions to the jury. The advisers of the appellant are in an advantageous position in that they can secure a typescript of the shorthand note taken at the trial. In this way they are able to pinpoint with some certainty any weaknesses on which they wish to rely.

Occasionally a convicted person wishes to appeal on the ground that he wishes to put further evidence forward. Under the 1907 Act the Court of Criminal Appeal had complete discretion whether to allow this or not [46] and it had evolved rules

40 *Whybrow* (1951) 35 Cr.App.R. 141 at p. 152.
41 *Neal* [1949] 2 K.B. 590.
42 *McKenna* [1960] 1 Q.B. 411.
43 See, for example, *Murtagh & Kennedy* (1955) 39 Cr.App.R. 72.
44 s. 1 (2).
45 Criminal Appeal Act 1966, s. 10 (1). Sched. 2 para. 1.
46 Criminal Appeal Act 1907, s. 9.

upon which it exercised this discretion. Evidence was only admitted if it had not been available at the time of the trial and the usual tests of relevance and credibility were applied. The first point was thought harsh [47] and the 1966 Act met this criticism by laying down the formula that there is a reasonable explanation for the failure to adduce evidence at the original trial.[48]

One special feature of appeals against sentence has been changed. The original basis was that the appellant was asking to be resentenced and so he might receive a greater as well as a lesser sentence. The paradox of being given leave to appeal—presumably upon the grounds that the sentence was wrong—and then having the sentence raised was criticised and now the court has no power to increase a sentence.[49]

A final improvement of the 1966 Act may be mentioned. Where leave to appeal was refused up to six weeks of any time spent in custody awaiting the application was not to count towards the sentence unless the court ordered otherwise.[50] This rule sprang from the fact that a prisoner awaiting the hearing of an appeal is subject to a less harsh prison regime. The rule has now been reversed and all time awaiting appeal in custody is to count unless the appeal court when turning down the application directs otherwise.[51]

The influence of this court on sentencing policy cannot be too highly stressed. Not only are dicta in individual cases often of great help in establishing judicial policy, a study of trends in the court's approach can be illuminating.

House of Lords

The pinnacle of the hierarchy of criminal courts of appeal is the House of Lords sitting as a court. The court consists of at least three Lords of Appeal and it is usual for five to sit. A Lord of Appeal is either a Lord of Appeal in Ordinary, that is to say a specially created judicial life peer, or a member of the House of Lords who has held high judicial office.

An appeal lies from the Divisional Court of the Queen's Bench and from the Criminal Division of the Court of Appeal. Appeals used to be regulated by the rule that the Attorney-General had to give his *fiat*, but since 1960 leave is given either

47 See, for example, the Donovan Committee.
48 Criminal Appeal Act 1966, s. 5, now Criminal Appeal Act 1968, s. 23 (2).
49 Criminal Appeal Act 1968, s. 3 (2).
50 Criminal Justice Act 1948, s. 38.
51 Criminal Appeal Act 1968, s. 29.

by the court against which the appeal is to be made, or by the House of Lords itself.[52]

An appeal may be made either by the person convicted or, where the earlier appeal ended in a conviction being quashed, by the prosecution. It is possible for an accused person to be convicted at his trial, to have his conviction quashed upon appeal and then have it restored by the House of Lords. This is obviously relatively rare; there are not a great number of cases involving points of law of importance. *D.P.P.* v. *Smith* is an example of the accused being found guilty of murder at his trial, having it reduced to manslaughter by the Court of Criminal Appeal and then restored to murder by the House of Lords.[53]

The House of Lords need not confine itself to the point of law certified as of importance. Once a case comes before it there may be a general review. It cannot, however, entertain argument about the sentence where the appeal is solely against conviction.[54]

It will be appreciated from the foregoing that the court rarely hears cases that have more than an indirect influence upon sentencing policy and practice. Although its decisions are of the greatest importance to the development of criminal law and the law of evidence, and incidentally manage on many occasions to arouse acute academic controversy, they have a relatively minor importance to the study of criminology.

The Trial of Criminal Offences

Although the purpose of this book is not to examine in detail the legal system or the rules of evidence there are certain features of English criminal trial which require attention because of their undoubted potential effect on sentencing. In the most general terms the very fabric of the trial is of importance. In this the English system is markedly different from that used in continental countries; the Scottish system is itself by no means similar in fundamentals to the English. The basic idea is simple. The prosecution makes an allegation against the accused which must be substantiated to the satisfaction of the court. On balance the rules favour the accused and hinder the prosecution. The distinctive flavour of the general attitude is that of a game played within the rules of law and evidence. This attitude, which is

52 Administration of Justice Act 1960, s. 1 (2).

53 [1961] A.C. 290. It is interesting that the Home Secretary announced before the determination of the appeal in the House of Lords that he would commute the death penalty if a murder verdict were restored.

54 *Jones* v. *D.P.P.* [1962] A.C. 635.

almost naturally assumed by lawyers, never fails to infuriate police and astound sociologists.[55] It can be defended without a great deal of difficulty if the approach is from the standpoint of individual liberty. To take just one point, it is obvious that the policeman who says, when a person he has charged is acquitted, " I know he did it, he should be found guilty " is asking for his own assessment of guilt to be accepted. The real aim must be to achieve a balance between protection of the individual epitomised by Bentham when he said " it is better that ten guilty men should escape than one innocent man be convicted " and protection of society by due conviction of criminals. At present some of the excesses are being corrected. For example, the defence's opportunity to spring on the prosecution an alibi during the course of a trial, when the possibility of it being bogus is hard to investigate through lack of time, has just been terminated by the Criminal Justice Act 1967, s. 11, which requires notice before an alibi can be put forward.

A further general point of English trial procedure is that it tends to restrict the area of inquiry. Points often arise which the intelligent observer feels he would like to know more about because he would increase his understanding of the crime and the criminal. The rules of relevancy and the abhorrence of wasting judicial time with speculation of a wide nature mean that a great deal passes by unexplained. It is rare that an English trial does not leave a large number of collateral loose ends, investigation of some of which might prove helpful. The contrast with the continental inquisitorial system serves to emphasise this peculiarity.[56]

Apart from these rather general considerations there are several rules which can be briefly examined with their effect on the whole shape of the criminal trial in mind.

Burden of proof

The general attitude is perhaps best crystallised by the evidential rule that the burden of proof in a criminal trial is on the prosecution. This has been put in a classic passage in *Woolmington* v. *D.P.P.*[57]

> " Throughout the web of the English Criminal Law one golden thread is always to be seen, that it is the duty of the

[55] See for example criticisms in the debates on the Criminal Justice Bill, 1966–1967.

[56] There are many books dealing with this but two can be highly recommended as bases for thought—Sybille Bedford, *The Faces of Justice*, on comparative methods of trial and Louis Blom-Cooper, *A.6. Murder*, for analysis of an English trial.

[57] [1935] A.C. 462, *per* Lord Sankey.

> prosecution to prove the prisoner's guilt subject to what I have already said as to the defence of insanity and subject also to any statutory exception."

It follows the defence can always submit that there is no case to answer when the prosecution has closed its case. At this stage mere suspicion or doubt of the accused's position will be of no avail unless the prosecution has covered, to the court's satisfaction, all the essential elements of the crime. One of the less pleasant " game " ploys of the defence is to seize upon the failure of the prosecution to establish a vital element of the crime charged. This could happen, as an oversight, in a case of careless driving where no witness ever formally identified the accused as the driver. Up till the close of the prosecution case the matter would proceed on an assumption that this was so and the accused's pleas of no case to answer would be a matter for consternation. This unfair use of the general principle has been stopped by a court allowing the prosecutor to reopen his case to cure slips of this sort.[58]

The basic principle reaches beyond the actual trial. During the period of investigation a suspected person is rarely[59] under an obligation to explain himself. He can take the neutral attitude of inviting the police to establish his guilt without his own assistance in any way. It is a well-known task of lawyers to advise their clients to say as little as possible at this stage. The number of cases which are only cleared up because of the confession of a suspected person must be very large—a great proportion of cases " taken into consideration "[60] fall into this group. It is again a matter of balance between the desire to clear up crime or to establish the truth and the need to ensure that preconceived views of the investigators are not forcibly stamped on the potential evidence. Perhaps the best starting point for a full consideration of all the delicate problems involved and a clear indication of the impossibility of an ideal solution is the Justice Report on Preliminary Investigation of Criminal Offences.[61]

Standard of proof

The discharge of the acquitted prisoner with a judge's admonition not to do it again is a traditional way of expressing the

[58] *Middleton* v. *Rowlett* [1954] 1 W.L.R. 831 was a timely reminder that the matter of reopening the prosecution was a matter for the discretion of the court. It would not be allowed for major omissions.

[59] There are statutory duties to disclose information.

[60] A useful procedure, sometimes abused.

[61] [1960] Crim.L.R. 793.

point that proof on a criminal charge must reach a particular standard which is higher than that normally used to determine everyday views and conduct. Every jury is instructed upon the standard of certainty they must reach before they pronounce guilt and not unnaturally what judges say to them has been often reviewed by the courts on appeal.

Two propositions are clearly established. The criminal standard of proof is higher than the civil. The criminal standard is best expressed by the phrase " beyond reasonable doubt " or in terms of the jury " feel satisfied." This is in contrast to the civil standard which merely requires that the balance should favour one side or the other. It is analysis of what these phrases really mean which causes greatest difficulty.

The phrase " beyond reasonable doubt " is well known to the layman and time-honoured. A previous Lord Chief Justice questioned whether it was as clear as it might be. He said:

> " I have never yet heard any court give a real definition of what is a ' reasonable doubt,' and it would be very much better if that expression was not used. Whenever a court attempts to explain what is meant by it, the explanation tends to result in confusion rather than in clarity. It is far better, instead of using the words ' reasonable doubt ' and then trying to say what is a reasonable doubt, to say to a jury: ' You must not convict unless you are satisfied by the evidence given by the prosecution that the offence has been committed.' " [62]

This passage is notable not for its proposal of a change in the formula but for the acceptance of the difficulty of explaining the standard of proof. Lord Goddard later modified his complete opposition to the phrase " beyond reasonable doubt " and it is customary now to use it along with the " feel satisfied " formula as a variation.[63]

The emphasis is, of course, on the term " reasonable " and an explanation which is consistent with the facts as established which offers an alternative version of what happened consistent with the accused's innocence will only raise *reasonable* doubt if the jury feel that the explanation is fairly probable. Otherwise all a defence lawyer would need to be successful would be the ingenuity of the detective story writer.

The term " benefit of doubt " is often used by defence lawyers in their address to juries. It is unfortunate in that it

62 *Summers* [1952] 1 All E.R. 1059 at p. 1060.
63 See *Hepworth & Fearnley* [1955] 2 Q.B. 600.

indicates the extension of " charity " to the accused when the law clearly gives an accused person the entitlement to an acquittal if the prosecution has failed to establish its case.

Where an issue is placed by law on the defence the standard of proof is the lesser civil standard. This is a point of great importance where the defence is insanity or diminished responsibility.[64]

Form of trial

Criminal trial, whether on indictment before a jury, or summarily in a magistrates' court, takes a standard form in its essentials. The fundamental feature is the division into two distinct processes; the first aimed at establishing guilt, the second at fixing the appropriate penalty. It is essential that these two functions should be kept separate although in practice it is fairly hard to achieve.

Two points can be used to illustrate this. The thought of the possible penalty that the accused may suffer if found guilty should not be considered when guilt is being determined, but it is fairly safe to assume that juries occasionally acquit on such considerations and magistrates convict when they have doubt because the trivial penalty they can impose will not be a great burden to the accused. Both attitudes are natural but wrong.

It is not unknown for courts, when they retire to determine guilt, also to consider the penalty. In most cases of, say, road traffic offences, all the relevant facts will have emerged during the trial but the accused is entitled to put forward points which may be irrelevant to the question of guilt or innocence, but which will be effective mitigation.

Trial opens with the prosecutor outlining the case to the court. The object of such an opening is to set a framework into which the court can fit the evidence as it emerges and in lengthy trials with complicated facts it is essential. Obviously the first words spoken about the matters in dispute will have advantageous weight. On the other hand, should the prosecutor in any way overstate his case he will find the defence able to underline the failure of his evidence to do what was promised. Where the plea is guilty the opening summary by the prosecution is of much greater importance. It then constitutes the basis on which the court will take its decisions. There has been recent criticism of the length and type of openings frequently heard. They are part of the trial which may be described as of help but not importance. Prosecutors need to be vigilant that they do not

64 *Dunbar* [1958] 1 Q.B. 1.

abuse their opportunities and courts that they do not accept from the prosecutor something which is subsequently not proved.

Following the opening the prosecution then calls its evidence. Each witness is examined, cross-examined if the defence wishes and re-examined where the prosecution wishes to re-establish a point. Consideration of this, the most important aspect of trial, is outside the scope of this book. There is no doubt that a study of psychology has a lot to give to the appreciation of testimony.[65] It cannot be doubted either that the court, which may later have to sentence the accused, is at this stage forming an assessment of the character of the accused. This factor may indeed be of importance to the conduct of the defence. In practice many considerations of this sort have to be faced. Thus a prolonged attack on the prosecution witnesses, particularly upon police witnesses, has some risk if it fails; the decision to attack witnesses will allow an attack upon the accused's character; calling witnesses for the defence of doubtful character—these are all decisions which are usually made with the possible sentence in mind. It is a well-known attitude that a plea of guilty may well achieve a lesser sentence than a protracted defence. It can only be said that all these notions are present in the minds of the defence. Whether they have any validity cannot be satisfactorily measured and no social scientist in England has studied these somewhat illusive attitudes.

After the evidence for prosecution and defence has been received the case ends, as far as trial is concerned, with closing speeches. Practice and theory diverge here. In theory the prosecution and the defence are both entitled to a closing speech. It is rare for the prosecution right to be exercised in magistrates' courts. Practice before a jury seems, inexplicably, to vary in different parts of the country. The Criminal Procedure (Right of Reply) Act 1964 removes the right of the prosecution to speak last. Its final speech, if made, follows the defence evidence and precedes the defence speech. By this time the matters in dispute have been rehearsed many times at various stages in the trial.

The final address to the jury is, of course, a feature only of trials on indictment. This is intended as guidance to the jury on the legal aspects of their task and an impartial review of the evidence. Judges are always careful to emphasise that juries are sole judges of fact and they adopt an attitude of balance in the treatment of the evidence to emphasise this, even at the risk of confusing the jury.

65 *e.g.*, see Peter McKellar, *Experience and Behaviour*, Pelican, 1968, especially Chap. 14, "Forensic Psychology."

Rules of evidence

The kernel of the criminal trial is the evidence and the rules of evidence establish the pattern which gives the trial its distinctive form. The two fundamental rules are those of relevance which quite strictly restrict the trial to issues already predetermined by the criminal law which delineates the elements of the crime charged and the rule which makes oral evidence on oath the normal method of presenting testimony. Within this framework there are other groups of rules aimed chiefly at protecting the accused. Thus the rules as to hearsay or the reception of similar facts are based on the idea that such evidence is usually far more attractive than its intrinsic probative value warrants. For this reason the general rule on both these types of evidence is exclusive and only in exceptional cases is evidence of this sort allowed. In the same way it is usual to look for corroboration of evidence of accomplices and of children so as to protect the accused. Finally there are protective rules governing the reception of admissions and confessions which the accused is alleged to have made.

Each of these rules has been developed in some detail. For our purpose it is merely necessary to look at the broad outlines to assess the impact of the rules on the shape of the trial. The shape of trial will itself help to determine the background against which the court will proceed to sentencing.

Relevance

The contrast with the inquisitorial system has already been made. It is the rule excluding irrelevant matter, and the fairly strict judicial interpretation of this rule which give the English criminal trial its introspective aspect. The real importance lies perhaps in the different depth of the two stages of trial. Matters of explanation which are relevant to the issues being tried are thoroughly established by testimony and tested by cross-examination whereas if they fall outside the rules of relevancy and are raised after conviction they tend to be treated far less thoroughly. This point is illustrated, in a slightly different context, by trials in which the only issue is the defence of diminished responsibility. The duty to test evidence was emphasised in *R.* v. *Ahmed Din* [66] where the Lord Chief Justice said:

"... the prosecution are only too ready in these cases to

[66] [1962] 1 W.L.R. 680.

> fall in with and support a defence of diminished responsibility. The court has already said that this is an issue which in every case must be proved."

If the rules of relevancy move a matter from the trial to the post-conviction phase then such a rigorous attitude is never adopted.

Oral evidence

Although oral evidence is still, and must always remain, the basic method of proof there is an increasing trend towards lessening the strict approach. The justification of the demand for oral evidence is usually put on three grounds—the oath, the opportunity of the court to observe demeanour and cross-examination. It is obvious that a strict requirement of oral evidence would create great practical difficulties and for many years exceptions have been created.

Perhaps the biggest single exception, although it is only a partial one, is the conditional binding over of witnesses who have given evidence at committal proceedings. This procedure enables a witness whose evidence is unchallenged to be excused from attendance at the trial where his deposition—that is his signed statement as given at the committal proceedings—will be read out to the jury.[67]

The latest step has been taken by the Criminal Justice Act 1967, s. 9, which allows admission of written statements under certain conditions. The statement must be signed, it must contain a statement by the maker that it is true to the best of his knowledge and belief and that he knows that he is liable to prosecution for wilful falsity. A copy of the statement must be served on other parties and they have the right to object within seven days to proof by this written statement. There are special rules requiring a maker under 21 to state his age, and one who is blind to declare that it has been read to him.

The Criminal Justice Act 1967 also provides for proof by formal admissions.[68] This is an exception to the general rule under which the prosecution must prove all the elements of the crime alleged and cannot rely on formal admissions (other than the fundamental one of the plea of guilty) to do so. Now a written admission, signed by the maker may be admitted and an oral admission may be made in court by the defendant or his legal representative on his behalf.

[67] There was an extension in the Criminal Procedure (Attendance of Witnesses) Act 1965.

[68] s. 10.

Hearsay

The rule against hearsay and its many technical exceptions is a large subject. Its chief interest for our purposes is in its application to the evidence given after conviction and prior to sentence. The rules are not applied with any strictness at this stage which means that those who wish to give evidence as to the character of the accused, or to report on him generally or perhaps medically, are much freer than in theory they appear to be. It is left to the good sense of those who prepare reports as to the care with which they check their information—a marked contrast to the attitude during the actual trial. It may well be that rules are needed and will develop to lay down broad guidance as to the quality of information to be used in such circumstances.

Similar facts

The rules which illustrate most clearly the different approach necessary before and after conviction are those dealing with evidence of similar facts. It is a fairly general assumption that once a person has offended he is more likely to offend again. The police certainly base one of their major detective methods on this assumption and they collect details of methods of work of criminals to use as a guide to the likely perpetrator of unsolved crime and they are always ready to interview known criminals to help them clear up crimes about which they have no lead. The same attitude in a jury, or bench of magistrates, would mean that the task of the accused who was known to have previous convictions would be very hard indeed and the prejudice against him may well be substantial. To avoid this there are strict rules about non-disclosure of previous convictions.

Thus every accused person begins with the advantage that his previous criminal record will remain unknown to the court until they have decided whether he is guilty. It is not an invariable rule, there are limited exceptions where previous convictions are admissible at the trial. An obvious example is where the crime is so framed that it requires the accused to be already a convicted person.[69] More interestingly the courts have developed a rule that the accused will lose his protection if he should attack the character of the prosecution witnesses. The character of a witness, unlike that of the accused, is always admissible for it goes directly to the point of credibility of that witness. If however, the accused decides to attack the characters of witnesses he does so with knowledge that his own character will be open to attack.

69 Prevention of Crimes Act 1871, s. 7.

The dividing line between an attack on a witness's testimony and his character may often be a fine one and has given rise to a corpus of case-law. If, for instance, the accused denied he ever made a statement a police officer is in evidence saying was made, it is obvious that although the cross-examiner may put it to the officer that he was mistaken, he is in reality saying that he is making it all up. The courts seem prepared to accept the first approach whereas they would regard cross-examination based firmly on the bad faith of the officer as opening the accused's character to attack.[70] In practice it is a matter of judgment with the courts on the whole favouring the accused as far as they feel they can.

The problem of keeping knowledge of this sort away from the court is extremely hard. In a small area court it will be impossible for the court not to know that they are dealing with a regular offender however hard the administration try to avoid the accused appearing before a bench known to him. Greater success can be achieved administratively in avoiding magistrates who have sat on the question of bail, when character is of the paramount importance, subsequently sitting to try the accused. There are unfortunately many small points which will indicate to a receptive judge that the accused has a record. The very fact that he has been kept in custody, the witnesses he calls, unfortunate pieces of evidence, often unwittingly given by the defence witnesses; all may give indication of a criminal record. It needs only to be said that the system goes as far as is conveniently possible to protect the accused and grosser breaches of the spirit of the law will lead to a successful appeal.[71]

It is not only previous convictions which are important. The prosecution may decide that it can best prove a man's guilt by relating the methods of his previous crime which bear a significant similarity to the crime charged. Or they may put together in the same trial several charges relating to different instances of the same crime which they feel the accused has committed. The rules relating to similar fact evidence are basically exclusive with exceptions where, for example, the prosecution can point to such a coincidence as to rule out chance as a reasonable explanation.[72]

[70] *Clark* [1955] 2 Q.B. 469.

[71] *Cook* [1959] 2 Q.B. 340.

[72] An attempt to put the rule the other way—that evidence of disposition was admissible unless excluded because of its danger—was made by Lord Goddard C.J. in *Sims* [1946] K.B. 302. The ability to make a logical scheme on the opposite proposition was demonstrated clearly by this case but it did not become the established law. It does illustrate the academic character of rules of evidence—their formulation is largely an intellectual exercise around basic principles.

The problem of separate charges is that a number of weak cases may look strong. An application for separate trials can be made in such circumstances but is hardly likely to succeed if the crimes charged have an obvious relationship. This was the position in the leading case of *Harris* v. *D.P.P.*[73] and the solution of the House of Lords was that the jury (it might equally be magistrates) must only use the evidence for each charge on that particular charge and this point must be emphasised to the members of the jury. The process of discounting what one knows is always a difficult one—indeed a genuine attempt to do so may lead to overzealous care and an unjustified aquittal.

After conviction

The duty of the prosecution, viewed narrowly, is to introduce the history of the accused so that the court knows the type of man it is dealing with. This evidence is usually given by the police, formally on oath in the higher courts, informally in magistrates' courts. The " history " or " antecedents " takes a fairly standard form with age, place of birth and sketchy summary of work record. The principal feature is the list of previous convictions—should the accused be already an offender.

In the same narrow sense the defence's task is to mitigate, that is to say to put before the court everything that can be said to lessen the gravity of the offence and establish the good points about the accused's character. All this is with a view to obtaining the least possible sentence. At its worst this can be second rate and shabby, with the advocate deferring to the position of the court, urging " a certain course " and hoping that this phrase will cover a discharge, fine or similar " light " sentence.

Fortunately the realities rarely stop at this. It is nonetheless a pity that there is not a greater body of rule and precept enjoining all to engage in an attempt to ensure that the court is in a position to select the appropriate sentence, appropriate that is both as to the crime and the offender. The position has moved from the time when the rules of evidence requiring, for example, sworn statements and debarring hearsay were strictly applied to this part of the hearing to a much more permissive situation. It is to be regretted that there has been no study of this part of the hearing with a view to isolating basic general principles upon which the various rules could be framed. The nearest approach has been Part B of the Streatfeild Report.[74]

[73] [1952] A.C. 694.

[74] 1961 Cmnd. 1289 "Arrangements for providing the courts with the information necessary to enable them to select the most appropriate treatment for offenders." Chaps. 9–11.

It is worthwhile setting out the principal recommendations as a basis for a discussion of the problems. The basis of the recommendations was neatly summarised as

> ". . . our cardinal principle throughout is that sentences should be based on reliable, comprehensive information relevant to what the court is seeking to do . . . it is important that the sentences imposed by the courts should have a sound factual basis and should not appear to be in any way speculative or based on vague impressions. . . . But information should not be proliferated for information's sake. . . . A mass of background information can be collected with comparative ease, but irrelevant information is not only useless but possibly harmful. . . . The test to be applied is whether the information can help the court to reach a better decision; and actual experience and the results of research (as it develops) should be used to check the relevance of particular facts about offenders as indicators of the likely effect of penal treatment." [75]

The first aim of the Committee was to ensure that those charged with the task of sentencing had full information about their powers and choices. This aspect has been tackled. The Home Office has published a pamphlet [76] and recent emphasis on training of magistrates has turned a great deal of attention to a consideration of these features.[77] One aspect, that of enabling courts to have a detailed follow-up of their own cases so that they can judge to some extent the effectiveness of their own decisions, does not seem to have progressed to the same extent.

Greater difficulty arises in securing the appropriate information about the individual offender who is to be sentenced. The traditional English system is that sentence should follow immediately upon conviction wherever possible. There is a healthy distaste for leaving an offender long in ignorance of his eventual fate. Wherever possible the Committee recommended that reports should be ready before conviction in case of need. Where this is not done then the Committee felt it was better to have a short adjournment of a few days. The figures of adjournments before sentence were stated by the Report to be 1 per cent. at assizes and 3 per cent. at quarter sessions other than the London and

[75] paras. 292–293.

[76] "The Sentence of the Court." First edition published 1964. This pamphlet has not been promoted with a great deal of vigour and is rather hard to come by.

[77] *e.g.*, the Lord Chancellor has encouraged magistrates to establish links with Universities and Colleges to facilitate training.

Middlesex sessions.[78] These figures clearly show the reluctance of courts to adjourn. No doubt the Streatfeild Committee recommendations have led to a greater number of adjournments.

The Streatfeild discussion of probation officers' reports is of great interest. They first of all attacked some of the apparent hostility to the use of the probation service. This sometimes took the form of restricting requests for reports to those cases where probation was a likely outcome. It sometimes took the more virulent form of resentment towards probation officers who attempted to discuss the appropriate sentence, an attitude which was identified, quite wrongly, with an attempt to usurp the sentencing power of the court. The use of reports and the expression of an opinion as to the suitability of different forms of punishment were both approved by the Committee. They summarised the basic advantages of reports under three heads:

> " (*a*) information about the social and domestic background of the offender which is relevant to the court's assessment of his culpability;
> (*b*) information about the offender and his surroundings which is relevant to the court's consideration of his culpability;
> (*c*) an opinion as to the likely effect on the offender's criminal career of probation or some other specified form of sentence." [79]

It must be remembered that the Streatfeild Committee was basically considering the position in the higher courts. It is almost inevitable that magistrates will not have as much time to spend on wide ranging inquiries and indeed in many instances the maximum sentence is such that to do so would be wasteful effort. There is, nevertheless, a growing awareness of the interrelation of crime and general anti-social behaviour and it would appear that the position is that magistrates' courts should be encouraged to spend more time on obtaining information prior to sentencing.[80] Whilst the greater attention paid to reports by a probation officer cannot be attacked there are certain points from the offender's point of view which tend to have been neglected.

It is entirely within the discretion of the offender as to whom he calls to give evidence on his behalf. It is not rare for at least one witness as to character, usually a wife, parson or friend, to be called. The probation officer may however use his wide power

78 para. 315.
79 para. 395.
80 This would raise the administrative problem of frequent adjournment.

of investigation to obtain information from many sources. If the offender's home life is unhappy he will probably not put this forward as mitigation, but the probation officer may well put it forward as useful information. If a situation of this type occurs there is plainly a conflict of interest between the probation officer and the offender. Unless the probation officer already knows the family most of his evidence will be hearsay, hearsay collected quickly for the purpose of the report. Under the rules of trial it would be excluded and it may indeed be, through no fault of the probation officer, prejudiced and unfair. It is not easy to challenge a probation officer. They are usually welcomed by the defence as experts who can help. When it is necessary to challenge a probation officer the task is a difficult one and a hazardous one too, for it may be resented by the court.

A far greater danger at this stage of the trial is the inability of the defence to put its case convincingly forward. Where the matter is complicated, a history of mental illness or family trouble would be an example, the collation of the necessary evidence is beyond the defendant who is not represented. He will probably try to make his point in a laboriously composed letter to the court. Even where there is legal representation the legal profession is not as a whole well organised to collect together quickly the necessary evidence. This raises the problem which is always present—whether to gather the necessary information at the cost of a lengthy adjournment or whether to allow a quick decision.

Legal representation

The methods of obtaining legal representation—legal aid, dock briefs and so on—have very detailed rules. It is only necessary here to consider whether legal representation is an important feature of the legal process. There is no doubt that it can be regarded as time consuming. Where the accused is legally represented his case will be fully presented and it may well be repetitively presented in the view of a court with a long list of cases. There can be little ground for objection where the accused pleads not guilty and there is a trial of the issues. It is a rare accused who has the skill or confidence to adequately present his case, and even if he has these lack of familiarity with the procedure may well prove an obstacle. Courts are generally extremely sympathetic and helpful to the accused conducting his own defence. Indeed, it would not be an exaggeration to say that there are marginal advantages to the unrepresented accused but these are far outweighed by the disadvantages. No one should have to face trial on indictment without legal assistance if he desires it. The fact that there appears to be no sensible defence is an argument for giving help rather than withholding it. The matter is not quite so clear in summary trial where the offences, and consequences, can be so much less serious. It is nevertheless a safe assumption that if an accused is determined to plead not guilty he does so either because he is convinced of his innocence or because he has a wrong-headed view of the position. In either case he is sincere in his desire to make a challenge and his sincerity deserves full support. The occasional vexatious plea of not guilty is inevitable but does not invalidate the general principle.

The matter is not quite so clear where the accused pleads guilty. If the job of the lawyer is regarded only as making an elegant plea in mitigation then there is little to be said for this being universal. On the other hand there are two factors which indicate that representation is beneficial. Although a fair number can make a very effective plea on their own behalf—far better than the second-hand speech of the lawyer—the vast majority of convicted persons have little idea of what to say. If the lawyer is given the opportunity to study the position of his client, to make his own inquiries (if counsel is retained, this presupposes the need for a solicitor who has the facilities for this), to talk with medical advisers and the probation service then he is able to give the traditional virtue of balance to the sentencing process.

Bibliography

Criminal law text books normally begin with a brief look at fundamental problems:

Cross and Jones, Introduction to Criminal Law (Butterworths, 6th ed., 1968).

Kenny, Ed. Turner, Outlines of Criminal Law (Cambridge 19th ed., 1966).

Smith and Hogan, Criminal Law (Butterworths, 1965).

There are two which concentrate upon general principles, the first English, the second American:

Glanville Williams, Criminal Law, The General Part (Stevens, 2nd ed., 1961).

Hall, J. Principles of the Criminal Law (Bobbs Merrill, 2nd ed., 1960).

The works dealing with the criminal/moral problem tend to be published lectures or essays:

DEVLIN, P., The Enforcement of Morals (Oxford, 1965).

HART, H. L. A., Law, Liberty and Morality (Oxford, 1963).
The Morality of the Criminal Law (Oxford, 1965).
Punishment and Responsibility (Oxford, 1968).

WOOTTON, B., Crime and the Criminal Law (Stevens, 1963).

There are similarly many books on the legal system all of which include considerable detail on the criminal courts. The best is perhaps:

JACKSON, R. M., Machinery of Justice in England (Cambridge, 5th ed., 1967).

Other useful reviews of the area of criminal law enforcement and trial are:

JACKSON, R. M., Enforcing the Law (Macmillan, 1967).

DEVLIN, P., The Criminal Prosecution in England (Oxford, 1960).

ALLEN, C. K., The Queen's Peace (Stevens, 1953).

Although there are a multiplicity of books on crime and the criminal trial there is a dearth of general works on the law of evidence. The basic work is now clearly:

CROSS, R., Evidence (Butterworths, 3rd ed., 1967).

A book that is more revealing than perhaps the author intended it to be is:

DU CANN, R., The Art of the Advocate (Pelican, 1964).

But the best analysis is:

GLANVILLE WILLIAMS, Proof of Guilt (Stevens, 2nd ed., 1960).

This is a field which at one time attracted little academic attention. This has changed and the most important journal devoted entirely to this area is the *Criminal Law Review*, published monthly by Sweet and Maxwell.

For two recent comparative works see:

COUTTS, J. A., The Accused (Stevens, 1966).

KARLEN, D., Anglo-American Criminal Justice (Oxford, 1967).

CHAPTER 2

DETECTION OF CRIME AND PROSECUTION OF OFFENDERS

Introduction

ONE of the important, and unfortunately elusive, factors which helps to determine the supply of convicted criminals is prosecution policy. It is an area of remarkably little regulation, of historical anomaly and of custom. Obvious problems are continually posed in this context and these vary from crime to crime. No one would expect to be seen committing murder or rape without a prosecution following and yet on the other hand a large proportion of the population commit regulatory crime, particularly road traffic offences, are seen to do so and yet are not prosecuted. The figures are remarkable. One commentator has highlighted these startling facts:

> "In 1961, for example, Manchester prosecuted 4,569 motorists for obstruction and parking offences, Liverpool 1,386. For neglect of traffic directions and prescribed route directions Manchester had 6,747 prosecutions as against 987 in Liverpool."[1]

These are mysterious regulatory factors which appear to affect all areas. Courts rarely have more criminal cases of this type than they can cope with. It is usual, for example, for there to be a constant backlog of some few months for road traffic cases but courts never seem to find themselves inundated so that they cannot cope at all. There must be several subconscious regulators. An individual policeman upon whom the initiative to report first falls plainly does not want to arrange his life so that it becomes completely cyclical—a few days reporting followed by a stretch in court. He no doubt aims at a balance and has his own standard of references as to what is reasonable. In the same way the higher officers who decide as between prosecution and caution must have in mind a balance between men in court and men on the beats.

It is not only the agencies of enforcement who give crime the characteristics of an iceberg. The incidence of complaints has the same effect. Many crimes, especially those involving offences

[1] Geoffrey Marshall, *Police and Government*, 1965, p. 116.

against property, lie on the borderline between civil and criminal law and fall into each category. It is often better, from the point of view of the complainant, to treat a crime as a civil matter and accept payment from the offender. It is often felt not to be worthwhile to prosecute, the time and effort required are not commensurate with the complainant's satisfaction in seeing the offender punished. So many who are found out in petty thefts are warned, or dismissed but not prosecuted.

Even when a complaint is made the success in turning it into a criminal prosecution depends upon the use the police make of their powers of investigation. Here the law attempts to hold some sort of balance of convenience. It is clear that an attempt to secure the greatest possible number of prosecutions would lead to intolerable pressure upon the police and this in turn would make their behaviour towards suspects intolerable. In general the law goes a considerable way towards protecting the suspect and we expect our police forces to act within the spirit of these rules.

It will be apparent that what in fact is achieved is a fairly delicate balance which is almost self-achieving. Given a certain number of courts we will tend to get a certain volume of prosecutions. Given very general laws which tend to cover the morally blameworthy and blameless there will be great use of the discretion to prosecute and wide variation in its use. This section of the book is an attempt to sketch in broadest outline the shape of the law covering some of these points so that its effect upon the state of crime at any time may be estimated.

The prosecution agencies

It is still theoretically true that the natural prosecutor of an accused person is the complainant who has himself been injured by the crime. Prosecutions are, of course, brought on behalf of the Crown, for all criminal trials take the form of a contest between the Crown and the accused. The complainant lays an information before a magistrate who, if satisfied that an offence is indicated, issues a summons. The summons is then served upon the accused and the court proceedings are in this way initiated.

In practice the number of private prosecutions is small. Serious crime is rarely left in the hands of the private prosecutor and a large part of the newer regulatory offences have no complainant in the usual sense of a victim. Most complaints are taken over by the police who lay the information and follow up with police prosecutions. Some government departments are in the habit of bringing their own prosecutions, those for breaches of food regulations and of factory safety rules are most frequent.

There are several minor crimes, assaults and similar disturbances between neighbours are good examples, in which the police usually decline to take action and in these cases the private citizen has to bring his own prosecution if he wishes to proceed.

Although the police are responsible for the bulk of prosecutions they are not without supervision. There has existed, since the middle of the nineteenth century, a Director of Public Prosecutions. His function is not only to prosecute, in certain cases, but also to advise the police and others who apply to him. The Director himself prosecutes all murder cases and any other cases which appear to have great importance or difficulty.[2] He will also prosecute for government departments who refer cases to him.

The police are under a duty to report certain serious offences to him and they follow his advice whether to prosecute or not. Some offences by statute can only be brought on the advice of the Director of Public Prosecutions. Thus the recent Criminal Law Act 1967 provides that the new offences of assisting offenders and concealing offences or giving false information shall only be brought with the consent of the Director of Public Prosecutions.[3]

Despite these provisions the real discretion to prosecute or not falls where it matters most—on the police. Offences with which the Director of Public Prosecutions is concerned are largely offences on which there is a policy to prosecute offenders as a matter of course if the evidence warrants it. The police are concerned with " routine " offences about which they are accustomed to use a great deal of discretion. Everyone is familiar with the police " caution." This is nothing more than a decision by the police not to prosecute an alleged offender who is happy enough, in most circumstances, to accept a warning not to transgress again. It is a usual way of dealing with a very large number of, for example, traffic offences of a relatively minor character.

The police are also likely to issue cautions instead of prosecuting in cases involving juveniles. In some forces these cautions are administered personally at a police station by a senior police officer with the juvenile and his parents present. The Criminal statistics give some account as shown by the table on p. 57, below.

Too little research into this aspect of law enforcement has been undertaken. The Royal Commission on the Police touched briefly on the topic. They had had evidence on the point, pointing out, for example, uneven treatment of homosexual offences. They acknowledged that road traffic laws constituted the major

[2] In 1967 the total number of such prosecutions was 2,134 out of 8,023 applications to the Director.

[3] s. 4 (4) and s. 5 (3).

NON-INDICTABLE OFFENCES OTHER THAN MOTORING OFFENCES, 1966 [4]

	No. of persons found guilty	*No. of persons found guilty and no. of persons cautioned*
Under 14	6,234	9,307
14–17	24,472	29,979
17–21	53,811	57,134
21 and over	230,342	256,529

CAUTIONS FOR INDICTABLE OFFENCES, 1966

	Male	Female
Under 14	11,222	2,385
14–17	6,459	1,942
17–21	2,554	392
21 and over	2,966	2,089

area of problem. They had recommended to them a system of public prosecution separate from the police along the Scottish pattern. They set out the advantages:

> "... first, that it would minister to good relations between the police and the public if the decision to prosecute were placed in other hands; secondly, that it would be in the public interest to relieve the police of their present unregulated discretion in this matter; and thirdly, that a system of independent public prosecution would make for greater uniformity in the enforcement of the criminal law." [5]

They later discussed road traffic problems and felt that it was the pattern of the law rather than the discretion of the police which led to most misunderstanding between police and public. The Commission did not feel that this problem fell within their terms of reference and merely recommended that the police should have more legal advice available and they suggested the appointment of a prosecuting solicitor for every force which was without one.[6]

Investigation of crime

The detection and investigation of crime are relevant to this work only in so far as the methods employed and framework of rules help to determine the pattern of accused persons presented to the courts. As with most parts of the machinery of the criminal

[4] *Criminal Statistics* 1966, Cmnd. 3332.
[5] Final Report, Cmnd. 1728, para. 379.
[6] *Ibid.* para. 380.

process English law aims at achieving a balance. It is clear that to encourage the police to search out and detect every possible crime would lead to intolerable interference with daily life. Similarly to allow the police unrestrained power to investigate suspected crime would infringe the liberty of the individual. Curbs have therefore been imposed on the police.

The most notable example of this process is contained in the so-called Judges' Rules.[7] These rules, which were revised in 1964, cover interrogation and the taking of statements by the police. They have their origin in a reply made by the Lord Chief Justice of the day, Lord Alverstone, in 1906 to the Chief Constable of Birmingham who had sought his advice. A brief résumé of the rules will indicate clearly that they are designed to protect the suspect and indeed they can be quite a hindrance to the police.

Rule I states that a police officer can question any person, whether suspected or not, from whom he thinks he can obtain useful information. This can be done even where the person is in custody provided that he has not been charged with the offence or told he may be prosecuted for it. Rule II, which is the crucial rule, provides that as soon as a police officer has evidence giving him reasonable grounds for suspecting a person has committed an offence he must caution that person in the well-known form before he asks him questions. The rule is framed objectively, that is to say, the test is whether evidence which should give rise to grounds of suspicion does not depend on the individual interrogator but on an objective standard. Rule III provides for a further caution to be given when a suspect is charged or told he will be prosecuted for an offence.
This too is in similar terms:

> Do you wish to say anything? You are not obliged to say anything unless you wish to do so but whatever you say will be taken down in writing and may be given in evidence.

It goes on to make the point that it is only rarely that a person who has been so charged or informed would thereafter be questioned. Such questions as may be put are only those which serve to clear up ambiguities in any statement made or which may serve to prevent or minimise harm to others. Before such questioning may take place a further form of words is laid down:

> I wish to put some questions to you about the offence with which you have been charged (*or* about the offence for which

[7] The rules are published as a White Paper by the Home Office.

> you may be prosecuted). You are not obliged to answer any of these questions, but if you do the questions and answers will be taken down in writing and may be given in evidence.

The rules go on to make provisions about the form of written statements, to provide for situations where statements are made by co-accuseds and they are followed by administrative directions which set out approved procedures.

The new rules have made " reasonable grounds for suspicion " the significant point in interrogation and in doing so have advanced the duty to warn the suspect. The immediate reactions of a police writer to the rules are perhaps summed up by his somewhat cynical last sentence, " I doubt whether any more thieves will be caught or convicted as a result of it." [8] There can be no doubt that the desire to protect the suspect has led to considerable limitation upon the interrogator even if, as the same writer mentions, some feel " that the new rules will be just as easy for police officers to honour in the breach as the old rules." [8]

A comparison between those rules and the rules governing search will serve to make the point that the whole area of investigation and detection is one which has never been given systematic logical analysis. The police right to enter private premises without a warrant has always been narrowly given. Yet case law has established that evidence which has been obtained by an illegal search may be used at a subsequent trial.[9]

It will be obvious that the police have to pay a great deal of attention to matters of this nature. They are also in a position in which they have to be continually mindful of their powers of arrest. Again, as with search, the normal situation is for the arrest to be effected under the authority of a warrant but the police have extensive powers of arrest without warrant. These powers were very much tied up with the category of crime known as felony and now that felonies have been abolished the Criminal Law Act 1967 has replaced them with " arrestable offences," the very name of which indicates the importance of the distinction. Arrestable offences are defined as " offences for which the sentence is fixed by law or for which a person (not previously convicted) may under or by virtue of any enactment be sentenced to imprisonment for a term of five years." [10] It also applies to atttempts to commit such crimes. This statute goes

[8] [1964] Crim.L.R. 173.
[9] *Elias* v. *Pasmore* [1934] 2 K.B. 164. See *Cross on Evidence*, 3rd ed., pp. 266 *et seq.*
[10] s. 2 (1).

on to set out the general rules covering arrest without warrant—the first time this has been incorporated in a statute.[11]

There is much in these preliminary stages on the way to criminal trial to interest the criminologist. Police procedures and attitudes can do much to alter the pattern of reported crime and it can affect the individual in numerous ways. There is a large area of " preventive crime " which ranges over attempts and a group of offences such as loitering whose chief element is the suspicion that crime may be committed by the accused. The details of this law are outside the scope of this book but its application has an important effect on the picture of current crime.

A combination of accurate and detailed record keeping by the police and investigation based on *modus operandi* can mean that a criminal who has previously committed crimes of a certain type will find that he is quite often visited by police who are checking that he cannot be responsible for a new crime they are investigating. This can have an unfortunate effect upon a criminal who is trying to reform, on the other hand it is undoubtedly a proven way of uncovering the perpetrators of crimes.

Remand in custody and bail

One feature of criminal process is the retention of accused persons in custody pending investigation and trial. On the other hand imprisonment without trial is obviously only justifiable under the most carefully regulated circumstances and its length must be kept to a minimum. The problem is easy to state. In 1962, for instance, 35,000 persons were in prison awaiting trial. They had either not been granted bail or had been unable to comply with the conditions. Of these over 1,000 were acquitted and of the remainder about half were not given a prison sentence. Early emphasis was placed upon the amount of the bail fixed—the Bill of Rights 1688 provides that bail should not be excessive. Recently emphasis has been on cutting down as far as possible unnecessary remands in custody. The Criminal Justice Act 1967 has, as we shall see, attempted to tackle this problem.

Bail is a process by which a person is released on condition that he presents himself at the time and place fixed for the next court hearing, usually the trial. A recognisance is fixed in terms of a certain sum of money which will be forfeited if the accused fails to turn up and sureties may be demanded to reinforce the

[11] ss. 2 (2)–(7), 3.

bail. Technically where there are sureties the accused is not set free but is released from custody of the court to that of the sureties who may subsequently hand him back before the time appointed. It is interesting to note that bail in England only involves putting a sum of money in jeopardy should there be a failure to appear, in the U.S.A. actual money or a bond has to be deposited at the time bail is granted.

This section is concerned principally with bail pending trial. It should be noted, however, that where a person has been taken into police custody without a warrant then a senior police officer may allow bail and must do so, unless on investigating the circumstances he feels that the case is a serious one, where it is impossible to bring the accused before a magistrate within twenty-four hours.

Once an accused appears before a magistrate it is the custom of the police to decide whether or not they will resist an application for bail whenever there is to be an adjournment because investigations are not complete or the trial is for some reason not ready to proceed. It is only natural that their judgment will tend towards resistance where they have any suspicion that their task, whether of completing inquiries or of securing the accused's attendance at the trial, may be difficult if he is released. The position caused concern and a new approach has been adopted by the Criminal Justice Act 1967.[12]

Magistrates have wide powers of remand and those powers enable a remand to be made either in custody or on bail.[13] They have previously had an unfettered discretion but now it has been laid down in certain restricted categories that bail must be granted except in certain specified cases. These categories cover all summary offences and all indictable and hybrid (*i.e.*, both summary and indictable) offences once a plea is taken in summary trial, the magistrates having decided to deal with the case in this way. They do not include, however, offences carrying a greater maximum punishment than six months' imprisonment.[14] The restrictions also apply to committals for trial of summary offences where trial on indictment has been chosen.[15]

The exceptional cases where the court may make its decision as to bail are set out in section 18 (5) and they relate basically either to the position and character of the accused or to the nature of the charge:

[12] "Justice" published the Interim Report of a Working Party on Bail and Remands in Custody in 1966.
[13] Magistrates' Courts Act 1952, s. 105.
[14] Criminal Justice Act 1967, s. 18 (1) (2).
[15] *Ibid.* s. 18 (3).

(1) the charge carries a term of imprisonment of at least six months and the accused has previously served a term in prison or Borstal;
(2) the accused has previously failed to comply with the terms of his release on bail;
(3) the offence charged was committed on bail;
(4) it is necessary to remand in custody to establish the accused's identity or address;
(5) the accused has no fixed abode or resides normally outside the U.K.;
(6) the crime charged is an assault or threat of violence; possessing a firearm or imitation firearm, an explosive or an offensive weapon; indecent conduct towards a person under sixteen;
(7) the accused is likely to commit an offence if released on bail;
(8) it is necessary for the accused's own protection that he remain in custody.

It will be appreciated that these are the instances where a court may decide to remand in custody—there is no suggestion that they *must* do so if any of the above criteria are present.[16] It is also privided that a court may remand in custody if the accused fails to provide a proper recognisance or to find the necessary sureties.[17]

The serious nature of refusal to grant bail is underlined by the provision that where bail is refused and the accused is not represented by a lawyer he must be given a written statement of the reasons for refusal.[18] It has always been possible to apply to a High Court judge for bail where this has been refused. A summons is issued to show cause before a judge in chambers why bail shall not be issued.[19]

Bail has also been made more flexible. It is now possible to attach to bail any conditions which the court feels will help to ensure the accused's appearance at his trial in due course, or may otherwise be necessary in the interests of justice.[20] The court cannot impose the requirement to find sureties as to these conditions. The most obvious condition and one which has been voluntarily used previously but will now have legal backing is the requirement that a passport be surrendered. In a similar category is the requirement of regular reporting to the police.

16 Criminal Justice Act 1967, s. 18 (5).
17 *Ibid.* s. 18 (4).
18 *Ibid.* s. 18 (8).
19 If bail is refused he must be told of this right.
20 *Ibid.* s. 21.

The new provisions have undoubtedly regularised and improved the requirements as to bail. It has made it clear beyond doubt that bail is to be regarded as desirable wherever possible and reasonable.

It is obvious that for a court to consider properly whether bail can be allowed or not the character and antecedents of the accused must be carefully investigated. It has always been a problem to hide from the court of trial information of this sort which ideally it should not have until after conviction. Courts have always attempted to ensure that a magistrate who has determined the question of bail does not sit at a subsequent trial. This is now given statutory force by the provision that a magistrate in such circumstances shall not sit at the trial if an earlier bail application has disclosed to that magistrate that the accused has earlier convictions.[21]

We have been dealing so far with remands which are made because the time for the trial has not yet come. There is provision for remands for a special purpose—for inquiry into the physical or mental condition of the accused.[22] It is possible for the remand to be on bail or in custody but there is a strong body of opinion that investigations of this sort are preferably carried out in the freer circumstances of remand on bail.

Reports

One of the most important features of the criminal process is the preparation of reports on those accused or convicted to assist the court in determining appropriate treatment or sentence. The preparation of antecedent history is the task of the police and they, in general, produce fairly stereotyped histories telling of the date and place of birth, employment and employment record, and centrally and importantly previous criminal convictions and appearances before courts. This is essential information which a sentencing court must have. It cannot be regarded as more than the absolute minimum. This should not be regarded as disparaging the work of the police. They are often able, either from their own careful inquiries or more usually from their own knowledge of the accused and his family and associates, to give a court a great deal of help in assessing not only the accused's complicity in the crime but also in judging his social background. This has particularly been marked in the medium-sized and smaller quarter sessions where the police have a wide and deep knowledge of a

21 Criminal Justice Act 1967, s. 19.
22 Magistrates' Courts Act 1952, s. 26.

large number of families in the area and have long experience with families whose members tend to find themselves before the criminal courts. The same is true of police help before magistrates' courts and it would be unwise to underestimate its importance. The bigger courts, and the tendency appears to be towards regionalisation, do not obtain these advantages and reports tend to rely more upon inquiry than upon the collective knowledge of a local police force.

The Streatfeild Committee on the Business of the Criminal Courts had quite a lot of importance to say about the putting of the necessary information before a sentencing court.[23] It stressed the importance of the attachment of the English trial procedure to immediate sentencing after conviction wherever possible and so it made the preliminary point that the necessary information should ideally be prepared ready for a court in case it may be required. It is nonetheless emphasised that it is more objectionable to sentence with inadequate information than to adjourn for the few days that will usually be required to secure the information. The Streatfeild Committee felt that police reports should be restricted to the factual account and cover the same matters as they have traditionally done. They felt that a deeper study of a person is best left to a trained social worker such as a probation officer. On the other hand they did not want to discourage the police from viewing the person against his wider social background and so producing more balanced and helpful antecedents.

There is no doubt that a probation officer's report is the kernel of the reporting process. The Streatfeild Committee thought that a probation report could helpfully cover these matters:

"(a) information about the social and domestic background of the offender which is relevant to the court's assessment of his culpability;

(b) information about the offender and his surroundings which is relevant to the court's consideration of how his criminal career might be checked; and

(c) an opinion as to the likely effect on the offender's criminal career of probation or some other specified form of punishment." [24]

The report considered each of these three heads in some detail but it is not necessary to set this out here.[25] The third head

[23] Cmnd. 1289. See particularly Chap. 11.
[24] para. 335.
[25] paras. 336–356.

shows the slow acceptance of advice by courts. It is true that the responsibility for sentencing is always that of the court and for many years some courts resented discussion by others of this aspect of the court's work. Even where it was allowed in some courts it was dressed up in phrases such as " if you take a certain course, then . . ." which did nothing for clarity nor did it protect the supposed position of the court. It is fortunate that these attitudes have almost now completely disappeared but it is remarkable that the Streatfeild Report could include a cross-heading " the propriety of including in probation reports opinions on the likely effect of sentences." [26]

The strength of probation officers' reports depends upon the training, ability and experience of the individual officer. It is clearly inappropriate to submit them to the same evidential rules as are applied to evidence at the trial. This has certain dangers which the Streatfeild Committee recognised when it said, for example, that

> " He [the probation officer] should always take care to confine himself to opinions founded on actual and substantial experience [whether his or his colleagues] of the effects of the sentence and should have regard to the results of general research into what sentences achieve, as they become available." [27]

The only important procedural rule about the reception of probation reports is that which insists that the offender must be given a copy.[28] This rule cannot, of course, apply to oral reports or answers to questioning by the court. Nothing is said in this statute about the right of the offender to challenge either the factual background to the report or the conclusions that are drawn. This is always allowed and the rules of the conduct of proceedings generally before a court are such to ensure that this must be done, indeed it is true to say that it would require statutory provision to remove the right of challenge. The only practical problem arises if a written report is submitted and given to the offender but the maker is not tendered for challenge. This would seem to deny the offender a fundamental right. The raising of this point should not obscure the more usual practice by which a probation officer is ready to discuss his report with the legal representatives of the offender before it is given in evidence. This most generally leads to a sense of co-operation and

[26] Before para. 343.

[27] para. 342.

[28] Criminal Justice Act 1948, s. 43. The report will not usually be read in full in court: see *Smith* [1968] Crim.L.R. 33.

indeed it would be wrong to regard the probation officer as in any sense in a similar position to a prosecution witness just because the offender should be allowed the right of challenge.

The position is not quite so satisfactory in relation to probation reports on juveniles before the juvenile court. It is governed by the Summary Jurisdiction (Children and Young Persons) Rules 1933 and does not provide for a copy of a report to be given to the juvenile offender's legal representative. This is particularly unfortunate since it is expressly provided that a written report may be received without its being read out in open court. This means that a legal representative may be faced with the task of addressing the court on behalf of the offender in ignorance of the recommendations of the probation officer. It will be readily imagined that few courts take advantage of the possibility of this happening and reports are shown on request. Where the juvenile appears before an adult court the report may be given not to him but to his parent or guardian.

Little need here be said of other types of report which may on occasion be put before a court. The need for and use of medical reports is, for example, obvious.

Bibliography

The two best general works covering some, but not all, of the topics raised in this chapter are:

Jackson, R. M., Machinery of Justice (Cambridge, 1967).

Devlin, P., The Criminal Prosecution in England (O.U.P., 1960).

Two blue books which are important are:

Report of the Interdepartmental Committee on the Business of the Criminal Courts (1961, Cmnd. 1289).

Royal Commission on the Police (1962, Cmnd. 1728).

Some of the topics, arrest and search for example, are usually treated in books on constitutional law. An interesting general treatment is:

Street, H., Freedom, the Individual and the Law (Pelican).

There is an interesting recent study of bail:

Bottomley, A. N., " The Granting of Bail, Principles and Practice," 31 M.L.R. 40.

CHAPTER 3

THE PENAL SYSTEM

CRIME IN ENGLAND [1]

THE start of any meaningful examination of crime, and of a penal system designed to control it, must be the acquisition of some basic information about the extent and nature of the problem. It scarcely needs saying that we need to know the number of criminal acts, how serious they are, how many offenders there are, and something about them. The list can be elaborated according to taste: the mobility of criminals about the country, the amount of " specialisation " in particular types of offence, the extent of highly organised group crime.

The sorry fact is that this is almost entirely wishful thinking. We have no precise, accurate information about crime in this, or any other, country. Although more elaborate explanations can be offered, the basic reason for this sad state of affairs is that almost all criminals hope either that their acts will pass unnoticed, or at least, that their responsibility will go undetected.[2]

Attempts have been made to overcome this basic problem. An offender may be willing to give an account of his criminal acts, provided that he can do so anonymously and to someone who has no connection with the police or prosecuting authorities. Various experiments have been made, using interviews or questionnaires, to discover the true extent of criminal experience amongst those with and those without official convictions. Even such experiments are open to some doubt: those willing to cooperate may not be representative, and they may be tempted to " over-report."

The results of these experiments are amazing, although a short period of self-examination often reduces the reader's amazement. An example is the work of Erickson and Empey.[3] They interviewed fifty American high school boys aged 15–17. None had made a court appearance. The boys reported that they had committed 1,031 thefts, of which 91·3 per cent. passed undetected,

1 Nationalists must forgive us: we use the term " England " to include Wales—and Berwick-upon-Tweed. See Wales and Berwick Act 1746.

2 Some offenders seek attention, *e.g.*, indecent exposers.

3 " Court Records, Undetected Delinquency and Decision-making " (1963) 54 J.Crim.L., C. and P.S. 456. For other work, see the summary in D. J. West, *The Young Offender*, pp. 39 *et seq.*

and 546 offences in a further category which included arson, malicious damage to property, and breaking and entering. 96·7 per cent. of these offences escaped detection; and, obviously, none led to court proceedings.

Criminal case mortality

This is a convenient phrase describing the process which leads 100 actual offences to appear in the official statistics as, let us say, ten " crimes known to the police," later as four crimes " cleared up," leading to three prosecutions and perhaps two convictions. At each stage, some offences disappear without trace.

As the self-reporting experiments demonstrate, the greatest mortality occurs between the commission of the offence and its becoming known to the police. It will only become known to the police if it is discovered, by someone other than the offender, and reported.

Many offences are simply never discovered. They may never be seen—a homosexual offence, a television set used without a licence in an attic bed-sitting room. Or the results of the offence may be seen, but may be put down to other, non-criminal causes: a fence pulled down by vandals might be thought to have been damaged by cattle, or by storm; a diamond ring stolen by a sneak-thief could always have been taken by a hoarding bird.

Even where an offence is seen, and some offences must be seen if only by the victim (*e.g.*, an assault) the police may not be informed. The observer may not wish " to get involved "; police-public relations may be bad generally or in a particular area; it may seem very unlikely that police action could lead to results. On the other hand, some offences are almost certain to be discovered and reported to the police; for example, the theft of a famous work of art, or a bank robbery.[4]

If an offence is reported, it will appear in the criminal statistics as a crime known to the police. These statistics are the most accurate we have of the pattern of crime. Presumably major changes in their figures will reflect real changes in criminal behaviour: this assumes that the " mortality rate " remains steady, an assumption which seems reasonable but cannot be proved correct.

An offence is regarded as " cleared up " when the police decide that they know the identity of the offender. He may not be prosecuted: he may be dead, or may be cautioned, or may

[4] Sellin, " The Significance of Records of Crime " (1951) 67 L.Q.R. 495.

ask that the offence be taken into consideration when he is sentenced for some other offence. Statistics for " persons proceeded against " must therefore be kept distinct, and only a proportion of those persons will be convicted and sentenced.

Some offences are more likely than others to be " cleared up." For example, any offence involving the possession of prohibited articles is almost certain to be one in which, if the crime is known to the police at all, the offender will be caught " red-handed." But where only the results of the offence are noticed, detection is unlikely. This can be illustrated by the " clear-up " rates for various offences in London.[5]

Offence	*Percentage cleared up*
Possessing housebreaking tools	100·0
Causing death by dangerous driving	100·0
Receiving	100·0
Manslaughter and infanticide	98·0
Larceny by a servant	95·1
Shoplifting	94·1
Larceny in a house (no breaking)	10·0
Larceny from unattended vehicles	8·0
Larceny of pedal cycles	6·4

Shoplifting is an interesting example. It is an offence which must very often pass unnoticed. If it is noticed and reported, the offender will almost always be known: hence the high " clear-up " rate.

In England, for all indictable offences, that rate was 40·2 per cent. in 1966 and 41·2 per cent. in 1967, improvements on earlier years after some years of steady decline.

Accuracy and suitability of criminal statistics

In many countries, including England, large volumes of criminal statistics are published. It must be asked how accurate are these statistics, and how suitable are they for criminological purposes.

We have already seen that the statistics cannot be an accurate reflection of the true crime rate. One might assume that they will at least be an accurate record of crimes known to the police.

[5] Report of the Commissioner of Police for the Metropolis 1966, p. 101; the overall clear-up rate is lower in London than elsewhere (22.3 per cent. for indictable offences in London; 45·8 per cent. outside London) but this does not affect the argument.

Unfortunately, there is a good deal of evidence that this is not always the case. Correct police procedure involves the recording of every offence brought to the notice of the police, however trivial, and however unlikely it is that the offence will be "cleared up." There is an obvious temptation to suppress some of these offences, to produce an impressively high "clear-up" rate.

So, in some police forces, at some periods of time, the practice has grown up of maintaining a secondary register of suspected offences which is not incorporated in the annual reports and returns of the force. The Metropolitan Police maintained such a register, a "Suspected Stolen Book," until 1932,[6] and the Kilmarnock police in Scotland had a similar practice concerning housebreakings until 1960.[7]

Similar variations in statistics can be due to particular bursts of police activity. A case in the local courts may excite public alarm about a particular type of offence, or a new Chief Constable may order a "drive" against certain offences. For a short time more offences will be discovered and recorded, while the actual number of offences may even decline.

Even if the statistics are accurate they suffer certain weaknesses from a criminological point of view. For good legal reasons, criminal conduct has to be classified into a number of carefully defined offences.[8] For procedural reasons, these offences may be grouped into categories, such as "indictable" and "non-indictable," or "felony" and "misdemeanour." These classifications often obscure the nature of the conduct involved.

For example, stealing an empty milk bottle is a felony and an indictable offence. Cruelty to children is non-indictable, and obtaining a million pounds by fraud may only be a misdemeanour.[9] Tyres may be stolen from cars parked in a secluded area, leading to several charges of larceny, and some for receiving. At the same time a department store is set alight by an arsonist; his single offence causes immense damage and danger to lives, but it makes only one entry in the statistics. If it could be produced, an index of crime in terms of damage caused, to persons and

6 See the Commissioner's Report for 1932.

7 Shields and Duncan, *The State of Crime in Scotland*, p. 62. More alarming illustrations can be found in the United States: in New York City 315 larcenies were recorded in July 1950 and 3,845 in November 1950; the police administration was changed in October.

8 Changes in legal definitions can distort apparent trends in crime statistics.

9 In England the felony-misdemeanour distinction does not affect the form of the *Criminal Statistics*, and disappeared on January 1, 1968: Criminal Law Act 1967, s. 1.

property, would be much more valuable than any totals of indictable offences; some work has been done by the American criminologist Sellin on this problem.[10]

English statistics

The principal sources of information in England is the *Criminal Statistics*, an annual Home Office publication. It contains annual tables relating to criminal proceedings, distinguishing between magistrates' and the higher courts of assize and quarter sessions. Further information about offences known to the police and cleared up, and the use of police cautions is contained in the long "introductory note" to the statistics, and in a section of comparative tables showing trends over a period of time, related to estimated population figures.

The Home Office also produces and distributes to interested organisations and individuals a mimeographed volume of *Supplementary Statistics*. These give information for each police district concerning known crime, the results of proceedings and the use of cautions, together with some information about the number of previous convictions of those convicted during the relevant year.

Further sources of information are the annual Reports of the Commissioner of Police of the Metropolis, of the Chief Inspector of Constabulary, and of the Prison Department of the Home Office. All are published by the Stationery Office.

Although much detailed information can be gathered from these sources, there are many anomalies. Information about criminal gangs is only available for London [11]; and while for indictable offences there are tables of crimes known to the police, for non-indictable offences there are figures only of persons proceeded against. These and other problems were examined by the Perks Committee,[12] which made recommendations for improvements.

Crime in England

We must now examine the pattern of crime revealed, however imperfectly, by the *Criminal Statistics*. The following Table gives

[10] See especially Sellin and Wolfgang, *The Measurement of Delinquency* (1964). On the whole subject, see McClintock and Avison, "Ways of Classifying Offences for Criminological Research," a paper presented at the National Conference on Research and Teaching in Criminology, 1964.

[11] In the Commissioner's Report. For example, in 1966, of those arrested when under 21, 57 per cent. were operating in the company of others. Tables indicate the number, size and age of the various groups. 1966 Report (H.C. 544), p. 67.

[12] Cmnd. 3448, December 1967.

figures of persons found guilty of offences in 1966 [13]; as it includes non-indictable offences, it cannot be based on crimes known to the police. They are obviously more numerous: 232,000 persons were convicted in 1966 of indictable offences, but over 1,199,000 indictable offences were known to the police.

	Number of persons	*Percentage of total*
INDICTABLE OFFENCES		
Larceny	135,611	9·4
Breaking and entering	48,688	3·4
Receiving	13,027	0·9
Frauds and False Pretences	6,181	0·4
(Sub-total)	(203,507)	(14·1)
Violence against the person	16,036	1·1
Sexual offences	5,622	0·4
Robbery	1,702	0·1
Other indictable offences	5,987	0·4
TOTAL	232,854	16·1
NON-INDICTABLE OFFENCES		
Traffic offences [14]	944,326	65·3
Drunkenness, liquor offences	74,205	5·1
Revenue offences [15]	70,486	5·0
Railway and by-law offences	34,892	2·5
Damage to property	17,668	1·2
Other non-indictable offences	71,517	5·0
TOTAL	1,213,094	83·9

The Table shows that the calendar of crime is dominated by motoring offences, which many people (including the offenders) would not regard as crimes at all. They would class these offences, with others such as failing to renew certain licences, as "breaches of regulations."

Such a distinction might be little more than a playing with words, reflecting the often irrational public attitudes to certain

13 Source: *Criminal Statistics* 1966, pp. xi, xii, Table 1 (a).

14 Includes taking and driving away without the owner's consent, which many would regard as akin to larceny though it is clearly distinct in law.

15 Includes offences relating to dog, car and wireless licences, and National Insurance offences.

offences. False pretences to obtain a pension is a mean trick; tax evasion is a moral triumph over bureaucracy. In the particular case of motoring offences, Willett has shown that some 23 per cent. of serious motoring offenders have convictions for non-motoring offences; to that extent, the assumption that motoring offenders are " not real criminals " is open to question.[16]

Even if we ignore motoring offences altogether, we still find that serious, indictable crime is less important numerically than the non-indictable offences. This serves to underline what has already been said, that measuring crime by counting the individual offences, without taking into account the damage they cause, is not really profitable. It is the indictable offences, by and large, which excite public alarm, and which fill the prisons and other institutions; 96 per cent. of non-indictable offenders are fined, and prison sentences for non-indictable crime are largely reserved for assaults, vandalism and vagrancy offences.

There are, of course, some non-indictable offences which touch on serious social problems. Drunkenness and vagrancy are examples, and it is unfortunate if the inevitable concentration on indictable crime prevents these problems from receiving the public attention they deserve.

Indictable offences

The Table shows that offences against the person, murder, wounding, sexual offences, all of which attract much attention, are very much out-numbered by property offences. The typical indictable offence, and the typical offence of anyone subjected to positive penal treatment,[17] is a property offence, usually a form of stealing. Because of the different clear-up rates, the dominance of property offences is much clearer in statistics of crimes known to the police. The Table overleaf [18] gives such figures related to population and showing trends over fifteen years.

The steady increase in crime is revealed all too clearly in this table. Some of the increase can be discounted to allow for increased police activity and other factors, but the size of the increase is so great that the underlying trend cannot be denied.

If individual offence-groups are examined, it is offences of violence to the person and robbery (which often includes the element of violence) which have increased most markedly in

[16] *Criminal on the Road*, Tavistock 1964. His category of " serious " motoring offenders includes offences which are indictable: see his pp. 48 *et seq.*

[17] *i.e.*, probation or some form of institutional treatment, accepting for the moment that imprisonment merits the adjective " positive."

[18] Source: *Criminal Statistics* 1966, Comparative Tables, Table E.

INDICTABLE OFFENCES KNOWN TO THE POLICE

Per 1,000,000 of the population

Offence	*Annual averages* 1950–59	1960–64	*Year* 1966
Larceny	8,787·6	14,798·8	19,267·7
Breaking and entering	2,518·4	4,826·3	6,852·3
Receiving	215·0	384·9	538·2
Frauds and false pretences	692·3	1,072·6	1,264·7
(sub-total)	(12,213·3)	(21,082·6)	(27,922·9)
Violence against the person	224·1	463·9	647·4
Sexual offences	268·1	368·3	407·4
Robbery	31·7	68·6	121·2
All indictable offences	13,264·4	22,547·7	29,792·4

recent years. This development is a most disturbing one, especially when coupled with the changes in the age distribution of offenders noted below.

The figures tend to mask detailed trends. Within the larceny class, for example, thefts from parked cars, from automatic machines, meters and telephone boxes, and from the person have all increased markedly, but the theft of bicycles is on the decline. Detailed examination of particular offence-groups will always reveal these changes in fashion.[19]

The sex and age of offenders

Criminal behaviour is largely the province of young males. That statement is open to many objections, especially for treating criminal behaviour as a single phenomenon; but the statement remains true, as the Tables on p. 75 show.

Of those found guilty of indictable offences, only 13 per cent. are women. The reasons underlying this remarkable fact remain surprisingly obscure; the implications for the penal system are enormous.[20]

So far as age is concerned, the largest concentration of offenders is in the age-groups 14–17 and 17–21. The period from age 13 to age 25 is the principal period for criminal behaviour, after which it dwindles. This suggests very strongly that

19 A list of recent studies will be found in the Bibliography to this Chapter.
20 See *infra*, pp. 258 *et seq.*

Persons Found Guilty of Indictable Offences, 1966, by Age and Sex [21]

Expressed (a) per 100,000 of the population in the relevant age-group
(b) as a percentage of all persons found guilty

Age-group	*Per* 100,000		*Percentages*	
	M	F	M	F
Under 14	1,622	194	9·3	1·1
14 and under 17	3,199	516	14·2	2·2
17 and under 21	2,944	318	19·4	2·0
21 and under 30	1,867	209	22·7	2·5
30 and over	385	93	20·9	5·7
All ages	1,039	150	86·5	13·5

offenders " grow out of " crime, but we have no real knowledge of the mechanisms involved. Meanwhile, the penal system has to make its most elaborate arrangements for the age-group we have identified.

If the rates per 100,000 of the population in the age-group are looked at for each annual age-group, an interesting pattern is seen [22]:

Age	*Males*		*Females*	
	1966	1950	1966	1950
13	2,725	2,101	422	173
14	3,528	2,303	600	206
15	3,158	1,540	523	188
16	2,932	1,415	430	184
17	3,181	1,292	400	171
18	3,104	933	338	158
19	2,779	958	272	149

For many years, the peak age for criminal behaviour has been age 14, the year before school-leaving for most children. When the school-leaving age was lower, so was the peak age for crime. This is true both for boys and girls. However, in the statistics for 1965 and 1966, a new peak, a subsidiary one, appears for youths aged 17 and 18. The reasons are obscure, and the pattern amongst girls remains unchanged. But it does seem that the

[21] Sources: *Criminal Statistics* 1966, p. xiii and App. II (Intro. Note).
[22] Source: *Criminal Statistics* 1966, App. III (a) (Intro. Note).

whole teen-age period may soon be a "plateau" of criminal behaviour. If this is accompanied by a tendency for crimes of violence to increase, then a bleak prospect presents itself.

We must now turn for a preliminary look at the penal system, our armoury against the rising volume of crime.

The English Penal System

It is obviously desirable that crime should be reduced,[23] for the damage and distress caused by criminal behaviour are enormous. Attempts to bring about this desirable reduction can take many forms. We are primarily concerned with the operation of the penal system, that part of the official apparatus of society which deals with the known offender.

The penal system operates in a number of stages. The enactment of criminal legislation, declaring and defining a number of prohibited acts, has a purpose and effect of its own. It indicates society's disapproval, and gives fair warning of the existence of criminal sanctions.[24]

The courts determine guilt or innocence, and select the proper form of treatment for the guilty. In selecting the sentence, and in the public commentary which often accompanies the pronouncement of the sentence, the courts also declare the policy of society.

We are now primarily concerned with the last stage, the treatment of the sentenced offender. We must review the available types of treatment, the use made of them, and their effectiveness, and then consider some basic questions as to penal policy and the whole purpose of punishment.

Forms of treatment—adults

The traditional punishments for criminal behaviour involve the death of, or physical injury to, the offender; his imprisonment or reduction to slavery; or the removal of some or all of his property, or of his public or other rights. In this century we must add the probation system, by which a free man receives the supervision, the advice, assistance and friendship of a court-appointed social worker.

Probation seems a misfit in that list of punishments. This illustrates the striking change in the treatment of offenders within the last hundred years, a change reflected in the use of the word

23 We ought, presumably, to seek to *eliminate* crime. But "to err is human," and life would be very dull without it! The actual elimination of crime is not a possibility which need trouble us.

24 *Cf.* American Law Institute's *Model Penal Code*, s. 1.02 (1).

"treatment" rather than the old word "punishment." Most penal systems have abandoned capital and corporal punishment, and have abolished all forms of slavery and the wholesale forfeiture of property. We are left with monetary penalties—fines, and with "treatment" in an institution—imprisonment new style, or in freedom—probation.

The introduction of probation also indicates a trend towards "individualised" treatment. Instead of punishment being meted out by reference to the offence committed, and to that alone, attention is now paid to the needs of the particular offender. This is obviously important in sentencing policy, but it has also influenced the forms of treatment available. Imprisonment is no longer a uniform, and thoroughly nasty, punishment. The term "imprisonment" now covers detention in institutions which have a range of different regimes, some of which place great emphasis on training the individual. Imprisonment is still unpleasant; but vocational training courses, and "group counselling," the use of group psychotherapy methods, are not punishments, but attempts to improve, to reform the prisoner.

As the Table below makes clear, the great majority of adult offenders are fined. Imprisonment is ordered in the second largest group of cases, of which most are in the higher courts. Probation takes the third group, while most of the rest are discharged without immediate penalty. Those who are conditionally discharged may be sentenced for their offence if they commit a further offence within a prescribed period.

TREATMENT OF OFFENDERS, 1966 [25]

Expressed as percentage of all persons in the same age-group convicted of indictable offences

(a) *Higher Courts*

	Under 17	*17 and under 21*	*21 and over*
Conditional discharge	5·0	3·2	3·1
Probation	30·5	22·3	12·9
Fine	7·2	13·2	23·5
Approved school	9·3	–	–
Detention centre	24·4	15·6	–
Borstal training	18·8 [26]	29·4	–
Imprisonment	–	11·3	57·2
Other sentence	4·8	5·0	3·3

[25] Sources: *Criminal Statistics* 1966, Intro. Note, Chap. VI, and Tables 1 (d) and 11 (d).

[26] Those aged 15 and 16 only.

(b) *Magistrates' Courts*

	Under 14	*14 to 17*	*17 to 21*	*21 and over*
Absolute discharge	2·6	1·6	0·8	0·7
Conditional discharge	25·2	17·4	8·8	9·0
Probation	32·5	28·3	15·8	9·2
Fine	20·2	33·4	55·2	61·0
Attendance centre	9·5	6·5	0·1	–
Approved school	6·0	7·3	–	–
Detention centre	–	2·1	6·4	–
Imprisonment	–	–	2·5	14·9
Committed, s. 28 MCA [27]	–	1·6 [26]	3·8	–
Committed, s. 29 MCA [28]	–	–	5·0	4·4
Other sentence	4·0	1·8	1·6	0·8

Young offenders

The introduction of individualised treatment methods had more spectacular results where young offenders were concerned. So long as attention was concentrated on the offence, the young offender needed little special attention, for the offence of those under 21 do not differ very much from those of adults. It was politic to separate young prisoners from older men, and it was humane to spare the young from the cruellest punishments; but that was all.

As soon as the qualities and needs of the offender are taken into account, special forms of treatment are seen to be necessary. The peak age for juvenile delinquency coincides with puberty and adolescence, periods of rapid physical and emotional development; and a young person may well be easier to educate, to "reform," than an older man.

So, during the last hundred years young offenders have been provided with special courts and special forms of treatment. Approved schools cater for all juvenile offenders, from the age of 10 (the lower limit of criminal responsibility) to 17 (the upper limit for the jurisdiction of the juvenile court). They provide schooling, and training for work, for offenders who are very young or who have not gone far in crime.

Borstal training caters for the older, more mature, offender,

[27] *i.e.*, committed to a higher court with view to a sentence of Borstal training.
[28] *i.e.*, committed to a higher court for sentence.

aged between 15 and 21; from the outset, it included both institutional training and supervision after release.

Short-term institutional treatment is provided by detention centres introduced in 1948. They have a brisk régime, usually a 3-month training period, and are available for offenders aged between 14 and 21.

Attendance centres, introduced at the same time, are an extension of "keeping in after school hours." They are a form of deprivation of leisure, for offenders aged from 12 to 17, or up to 21 in some parts of the country.

For young offenders in need of supportive residential accommodation, probation homes and hostels are available; or by a "fit person order," a child can be committed to a local authority and by them to foster-parents, or to a relative.

Each type of treatment is considered in much more detail later. All exist as a result of the attention given to the needs of the offender. Their use, for those of juvenile court age, is governed by the principle that the welfare of the child or young person is paramount.[29]

Effectiveness of penal treatment[30]

How successful is the penal system in reducing crime? This is obviously an important question, and one which becomes more important when there exist a number of different types of treatment. Those responsible for administering the system are anxious to discover the most promising area into which to channel the available resources. The courts in sentencing, although other factors may weigh with them, must also take account of the relative effectiveness of the various forms of treatment open to them.

We have already seen that the early and mid teens are the peak age for criminal behaviour. The older person is much less likely to offend. It would be very pleasant if this falling away from crime could be attributed to the beneficent workings of the penal system. In fact it is more likely that crime is something that most people "grow out of." Certain types of penal treatment may speed the growth to maturity; conceivably some may retard it.

Looking at the matter in another way, we can note the rising figures of crime, even when expressed proportionately to the

[29] Children and Young Persons Act 1933, s. 44 (1).

[30] See Hood, "Research on the Effectiveness of Punishments and Treatments," *Collected Studies in Criminological Research* (Council of Europe, 1967), Vol. 1, p. 73.

growing population.[31] So long as each successive year sees new records set for the volume of crime, and even allowing for all the doubts as to the reliability of criminal statistics, no great success can be claimed by the penal system.

More useful, perhaps, is the attempt to assess the relative effectiveness of different forms of penal treatment. This can be done in a number of ways.

Reconviction rates

Reconviction rates are a deceptively simple measure of the success of a form of penal treatment. The rate is obtained by counting the number of offenders released from prison, or completing some other form of treatment, in a given period, and calculating the proportion who are reconvicted within a certain time, the follow-up period, often fixed at three years. Prima facie, a form of treatment with a reconviction rate of 70 per cent. is less successful than one with a rate of only 30 per cent.

Quite apart from the problems of obtaining accurate information, these rates are clumsy. They are usually calculated for a single form of treatment, overlooking at least some of the many variables in the situation. For example, to be useful the rates should distinguish between different types of offender, by record, previous penal treatment, background, personality; and they should also reflect variations in the application of the treatment.

This latter factor, " intensity of treatment " we might call it, is a very difficult matter. There is obviously a great difference between a fine of £5 imposed on a wealthy man, and a fine of £100 on a poor man. A reconviction rate for " fines " is patently superficial. The same applies to institutional treatment: it is possible to distinguish between, for example, different types of prison, open or closed, but this still assumes that imprisonment makes an impact, tolerably uniform, on the prisoner. It probably does not: the sensitive man whose family suffers greatly from his imprisonment may go through an experience quite distinct from that of the cunning prisoner, with no commitments outside and a gift for " shirking." This sort of variation is almost impossible to measure.

There are further difficulties concerning the offences counting as " reconvictions." A man with a long record of housebreaking offences leaves prison. He never commits another housebreaking

[31] *e.g.*, 13,264·4 indictable offences per million of the population in the 1950s; 29,834·8 in 1967.

offence, but two years later is convicted of a minor assault. Is his reconviction to count as a failure for the system? Would it make any difference if his later offence was murder or rape?

Prediction studies

Another technique is the use of prediction methods.[32] A careful analysis of the available information concerning samples of offenders for whom a treatment method seems to have succeeded or failed identifies particular factors whose presence or absence points most clearly to a particular outcome.

The use of this technique does not avoid the difficulties of assessing success and failure. And, while it becomes possible to predict the outcome if a particular form of penal treatment is applied, it is difficult to tell whether the outcome would be any different if some other treatment were used, or if nature were left to take its course.

Comparing effectiveness

The sad truth is that most studies reveal considerable similarities between the effectiveness of penal treatments of various types. In other words, imprisonment has the same proportion of successes as probation. Even when a closer examination is made, it becomes apparent that in many individual cases the outcome will be the same whatever treatment is used.

So, reconviction rates reveal that a large number of previous convictions indicates a strong likelihood of failure, of further reconviction, whatever penal treatment is applied. Prediction studies would give the same result for the young offender who for example, never held a job down for longer than a few days and had a record of truancy at school.

Even if there is some difference between the success of two different types of treatment, so that, for example, fines are more successful with first offenders than probation, this is still unhelpful. This is because the calculations are based on actual experience; the courts do not make sentencing decisions on a random basis but in accordance with some policy decisions worked out over a period of time. Probation officers are in short supply, so their use tends to be limited to cases where their guidance and help is really needed.

Two young offenders are convicted of their first housebreaking offence. One seems a stable boy, with sensible parents; he acted

[32] *e.g.*, Mannheim and Wilkins, *Prediction Methods in Relation to Borstal Training* (1955).

more out of a sense of adventurous mischief than anything else, and is now full of remorse. His companion comes from an unhappy home, from which his father is often absent, leaving financial crises behind him. The court may well be reluctant to order institutional treatment for these first offenders, but some strong steadying influence is needed in the second case. So the decision is a fine for the first boy, and probation for the second.

Because of the circumstances, the first boy is unlikely to offend again, and the second boy much more likely to be reconvicted. For this very reason, the fine and the probation order were made. Can one then say that a fine, leading to a success, is " better " than probation, which may have been a failure?

It is this which makes difficult the interpretation of some official statistics in the Home Office paper *The Sentence of the Court.*[33] Starting from the known pattern of reconviction rates, that the younger the offender and the larger the number of his previous convictions, the more likely he is to be reconvicted, it was possible to calculate " expected reconviction rates " for first offenders and other offenders in each age-group. The actual rates for a large sample were then compared with these expected rates; fines and discharges were the most flattered by the comparison. But this seems to mean very little, for in practice the most hopeful cases are dealt with in this way.[34]

Perhaps the most promising line of research involves detailed examination of the effect of treatment, developing both a typology of treatment as to type and intensity, and typology of offenders. A start is being made on this in the Home Office Probation Research Project.[35]

Penal policy

The melancholy but inevitable conclusion that we know very little about the success or otherwise of the penal system makes it possible to argue that the whole system is misconceived. This would be an extreme view, one which would ignore the experience of the very intelligent and critical people who direct the system, but more limited criticisms can be raised.

A great deal of work has been done to investigate the causes

33 p. 50: reproduced opposite.

34 For a different view, see Walker, *Crime and Punishment in Britain*, pp. 252 *et seq.*

35 See Grant, "Interaction between Kinds of Treatment and Kinds of Offender" (California Bd. of Corrections: *Inquiries Concerning Kinds of Treatment for Kinds of Delinquents*, 1961).

RESULTS OF SENTENCES COMPARED WITH EXPECTATION

100 = expected reconviction rate over 5 years

	Under 17		17 and under 21		21 and under 30		30 and over	
	1st offenders	Others	1st offenders	Others	1st offenders	Others	1st offenders	Others
Discharge	89	100	89	98	109	90	133	104
Fine	75	83	75	94	63	99	84	65
Probation	118	101	122	101	153	115	(150)	121
Imprisonment	–	–	–	106 [36]	146 [37]	111 [36]	(91) [37]	104 [36]
Approved school	138	102	–	–	–	–	–	–
Attendance centre	–	119	}	–	–	–	–	–
Detention centre	–	106	} 150	110	–	–	–	–
Borstal training	–	101	}	95	–	–	–	–

Note: Round brackets indicate that the calculation involved a very small number of offenders.
[36] Based on a 3-year follow-up; and sentences of over 3 years excluded.
[37] Six sentences of 3 years or more excluded.

of criminal behaviour. It is outside the scope of this book to review that work,[38] and it must be said that few facts have been established. The search for a single " cause " of crime has proved as chimerical as the search for a single form of penal treatment. There are many types of crime, many types of offender; modern work is much more likely to be examining the interaction of contributory factors in a situation which led to criminal behaviour than to be searching for " causes." It remains a valid question whether the penal system is designed to deal with the criminogenic factors discovered by the research workers.

These theories of crime which are supported by scientific evidence are mainly concerned with the relationship between delinquent behaviour, physique and personality. So, for example, there is evidence that delinquents are likely to be mesomorphs, having a particular body-build, solid and muscular, and an aggressive temperament.[39] Eysenck suggests that a delinquent is also likely to be an extrovert, and resistant to social " conditioning," and a neurotic rather than a stable person.[40] To some extent, these factors may be inherited.

Some of these factors are obviously unalterable, but Eysenck has proposed that, granted his theories' validity, penal treatment should include a definite process of positive conditioning, where necessary coupled with the administration of drugs designed to assist the process.[41] As he realises, this looks rather like " brainwashing "; but equally, it is true " reform," helping the offender to learn socially-acceptable behaviour, a learning process which non-delinquents have completed at an earlier age.

The penal system can be regarded as a rather clumsy, conditioning device. If an offender is punished often enough, he may eventually realise that his behaviour is unprofitable and socially undesirable. Within institutions, and to some extent in probation, this effect is being reinforced by the use of group therapy methods. This involves the guided discussion of the offender's problems, personality and behaviour, in a group of other offenders: each learns from the experiences of the others.

Another important group of theories of criminal behaviour concentrates more on the social environment. It is a well-documented fact that criminals tend to be concentrated in small

[38] See, *e.g.*, West, *The Young Offender*, Chaps. 3–7; Walker, " A Century of Causal Theory " in *Frontiers of Criminology* (Pergamon, 1967).

[39] Glueck and Glueck, *Physique and Delinquency* (1956).

[40] Eysenck, *Crime and Personality*; see also Trasler, *The Explanation of Criminality*.

[41] *Op. cit.*, Chap. 8.

areas in working-class districts. This is explained in a variety of ways, as being a result of the class structure of society, as a result of the inadequacy of public welfare facilities, as working through imitative learning processes.[42] These theories lack real supporting evidence.

If these views are accepted, the penal system itself is a very inadequate answer to the crime problem. A small revolution in society is needed. In practice, this sort of thinking has led to the growth in the United States of a number of prevention programmes aimed at improving work and welfare facilities in poorer areas of cities. An example is the Mobilisation for Youth project in New York's Lower East Side, and earlier experiments included the Cambridge-Somerville Youth project, which placed greater emphasis on counselling and guidance. The lack of success of these large projects has led to even more valiant attempts by individual workers to reach the potential delinquent whom an official project would miss.[43]

It seems fair to say that no real alternative to present penal methods is suggested by these studies, theories and experiments. It is reasonable to hope that the penal system is on the right lines, at least until the contrary is proved. But, as Professor Cross has observed, " If only it were more widely recognised that most penal reforms are based on guess work, there might be less disappointment at their comparative lack of success." [44]

Philosophy of punishment

In view of the marked shortage of factual information about the effects of penal treatment, it is not surprising that punishment has long been a favoured topic for philosophical speculation. This cannot be ignored for the practical business of sentencing is influenced by it, at least in matters of terminology. The terms used today are not dissimilar from those of Sir William Blackstone: he discusses the purpose of punishment, rejecting ideas of atonement and expiation as not fit for human determination, and regarding it

> " as a precaution against future offences of the same kind. This is effected three ways: either by the amendment of the offender himself; . . or, by deterring others by the dread of his example from offending in the like way; . . . or, lastly,

[42] *e.g.*, Cohen, *Delinquent Boys;* Sutherland and Cressey, *Principles of Criminology* on " differential association."
[43] *e.g.*, Morse, *The Unattached.*
[44] " Penal Reform in 1965, A Mass of Unexplained and Unfounded Assumptions " [1966] Crim.L.R. 184.

> by depriving the party injuring of the power to do future mischief. . . The public gains equal security, whether the offender himself be amended by wholesome correction, or whether he be disabled from doing any further harm: and if the penalty fails of both these effects, as it may do, still the terror of his example remains as a warning to other citizens.[45]

To these notions of reform, deterrence and prevention, we must add the idea of retribution or denunciation. This idea was adopted by Lord Denning in his evidence to the Royal Commission on Capital Punishment, though it can take a number of forms:

> " The ultimate justification of any punishment is not that it is a deterrent but that it is the emphatic denunciation by the community of the crime." [46]

Prevention

Little need be said about this justification for punishment. To prevent an offender from repeating his offence he must be killed or incarcerated for a very prolonged period. If either of these courses is to be justified, his offences must constitute a serious problem, by their nature or quantity, and it must be clear from his record that the likelihood of repetition is great. In practice, prevention is relied on when certain persistent offenders come before the courts; and the application of the principle is attended by some difficulties.[47]

Retribution

Few people would base a justification of punishment on ideas of retribution,[48] certainly not if this means vengeance. It is true that the thinking of the criminal law is essentially concerned with moral blameworthiness, and that acts are defined as criminal because they are seen to be blameworthy. In practice, retribution may have a part in sentencing, but not as the basis of the whole operation.[49]

45 *Commentaries on the Laws of England*, (16th ed.), Vol. 4, Chap. 1, pp. 11–12.

46 Report, Cmd. 8932, para. 53.

47 See *infra*, pp. 133 *et seq.*

48 But see Hawkins, " Punishment and Moral Responsibility " (1944) 7 M.L.R. 205; and Mabbott, " Punishment " (1939) *Mind* 152.

49 Brett, *An Inquiry into Criminal Guilt;* see H. L. A. Hart, " Prolegomenon to the Principles of Punishment " (Aristotelian Society, 1959–60).

Deterrence

There is much greater support for the idea that punishments are imposed to deter. The deterrence is aimed at anyone who may be tempted to commit an offence, including the sentenced offender who may be tempted to repeat his offence.

Some argue that deterrence cannot be the true justification of punishment, for a deterrent effect could be produced by punishing alleged offenders, whether guilty or not; and that if deterrence were paramount, some offences presently attracting small penalties, such as motoring offences, would be met with much stiffer punishment. The answer seems to be that the effect of deterrence is not only in observing the plight of the guilty, but in the contrast between that and the happier state of the innocent. This may mean that gradations of guilt, of moral blameworthiness, will have to be recognised, but this is not to base punishment on retributive ideas.[50]

Reform

We have already noted the changing attitude to penal treatment, with greater individualisation of punishment, more attention to the needs of the offender. Institutional treatment is now clearly seen as an opportunity for reformative action; probation proceeds on the same lines.

The difficulty, practical and not just theoretical, is that a wholly reformative penal system would not be deterrent. If convicted offenders are dealt with entirely in their best interests, crime might even become profitable, an avenue to favoured social treatment. In practice, a balance must be maintained between deterrence and reform.[51]

Sentencing in practice [52]

The practical aspects of the problems have received much closer attention since the discussion of the aims of sentencers in the Report of the Streatfeild Committee on the Business of the Criminal Courts in 1961 [53]:

[50] See Hart, *Punishment and the Elimination of Responsibility*. Thomas in an illuminating review of "Theories of Punishment in the Court of Criminal Appeal" regards the question of gradations of guilt, of "just deserts," as an aspect of the retributive theory; but he points out that denunciation and deterrence are so closely related that a definite distinction between their operation is difficult: (1964) 27 M.L.R. 546, 548.

[51] There is, of course, no scientific evidence as to the alleged deterrent effect of punishment; even this is an unproven assumption.

[52] See Thomas, "Sentencing—the Basic Principles" [1967] Crim.L.R. 455, 503, and the earlier studies there referred to.

[53] Cmnd. 1289, paras. 257 *et seq.*

"Sentencing used to be a comparatively simple matter. The primary objective was to fix a sentence proportionate to the offender's culpability, and the system has been loosely described as the 'tariff system.' The facts of the offence and the offender's record were the main pieces of information needed by the court, and the defence could bring to notice any mitigating circumstances. . . .

"In addition, the courts have always had in mind the need to protect society from the persistent offender, to deter potential offenders and to deter or reform the individual offender. But in general it was thought that the 'tariff system' took those other objectives in its stride. Giving an offender the punishment he deserved was thought to be the best way of deterring him and others and of protecting society.

"Over the last few decades, these other objectives have received increased attention. The development has been most obvious in the increased weight which the courts give to the needs of the offender as a person. It is realised that whatever punishments are imposed, he will eventually return to society, and sentences are increasingly passed with the deterrence or reform of the offender as the principal objective: and in assessing the offender's culpability his social and domestic background is more closely examined."

This sort of development led to improved arrangements for social inquiry reports, and ultimately to the enactment of section 57 of the Criminal Justice Act 1967. When this is brought into force, rules may be made prohibiting the passing of a custodial sentence in the absence of such a report.

This leaves untouched the basic question whether the particular case is one in which the needs of the offender can be regarded as paramount or is one which calls for a sentence reflecting his apparent moral blameworthiness, an exemplary, deterrent sentence. The dilemma is openly recognised by the courts. In connection with remission, for example, Lord Parker C.J. has ruled that,

"It is no doubt true that when one is considering *punishment* it is quite wrong for the court to take into consideration the matter of remission, but it has long been recognised that when one is considering not punishment but considering *reform* or mental treatment, something which is in the interests of the prisoner, it would be obviously right for this court to take remission into consideration." [54]

A clear example of the dilemma is *Coleman*.[55] An accounts manager stole several thousands of pounds from his employer. He was of previous high character, ruined by the conviction alone, and admittedly unlikely to offend again. The principles of reforming and of deterring the offender himself would point to a lenient sentence. Despite all this, a sentence of four years' imprisonment was upheld, in view of the serious breach of trust involved.

An examination of the cases soon reveals that certain types of offence will attract a deterrent, exemplary sentence, despite other circumstances concerning the offender. Offences involving abuse of a position of trust, such as *Coleman*, provide one example.[56] Others are sexual offences which are also seen as causing danger to the public, which needs the protection of a heavy deterrent sentence [57]; and offences seemingly directed against the law itself, perjury,[58] and even driving while disqualified.[59]

Deterrent sentences are also likely when the particular offence is particularly prevalent. This is rather a dangerous argument, for a glance at the criminal statistics reveals the prevalence of most offences; it is difficult to avoid the impression that " prevalence " is automatically prayed in aid whenever a court decides on a deterrent sentence. The argument has been applied to violence,[60] taking and driving away vehicles,[61] assaults on police officers,[62] and even sexual intercourse with young girls which was apparently committed wholesale in Lincolnshire in 1964.[63]

When a deterrent sentence is selected, the " tariff system," with allowance for mitigating circumstances, applies. Remorse,[64] or low intelligence,[65] can mitigate even where the offence is very

[54] *Turner* (1966) 51 Cr.App.R. 72, 73; italics added. To illustrate the co-existence of various approaches, cases decided in late 1966 and early 1967 have, so far as possible, been used.
[55] (1967) 51 Cr.App.R. 244.
[56] *e.g.*, *Matthews* [1967] Crim.L.R. 66 (warehouse-breaking by a security officer).
[57] *Lee* [1967] Crim.L.R. 548.
[58] *McCarthy* [1967] Crim.L.R. 117.
[59] *Superstein* [1967] Crim.L.R. 548.
[60] *Baker and Hawkins* (1966) 51 Cr.App.R. 74.
[61] *Harrison* (1967) 51 Cr.App.R. 371.
[62] *Hayden* [1967] Crim.L.R. 185.
[63] *Murphy* [1964] Crim.L.R. 155.
[64] *Alcock* [1967] Crim.L.R. 66 (manslaughter).
[65] *Smith* (1967) 51 Cr.App.R. 376.

serious. But unhappy circumstances can have seemingly inconsistent effects: dreadful domestic difficulties may so influence a court that a receiver is released as "needing all the help she can get," [66] but the unfortunate man whose brain abnormality makes him dangerous when drunk faces indefinite detention in the interests of himself and the public.[67]

No one would quarrel with these sentencing decisions, but they may be used to criticise the courts for acting inconsistently. It is an important principle that "like cases should be treated alike," that the sentence imposed should be an accurate reflection of the degree of guilt. The appeal courts are often called upon to correct inconsistencies of this sort, where offenders have been tried at different times, or where there is no discrimination between co-defendants with different degrees of guilt.[68] It is a statutory principle that a man convicted of an attempt may not receive a heavier sentence than he could have received had he completed the offence.[69]

This sort of argument is only valid as between two sentences both imposed in accordance with the deterrent principle. It cannot legitimately be used as between deterrent and reformative sentences; it is so used, but the courts must bear it with patient resignation. In some minor offences, especially road traffic cases, where reformation is not an important factor, many courts make use of agreed "standard" sentences for average cases to avoid the most obvious cases of inconsistency.

Theory and practice

There is a very real danger that discussions of sentencing policy, and the actual business of deciding what a sentence should be, will be influenced too much by theoretical and philosophical considerations. At least as important is accurate information, for the sentencer, concerning the availability of different types of penal treatment and what they involve. It is to ensure that this information is available that conferences between judges, magistrates and penal administrators are organised with increasing frequency in many parts of the country, with an annual conference in London for judges of the superior courts.

The same danger can exist when reform of the penal system is under consideration. It is to avert this that there exists the

[66] *Neale* [1967] Crim.L.R. 314.
[67] *Whittaker* [1967] Crim.L.R. 431.
[68] *Daly* [1967] Crim.L.R. 547 illustrates both points.
[69] Criminal Law Act 1967, s. 7 (2).

Home Secretary's Advisory Council on the Penal System, successor of the abortive Royal Commission on the Penal System dissolved in 1966, and of the Advisory Council on the Treatment of Offenders, which produced many valuable reports in the preceding decade.

Bibliography

Official statistical publications containing information about crime include:

Criminal Statistics
Supplementary Statistics relating to Crime and Criminal Proceedings
Offences of Drunkenness
Offences relating to Motor Vehicles
Report of H.M. Chief Inspector of Constabulary
Report of the Commissioner of Police for the Metropolis.

All the above are annual publications, obtainable from H.M.S.O. except for the supplementary statistics which are produced in mimeographed form and distributed to applicants by the Home Office.

See also

Shields, J. V. M., and Duncan, J. A., The State of Crime in Scotland (Tavistock, 1964). An English counterpart is being produced by the Cambridge Institute of Criminology.

On criminal statistics in general, see:

Grunhut, M., " Statistics in Criminology " (1951) *Journal of Royal Statistical Society*, Ser. A., Vol. 115, p. 150.

Sellin, T., " The Significance of Records of Crime " (1951) 67 L.Q.R. 495.

An admirable introduction to studies of the " causes " of criminal behaviour is

West, D. J., The Young Offender (Penguin Books, 1967).

Studies of particular types of crime in England:

Gibbens, T. C. N., and Prince, J., Shoplifting (I.S.T.D., 1962).

McClintock, F. H., and Gibson, E., Robbery in London (Macmillan, 1961).

McClintock, F. H., Crimes of Violence (Macmillan, 1967).

MARTIN, J. P., Offenders as Employees (Macmillan, 1962).

Sexual Offences (prepared by the Cambridge Institute) (Macmillan, 1957).

On the effectiveness of the penal system see the following, each with full bibliography:

HOOD, R., " Research on the Effectiveness of Punishments and Treatments " in Collected Studies in Criminal Research, Vol. 1, p. 73 (Council of Europe, 1967).

" The Effectiveness of Punishment and Other Measures of Treatment " (Council of Europe, 1967).

The Sentence of the Court (H.M.S.O., 1964).

Material on the effectiveness of particular forms of penal treatment is also contained in the Reports of the Prison Department, in other official publications (*e.g.*, " Statistics relating to Approved Schools, Remand Homes and Attendance Centres " (annual) and in monographs listed in the bibliographies to later parts of this book).

On sentencing and related matters see:

Report of the Committee on the Business of the Criminal Courts (Cmnd. 1289).

BRETT, P., An Inquiry into Criminal Guilt (Sweet & Maxwell, 1963).

HART, H. L. A., Punishment and Responsibility (Oxford, 1968).

HOOD, R., Sentencing in Magistrates' Courts (Stevens, 1962).

THOMAS, D. A., " Theories of Punishment in the Court of Criminal Appeal " (1964) 27 M.L.R. 546.

——, " Sentencing—the Basic Principles " [1967] Crim.L.R. 455, 507.

CHAPTER 4

ADULT OFFENDERS

IMPRISONMENT

IT scarcely needs to be said that imprisonment, the detention of an offender within a special institution, has a major role in the English, and in every other, penal system. Although this has not always been the case, it now seems an inevitable and unalterable fact.

Yet it is still worth speculating whether the founders of a Utopia, surprised to discover that crime was a feature of their perfect society, would think of imprisonment as a method of meeting the problem. There have always been some writers on penal matters who have been convinced that the whole idea of imprisonment is wrong, or at least bound to fail.

So, the Gladstone Committee set up to examine the prison system and reporting in 1895 cited as being accurate " as a broad description of prison life " this comment by Sir Godfrey Lushington [1]:

> " I regard as unfavourable to reformation the status of a prisoner throughout his whole career; the crushing of self-respect, the starving of all moral instinct he may possess, the absence of all opportunity to do or receive a kindness, the continual association with none but criminals, and that only as a separate item amongst other items also separate; the forced labour, and the denial of all liberty. I believe the true mode of reforming a man or restoring him to society is exactly in the opposite direction of all these; but, of course, this is a mere idea. It is quite impracticable in a prison. In fact, the unfavourable features I have mentioned are inseparable from prison life."

Two more recent critics, under the heading " Why Imprisonment Must Go " [2] have written:

> " Rule 2 (3) of the English Prison Rules (1964) specifies

[1] Report, Cd. 7702, para. 25.
[2] Chap. 1 of Playfair and Sington, *Crime, Punishment and Cure* (1964) at p. 42. For an earlier view, see Lord Auckland, *Principles of Penal Law* (1771): " Imprisonment . . . is not according to the principles of wise legislation " (at p. 50).

that the 'treatment of prisoners shall be such as to encourage their self-respect and a sense of personal responsibility.' This rule is flagrantly violated in every closed prison, unless it can be seriously maintained that to sunder a man from wife and children, thus flinging them into utter penury, to strip him in all his democratic rights (and duties), to deny him any say in the management or organisation of the society in which he is compelled to live, to regulate his life by orders and hardly ever to permit him to act on his own initiative, to lock him up in a cell, as though he were some dangerous animal who might otherwise get loose, and even then to continue to watch him through a spy-hole—that such treatment is to encourage his self-respect and sense of personal responsibility!"

Most observers see a great deal of truth in these and similar criticisms, but very few would conclude that imprisonment should be abandoned. The Gladstone Committee assumed without argument that prisons were essential, but advised some modification of the prison system to reduce its unfavourable features. This was, and remains, the position of many who are actively interested in penal reform. More recently the courts have been under pressure to be more discriminating in their use of imprisonment, and not to use it for first offenders, or young offenders, and not to impose sentences which are too short, or too long, to be useful. There are still many who are sent to prison because they have committed a serious offence for which no other form of treatment is available; the next stage in penal history may be the development of alternatives to imprisonment.

There remains to be answered the fundamental question: why do prisons exist? What are they meant to do?

At one time, serious offenders were hanged or transported. These methods of treatment combined punishment of the offender for his wrongdoing with his removal from society so that he could not offend again. Imprisonment is largely a development of the nineteenth century, when humanity worked against capital punishment and incipient nationalism against the transportation system. It retained the twin functions of punishment and removal.

A popular answer to the question "Why imprison?" would still be that imprisonment punishes; it deters the imprisoned from offending again; it deters others from offending and sharing the prisoner's fate.

This was the prevailing attitude in official circles in the last century. The House of Lords, going through one of its reactionary phases, accepted in 1863 the report of a committee which advocated " hard labour, hard fare and a hard bed " as the basis of an adequately punitive regime. The Gladstone Committee set themselves to answer the question " Is the present prison system sufficiently deterrent? "

The current view of the prison authorities, summarised in the Home Office booklet *Prisons and Borstals* [3] distinguishes between two aspects of the question. On one side is the deterrent and punitive effect of the whole judicial and penal system, the wholesome fear excited by the sight of scarlet robes and by the thought of a cell door clanging shut behind one. But " an offender is sent to prison *as* a punishment and not *for* punishment." Once he is inside a prison, the emphasis moves away from punishment towards constructive " training for freedom."

This approach does much to explain the persistence of judges in thinking in terms of punishment, of giving an offender his " just deserts." As we shall see later,[4] the legislature has presented to the judges special forms of sentence to use when they are concerned not so much to punish as to order training, or the prolonged custody of a persistent offender; but in each case, difficulties have arisen because of the conflict between these objectives and the principle of " just deserts."

So far as the experience of imprisonment itself is concerned, the modern approach is expressed in the Prison Rules:

> " The purpose of the training and treatment of convicted prisoners shall be to encourage and assist them to lead a good and useful life," [5]

or more fully, in the United Nations Standard Minimum Rules for the Treatment of Prisoners:

> " Imprisonment and other measures which result in cutting off an offender from the outside world are afflictive by the very fact of taking from the person the right of self-determination by depriving him of his liberty. Therefore the prison system shall not, except as incidental or justifiable segregation for the maintenance of discipline, aggravate the suffering inherent in such a situation.
>
> " The purpose and justification of a sentence of imprisonment or a similar measure deprivative of liberty is ultimately to protect society against crime. This end can only be

[3] 4th ed., 1960, p. 2.
[4] *Infra*, pp. 133 *et seq.*
[5] Prison Rules 1964 (S.I. 1964 No. 388), r. 1.

achieved if the period of imprisonment is used to ensure, so far as possible, that upon his return to society the offender is not only willing but able to lead a law-abiding and self-supporting life.

"To this end, the institution should utilise all the remedial, educational, moral, spiritual and other forces and forms of assistance which are appropriate and available, and should apply them according to the individual treatment needs of the prisoners." [6]

In many countries, penal reformers have succeeded in reducing the physical discomforts and indignities of imprisonment to a minimum. Some prisoners may have keys to their own cells to give them privacy; they may grow or select and cook their own food; they may wear their own clothes. But the psychological effects of the loss of freedom are almost irreducible.

Most men deprived of their freedom are tempted to regain it, to escape. Prisons can only carry out their present function if they contain these men. This means that the security of the establishment is of primary importance. Security means walls or fences, locks and bars. However carefully security devices are concealed or disguised they will be seen; this indignity must remain.

"A constructive liberal prison regime and secure prisons are not necessarily incompatible" [7]; but there is an element of conflict which must affect personal relationships within a prison. All members of a prison's staff are concerned in the special type of social case-work which is prison training, but equally they are concerned with the security of the prison. An officer may seek to help, to befriend, to influence a prisoner, but he may also have to count him, search him, and lock him in his cell. There is a conflict and the nature of many English prisons makes its resolution doubly difficult.

Prison design and penal policy

The features of a prison which have the greatest immediate impact on the individual prisoner are its architecture, the daily routine, and, intangible but all-pervading, that which Brendan Behan described as "a heavy smell of well-washed stuffiness." [8] Most prisoners would apply a more critical and more exact description.

[6] Rules 57, 58 and 59; adopted at the first UN Congress on the Prevention of Crime and the Treatment of Offenders, August 30, 1955.
[7] Mountbatten Report, Cmnd. 3175, para. 202.
[8] *Borstal Boy* (p. 51, Corgi edition).

Most English prisons, especially the closed local prisons, were built in the nineteenth century; it was then that the alternative methods of disposal, hanging and transportation, gave way to more humane methods. Inevitably, the buildings reflect the penal ideas of the times, the English conclusions drawn from the great debate over the relative merits of the " separate " and the " silent " systems of imprisonment.

The state of prisons before the appearance of these rival systems was quite deplorable. Many prisoners died from gaol-fever; many remained in prison longer than the law required as they could not pay the discharge fees demanded by their keepers. In 1702, the worst features of prisons were said to be " the personal Lewdness of the Keepers and under Officers themselves who often make it their business to corrupt the prisoners especially the women; their Confederacy with Prisoners in their vices allowing the men to keep company with the women for money; the unlimited use of Wine, Brandy and other Strong Liquors even by condemned Malefactors; Swearing, Cursing, Blasphemy and Gaming; Old Criminals corrupting Newcomers; and the Neglect of all Religious Worship." [9] Prisoners of both sexes, and of all types of criminal experience were together by day and night.

Reformers like John Howard and Elizabeth Fry did much to alleviate the misery of English prisoners. The theoretical bases for new prison methods were laid in America, in Pennsylvania and in New York.

The Pennsylvanian system owed much to the work of members of the Society of Friends. It was based on the separation of prisoners from one another, so as to avoid the old evils of corruption and contamination.

This was achieved by the use of solitary confinement; the prisoner lived, worked and slept in his cell, exercised alone, and wore a hood when it was essential for him to be in the company of other prisoners. A prison operating this system required a large number of roomy cells, but virtually no other accommodation: the most famous example was the Cherry Hill Penitentiary, built near Philadelphia in 1829.[10]

The rival " silent " system is usually associated with Auburn Prison, in New York State, built a few years earlier. Prisoners were still given individual cells, but these were very small being

[9] *An Essay towards the Reformation of Newgate* . . . . , S.P.C.K., reproduced in Hinde, *British Penal System 1773–1950*, at p. 21.

[10] See on the whole of this topic, Madge, " Prison Design and Penal Reform," *International Review of Criminal Policy*, No. 17, p. 1.

used only for sleeping. The day was spent in workshops where strict silence was enforced. This principle and the type of prison that accompanies it, became prevalent in the United States.[11]

English prisons contrived to get the worst of both systems. The prisons were often designed on the lines of Cherry Hill; this gave them large cells, and no workshops. The routine came to be that of Auburn, shorn of its repressive features. This routine requires workshops, and does not require large cells; workshops have had to be built as money and space have allowed, the cells have been used to house not one but three prisoners, with all the discomfort and loss of privacy this entails.[12]

Similarly, the design of nineteenth-century English prisons relied on cells for security. " In effect, imprisonment was solitary confinement and all security depended on this fact." [13] As soon as the routine of the prison involved much movement of prisoners about the prison, and the provision of facilities for time to be spent together " in association," the security of the prison could no longer be based entirely on the cell. The perimeter defences became more important, and, as was revealed by Lord Mountbatten's inquiry in 1966, those defences were not adequate. As he concluded,

> " A constructive liberal prison régime and secure prisons are not necessarily incompatible, but conflicts arise if an attempt is made to conduct a liberal régime in buildings designed in accordance with the 19th-century philosophy of penal treatment. Treating prisoners by modern methods in out-of-date buildings inevitably means that some of them can escape." [14]

Classification

There are over sixty establishments in which a sentence of imprisonment may be served. This permits a degree of specialisation; a particular prison will take a certain type of prisoner. The process whereby a prisoner is allocated to a particular prison is the process of classification.

[11] See the 1961 Rules of Iowa State Penitentiary, reprinted in Johnston, Savitz and Wolfgang, *Sociology of Punishment and Correction*, p. 87; for example on the dining hall: "On entering the dining hall, take your seat promptly, position erect with eyes to the front until the signal is given to commence eating. Strict silence and decorum must be observed during the meal. Talking, laughing, grimacing or gazing about the room is strictly forbidden."

[12] For a detailed description of the buildings and routine of one such prison, see T. and P. Morris, *Pentonville*, especially Chaps. 2 and 5.

[13] Mountbatten Report, Cmnd. 3175, para. 201.

[14] *Ibid.* para. 202.

It may be doubted whether the English classification machinery is adequate. Most of the work has to be done at some speed in the crowded conditions of the local prison which receives the convicted prisoner direct from the court. In many cases, the success or failure of prison training may depend on the correct decision being taken at the classification stage; yet, by comparison with some other countries, England has inadequate staff, buildings and other resources for the task.

A basic difficulty in classification is the conflict between training considerations—the régime of a particular institution, the trades available there—and the overriding need to take security into account. The prison authorities must take into account the prisoner's record and previous institutional experience, his personality and aptitudes, geographical factors, and security needs. The application of the different criteria may well give different results.

Prisons may be classified as " local " or " training "; as " open " or " closed "; and by standards of security.

The local prison to which all prisoners are committed by the courts is the worst sort of institution in the penal system. Most criticisms of prisons are made with this type of prison in mind. Even the official view is that such prisons are highly unsatisfactory:

> " The buildings of . . . local prisons are for the most part old and unsuited to modern methods of treatment. Many lack better class workshops and have unsatisfactory amenities for association, educational activities and visits. The rapid turnover of the population makes efficient planning of training and work difficult." [15]

The local prisons receive the unselected mass of prisoners direct from the courts. There is no way of controlling the numbers sent to imprisonment by the courts, so that numbers may fluctuate alarmingly. If there are an excessive number of committals, the local prison must nonetheless find room, even at the cost of sleeping three in a cell: at the time of greatest pressure in 1962, 8,000 prisoners were so detained, but the current figure is nearer 7,000.[16]

From this intake, those suitable for open conditions are selected and moved elsewhere. Of the rest, some will have received long sentences and will be moved in time to start the main part of their sentence elsewhere; for them, the year in a local prison,

[15] *The Sentence of the Court*, p. 26.
[16] 6,954 on January 31, 1967.

or whatever period it may be, is one of marking time. The remainder are in for a few months only: the table of lengths of sentences shows what a large group they are.[17] For these short-term prisoners no training is possible. Their sentences are too short, and the pressure of work in the prison with great numbers of receptions, escort duties for court appearances and discharges does not allow the staff time to find out enough about the prisoner to design a training programme where one is possible.

The remaining prisons were formerly classified in the Prison Rules as "central" or "regional training" prisons. These terms have disappeared from the latest Rules [18] but the distinction exists. Central prisons are for the longest-term prisoners, with sentences of five years or more; the numbers are such that they have to be organised with a country-wide catchment area. The régimes vary slightly depending on the type of prisoner, for some are more responsible to training than others; some even enjoy open conditions at Leyhill.[19] Regional training prisons, for offenders serving medium terms, have smaller catchment areas.

An open prison [20] is essentially one in which there are no locks, and no surrounding security fence. The prisoner is trusted to remain inside the prison—or in its immediate neighbourhood, for in many open prisons much time will be spent working outside the area in which there are prison buildings.

The absence of locks is much more than a detail of building design; it changes the whole atmosphere of the prison. The prisoner is less conscious of being detained, the staff are less preoccupied with security, the atmosphere of trust is one in which it is much more realistic than in a local prison to talk of the development of individual responsibility. In practice, most open prisons are in rural settings; often they are hutted camps. This means that they are brighter and healthier than the older closed prisons, that work outside is usual, and that life is generally pleasanter in every way.

The population of an open prison must be a carefully selected one. Anyone who is regarded as an escape risk is clearly unsuited for open conditions. So are those prisoners who through inherent inadequacy or institutionalisation would find open conditions

17 See *infra*, p. 105.

18 Though "local" remains: see r. 65.

19 For the classification of prisoners, see below; for details of the use of particular institutions see the latest annual Report of the Prison Department.

20 See the discussions on open institutions recorded in the Report of the First UN Congress on the Prevention of Crime and Treatment of Offenders; and the document at p. 76.

intolerable, as forcing on them too much responsibility. So are violent and sexual offenders. Many sexual offenders are probably well suited to open conditions, but there is pressure against their selection in any numbers in the form of opinion amongst local residents with whom open prisons have close and valued links. The selection of prisoners for open conditions is carried out at the local prison.

Security [21]

The importance of security in classification or allocation decisions is most obvious where selection for open conditions is being considered, but it affects every decision. This has been given greater emphasis since the Mountbatten Report, commissioned in 1966 after a series of prison escapes had attracted public attention to the issue.

There are four categories of prisons and prisoners based on security considerations. Category A prisoners are for "those prisoners who must in no circumstances be allowed to get out, whether because of the security considerations affecting spies, or because their violent behaviour is such that members of the public or the police would be in danger of their lives if they were to get out." [22] Category B includes prisoners who need very secure conditions, but for whom the very costly devices required for full security would not be justified. Category C comprises prisoners "who, although they lack the resource and will to make escape attempts, have not the stability to be kept in conditions where there is no barrier to their escape." [23] Category D consists of prisoners suitable for open conditions.

At the time of Lord Mountbatten's Report the perimeter security of most English prisons was so defective that they were only really suitable for Category C. His report contained elaborate recommendations for improving security, including the removal of outbuildings close to the perimeter wall, the use of floodlighting and dog patrols at night, electronic devices on the walls, and radio links between the prison control office and the local police headquarters. With these improvements most prisons would be raised to the standard required for Category B. The improvements will supplement the existing, and rather more primitive,

[21] On this whole topic, see the Report of the Inquiry into Prison Escapes and Security, 1966, Cmnd. 3175 (hereafter "the Mountbatten Report"), and the Commons debate at 741 Parliamentary Debates (5th series), col. 828.

[22] Mountbatten Report, para. 212.

[23] *Ibid.* para. 217.

precautions taken as regards "escapers." Such prisoners, suspected of being likely to attempt to escape are watched with especial care, work in secure workshops, and wear distinctive markings on their clothes.

Category A prisoners present a much more difficult problem. The rescue of a notorious train robber from Winson Green Prison, Birmingham, in 1964 drew attention to the existence of this group. A review of prison security was carried out,[24] and special security blocks were established at Durham, Leicester and Parkhurst prisons. At one time in 1965, armed troops were stationed in Durham prison. Lord Mountbatten's trenchant comment was, "The conditions in these blocks are such as no country with a record of civilised behaviour ought to tolerate any longer than is absolutely necessary as a stop-gap measure." [25]

He recommended the establishment of a prison on the Isle of Wight containing some 120 category A prisoners in secure conditions.[26] The Advisory Council on the Penal System, in a well-argued report published in mid-1968,[27] preferred to see a number of existing prisons raised to a high level of security; segregation blocks would exist, but would be for short term use as far as possible. The government has accepted this advice, but rejected the proposal of a majority of the Council for firearms to be available for perimeter security guards at those prisons.

Types of prisoner

Yet another classification is that of prisoners into "stars" and "ordinaries." The star class consists essentially of those serving their first sentence of imprisonment. The ordinary class contains the remainder. Although still very much a part of the vocabulary of the prison service, this distinction which was never a very exact one, is of declining importance. It is now merely a factor in allocation.

What has been said so far ignores the fact that many prisoners are not convicted offenders. At any one time, some 10 per cent. are there awaiting trial, or are non-criminal prisoners. The table which follows gives a picture of the prison population at a

24 R.P.D. 1965, p. 12.

25 Report, para. 212.

26 Described in detail in his Report, paras. 272–287.

27 *The régime for long-term prisoners in conditions of maximum security* (1968). The report, published as this book was in the press, contains valuable recommendations covering many aspects of prison life.

particular time; the overall number of prisoners varies very considerably. The figures given are expressed both in terms of average population in 1965 and of receptions during the year.

PRISON [29] POPULATION AND RECEPTION FIGURES, 1965

	Average Population		*Receptions*	
Untried Prisoners	Male	Female	Male	Female
For trial, or being tried	1,349	50	27,540	1,081
Recommended for medical examination [30]	160	46	3,020	983
Convicted Prisoners				
For inquiry, or awaiting sentence	926	45	16,636	805
Sentenced to imprisonment	18,500	483	32,043	1,379
Imprisoned in default of payment of fine	832	24	11,336	694
Sentenced to corrective training	287	4	125	1
Sentenced to preventive detention	542	9	40	0
Non-Criminal Prisoners				
Civil process prisoners	–	–	7,336	110
Contempt of court prisoners	–	–	263	26
Aliens [31]	–	–	87	3
Others	–	–	146	26
All non-criminal prisoners	456	6	–	–
All Prisoners	23,077	666	–	–

The most disturbing feature of these figures, apart from the size of the numbers involved, is the very high proportion of receptions otherwise than under sentence. In many cases, those

29 Excluding persons sentenced to Borstal training or to detention in a detention centre. Source: R.P.D. (Tables) 1965, p. 2, and Table C.9.
30 Magistrates' Courts Act 1952, s. 26.
31 Aliens Orders 1920, 1953.

people should not be in prison at all; quite apart from other considerations of justice and convenience, they put an enormous burden on the local prisons.

For example, the 1965 figures include over 5,000 persons under 21 who were received as untried prisoners and who, having been tried, did not receive a prison sentence.[32] What justification can there be for their having been in prison at all? A few might have been heading for imprisonment only to be saved by a decision of a jury; but in many cases this cannot have been the case. The figures point to an inadequate use of bail.

Similarly 5,700 of those convicted prisoners detained for inquiries, or awaiting sentence, did not receive a sentence of imprisonment.[32] Much the same observations apply in their case.

Non-criminal prisoners are mainly those who have failed to comply with the judgment of a civil court, are in arrears with payments under maintenance or affiliation payments, rates or taxes, or are in contempt of court.

It will be noticed that non-criminal and untried prisoners, whose period of detention is short, are almost certain to be housed in the worst conditions. This is particularly unfortunate where a man is detained pending trial and does not then receive a prison sentence. He has already experienced a local prison, which must have lost a little of its terror; the deterrent value of the prison system will be that much less. This is one of the considerations behind the establishment of special "remand centres" for this type of prisoner.[33] The Prison Rules require that unconvicted prisoners shall be kept out of contact with convicted prisoners as far as can reasonably be done; but this is not easy in crowded local prisons.[34]

We are primarily concerned with those received into prison under sentence of imprisonment, more than 30,000 every year, some returning several times in the single year. The overwhelming majority have committed offences against property; the various other types of offence account for only one-sixth of prison sentences.

The following Tables indicate their age and sex, and the length of time for which they have been sent to prison. It will be seen that most are under 30; and that 85 per cent of all prisoners are in prison for 12 months or less—the corresponding figure for women is 94 per cent.

32 R.P.D. (Tables) 1965, Table C.11.
33 See *infra*, p. 212.
34 r. 3 (2).

Age of Prisoners received under Sentence of Imprisonment,[35] 1965

	Male	Female
Under 21	2,957	180
21–24	8,706	280
25–29	7,256	251
30–39	7,497	332
40–49	4,190	242
50–59	1,656	140
60 and over	564	43

Imprisonment: Length of Sentence, 1965 (Men)[36]

Length	Percentage of sentences of imprisonment	Cumulative percentage
Not exceeding 1 week	2·3	2·3
1–2 weeks	4·2	6·5
2–5 weeks	14·8	21·3
5 weeks—3 months	27·6	48·9
3–6 months	25·0	73·9
6–12 months	11·8	85·7
12–18 months	5·4	91·1
18 months–2 years	3·3	94·4
Over 2 years	5·6	100·0

The prison staff

We have so far concentrated on the prisoner. Necessarily so, for we are concerned with his experience of imprisonment, rather than with the penal institution itself, however fascinating such institution may be as a sociological phenomenon. But the experience of imprisonment is not just a matter of doors and locks and smells. As the emphasis moves from custody to training, the relationships between prisoner and prison staff grow in importance. We must know something of the nature of the prison staff.

The position of every member of the prison staff is one of very considerable stress. There is the inevitable tension between

[35] *i.e.*, without option of a fine. Source: R.P.D. (Tables) 1965, Tables C.10, D.1 and D.2.

[36] Source: *ibid.*, Table C.5. These figures should be greatly affected by the suspended sentence provisions of the Criminal Justice Act 1967: see *infra*, pp. 126 *et seq.*

staff and prisoners; tension created partly from the nature of their roles, but also through the officers' fears of violence or a breakdown in routine and order. There is also, as we shall see, tension within the staff, as a result of the structure of the prison hierarchy. Finally, at this particular period, there is strong feeling of insecurity within much of the prison service as a result of doubts as to the role of the prison officer.

The prison hierarchy [37]

No two penal institutions are organised in precisely the same way; there are obviously enormous differences between an old overcrowded local prison and a modern spacious open borstal. But all institutions are staffed by the same Prison Service, and the staff hierarchy in each prison or borstal is a variation of a common pattern. The Table on page 107 is an attempt to set out the main features of that pattern.

It is helpful to begin by examining the left-hand side of the Table, which contains those members of the staff who are responsible for the general operations within the prison. In structure, this group shows many similarities to one of the armed forces, in which many of its members have served. In particular there is the same division between superior and subordinate staff, as between commissioned officers (Governors and Assistant Governors) and non-commissioned officers. As in the armed forces it is possible, but not easy, to work your way from the ranks to the highest positions in the service. Entry into the service is either as a prison officer, the basic grade, or as an Assistant Governor, Class II.

Assistant Governors are generally recruited through an open competition on the lines of a Civil Service entrance competition. Many are recent university graduates, but a degree is not essential, and the maximum age is, at present, 40. As a result of pressure from the Prison Officers' Association, the Home Office is bound to try to fill vacancies at the Assistant Governor level from within the officers grades, and only where these attempts are unsuccessful are vacancies advertised for open competition. In practice only a few internal promotions are made each year. All newly appointed Assistant Governors attend an eight-month course at the Prison Staff College, Wakefield, for training in such things as psychology, casework techniques and group theory. There are two classes of Assistant Governor, and three of Governor. Above the Governor level are the Prison Board at the

[37] See R.C.P.S., Vol. 3, pp. 54–66 (Soc. of Civil Servants).

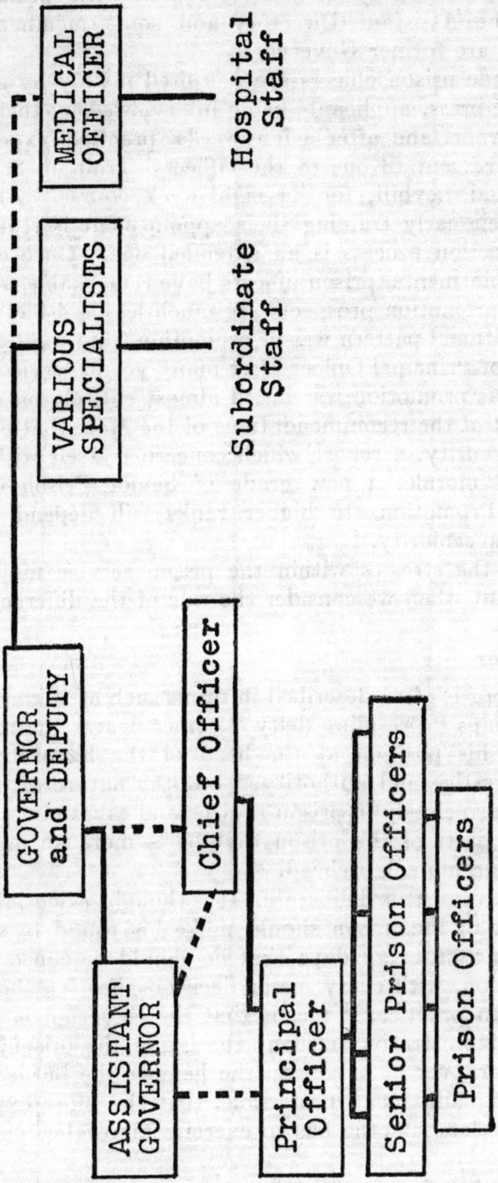

THE PRISON HIERARCHY

Home Office, assisted by Assistant Directors with special responsibilities. The Assistant Directors and some members of the Board itself are former Governors.

Basic grade prison officers are recruited mainly by advertisements in the press, applicants being interviewed by their nearest prison Governor, and after a few weeks' practical experience in the prison are sent to one of the Officers' Training Schools, at Wakefield and Leyhill, for an eight-week course. At various points in their early training their appointment is reviewed, so that the selection process is an extended one. Once confirmed in their appointments, prison officers have remarkable security of tenure, but promotion prospects are much less satisfactory.

The traditional pattern was of promotion from the basic grade to the rank of Principal Officer after many years' service, latterly 16 or 17. This promotion was based almost entirely on seniority. As the result of the recommendations of the Mountbatten Report on Prison Security, a report which concerned itself with general questions of morale, a new grade of Senior Prison Officer is interposed. Promotions to higher ranks will depend more on merit than on seniority.[38]

Some of the stresses within the prison service may become more apparent when we consider the role of the different grades.

The Governor

The Governor is often described in terms such as " king " of the prison; perhaps " presiding deity " comes nearer the mark. For not only is his position at the head of the hierarchy one of enormous prestige and authority,[39] but the nature of his duties involves him so closely in prison routine and takes him physically to so many parts of the prison that he is more an omnipotent power than a remote figurehead.

This involvement is deliberate. It is thought essential that the senior officer of the prison should make his round to see every part of the prison every day; that he should be concerned with every reception, with every major decision affecting those under his charge. In practice, it means that the Governor is under an enormous administrative burden; the larger the prison, and the swifter its turnover of prisoners, the heavier the burden. It is a common complaint in all professions that the more experienced the man, the less time he has to exercise his professional skills;

[38] Mountbatten Report, paras. 224–229.

[39] Joanna Kelley in *When the Gates Shut* records the admission of one Governor that, when jostled in Woolworth's, he had to stifle the thought: " How dare they? Don't they realise I am the Governor? "

but it is especially frustrating in organisations like the prison service, whose members often feel a strong sense of vocation.

By his decisions, a Governor can make very real changes in a prison, and even more in a Borstal where there is more room for experiment. To give a simple example, one Governor may believe that tidiness is best enforced by keenness on the part of the staff, and the day will begin with an inspection of the dormitories, boys standing by their beds. His successor may believe in self-discipline: inspections will disappear, and faults will be gently pointed out, with perhaps some collective loss of privileges if a good standard is not maintained. Such small alterations can alter the whole atmosphere of a prison.

Assistant Governors

Even a newly appointed Assistant Governor has some administrative duties. In a Borstal, for example, he may have responsibility for overseeing sporting activities for the whole institution. His principal task is the immediate charge of a Borstal house or a prison wing, of perhaps sixty inmates. He is responsible for their training as a group and as individuals. He has to "get to know the chaps,"[40] to help them with their particular problems, to assess them and report on them as need arises.

This is a challenging responsibility for a newly appointed man of twenty-two. In addition he has to find his own position within the prison. This means not only his relationships with the Governor and the other senior members of staff, but also with the officers working under him in his prison wing or Borstal house. He will probably have a Principal Officer, a seasoned professional perhaps thirty years his senior, and a handful of prison officers of varying ages and experience. As the Assistant Governor may be responsible for training these men, and reporting on them, the relationship can be full of problems.

Chief Officer

The Chief Officer is the mainspring of the mechanism of prison routine. His main task is the deployment of men in the lower officer grades. He makes sure that officers are kept informed of changes in routine; that officers are available for escort duties when prisoners are due for transfer or appearance in court; that officers are available for the various parts of the

[40] *Cf.* J. F. Conrad "The Assistant Governor in the English Prison" (1959–60) 10 B.J.D. 245 *et seq.* This article also contains valuable information on the motivations of recruits to the Assistant Governor grade.

prison as needed. In all matters affecting the officer grades he is in direct contact with the Governor.

Here again there is a source of some stress. An Assistant Governor has his team of officers under his command. They are also under the command of the Chief Officer, who may need them for tasks within his sphere. Good personal relationships are clearly essential if the machinery is to run smoothly.

The officer grades

Prison officers were once " turnkeys," or " warders." The distinctive feature of their uniform is the silver chain from which hangs their great bunch of keys. Their role is still primarily a custodial one. They must constantly maintain the security of the prison, and keep a strict control on the movement of prisoners within it, and on receptions and discharges. This is an inevitable task so long as there are prisons; and it is a role which the officer can readily understand.

The Prison Officers' Association describes a day's duty for a uniformed officer as consisting of

> " nothing more or less than unlocking the men and locking them up again; escorting them to exercise, to the workshops and back again inside the prison; feeding them and, at the end of the day, finally locking them up and checking them in for the night. Indeed, there is little in this procedure that is different from the work of the turnkey in the last century and the Prison Officer class as a whole is tending to become thoroughly institutionalised as a result." [41]

In recent years, prison officers in this and other countries have been seeking a new role, as part of a genuinely rehabilitative process. The Prison Officers' Association has declared itself in favour of this new role, incorporating some elements of casework.[42] In some institutions, where activities in association, and group work, are emphasised, officers can play this part.

For the older officer, discussion of his " changing role " is very disturbing: he may well imagine that the whole settled routine of his work is to be swept away. Certainly, the greater emphasis on a rehabilitative role means that the officer must take many more decisions for himself, and cannot simply rely on the rules.[43]

[41] Memorandum on " The Role of the Modern Prison Officer," submitted to the Prison Department in 1963 (reproduced, R.C.P.S., Vol. 3, p. 94).

[42] See the memorandum referred to above; and the Mountbatten Report, para. 228.

[43] See Morris, in *Collected Studies in Criminological Research* (Council of Europe), Vol. 1 at pp. 142–144.

At its simplest, of course, this new role may only amount to a slight change of emphasis. To give a simple illustration, an officer on escort duty taking a man to or from court can remain silent, performing his security function and that alone. Equally, as a sympathetic listener, he can do much to relieve the anxieties of the prisoner he is escorting; it is not too difficult to call this rudimentary casework.

Recruitment of prison officers [44]

From what has already been said, the career of a basic grade prison officer may seem unattractive. One might well ask how it is possible to recruit an adequate number of candidates. The current advertising literature emphasises the security of the job—" it offers you and your family real security, not only during your time in the service but in retirement " [45]—and the provision of free quarters. Understandably, nothing is said about the frequency of transfers to other establishments; and the information on promotion prospects mentions two-year and three-year periods,[46] but nothing about sixteen or seventeen years in the basic grade.

The Pentonville study [47] showed that the officers in that prison had joined the service either as an extension of their service in the armed forces, prisons offering a similarly disciplined career, or for financial security. The same study also revealed a marked cultural identity between officers and prisoners; that some officers were institutionalised and identified more with the inmates than with the senior staff.[48] It must be remembered that Pentonville is only one of many establishments; generalisations based on a single study may be misleading.

Night patrols

Very few prison officers remain on duty at night. The prison is staffed only by " night patrols," watchmen who have no keys and no real place in the prison hierarchy. They are often elderly; in any case they have no promotion prospects. Their

44 See two Council of Europe reports: *The Status, Selection and Training of Prison Staff* (1963) and *The Status, Selection and Training of Basic Grade Custodial Prison Staff* (1967).

45 " A new job—a brighter future," p. 12.

46 These refer to eligibility to take the limited competition for Assistant Governorships, and promotion in the Trade Assistant grade.

47 T. and P. Morris, *Pentonville*, p. 78.

48 *Ibid.* pp. 99–101. Several parts of this study are very illuminating on the matters touched on in this section: see especially Chap. IV.

justification is the negative one that their existence prevents regular prison officers having to carry out night duties.

The system was criticised in the Mountbatten Report,[49] and it seems likely that the patrols will eventually be replaced by officers aided by new security devices. The effect on recruiting remains to be seen.

Specialists

In the Table on page 107 the right-hand portion includes an entry " Specialists." At one time the only person in this category would be the chaplain [50]; it now includes a number of members of the prison staff with special tasks. They include the tutor-organiser who has taken over much of the educational work of the chaplain; the welfare officer or social worker; the psychologist in some institutions; the foreman of works in charge of the prison industries; and the administration officer in charge of executive and clerical staff.[51]

No one denies the value of these specialists, or the importance of their work. But from the point of view of the ordinary discipline officers the existence of their departments of the prison has certain disadvantages. There are more places in the prison to which prisoners have to go; and this complicates the security problem. It usually means that prison officers spend a lot of time taking prisoners to and from these various places; the prison officer sometimes kicks against being " a mere messenger-boy."

There are other difficulties of a career nature. Several of the specialist officers have their own staffs. This is especially true in the prison workshops. There are numerous trade assistants, " free-workmen," and others whose prospects of promotion are better than those of the ordinary discipline officer.

Medical staff

The medical officer and his hospital staff are mentioned separately because they enjoy an unusual autonomy within the prison. Although the Governor retains full responsibility for the whole prison, the medical officer within his own sphere is not subordinate to him; his allegiance is primarily to his profession.

Recruitment to the Prison Medical Service and its relationship to the National Health Service were examined by a Government Working Party whose report was published in April 1964.

49 Report, paras. 234–235.
50 *Infra*, pp. 118–119.
51 See R.C.P.S., Vol. 3, p. 75 (Soc. of Civil Servants); Vol. 4, p. 68 (Jones).

This made important recommendations designed to strengthen the service by improving arrangements for training, research and supervision, and by creating specialist appointments at consultant level in some prisons.[52]

Central direction

The Table on p. 107 is concerned with the hierarchy within an individual prison. General direction of the prison service, including Borstals, detention centres and senior attendance centres is in the hands of the Prison Department of the Home Office. The head of the prison service is the Inspector-General, whose post was created in 1967 following the Mountbatten Report. There is also a Chief Director and other officers.

Below Head Office there is a recently developed regional organisation in the North, Midlands, South-East and South-West, headed in each case by an Assistant Director, who acts as a sort of area superintendent. The eventual aim is to provide as much of the full range of prison facilities as possible within each region. The existence of regional offices does complicate the communications problem within the prison service; it is a standing source of complaint *either* that communications are too slow, owing to the number of links in the chain, *or* that individuals in the chain have been left uninformed owing to the need for quick communications.

Prison routine

The actual daily routine of a prison will vary from one establishment to another. That of a local prison may perhaps be taken as an example, as being the one routine experienced at some time by all prisoners.

The procedure of locking prisoners in their cells, unlocking them, and counting them is a staple feature of local prisons. It takes place at least four times a day for most prisoners, as they have to be locked up while the staff have meal-breaks, and for the night. At all times, of course, some staff are on duty.

The day begins at about 6.30 a.m. Cells must be tidied, the prisoners must dress, wash and shave in cold water, be unlocked to empty their chamber-pots, and have breakfast. An extraordinary amount of time has been devoted by penologists to the chamber-pot question; it certainly is one of the most offensive aspects of prison life. Although some prisons in the nineteenth century had water closets in cells, this was discontinued as a

[52] See the report; and R.P.D. 1964, pp. 51–52.

result of their misuse by prisoners unused to such modern devices. Now that all prisoners could use them properly, sanitary facilities are reduced to " recesses " on each landing where pots can be emptied each morning. More normal facilities are available in workshops and exercise yards, but not in any quantity; and in many prisons, the inmates will spend twelve hours in their cells at night, perhaps sleeping three pots to a cell —and eating breakfast there. The arrangement continued in the most modern prisons until 1967, when the implementation of the Mountbatten Report on Prison Escapes and Prison Security included, strange as it may seem in that context, a decision to instal proper sanitary fittings.

The morning and afternoon are occupied with work, but it is in very few prisons that a full eight-hour day exists. Some of the special problems in obtaining and organising work for prisoners are discussed below; they exist alongside general staff shortages which are responsible for the greatest reductions in the working day.[53]

In the evening, most prisons have some time in association, attending educational classes, or watching television until an early bedtime at 9 p.m.

Against this background occur the other regular events of prison life. Each afternoon the Reception block receives its intake, new prisoners being stripped, bathed, registered and issued with their prison clothing and New Testament. A reverse process accompanies discharges each morning.

Every day, too, a number of " boards " meet; a Reception Board may see all new prisoners and make some essential decisions about the type of work they should do; an Allocation Board may meet to make classification decisions. The Governor will preside at a staff meeting, do his round, deal with prisoners on report for offences, and see those prisoners who have applied to see him as he is bound to do by Prison Rules.[54] Others will be called up by him to be given information.

In other parts of the prison, prisoners will be having interviews with the chaplain, welfare officer or medical officer. In the bath-house, prisoners will be receiving, under supervision, the weekly hot bath prescribed in the Rules.[55]

All these activities have to take place in secure conditions: it

[53] *e.g.*, one period in early 1966, when at Pentonville working time during the morning was 15 minutes one day and none at all the next (741 Parliamentary Debates, col. 926).

[54] Prison Rules 1964, rr. 8 (2), 48 (3) (4).

[55] *Ibid.* r. 26 (1).

is easy to see why in local prisons the whole effort of the staff is taken up with these routine tasks. In addition, some aspects of prison routine present special problems or raise special issues, and they will be considered in turn.

Work for prisoners

> " A convicted prisoner shall be required to do useful work for not more than ten hours a day, and arrangements shall be made to allow prisoners to work, where possible, outside the cells and in association with one another." [56]

So the Prison Rules express the modern attitude to prison work, which is that a full day's work in conditions as far as possible similar to normal industrial conditions should be the heart of any prison sentence. The Gladstone Committee could still discuss the merits of the crank, the tread-wheel and of oakum-picking as forms of hard labour, as a " punishment of hard, dull, useless, uninteresting, monotonous labour." They were persuaded that this might be undesirable. A quite different approach was adopted by the Advisory Council on the Employment of Prisoners (A.C.E.P.) in its first report in 1961 [57]:

> " We believe, first, that the fundamental reason why prisoners should work is that every person should make the best contribution he can to the community; secondly, that suitable work, if properly organised, is a most valuable part of a prisoner's training; and thirdly, that prisoners represent a considerable labour force which ought not to be wasted."

There are some very real difficulties in providing suitable work for prisoners. The overcrowding of local prisons applies not only to cells but to workshops as well. The labour force, although large, is selected on criteria which would not appeal to the average employer. A proportion of prisoners are unfit for heavy or complicated work; the great majority are serving short sentences which preclude their attending training courses for skilled work. The nature of the prison routine, with constant interruptions for baths and interviews, and the transfer to other prisons of men who have held key roles, all make for inefficiency. This in turn prevents the prison manufacturing industries from producing goods of satisfactory quality at the agreed date. Disappointed customers do not give repeat orders. A shortage of work results, and deliberately inefficient methods have to be

56 *Ibid.* r. 28 (1).
57 *Work for Prisoners.*

resorted to to fill the working day. The vicious circle is hard to break, especially when there is an undercurrent of opposition to prison work through fears, however groundless, that giving priority to prisoners will cause unemployment outside the prisons, or will damage the interests of " sheltered workshops " for disabled men.

Some of these problems were examined by a Departmental Committee in 1933. Nothing much came of that report, but great changes are following the more recent reports of A.C.E.P., which was set up in 1960.[58]

The average labour force available in the prisons is 25,000. One half is employed in the manufacturing industries, making mail-bags, tailoring, metal-recovery, mat-making, carpentry, and a large number of small industries. Another third are employed on domestic work, principally cleaning and maintenance tasks, but also cooking, baking and laundry work. Two thousand men are in the works department, adding to or maintaining the prison buildings. One thousand are on prison farms.

The Advisory Council has made a number of important criticisms of this system. Its members were not even satisfied that the present industries were the right ones. For example, some small industries are uneconomic, but retained because they supply goods needed within the prison service. The Council took the view that preference should be given to the development of larger, profitable industries, even at the expense of buying some goods from outside.

So far as the industrial work, the manufacturing trades, was concerned, the inefficiency of many workshops, the failure to develop line or group production methods had led to an atmosphere of " desultory activity rather than ' a hive of industry,' " so that a prisoner used to the tempo of the workshop would feel bewildered and inadequate in a normal factory.[59]

Non-industrial work, the farming, domestic and maintenance work, was also reported as being in need of review. Prisoners were allocated to such work without any precise assessment of what tasks were essential, how many men were needed to perform them or how the work could be most efficiently organised.

To remedy this situation, the Council made suggestions for the modernisation of the whole prison industrial system. The system should be rationalised and adapted to the needs of the prisoners, with the use of work study methods, and the introduction of

[58] *Work for Prisoners* (1961), *Work and Vocational Training in Borstals (England and Wales)* (1962), and *The Organisation of Work for Prisoners* (1964).

[59] 1961 report, para. 62 (a).

proper costing. Modern methods of production scheduling and control, market research and bulk-buying were recommended for the major manufacturing industries, each of which should be under specialist management. Greater use should be made of outside resources, training schemes and good will.

The reports of the Prison Department in recent years show that these recommendations are being put into effect, and with good results. This was particularly true of a new incentive earnings scheme introduced in 1961, which helped to raise the contract value of prison work to its present figure of £2,500,000 per year. An elaborate market research survey on possible new prison industries was completed in 1967, and in several prisons modern workshops have been equipped by local industrial firms which can offer training and, to some prisoners, jobs on release.

One major rationalisation programme is reducing the number of prison industries. In future, most labour will be concentrated in six industries: metal recovery, carpentry, light engineering, weaving, tailoring and laundry work.

On the other hand, little progress seems to have been made in non-industrial fields. For example, the House of Commons Estimates Committee, reporting in 1967, found that it was almost impossible to assess the profitability of prison farms; no review had been carried out.[60]

Prisoners' earnings

Although closely related to the question of prison work this requires some special attention. Despite some recent changes, prison earnings are still at the " pocket-money " level. In prison industries, the average weekly earnings in 1966 were just over 6s., though in a few prisons experimental schemes for higher wages (averaging 16s.) were introduced early the following year.

Many writers have objected to this. Prison training is intended to develop a sense of personal responsibility. In normal life, the management of money is a large part of this, but in prison there can be no training given, except for those few prisoners in hostels, who work outside at the full rate for the job.

The ideal is that prisoners working inside the prisons should have the normal rates of pay and conditions of work. National wage agreements, and all the provisions of the Factories Act would apply [61]—though not the right to strike. Out of his

60 Eleventh report, para. 223.

61 Prison workshops are not within the present factories legislation; prisoners are not employees. *Pullin* v. *Prison Commissioners* [1957] 1 W.L.R. 1186; Fridman, *Modern Law of Employment*, 980–981.

earnings, with deductions for the cost of food and lodging, a prisoner could send money to his family and save for his release. It may be that this ideal will come nearer when the modernisation of prison industries is complete; but that probably entails the rebuilding of the majority of local prisons, a long and enormously expensive task.

In some foreign countries, this system is already in operation. In Sweden, which is possibly the most advanced in its penal system, new institutions are built around the factory, rather than the workshops following the cell-blocks. Modern industrial methods have led to the growth of some highly successful ventures, especially in making prefabricated houses. In at least one prison, full civilian wages are paid to all prisoners, who pay income tax and a charge for room and board.[62] There seems no reason why this should not come, one day, in England.

Education, religion and welfare

These matters can be grouped together, if only because they were once all within the province of the chaplain, who with the Governor and the medical officer used to head the prison hierarchy. He was responsible for some rudimentary welfare work, now developed under welfare officers as part of after-care; he organised educational work, now in the charge of tutor-organisers; he arranged entertainments for the prisoners. All these functions have been lost to him in the last fifty years, though in most institutions he still ranks as a permanent member of prison boards.

Speaking on this change in function, a Prisons Commission of the Church Assembly commented: " In some ways this may be a disadvantage to him in that he has lost certain points of contact with the prisoner, but it is an inevitable, and on balance probably a desirable, development, as it gives more time for his pastoral work." [63] This work takes the form of the conduct of services, of discussion and study groups, and of individual work with prisoners. Most chaplains would regard the last as being of greatest importance, but the growing practice of giving prisoners time " in association " makes the old pattern of chaplains visiting men in their cells difficult to continue.

Anglican chaplains are appointed by a Board from the Civil

[62] Eriksson, *The Correctional System in Sweden*, pp. 60 *et seq.*

[63] *The Church and the Prisoner* (1960) C.A. 1332, p. 33; on the whole subject see this report and the annual, and rather innocuous, reports of the Prison Chaplaincies Council of the Church Assembly set up in 1962, and the chapter on " Religion " in Joanna Kelley, *When the Gates Shut*.

Service and Prison Commissions and the Prison Chaplaincies Council. They are appointed for two terms of five years, renewable for periods of three years: chaplains, like prisoners, can suffer " prisonisation " and lose their effectiveness. Ministers of other denominations are appointed in similar ways. The Church is also active through the Church Army, whose officers are attached to several prisons, through religious orders which conduct missions, and through the Guild of St. Leonard, of interested laymen.

Educational classes are one of the evening activities open to prisoners, though illiterate prisoners or, at the other extreme, prisoners preparing for external examinations may be given special day-time instruction. In physical education, there are both remedial classes and opportunities to win proficiency awards or take examinations.[64]

Discipline

All members of the staff of a prison are concerned with the maintenance of order and discipline. The nature of the task in the various types of prison is well expressed by a group representing the Governor grades in the prison service [65]:

> " In training establishments, provided that they are of manageable size and adequately staffed, that the initial selection of prisoners has been carefully made in accordance with sound principles, and that staff have been properly trained, it should be possible to evolve a system of control and discipline which, while maintaining good order and security, puts as much responsibility as possible on the shoulders of the inmates themselves; and which, while retaining effective control by the staff permits of such control being unobtrusive.
>
> The problem is very much more difficult in the case of local prisons and those for long term ordinaries and persistent offenders. Here it is not only essential for the staff to have complete and unquestioned control, but they should clearly be seen to have it. Such prisons contain many men who are malicious, cunning and often violent, whose only interests, throughout their sentences, are to score points off authority and to bend to their purposes such weaker prisoners as they can dominate."

[64] See the evidence of the Association of Teachers in Penal Establishments, R.C.P.S., Minutes of Evidence, pp. 1–32.
[65] Society of Civil Servants: R.C.P.S., Vol. 3, p. 47.

Indiscipline is punished by the Governor, or in more serious cases by the Visiting Committee or Board of Visitors of the prison. This committee or board is a reminder of the period before the establishment of any central prison authority when the local magistrates were responsible for the administration of prisons. As a general rule, the committee or board meets monthly,[66] and is under a duty to satisfy itself "as to the state of the prison premises, the administration of the prison and the treatment of the prisoners." [67] Visits by individual members must take place more frequently, and they can speak in private with any prisoner.[68] The full board or committee must hear any application or complaint addressed to them by a prisoner.[69]

The distinction between committee and board is, inevitably, a matter of history. In practice, visiting committees are provided for local prisons and consist entirely of magistrates elected by local benches or by quarter sessions.[70] Other prisons have a board of visitors, which must have at least two members who are justices.[71]

Disciplinary charges are normally heard by the Governor; but in certain serious cases he must refer the matter to the committee or board, and in any case he may do so if he feels that his powers of punishment are inadequate. The punishments available to the Governor and the committee or board, and their use in men's prisons in 1965 are summarised in the Table.

GOVERNOR'S POWERS	BOARD / COMMITTEE	*Number* 1965 [72]
Caution	ditto	1,865
Loss of privileges for 28 days	for any period	7,484
No work in association for 14 days	for 56 days	4,077
Loss of earnings for 14 days	for 56 days	7,336
Punishment cells for 3 days	for 56 days	4,657
Restricted diet for 3 days	for 15 days [73]	4,099
Loss of remission for 14 days	for 180 days [74]	4,167

66 Prison Rules 1964, r. 93.
67 *Ibid.* r. 94.
68 *Ibid.* r. 96.
69 *Ibid.* r. 95.
70 Prison Act 1952, s. 6 (1); Prison Rules 1964, rr. 89, 90.
71 Prison Act 1952, s. 6 (2); Prison Rules 1964, r. 92.
72 Source: R.P.D. 1965, Appendix No. 8C.
73 Bread and water diet is never given for more than three consecutive days; there follow three days' normal diet: Prison Rules 1964, r. 55.
74 No limit for mutiny, incitement to mutiny or doing gross personal violence to an officer.

Corporal punishment was formerly available for certain very serious offences, but could only be imposed after a special procedure including confirmation by the Home Secretary. After several years in abeyance, it was abolished in 1967.[75]

The effect of imprisonment

It is almost impossible to measure the effect of imprisonment as a general deterrent, in dissuading individuals from offending. It is easier to say something about its effect on those who are or have been imprisoned. Such comment can be based either on an examination of statistics, principally those of reconvictions of ex-prisoners, or on a closer examination of the reactions of prisoners to their prison experience.

Reconviction rates

We have already seen that reconviction rates are a deceptively simple measure of the success of any form of penal treatment. But they do provide some guide. The following Table shows the percentage of male prisoners released from regional and central prisons in 1962 who had been returned to prison under sentence within three years; reconvictions not leading to imprisonment are ignored.

Category			*Number discharged*	*Percentage returned*
Central prisons	—Open		89	7
	Closed		376	18
Regional prisons—				
	Open—	" Stars "	58	15
		" Ordinaries "	31	16
		Corrective trainees	34	27
	Medium security—	" Stars "	119	33
		" Ordinaries "	75	60
		Corrective trainees	42	41
	Closed—	" Stars "	359	21
		" Ordinaries "	170	35
		Corrective trainees	331	60

The success rates for " stars," those serving their first prison sentence, are good, but results for " ordinaries " and corrective trainees are markedly worse; and these figures do not include local prisons. The overall reconviction rate for prisoners between

75 Criminal Justice Act 1967, s. 65.

21 and 30 years of age is close to 70 per cent. over a five-year period.[76]

The prisoner and his environment

More important, at least in the present state of knowledge, are studies of how prisoners react in the prison environment, to the prison staff, their fellow prisoners, the deprivations of imprisonment, and their surroundings generally. This is an enormous subject in itself; here we can touch upon only a very few aspects of it.[77]

The key relationship from the point of view of the prison authorities is that between the prison officers and the prisoners. It is easy to see the difficulties of this relationship. When one man has control over another, even in small and personal matters, there is a great deal of room for friction over real or imagined injustice. To this must be added the fear, and sometimes the fact, of physical violence on both sides. From the authorities' point of view, there is the fact of the corruption of officers by prisoners, the creation of " bent screws." This no doubt accounts for the disciplinary rule, relaxed in 1966, forbidding " undue familiarity " between officer and prisoner. Yet it is through the personal influence of the staff that imprisonment is meant to be a reformative experience.

The resulting relationship inevitably varies enormously from one institution to another. An open prison, where anxieties about violence and security are few, and prisoners stay for lengthy terms so that they can be known as individuals produces a wholly different relationship from that in a busy closed prison where there is an unselected and constantly changing population.

From the point of view of the prisoner, it is probably the other prisoners who matter most, and not the staff at all. It is with the other prisoners that he must work, eat, watch television, and probably sleep. To the sensitive soul, and there are some in prisons, the constant exposure to his fellow-prisoners must be the worst torment of all. Some prisoners, in fact, find it intolerable; they can be removed under rule 43 from association with their fellows. They are sent to a special wing at Manchester Prison, and many are later sent out again to another normal prison. This group consists principally of sexual offenders, many of whom are victimised by other prisoners, informers, and those

[76] *The Sentence of the Court*, Table 3. See also *supra*, p. 82, for further discussion of the evidence in that publication.

[77] See Sykes, *The Society of Captives*; T. and P. Morris, *Pentonville*, esp. Chaps. VII, XI and XII.

who have in other ways fallen foul of the prison's leaders, especially the "tobacco barons"[78] and bookmakers.

Over and above these special problems is the question of how a prisoner adjusts to the whole situation in which he finds himself, how he accepts the virtually complete loss of personal responsibility, and reacts to the official demands of the institution and of the inmate culture. It is possible to classify prisoners as conformers, or rebels or retreatists. What is not clear is how far the various groups "benefit" from their differing methods of adjustment, and how far the different patterns of behaviour are reflected in long-term results.[79]

Imprisonment—Forms of Sentence

Imprisonment is not a uniform system of treatment. There are great differences between imprisonment in open conditions and imprisonment in a closed local prison, between one closed prison and another, between different wings of the same prison. These differences are of great importance to the individual prisoner, to the prison staff and to prison administrators, but they are not the concern of the courts. This section is concerned with the function of the courts.

The courts must decide whether a sentence of imprisonment is to be imposed. Although every case is different and must be considered on its merits, there are inevitably, and properly, well-defined patterns in sentencing practice. It is possible, for example to list a number of types of sexual offences which will almost certainly attract a sentence of imprisonment.[80]

If imprisonment is to be ordered, the court must also decide on a period of time to be specified in the sentence. Here again the practice of the courts is to some extent predictable. An experienced practitioner comes to be aware of a rough "scale" of sentences: a particular type of fraud may attract a sentence of three or four years; a rape may deserve five; and so on. This scale is largely a measure of the "just deserts" of one who has committed a particular type of offence. The judges' scale measures moral wrong, and attaches an appropriate penalty.

This is, of course, to oversimplify the sentencing process; many other factors are taken into account. Nonetheless the judges

[78] *i.e.*, the organisers of illicit, but profitable, trading in tobacco; for r. 43, see R.P.D. 1965, paras. 15–18.

[79] On the whole subject see T. and P. Morris, *op. cit.*, Chap. VII and literature there discussed; see also, for analysis of the social structure of a Borstal institution, a series of papers by Rose, B. J. D., Vols. 6 and 9.

[80] See *Sexual Offences* (ed. Radzinowicz), Macmillan, 1957.

are reluctant to give so much weight to other factors that a sentence is far removed from that fixed by the scale of "just deserts." It is easy to criticise the judges on this score. How can they really measure "just deserts"? Ought they not, in any case, to give more weight to the likely effect of penal treatment than to the offence which occasions it? The judges' answer must be that some sort of agreed practice is necessary to secure consistency in sentencing,[81] and that inconsistency is interpreted as injustice by the public whom the judges in a sense represent.

In practice, the judges' scale of sentences is open to objection on the grounds that it produces many sentences which are too short for prison training to be effective. It is this fact which has led to the excessive number of short-term prisoners; to the introduction of suspended sentences; and which led in 1948 to the introduction of "corrective training," an attempt to persuade the judges to depart from their scale in some cases to give training methods a chance to succeed.

Short-term prisoners

We have already seen what a large proportion of prisoners are serving sentences of less than six or twelve months.[82] For them little constructive training is possible, but imprisonment has its full disrupting effect on the offender's employment and family. Where an offender's first prison sentence is a short one, there is the added disadvantage that he becomes familiar with prison, losing his fear of the unknown. These considerations led the second United Nations Congress on the Prevention of Crime and the Treatment of Offenders, in 1960, to urge a reduction in the use of short sentences, especially for trivial offences. The Congress suggested an extended use of probation, fines, "extramural labour," "suspended sentences" and "other measures that do not involve the deprivation of liberty."[83]

Another possible alternative to short prison sentences is the "Reconstruction Centre," which offenders would attend for twice-weekly sessions at which "clinical-type therapy could be given, together with vocational training, occupational therapy, group activities, etc." This proposal was put forward by Andry in his psychological study of short-term prisoners.[84] He would

[81] *Cf.* the scale of damages for personal injuries in civil cases; see 4 Sol.Q. 7 *et seq.*

[82] See Table, *supra*, p. 105.

[83] Report (UN Sales No. 61.IV.3), p. 63.

[84] R. E. Andry, *The Short-Term Prisoner* (1963). See also the rather shallow A.C.T.O. report, "Alternatives to Short Terms of Imprisonment" (1957).

provide an element of deterrence by combining this form of treatment with punishment in the form of heavy fines; the combination might well prove a very difficult one in practice.

First Offenders Act

An attempt was made in 1958 to deal with one aspect of this problem by legislation. The First Offenders Act of that year prohibits magistrates' courts from passing a sentence of imprisonment on a first offender [85] over 21 years of age unless the court considers that no other method of dealing with him is appropriate.[86] The court is under a duty to obtain full information about the offender, and if imprisonment is ordered must state its reasons and have them recorded in the register of the court and the warrant of commitment.[87]

In effect, the Act is a means of persuasion, and has not proved very effective. In 1964 magistrates' courts sentenced nearly 7,000 first offenders to periods of imprisonment. The provisions of the Criminal Justice Act 1967 dealing with suspended sentences do not, at least in theory, detract from the force of this 1948 Act.

Suspended sentences

A suspended sentence can take a number of forms. It can take the form of the postponement of any sentencing decision, so that only a conviction is recorded and no further action taken so long as the offender is of good behaviour; the result is much the same as a conditional discharge.[88] Alternatively, sentence may be pronounced but its execution similarly suspended.

The former system has the advantage that if a sentence has to be passed, it can be selected with the benefit of knowledge of the offender's behaviour to date, including the period of suspension. The latter system is thought to have greater deterrent effect, for the offender knows the gravity of the penalty which would follow further conviction. In practice there is frequently a compromise: a sentence is pronounced, but is capable of variation at the time of the subsequent conviction. The deterrent value of such a compromise system will presumably vary with the extent to which courts actually enforce the suspended sentence, or reduce it before execution.

In the early part of this century, this system of *sursis* was

[85] Offences committed as a juvenile, or not punishable with imprisonment, are to be ignored: First Offenders Act 1958, s. 1 (3).

[86] *Ibid.* s. 1 (1).

[87] Criminal Justice Act 1948, s. 17 (2) and Magistrates' Courts Act 1952, s. 107 (3) as applied by First Offenders Act 1958, s. 1 (1) (2).

[88] See pp. 149–150.

introduced in many European countries. The corresponding developments in England led instead to the introduction of probation, which combines casework supervision with a suspension of sentence.[89]

Some English judges felt the need for a form of suspended sentence. In *West*, for example, a recorder postponed sentence for six months to see if the accused would carry out a promise to repay sums obtained by fraud. In the event, he paid nothing and was sent for three years' corrective training. Speaking of the suspension of sentence, Lord Parker C.J. said,

> "That is just what this court has said ought not to be done. If a prisoner is thought fit to be put on probation, let him be put on probation. If it is not a matter for probation, let him be sentenced there and then, but it is highly objectionable to postpone sentence, and at the same time to turn the court into a money-collecting agency." [90]

By 1967, official attitudes had changed, and suspended sentences were introduced in the Criminal Justice Act.[91] Evidence given to the abortive Royal Commission on the Penal System had revealed a substantial body of informed opinion in favour of such a change, but for a variety of reasons. The courts felt that suspended sentences would be a useful addition to choices open to them. Others were anxious to use suspended sentences as a means of reducing the number of offenders who received, as their first prison sentence, a sentence too short to do more than acclimatise them to prison life. This difference of emphasis is reflected in the Act, which gives a wide discretionary power of suspension, and makes suspension mandatory where a short sentence would otherwise be passed on an offender with no prison experience. The change was also designed to reduce the alarming level of overcrowding in the prisons; for once, administrative convenience and penal policy were allied.

DISCRETIONARY POWERS. A court which passes a sentence of imprisonment for a term of not more than two years may make an order suspending sentence. The only qualifications are that a court may not, at the same time, make a probation order or impose an effective prison sentence.[92]

89 See *Suspended Sentence, Probation and Other Alternatives to Prison Sentences* (Council of Europe, 1966); Ancel, "The System of the Conditional Sentences or Sursis" (1964) 80 L.Q.R. 334.

90 (1959) 43 Cr.App.R. 109, 110.

91 The relevant sections effective from January 1, 1968.

92 C.J.A. 1967, s. 39 (1) (2). *Sapiano*, *The Times*, July 26, 1968. While each sentence is of less than two years, there seems no reason why several sentences cannot be suspended on the same occasion.

MANDATORY SUSPENSION. Where a court passes a sentence of imprisonment for a term of not more than six months, and the offender has no previous experience of imprisonment or Borstal training, suspension of sentence is mandatory.[93]

The principle is not fully pressed, for the mandatory provisions do not apply to cases where the offence involved is one which creates a certain amount of public alarm. This category includes offences of violence, or of indecency with young people, and offences of possessing firearms, imitation firearms, or explosives.[94]

The requirement of mandatory suspension is also excluded when

(i) the offender is receiving on the same occasion a sentence of imprisonment which may take immediate effect, *e.g.*, one for longer than six months; or
(ii) the latest offence was committed when the offender was subject to a probation order, conditional discharge, or an earlier suspended sentence; or
(iii) he is being sentenced in respect of the offence which led originally to the making of a probation order or order for conditional discharge.[95]

These provisions as to mandatory supervision are regarded as experimental. The Home Secretary is given power to extend their application, with parliamentary approval, if the experiment is a success. In particular, he may extend the provisions to cover all sentences for terms of not more than *twelve* months.[96] He may also apply them to cases where the offender *has* had some experience of imprisonment or Borstal training; for example, where this was many years previously.[97]

EFFECT OF SUSPENSION. The order suspending the sentence of imprisonment prescribes a period of between one and three years, during which the offender remains subject to the sentence. If he commits no further offence punishable with imprisonment during that period, the sentence lapses. If he does commit such an offence during the prescribed period, he must be brought before the court [98] so that a decision may be made as to the suspended sentence.

[93] *Ibid.* s. 39 (3). Note that detention centre experience is immaterial.
[94] *Ibid.* s. 39 (3) (*a*).
[95] *Ibid.* s. 39 (3) (*b*) (*c*) (*d*).
[96] *Ibid.* s. 39 (5).
[97] *Ibid.* s. 39 (4); he may not render immaterial custodial treatment within the last three years.
[98] Whether this will be a magistrates' or a superior court depends on which court passed the original sentence. See Criminal Justice Act 1967, s. 41.

The court is required to order that the suspended sentence take effect unless it is satisfied " that it would be unjust to do so in view of all the circumstances which have arisen since the suspended sentence was passed, including the facts of the subsequent offence." [99] If the court is so satisfied, it may adopt one of three possible courses of action. It may

(i) order that the suspended sentence take effect, but substituting a shorter term of imprisonment for the term originally ordered; or

(ii) decide not to order that the suspended sentence take effect, but to extend the period during which the offender remains subject to it, the maximum extension being that which would preserve the original order in force for three years from the date of the extension; or

(iii) take no action.[1]

Alcoholics

There are a number of persistent petty offenders, including drunks and prostitutes, who return to prison under short sentences with monotonous regularity. The system of suspended sentences may slightly delay their first experience of imprisonment, but the real problem will be left quite untouched.

In the present state of medical knowledge there is no " cure " for alcoholism. It is equally clear that a short prison sentence, especially if it has to be served in a local prison, serves no useful purpose. This is recognised in section 91 of the Criminal Justice Act 1967 which would abolish imprisonment for offences of being drunk and disorderly.

The section is not to be brought into force until hostel accommodation is available as an alternative to imprisonment, and the intention is that the courts will be encouraged to make use of the power to order residence in a hostel as a condition of probation.[2] It seems inevitable that many years will pass before an adequate number of hostel places is available.

Indeterminate sentences; parole

Critics of the sentencing policy of the courts sometimes suggest that the courts should be deprived in whole or in part of the sentencing function. It has been suggested that sentencing functions in England should be transferred to some executive

[99] *Ibid.* s. 40 (1).
[1] *Ibid.*
[2] See pp. 166–167.

authority, such as has been established in California.[3] There is wider support for the view that the courts should continue to decide whether imprisonment is necessary, but that the length of the sentence should not be determined at the outset by the courts, but fixed at a later stage by the penal authorities. Those authorities already control the conditions under which the sentence of imprisonment will be served; the length of imprisonment can be regarded as one aspect of that question.

The form of this proposal can vary a great deal. It is possible that a court would make a wholly indeterminate sentence, simply of " imprisonment "; the existing life sentence is an example. Or the trial judge could fix the maximum,[4] or minimum, or both [5]; Borstal training for young offenders is an example of a sentence with fixed minimum and maximum periods of institutional treatment.

Whatever the form of the scheme, the object is to secure that the prisoner is released at the most opportune moment. " A considerable number of long-term prisoners reach a recognisable peak in their training at which they may go downhill. To give such prisoners the opportunity of supervised freedom at the right moment may be decisive in securing their return to decent citizenship." [6]

A substantial body of opinion holds that this notion of " the right moment " for release is illusory; or, at least, that it is impossible to identify it. The element of indeterminacy in the old sentence of preventive detention was abandoned in 1963, on the advice of the Advisory Council on the Treatment of Offenders, because it was found impossible to determine, for preventive detainees, the right moment for release.

There are similar difficulties in devising suitable machinery for making the decision. Decisions taken by the prison authorities themselves are likely to be well informed, and to accord with other decisions as to the prisoner's treatment, the responsibilities and training he is given. Objectors argue that the release decision is so important to the prisoner that unbearable tensions will arise when this decision is to be taken within his own prison, by those with whom he has to live. Again, there are objections to these decisions resting solely with the prison administration, with

3 See Hall Williams, " Alternatives to Definite Sentences " (1964) 80 L.Q.R. 41, esp. 54 *et seq.*; Walker, " The Sentence of the Court " (1962) 67 *The Listener* 1099.

4 Cross, " Indeterminate Prison Sentences " (1962) 67 *The Listener* 289.

5 Found frequently in the U.S.A.; included in Model Penal Code.

6 *The Adult Offender*, Cmnd. 2852, para. 5.

the executive arm of the state; an independent Parole Board is the alternative.[7]

When the release decision is made, the prisoner will be released on licence, " on parole." If he offends again, or breaks the conditions of his licence, he may be recalled. Once again, there are problems in determining the machinery by which he is to be recalled; the courts, the prison authorities, or the Parole Board are all possibilities.

Parole in England

A parole system was introduced in England in the Criminal Justice Act 1967; the first parole decisions were to be made in April 1968. The essential provision in section 60 (1), which provides that

> " The Secretary of State may, if recommended to do so by the Parole Board, release on licence a person serving a sentence of imprisonment, other than imprisonment for life, after he has served not less than one-third of his sentence or twelve months thereof, whichever expires the later."

The licence will normally contain conditions, particularly as to supervision by the Probation and After-Care Service, and the Parole Board has advisory functions in connection with the formulation of the conditions.[8]

Legal background to parole

From one point of view, parole is a method of providing compulsory after-care for certain discharged prisoners: it is not just a matter of early release, but of release to " supervised freedom." Confusingly, release on licence, with conditions as to supervision, is used in other cases than those which are parole cases in a strict sense, and other forms of compulsory after-care look very similar. It is necessary, then, to see how parole fits into this context.

(a) REMISSION. Under the Prison Rules, most prisoners are entitled to remission.[9] In effect, so long as he serves 31 days as a minimum, a prisoner gets remission of one-third of his sentence, assuming he has not forfeited remission on disciplinary grounds. Although released early, there is no element of compulsory supervision in this situation.

[7] *Cf.* the Advisory Board under the preventive detention system.
[8] Criminal Justice Act 1967, s. 60 (4) (5).
[9] Prison Rules 1964, r. 5.

(b) RELEASE ON LICENCE, OLD STYLE. The after-care agencies have never had adequate resources.[10] Only selected categories of ex-prisoners can be provided with compulsory after-care supervision. This could be achieved by refusing remission to these prisoners, but releasing them on licence, with a condition as to supervision, the licence to remain in force for the remaining period of the sentence. This type of release on licence, in which the release decision involves no parole procedures, applies to those serving extended prison sentences as persistent offenders,[11] and to young prisoners under 21 when sentenced to imprisonment for eighteen months or more.[12]

(c) SUPERVISION FOR YOUNG OFFENDERS. In the case of some young offenders, there is no "release on licence." Instead a period of supervision automatically follows the period spent in the institution. To some extent this is merely a difference in terminology; instead of "conditions in a licence" one speaks of "requirements in the notice relating to supervision handed to the offender." But there are some more substantial differences, especially in the case of Borstal training, for there the supervision is a part of the training itself and not a mere appendix; and there are other differences as to duration and recall procedure.

The main group subject to this form of after-care consists of Borstal trainees.[13] They now have supervision for a fixed period of two years and for breach of the terms of their supervision can either be recalled by the Home Secretary or, if an offence is involved, be sent back to Borstal under a court order.[14]

Supervision for a period of 12 months applied to those released from detention centres,[15] and, since the Criminal Justice Act 1967, to young prisoners sentenced while under the age of 21 to a term of less than 18 months.[16] Recall powers are exercised by the Home Secretary.

Those released from approved schools are also subject to supervision usually for two years, but ending in any case at the age of 21.[17] Recall powers are vested in the managers of the approved school concerned, subject in some cases to Home Office control.

10 See the next section.
11 *i.e.*, under Criminal Justice Act 1967, s. 37.
12 *Ibid.* s. 60 (3). Recall procedures in these cases are the same as for parolees: *infra.*
13 Prison Act 1952, s. 45; Criminal Justice Act 1961, s. 11.
14 Criminal Justice Act 1961, s. 12.
15 *Ibid.* s. 13, and First Sched.
16 Criminal Justice Act 1967, s. 63, and First Sched. to the 1961 Act, as modified.
17 Criminal Justice Act 1961, s. 14 and Second Sched.

(d) Parole proper. The final group of cases is where there is release on licence, on the advice of the Parole Board, either before the time at which release would be granted on remission, or in cases where no remission can be granted. This second category includes persons serving sentences of life imprisonment and young prisoners convicted of murder or other grave crimes and ordered to be detained under section 53 of the Children and Young Persons Act 1933 [18]; in all such cases where the sentence is for life or " during Her Majesty's pleasure," the Lord Chief Justice, and if possible the trial judge, must be consulted as well as the Parole Board.[19]

Where there is a fixed sentence, and this applies to the great majority of parole cases, supervision extends from the time of release on licence to the date on which the prisoner would have become eligible for release as a result of remission, after two-thirds of the sentence had expired.[20]

Putting it in a nutshell, most parole cases involve prisoners who are released at some moment during the second third of their sentence, and they remain under supervision for the remainder of that third.

The parole decision

The Home Secretary is advised by a Parole Board, which must include a judge or former judge, a psychiatrist, a specialist in after-care and a criminologist.[21] This is a part-time body, dealing with an estimated 750–1,000 cases a year which have already passed a preliminary filtering process.

This process is to be carried out by local review committees at each prison. These committees will review the cases of all those eligible for parole, estimated at numbering 4,000 at each six-monthly review. A member can interview the prisoner concerned, and reports will be provided by the staff of the institution. The committee will advise the Home Secretary which cases should be referred to the Parole Board.

That board will decide the case on the basis of the written reports and documents which may include further representations by the prisoner. If the board thinks it necessary, it can send one of its members to interview the prisoner.

The precise procedure [22] is governed by the Parole Board Rules and the Local Review Committee Rules 1967.

[18] For details, see *infra*, pp. 253–254.
[19] Criminal Justice Act 1967, s. 61.
[20] *Ibid.* s. 60 (6) (*b*).
[21] *Ibid.* Sched. 2.
[22] Outlined, *ibid.* s. 59.

The first task of the Parole Board and committees will be the formulation of criteria on which to base their decisions, and this should provide a fruitful source for research. One possible criterion, arrival at a "peak" in training, may conflict with another, that those most in need of compulsory after-care should be paroled. The earlier policy, now abandoned, of extending compulsory after-care to new classes on a scheme of priorities [23] may still prove influential.

Recall from parole

The Criminal Justice Act's provisions as to recall from parole are an ingenious combination of all possible systems. The normal procedure will be for recall to be recommended by the Parole Board.[24] Inevitably, this will involve some delay, and provision is made for recall without prior consultation with the Board where it is "expedient in the public interest to recall that person before such consultation is practicable." [25] The Board will review all such cases when recall has taken place.

Where a parolee is charged with a further offence punishable on indictment with imprisonment, he may be committed to assizes or quarter sessions, and those courts may revoke his licence. In such a case no further parole can be granted for a year, or until one-third of the licence period has elapsed whichever is later.[26]

Sentencing recidivists

The persistent offender presents sentencing problems which are not dissimilar to those discussed earlier in this chapter. His offences may not be very serious in themselves, but his record viewed as a whole certainly is. By the scale of just deserts, the sentences he receives may not be very heavy, but if an offender is to be prevented from becoming a hard-core recidivist, there may come a time when he must be detained for a long period as a measure of protection for the public. These ideas lay behind the forms of sentence known as "corrective training" and "preventive detention," and also justify extended sentences under section 37 of the Criminal Justice Act 1967.[26a]

23 Under s. 20 of Criminal Justice Act 1961, never brought into force, the priority classes were those released from a sentence of four years or more, those released from a second custodial sentence, and those under 26 when sentenced. For the rationale of this, see the A.C.T.O. report on After-Care and Supervision of Discharged Prisoners (H.M.S.O. 1958).

24 Criminal Justice Act 1967, s. 62 (1).

25 *Ibid.* s. 62 (2).

26 *Ibid.* s. 62 (7) (10).

26a *D.P.P.* v. *Ottewell* [1968] 3 All E.R. 153, H.L.

Corrective training [27]

Corrective training was a new form of sentence introduced in 1948. It was invented " to give the courts power to pass sentences long enough to enable methods of training already developed in training prisons to be effectively applied." [28] The actual content of the training was not new. It was described in the Prison Rules 1949 as including

" (i) the provision of work which will so far as practicable help to fit [trainees] to earn their living after release, with technical training in skilled trades for suitable persons [29];
(ii) special attention to education;
(iii) the exercise of personal influence on the character and training of individuals by members of the prison staff;
(iv) the provision of every opportunity for the development of a sense of personal responsibility, including, for suitable prisoners, training in open conditions." [30]

This is a description of the normal aims of prison training; the effect of a corrective training sentence was that the trainee was likely to receive training of a better quality, and for longer, than a man serving a normal sentence of imprisonment.[31]

The use of corrective training was governed by section 21 (1) of the 1948 Criminal Justice Act, which provided:

" Where a person who is not less than 21 years of age:
(*a*) is convicted on indictment of an offence punishable with imprisonment for a term of two years or more; and
(*b*) has been convicted on at least two previous occasions since he attained the age of seventeen of offences punishable on indictment with such a sentence,

then, if the court is satisfied that it is expedient with a view to his reformation and the prevention of crime that he should receive training of a corrective character for a substantial time, followed by a period of supervision if released before the expiration of his sentence, the court may pass, in lieu of any other sentence, a sentence of corrective training for such

[27] See McClean, " Corrective Training—Decline and Fall " [1964] Crim.L.R. 745.
[28] R.P.C. 1949, p. 31.
[29] The courts at one time regarded vocational training as the essence of corrective training, but later corrected this view: *Chipchase* [1962] 1 W.L.R. 291; Practice Direction [1962] 1 W.L.R. 402.
[30] Prison Rules 1949, r. 154; now rescinded.
[31] See Bottoms, " Towards a Custodial Training Sentence for Adults " [1965] Crim.L.R. 584–587.

term of not less than two nor more than four years as the court may determine."

Over the years the Court of Criminal Appeal put a gloss on this section. The use of corrective training was generally limited to those under thirty, who had not served a sentence of Borstal training.[32] Unless there were special circumstances, the sentence was normally one of two years.[33]

One difficulty experienced in some cases was caused by the courts' reluctance to depart from the principle of just deserts. They sometimes refused to impose a corrective training sentence for an offence which was not so serious as to " deserve " two years in prison.[34] The form of the legislation may have encouraged this attitude, giving more prominence to the offender's previous record than to his likely response to a training programme. The 1967 legislation has the same fault.

In its last few years, corrective training was heavily criticised, as unjustified by its results, as unnecessary in the light of improved training methods and standards in prisons generally, and as demanding impossible standards of selection.[35] Its use greatly declined after an enthusiastic start, as the Table makes plain:

Year	*Sentences of C.T.*
1950	1,234
1955	403
1960	319
1965	152

Source: *Criminal Statistics*, Table II (a).

Preventive detention

Similar issues are raised in connection with prevention detention, designed for the persistent offender.

Every penal system has its failures, who receive every available form of penal treatment, including quite lengthy terms of imprisonment, but who offend again and again. There comes a

32 See Practice Direction [1966] 2 All E.R. 905, giving the effect of much case-law.

33 This reversed earlier rulings. Practice Direction [1961] Crim.L.R. 249; *Palmer* [1963] Crim.L.R. 709.

34 *McCarthy* [1955] 1 W.L.R. 856; *Wasley* [1958] Crim.L.R. 484. *Cf. Evans* [1959] Crim.L.R. 139.

35 For a debate, see Hall Williams (1964) 80 L.Q.R. 41; McClean [1964] Crim.L.R. 745; Bottoms [1965] Crim.L.R. 582; Sparks [1966] Crim.L.R. 84, 155.

time when "to punish them for the particular offences of which they are detected is almost useless."[36] Most penal systems resort to sentences of prolonged detention, not designed to punish, nor expected to reform, but intended to keep the offender out of circulation. This century has seen two English experiments under the name preventive detention.[37]

The first was introduced in Part II of the Prevention of Crime Act 1908, as a belated consequence of the Gladstone Report,[38] and has come to be known as the "dual system." Whenever an offender with three convictions on indictment since the age of sixteen received a sentence of penal servitude he could be charged with being an habitual criminal; if convicted, he could be sentenced to preventive detention for between five and ten years, to be served immediately after his sentence of penal servitude. This imposition of a second sentence justified solely by reference to the offender's record came far too close to punishing a man twice over for the same offence. This form of preventive detention fell into disuse and was abolished in 1948.

The second type of preventive detention was introduced by section 21 (2) of the Criminal Justice Act 1948, which provided:

> "Where a person who is not less than 30 years of age:
>
> (*a*) is convicted on indictment of an offence punishable with imprisonment for a term of two years or more; and
>
> (*b*) has been convicted on indictment on at least three previous occasions since he attained the age of 17 of offences punishable on indictment with such a sentence, and was on at least two of those occasions sentenced to Borstal training, imprisonment or corrective training;
>
> then if the court is satisfied that it is expedient for the protection of the public that he should be detained in custody for a substantial time, followed by a period of supervision if released before the expiration of his sentence, the court may pass, in lieu of any other sentence, a sentence of preventive detention for such term of not less than five nor more than 14 years as the court may determine."

36 Gladstone Committee, Report (C. 7702).

37 Note the earlier Criminal Law Act 1827, s. 11 of which authorised life imprisonment for a second conviction of felony. Long obsolete, this was only repealed in 1967. For a review of some foreign systems, see Grünhut, *Penal Reform*, Chap. 14.

38 See Rose, *The Struggle for Penal Reform*, pp. 79 *et seq.*

As with corrective training, the section received a substantial gloss from the Court of Criminal Appeal, which severely limited the application of preventive detention.

So the minimum age was, in effect, raised to 40, to avoid the institutionalisation of younger men.[39] The minimum length of sentence was raised to seven or eight years in most cases.[40] The courts were reluctant to order preventive detention where the offender had not had a long sentence, three or four years, of ordinary imprisonment, or where there was some evidence that the offender was trying to keep out of trouble. The sentence was reserved for the virtually hopeless cases.[41]

The legislation requires the court to consider " the protection of the public." The 1908 Act used the same criterion, and it appears in the provisions governing extended sentences under the Criminal Justice Act 1967. The phrase suggests that preventive detainees were violent, dangerous criminals. A Home Office memorandum on the 1908 Act[42] spoke of " the persistent dangerous criminal," and of " violence or treachery." The actual use of preventive detention was completely different.

The Advisory Council on the Treatment of Offenders, reporting in 1963, reported, " The majority of preventive detainees are of the passive-inadequate type, feckless and ineffectual in every sphere, who regard the commission of crime as a means of escaping immediate difficulties rather than as part of a deliberately anti-social way of life. Very few of them are of the seriously violent or aggressive type of personality."[43] Fewer than 10 per cent. had committed violent or sexual offences.

Preventive detainees were clearly a special group of socially inadequate people who needed special attention. The A.C.T.O. report concluded that preventive detention was not the answer to their needs. Prolonged imprisonment, often in secure conditions, for minor offences not only offended against the " just deserts " principle, but was undesirable in itself. The Council suggested a new type of regime, which would include initial confinement in a secure prison, but would lead progressively to treatment in open conditions, involving work outside the prison. For some a self-supporting farming community, more a shelter than

39 Practice Directions [1962] 1 W.L.R. 402; [1966] 2 All E.R. 905.

40 See *Sedgewick* [1950] 2 All E.R. 397, criticised [1963] Crim.L.R. 731.

41 See Jones, " Preventive Detention in 1961 in the Court of Criminal Appeal " [1962] Crim.L.R. 352; Thomas [1963] Crim.L.R. 248–250.

42 Quoted in the A.C.T.O. report, Preventive Detention, para. 8.

43 *Ibid.* para. 21. See West, *The Habitual Prisoner*; Hammond and Chayen, *Persistent Criminals*; and Taylor, " The Habitual Criminal " (1960) 1 B.J.Crim. 21–36.

a prison, might be possible.[44] There are of course some inadequate offenders who cannot accept the responsibilities of open conditions.

The Council was satisfied that the really violent or dangerous offender could receive a sentence of adequate length under the existing law, but put forward a scheme for extended sentences which forms the basis of the scheme introduced in 1967, when preventive detention was abolished. The extent to which the courts anticipated this is clear from the Table.

Year	*Sentences of P.D.*
1950	221
1955	197
1960	214
1965	42

Source: *Criminal Statistics*, Table II (a).

Extended sentences

After prolonged discussion,[45] the A.C.T.O. proposals were incorporated in the Criminal Justice Act 1967. Under the Act, certain persistent offenders can receive extended terms of imprisonment.

For an extended term to be possible:

(a) the offender must be convicted on indictment of an offence punishable with imprisonment for a term of two years or more; and

(b) the offence must have been committed within three years of a previous conviction for such an offence *or* his release from a sentence of imprisonment, corrective training or preventive detention passed for such an offence; and

(c) the offender must, since the age of 21, have been convicted on at least three previous occasions of such offences; and

(d) he must have received custodial sentences totalling five years, including *either* a sentence of preventive detention *or* two sentences of imprisonment or corrective

44 A.C.T.O. Report, paras. 65–73.

45 See the earlier scheme at 699 Parliamentary Debates (5th series), col. 127; McClean [1964] Crim.L.R. 760–762; *The Adult Offender*, Cmnd. 2852, paras. 9–17.

training, including one three-year or two two-year terms.[46]

If these conditions exist, the court may sentence the offender to imprisonment for an extended term if it is " satisfied, by reason of his previous conduct and of the likelihood of his committing further offences, that it is expedient to protect the public from him for a substantial time." [46]

An extended term may be longer than the normal maximum for the offence. If the normal maximum is between five and ten years, the extended term is up to ten years; if the normal maximum is less than five years, the extended term is up to five years.[47] It seems likely that such extended sentences will be used rarely; the normal maxima are generally adequate.

The provisions also permit judges to impose sentences greater than those they would otherwise have imposed, in order to protect the public; this is even if the resulting term is well below the normal maximum.[48] This may well have a greater effect on sentencing policy.

Conclusion

It is difficult to avoid the pessimistic conclusion that all this experimentation with forms of sentence is carried out on the outer fringes of the problems. It is possible that the use and form of imprisonment will one day be radically affected by the results of psychological research. It is becoming clearer that certain types of personality are likely to respond to firm discipline in institutions not unlike present prisons; and that other types of personality require wholly different treatment methods. But work in this field is in its infancy.[49]

Imprisonment and After-Care

In theory, a prisoner's only punishment is his loss of liberty. When he is discharged from prison, his punishment is over, and he is fitted by the constructive training he has received to lead a good and useful life. In contrast stands the official observation that in practice " many a prisoner approaches the end of a long sentence in a state of bewilderment and fear as to what the future will hold for him." [50]

[46] Criminal Justice Act 1967, s. 37 (2) (3) (4).
[47] *Ibid.* s. 37 (3).
[48] *D.P.P.* v. *Ottewell* [1968] 3 All E.R. 153, H.L.
[49] See the work of Grant, " The Treatment of Non-conformists in the Navy," *Annals* (322), 1959, discussed by Eysenck in *Crime and Personality*, p. 160, and Andry, *The Short-Term Prisoner*.
[50] Annual Report of the Central After-Care Association, 1959, p. 4.

It is easy enough to see why the ideal is never approached. A prisoner is deprived of far more than his liberty. The fact of his imprisonment almost inevitably loses him his job; the stigma of conviction or physical separation may estrange his friends and family; and that in turn may leave him without a home to which he can go on discharge, and with nowhere to turn for financial help. Some of these may be inevitable results of institutional treatment. They can be alleviated by careful attention to the conditions under which the sentence of imprisonment is served, and to the provisions of adequate after-care on release.

The prisoner and the outside world

Despite their detention, many prisoners retain important responsibilities outside the prison. A humane prison system must recognise this fact. For many offenders leading a hand-to-mouth existence or living off crime, their " business affairs " are virtually non-existent. Matters may be more complicated for the motorist unexpectedly imprisoned for a serious driving offence. In all cases, prison sentences begin as the trial court rises for the day, and the prison van drives off. It is difficult to see why some offenders at least should not be instructed to report to a prison after a short period in which they could attend to their affairs.

Much more important is the relationship between a prisoner and his wife and family. This relationship may have been under strain before, or as a result of, the prisoner's conviction. It will be crucial at the time of his release. So far as possible, then, it must be sustained during the period of imprisonment.[51]

During this period both parties must suffer. In the case of a married prisoner, both parties will feel loneliness and sexual frustration. The wife will experience financial difficulties, only partly relieved by grants from the Ministry of Social Security, and will carry the added burden of running the home and caring for the children alone. The husband will suffer from his very inability to do anything to help. Although few marriages seem to founder as a result of imprisonment, a marriage must suffer when there is inadequate communication between the parties.

Letters and visits are the means of communication available. Although the rules are generously interpreted both are sharply limited. Letters are limited to one a week, and are usually censored. Visits are normally limited to once a month. Even then, it is often difficult for a wife to visit as often as she is allowed. This may be because her husband is imprisoned in a

[51] See, on the whole topic, P. Morris, *Prisoners and Their Families* (1965), and *The Place of Voluntary Service in After-Care* (1967) paras. 62 *et seq.*

remote part of the country; the cost of the journey, the problems of providing for the children, the poor conditions under which visits still sometimes take place; all these are discouragements.

Most of these problems are being tackled. Visiting facilities are being improved everywhere: most prisons now have attractive visiting rooms with small tables and chairs in place of the frightful "visiting-box" system [52]; prisoners can sometimes be transferred to a prison nearer their home, either permanently or to receive visits; the "regionalisation" of prisons should help reduce distances.

The prisoner's adjustment to sexual deprivation all too often takes the form of homosexual behaviour. Although not so great a problem as in some United States prisons, with their different pattern of supervision,[53] homosexuality is one of the disturbing features of English prison life, adding to the tension. Its prevalence accounts in part for the UN Standard Minimum Rules forbidding the housing of *two* offenders in one cell; since 1964, some English prisoners have been so housed, but they are carefully selected.[54]

Generous provision of home leave, where this is possible, is the answer to many of these problems. At present, many prisoners serving relatively long terms have one short period of home leave near the end of their sentence. It is intended to be used in seeking employment and making other arrangements for release. In many countries regular home leaves are allowed, at intervals throughout the sentence. In his Report in 1966, Lord Mountbatten recommended the extension of home leave in England.[55] An alternative is the provision of facilities for prisoners to be alone with their wives in conditions of privacy during visits, perhaps for several hours at a weekend. Lord Mountbatten referred obliquely to this possibility as one to be explored.[56]

After-care

A long sentence may greatly reduce the prisoner's power to deal with the urgent problems which face him on release. During

52 Not unlike railway booking office windows, and even more difficult to speak through.

53 Sykes, *Society of Captives*, pp. 95–99; Patterson and Conrad, *Scottsboro Boy*, pp. 79–85. Both are reproduced in Johnston, Savitz and Wolfgang, *Sociology of Punishment and Correction*. For English material, see T. and P. Morris, *Pentonville*, Chap. VIII.

54 R.P.D. 1965, para. 2.

55 Report, Cmnd. 3175, para. 324. See also Eriksson, *Correctional System in Sweden*, p. 62. For details of the operation of the home leave system in England, see the Home Office memorandum to the Royal Commission on the Penal System, *Written Evidence*, Vol. 1, p. 94.

56 *Cf.* Hooper, "The Conjugal Visit at Mississippi State Penitentiary" (1962) 53 J.Crim.L.C. & P.S. 340.

his sentence, he will have adapted himself to the demands of prison life: he will have developed new attitudes and habits suited to the prison regime, but totally unsuited to life outside the institution. For such a man, release from prison may be psychologically more harmful than entry into it, and the process of "prisonisation" may have gone so far that his problems may be quite insoluble without outside help.

The Maxwell Committee on Discharged Prisoners' Aid Societies described the plight of many persistent offenders [57]:

> "Such offenders often have no home or family ties, or no such home or family ties as will supply the support and stimulus they need: no trustworthy friends; no niche in society to buttress any legitimate self-esteem: there is merely a bewildered and frustrated malcontent floundering in a sort of social limbo between prison and a world with which he cannot come to terms—a man not confirmed in criminality but with no strength or standards upon which to build a useful and honest life."

After-care, in the wider sense of the term, includes all efforts made to assist the discharged prisoner in overcoming these difficulties, not only from humanitarian motives, but also to prevent him seeking a solution to his difficulties in an immediate return to crime. It includes special provision within the institution for the preparation of prisoners for release; it includes "aid-on-discharge," the supply of money, clothing and other material needs; and "after-care," in the narrower sense, guidance and moral support for a period of time after discharge.

In this narrower sense, after-care is not unlike probation.[58] It involves supervision by a social case-worker, who will often be a probation officer. As in the case of probation, it involves the client in certain obligations to his supervisor. As in probation, these obligations need to be supported by the provision of sanctions in case of their breach.

Yet while probationers are selected by the courts as being suitable for such supervision, after-care is not a form of penal treatment for which convicted persons can be selected. Everyone discharged from a penal institution may need after-care, but there is no social service capable of taking on such a task. The result is that while all discharged prisoners now receive material aid-on-discharge, and all *may* seek help from the various after-care

[57] Report, Cmd. 8879, p. 17.

[58] See *Evans* [1959] 1 W.L.R. 26, for attempts by the courts to use probation as a form of after-care.

agencies at any time after their discharge, only certain selected classes of prisoners receive compulsory supervision as a matter of course.

Legal framework of after-care

The provision of material aid-on-discharge is now largely a matter for the ordinary social services such as the Departments of Employment and Productivity, of Social Services and the Supplementary Benefits Commission.[59] The prison authorities provide each discharged prisoner with suitable and adequate clothing,[60] a new outfit if the sentence is a long one, with his fare home or a travel warrant, and with some money in the form of a discharge grant to make his available ready money up to £4,[61] The probation authorities can also make money available from their " befriending funds."

Subsequent compulsory supervision, " compulsory " or " statutory after-care " is governed by detailed provisions of the Criminal Justice Acts. These have already been examined.[62]

Administration of after-care

An examination of the legislative provisions on after-care may well be misleading, because they are almost wholly concerned with compulsory after-care, for which the great majority of discharged prisoners are ineligible. They may instead seek " voluntary after-care " which was originally provided by charitable bodies founded as a result of private initiative, which was much more important in developing after-care in this country than any form of state initiative.

Voluntary after-care agencies

In the early nineteenth century, there was hardly any provision for material aid-on-discharge for prisoners. The Gaols Act 1823 authorised local justices to make small payments for travelling expenses, clothing and tools, but these payments were quite inadequate. To meet the needs of discharged prisoners, there grew up a large number of local societies, the Discharged Prisoners' Aid Societies, which until recent years were responsible for almost the whole field of voluntary after-care.

[59] For details see the Home Office evidence to the Royal Commission on the Penal System, *Written Evidence*, Vol. 1, pp. 90 *et seq.*; Circular 144/1965, reprinted *ibid.* p. 99.
[60] Prison Rules 1964, r. 20 (5).
[61] Prison Act 1952, s. 32; and *cf. ibid.* s. 31.
[62] *Supra*, pp. 130–133.

At first the societies had no official status, and small funds. The Discharged Prisoners' Aid Act 1862 greatly improved their financial position by introducing a system under which societies which received a certificate of approval were allowed small grants of money from state funds. Although its form changed repeatedly, the principle of contribution to the societies from the Exchequer remained, and by 1961 amounted to nearly 40 per cent. of the societies' income.[63]

The history of these societies was one of gradual change from a number of essentially local bodies concerned with material aid to something much closer to being a national organisation providing after-care in the wider sense.

Originally each society was based on a single local prison which handled prisoners from the area around it. In this century, many local prisons have been closed, and there has been much greater emphasis on prisons dealing with special types of prisoner, drawn from a wide region, or even the whole country. This means that the regional prisons had to deal with a large number of societies and also that some societies ("closed prison societies") had no prison in their area, and dealt exclusively with discharged prisoners returning from prisons elsewhere. These difficulties were gradually overcome by the increased activity of the National Association of Discharged Prisoners' Aid Societies (N.A.D.P.A.S.).[64] On its formation in 1936, N.A.D.P.A.S. took over direct responsibility for after-care at regional[65] prisons, appointing their own welfare officers who make arrangements with all the local societies involved. As a result of the recommendations of the Maxwell Committee, N.A.D.P.A.S. appointed its officers in local prisons also, acting as agents for the various societies.

The local Aid Societies were originally formed to provide material aid. Government committees had repeatedly exhorted them to attempt more after-care, guidance and supervision for a longer period. It was hoped that the presence of full-time welfare officers in the prisons would encourage this development; the officers would be in a better position to select those in need of after-care than the Case Committees of the societies which had

63 For certification, see the Prison Act 1952, s. 30 (now repealed). A full account of the various systems of financial support is given in the Maxwell Report, 1953 (Cmd. 8879), Chap. 1 and Appendix B.

64 Formed as a result of the reorganisation of the Central D.P.A. Society (1918–36) which undertook direct responsibility for after-care in a few cases only. Co-ordinating machinery existed in some form from 1863.

65 Voluntary after-care at central prisons was from an early date the responsibility of one of the compulsory after-care agencies.

formerly visited the prisons to hold brief interviews with those prisoners due for discharge.

Unfortunately, almost all the societies lacked the staff and financial resources necessary for effective after-care. In 1962, forty full-time and fifteen part-time officers faced a potential case-load of over 48,000 discharged prisoners, and in almost every case the societies' expenditure considerably exceeded their income. It was inevitable that the work of after-care should be placed on a firmer footing: how this was accomplished is considered below.

Compulsory after-care agencies

Compulsory after-care began in 1908 with the introduction of Borstal training which includes a period of supervision after release from the institution. This supervision was by Borstal Associates, almost all of whom were probation officers. Their work was co-ordinated until 1948 by the Borstal Association, originally a voluntary society but soon wholly financed from public funds.

In 1910 a similar system was introduced for men released from penal servitude and preventive detention. Again the probation service was used, and co-ordination was entrusted to a Central Association for the Aid of Discharged Convicts. Although financed through, and generally supervised by, the Home Office, this association adopted the guise of an autonomous society.

A similar body was established in 1928 to take over compulsory after-care of women and girls and named the Aylesbury Association after the prison in which almost all its charges were detained.

This threefold division persisted despite changes introduced after the passing of the Criminal Justice Act 1948. In form the three bodies just described were abolished and merged into a new Central After-Care Association (C.A.C.A.). In fact, they became the three divisions of that body, and continued to work independently, for the association as distinct from the divisions had no executive staff. There also existed a distinct after-care body, the Approved School Welfare Service, which dealt with some of those discharged from approved schools.

A unified after-care service

In 1963, after a prolonged period of gestation, the Advisory Council on the Treatment of Offenders produced proposals for a new pattern of after-care organisation.[66] Believing that

[66] "The Organisation of After-Care," 1963.

"the nature and quality of the after-care service provided should be fundamentally the same and available for all offenders, irrespective of the particular type of sentence which they may have served," [67]

the Council proposed that all after-care should be provided by one body, a Probation and After-Care Service—in fact the Probation Service renamed, and slightly enlarged.

The proposals were summed up as amounting to unification with decentralisation. Unification in that while the distinction between compulsory and voluntary after-care must remain, both should be provided by a single service. Decentralisation in that the professionalism of the service will largely remove the need for elaborate central organisations; the necessary central control and co-ordination is provided by the Probation and After-Care Department of the Home Office.

The A.C.T.O. report emphasised that

"after-care, to be fully effective, must be integrated with the work of the penal institutions in which the offender serves his sentence, and must be conceived as a continuing process throughout his sentence, and for as long as necessary after his release." [68]

In the result, and against the advice of the Council, prison welfare officers have become members of the Probation and After-Care Service, responsible to a particular probation area but on secondment to the institution.[69]

The result is that all after-care work is now concentrated in the hands of the Probation and After-Care Service.[70] The Aid Societies have all handed over their after-care functions, some having dissolved themselves, others taking up other work in the same field. The Approved School Welfare Service has run down, and the central after-care organisations have disappeared, except for the Borstal Division of C.A.C.A. which is handing over its functions gradually.[71]

This does not mean that there is no longer any place for volunteer workers such as the members of the former Aid

[67] *Ibid.* p. 16.
[68] *Ibid.* p. 16.
[69] *The Adult Offender*, Cmnd. 2852, p. 10; see Home Office Circular 144/1965 (printed in Royal Commission on the Penal System, *Written Evidence*, Vol. 1, p. 99); Report on the Probation and After-Care Department 1962–65, paras. 102–107.
[70] See McClean, "Probation and After-Care: The State of the Union" [1967] Crim.L.R. 690.
[71] *Prison and Borstal After-Care 1964*, pp. 11–12.

Societies. The Advisory Council recommended the appointment of volunteer "after-care auxiliaries" to help the probation officers, to act as friends and advisers to some of his clients. In many ways, this is similar to the work done through various volunteer associate schemes in different parts of the country, organised by Aid Societies, the W.R.V.S., or special bodies such as the Blackfriars Settlement.

These schemes have the advantage that discharged prisoners may prefer to seek help from someone who is not visibly associated with the "authorities," into which category probation officers as well as prison officers may come. But the schemes' difficulty, in many cases, is that they can do little towards giving material aid, and not surprisingly many prisoners can see little reason for meeting an associate if they "get nothing out of it."

The other principal area for voluntary effort is the hostel movement. Hostels of various sorts are an increasingly important feature of the penal system. For many years there have been approved probation hostels,[72] and more recently pre-release hostels for long-term offenders. After-care hostels are a more recent development still, and the main area for private initiative.[73]

The first after-care hostels were "half-way houses" for discharged prisoners of inadequate personality. These houses, the best known being Norman House, not only provide a home for men who might otherwise be homeless but are also a transitional stage between the institution, where the inmate has few responsibilities and few decisions to make, and the complete and sometimes frightening freedom of life outside. They provide the element of order needed by a man who has become institutionalised while he adjusts to the conditions of liberty, and the staff can provide the friendship and advice which he needs more easily than a probation officer working in an official setting.

Many organisations have now established hostels, catering not only for men of inadequate personality but for many other types. Lady Reading's Working Party on the Place of Voluntary Service in After-Care, in a report on "Residential Provision for Discharged Homeless Offenders," [74] devised a number of categories of need. For example, some discharged prisoners may need sheltered work facilities, but most are expected to work outside their hostel. Some hostels may accept men for indefinite periods or as permanent residents, whilst "multi-purpose" hostels are

[72] See p. 167. [73] See the Manual and Directory published by N.A.C.R.O.
[74] H.M.S.O., 1966. A second report, *The Place of Voluntary Service in After-Care* was published in 1967.

designed for short-term use, for emergency and classifying purposes.

The various voluntary bodies and interested individuals are now associated in the National Association for the Care and Resettlement of Offenders (N.A.C.R.O.), an independent body which arose from the ashes of the N.A.D.P.A.S.

Statistics of after-care

The significance of statistics relating to after-care is limited; they are inevitably a reflection of trends in the use of the various forms of institutional treatment.[76] Similarly, it has so far been found impossible to devise a method of assessing the success of after-care. Official publications often rely on reconviction rates, but, quite apart from the inherent weaknesses of such figures, the reader cannot tell whether he should allot the praise (or the blame) to the institution, or to the after-care worker.

There has been little research in this field in England. The Home Office Research Unit prepared a report[77] for A.C.T.O. in 1958, based on prisoners' accounts of the after-care given to them on previous discharges; all the informants were therefore "failures" in so far as they had been reconvicted. The report confirms that employment, at least in the prisoners' opinion, presents the greatest difficulties, although some one-third of the sample had no accommodation available on discharge. The only other fact which emerges is that where after-care is voluntary a negligible proportion seek help other than immediate aid-on-discharge.

Non-Custodial Sentences

Penal policy requires that judges and magistrates refrain as often as possible from passing a sentence of imprisonment. We must examine, in this and the following chapters, the alternatives to imprisonment.

The most common of all sentences is the imposition of a *fine*. The fine as a means of punishment is fully examined below but in many cases its use is inappropriate because of the nature of the offence or the indigence of the offender.

In many cases, the real choice facing the court is between a fine and *probation*, a period of supervision by a probation officer.

[76] For the case-load borne by probation officers, see p. 171.
[77] Published as Appendix A in the Report on After-Care and Supervision of Discharged Prisoners (A.C.T.O.) 1958.

This form of treatment is also sufficiently important to require separate treatment in a later section (pages 157–171).

In this section we examine some other forms of sentence, used mainly in magistrates' courts, and for trivial offences.

Absolute discharge

Section 7 (1) of the Criminal Justice Act 1948 provides:

> " Where a court by or before which a person is convicted of an offence (not being an offence the sentence for which is fixed by law) [78] is of opinion, having regard to the circumstances including the nature of the offence and the character of the offender, that it is inexpedient to inflict punishment and that a probation order is not appropriate, the court may make an order discharging him absolutely. . . "

Here, for once, is a statutory provision which is almost self-explanatory. Having convicted the offender, the court feels that punishment is unnecessary; conviction, especially if it is noted in the columns of a local newspaper, is often an adequate punishment in itself. Even the conviction has limited effects: it is ignored in future proceedings and, outside road traffic cases,[79] attracts none of the disqualifications and disabilities which may follow a normal conviction.[80]

Because of the number of other forms of treatment available, absolute discharges are used much less frequently than in the past. They are used in about 1 per cent. of all cases, the percentage being highest for very young offenders. So 3·1 per cent. of children under 14 found guilty of indictable offences in 1965 were absolutely discharged. In 1938, the corresponding percentage was 27·8 per cent.; what has happened is that courts now prefer conditional discharges, little used in 1938.[81]

Conditional discharge

The circumstances in which an order for conditional discharge may be made are very similar to those in the case of absolute discharge. The same statutory provision governs both, for section 7 (1) of the Criminal Justice Act 1948, quoted above in part, continues

> " . . . or, if the court thinks fit, discharging him subject to the condition that he commits no offence during such period,

[78] *i.e.*, not murder or treason.
[79] Criminal Justice Act 1967, s. 51 (2).
[80] Criminal Justice Act 1948, s. 12 (1) (2).
[81] Source: *Criminal Statistics* 1965, p. xxiii.

not exceeding three years [82] from the date of the order, as may be specified therein."

In this case, the court still takes no immediate action on conviction, which has the same limited effects as on an absolute discharge.[83] Where the discharge is conditional the court retains a sanction. If the offender commits another offence within the prescribed period he can be sentenced, not only for that further offence, but also for the offence which led to his conditional discharge. This is explained to him at the time of his first appearance [84]; when he is subsequently convicted a sentence will normally be imposed for the first offence,[85] and that conviction will no longer be ignored in future proceedings.[86]

There are complex provisions governing the choice of the court before which subsequent hearings under an order for conditional discharge should take place. In the usual case, where one magistrates' court makes the order and another court convicts the offender of a further offence, the second court may, with the consent of the first, deal with both convictions.[87]

Binding over

The procedure of binding over is used a great deal in English criminal procedure, and, to a lesser extent, as something akin to a sentence. Despite this, the law is ancient and obscure, and the matter is not made any clearer by the confusing terminology. It should be said at once that "binding over," "requiring sureties" or "requiring someone to enter into recognisances" are all part of the same thing; for all useful purposes they can be equated.

What is involved is that the person concerned, for our purposes usually the offender, promises to do or refrain from doing something; and further promises to forfeit a stated sum of money should he fail to keep the promise. It takes the form of a statement recognising a debt, payable if the stated condition is not fulfilled. "A recognisance is an obligation of record, which a man enters into before some court of record, or magistrate duly

[82] The three-year limit was substituted for the former maximum of 12 months by Criminal Justice Act 1967, s. 52.
[83] Criminal Justice Act 1948, s. 12 (1) (2).
[84] *Ibid.* s. 7 (3).
[85] *Fry* [1955] 1 W.L.R. 28; *Whitehead* [1961] Crim.L.R. 109.
[86] Criminal Justice Act 1948, s. 12 (1), proviso, applicable only when the offender is over 17 at the time of the first offence.
[87] *Ibid.* 1948, s. 8, especially s. 8 (7).

authorised, with condition to do some particular act, as, to keep the peace." [88]

This power of binding over was formerly used to secure the attendance of prosecutor and witnesses at a trial.[89] We are concerned with three of its uses, the first two of which are closely related.

All justices of the peace, and this includes the judges as well as magistrates, have the power to bind someone over "to keep the peace," and also the power to bind over "to be of good behaviour" for a stated period. The former seems to be a common law power, and is used to restrain anticipated breaches of the peace.[90] The term " breach of the peace " almost defies definition: in practice, a fight or assault is the usual occasion for the use of this power. The power to bind over to be of good behaviour derives from the Justices of the Peace Act 1361 and can be used in any case where it is apprehended that a person will do something contrary to law.[91] To some extent, the two powers cover the same ground.

These powers can be exercised by justices on the complaint of any individual,[92] but can also be used when anyone is before the court, charged with an offence,[93] or even as complainant or witness so long as they are given a chance to make answer.[94] If someone refuses to enter into a recognisance, he may be imprisoned for up to six months or until he does so within that time.[95]

If someone breaks the recognisance, he may be required to forfeit some or all of the sum stated.[96] In some cases, the courts have ordered imprisonment for breach of recognisance, but there seems no authority for this practice which has been heavily criticised.[97]

These powers have proved of value in connection with offences for which the penalty is grossly inadequate. It is legitimate to

[88] Blackstone's classic definition: 4 *Commentaries* (17th ed.), 341.
[89] See now Criminal Procedure (Attendance of Witnesses) Act 1965.
[90] *Wilkins* [1907] 2 K.B. 380.
[91] *Bamping* v. *Barnes* [1958] Crim.L.R. 186; *Everett* v. *Ribbands* [1952] 2 Q.B. 198.
[92] Magistrates' Courts Act 1952, s. 91; for superior courts' powers see Criminal Justice Act 1948, ss. 14, 15.
[93] Even if acquitted: *Ex p. Davis* (1871), 24 L.T. 547. See also Criminal Law Act 1967, s. 7 (4).
[94] *Wilkins*, *supra*; *Sheldon* v. *Bromfield Justices* [1964] 2 Q.B. 573.
[95] Magistrates' Courts Act 1952, s. 91 (3). On practice, see Jones, "Binding over on complaint and otherwise" [1955] Crim.L.R. 484.
[96] Magistrates' Courts Act 1952, s. 96; Criminal Justice Act 1948, s. 14; Criminal Justice Act 1967, s. 47.
[97] See *Sharpe* [1957] 1 Q.B. 552; [1958] Crim.L.R. 738; Chislett, "Recognisances and Conditions" [1958] Crim.L.R. 734; *Finch* (1962) 47 Cr. App.R. 58; *Younis* [1965] Crim.L.R. 305.

fix as the amount of the recognisance a sum larger than the maximum fine.[98] Fears of abuse in this connection have been reduced since the granting of the right of appeal from binding over orders in 1956; formerly there was no appeal.[99]

The remaining power to be examined is also controversial. This is the power to bind over " to come up for judgment " exercised by the higher courts. The practice has grown up of inserting further conditions in the order; in particular, courts order an offender to remain out of the country, or to return to the Irish Republic, and to come up for judgment if he returns.[1] This is a form of transportation, or deportation, used when no statutory authority for deportation exists, and it seems wholly without merit. Despite much academic criticism,[2] the power is still used, even for " confirmed recidivists." [3] It is good to know that the Irish judges sometimes return the compliment and transport their undesirables to England !

Fines and Monetary Penalties

A fine is " any pecuniary penalty or pecuniary forfeiture or pecuniary compensation payable under a conviction." [4]

It is necessary to consider monetary payments of this type under two heads—as punishments and as means of compensating victims of crime. The narrow definition of a fine covers only punitive penalties.

Fines

Since the Criminal Justice Act 1948 a fine has become a possible penalty in all but a few crimes, those crimes such as murder which have a fixed penalty.[5] Before 1948 the courts had had power to fine in cases of misdemeanour but not in cases of felony with the exception of manslaughter. Now the only limitations upon fining are the various maxima imposed by statute in respect of particular crimes [6] and the general limitation of

98 *Sandbach* [1935] 2 K.B. 192.
99 Magistrates' Courts (Appeals From Binding Over Orders) Act 1956.
1 *Flaherty* [1958] Crim.L.R. 556; *McCartan* [1958] 1 W.L.R. 933; Chislett, *op. cit.*; *Ayu* [1958] 1 W.L.R. 1264 (a case involving return to Nigeria). For some practical difficulties, see [1960] Crim.L.R. 113.
2 See Williams, " Suspended Sentence at Common Law " [1963] *Public Law* 449; O'Higgins, " Voluntary Deportation " [1963] Crim.L.R. 680.
3 *Hodges* (1967) 51 Cr.App.R. 361.
4 Magistrates' Courts Act 1952, s. 126.
5 s. 13. The power to fine is " in lieu of or in addition to " other specified punishments.
6 The steady inflation has led to a re-enactment of individual maxima in a large number of crimes—they are set out in Sched. 3, Criminal Justice Act 1967.

powers placed upon inferior courts.[7] Despite this apparent freedom the courts have laid down few general principles to be used to assist in fixing the appropriate fine.

Amounts

There are some isolated statutory rules such as that restricting a magistrates' court from fining a child under fourteen years of age more than £10.[8] Since, as will be seen, the ultimate results of failure to pay a fine will be imprisonment the most obvious factor to be considered in fixing an appropriate fine is the means of the criminal. The Criminal Justice Act 1967 has made a genuine attempt to ensure that every effort is made to avoid the necessity of imprisonment for non-payment and it has placed great emphasis upon a means inquiry.

The usual practice has been to fix a term of imprisonment to be served on default at the same time as the fine was fixed—£10 or seven days, for example. The Criminal Justice Act 1967 has prevented this from being done except where the court has power to use its power of imprisonment forthwith.[9]

The emphasis is now upon the means inquiry and it is clearly the intention of the statute that this should be an effective and realistic one. Often up till now inquiry as to a convicted person's ability to pay a fine has rarely gone beyond questioning as to his weekly wage—" how much do you have in your wage packet?" It is usually left to the accused to put forward any special commitments he may have and these are seldom advanced. There has been a marked contrast to the procedure in fixing a fine and that of fixing weekly maintenance payments in the matrimonial court where great care is usually taken. The Act now provides that a person who is having a means inquiry may be required, by the court, or by a magistrate before the hearing, to furnish to the court a statement of means. Failure to comply is a summary offence itself attracting a maximum fine of £50.

It would appear that if a fine is out of all proportion with ability to pay, the Court of Appeal (Criminal Division) will substitute a more realistic punishment. In a case where a fine of £3,000 was made against a man, who had been in the motor trade but was now in grave financial difficulties, for the crime of larceny-bailee the court said that ability to pay must be taken

[7] *e.g.*, that of magistrates' courts, recently raised to £400 for indictable offences dealt with summarily. Criminal Justice Act 1967, s. 26.

[8] Magistrates' Courts Act 1952, s. 32; Criminal Justice Act 1961, s. 8.

[9] s. 44 (3).

into account. It substituted a binding-over order and the payment of £150 towards the costs of the case.[10] It was emphasised recently that a fine must be in the person's capacity to pay but not necessarily in his immediate capacity.[11] In other words, it may be a reasonable charge upon his future income.

The exact legal nature of a fine is interesting. It is personal to the criminal in that he will suffer the alternatives if it is not paid. It has even been held that it may be recovered from his estate after his death though the crime itself may not have benefited his estate.[12] On the other hand, in marked contrast to other forms of punishment it can be discharged by others. Anyone is free to pay another's fine and some intending martyrs have been denied their desire to protest by going to prison, through others paying their fines unasked. It is of course illegal to agree to pay another's fines in the future—such a contract is contrary to public policy and so illegal and void.

In *Dodd* [13] the Court of Criminal Appeal made strange use of this position. Dodd had been fined £100 and ordered to pay £50 costs for using premises for gaming. He was a cripple with no resources and little clear prospect of paying. The court thought that the fine was " clearly imposed by the trial judge on the assumption that the person employing Dodd would pay." Surprisingly they approved of this reasoning and so Dodd was in a position in which his liberty depended upon the willingness of his employer to pay. This is an unhappy decision.

The relationship between imprisonment and fining has never been systematically explored by the courts. In 1953 by coincidence two cases were reported concerning larcenies in golf clubs in both of which the original sentence was changed in character. In *Markwick* [14] money had been missed and Markwick was found with a marked 2s. 6d. piece in his possession. He was fined £500. In *Morris* [15] four balls worth 5s. had been stolen by the accused. He was sentenced to one month's imprisonment even though he said he had merely " borrowed " the balls and had indeed returned them by post. On appeal Markwick's sentence was altered to two months' imprisonment on the ground that " the gravamen of the offence was not only its essential meanness, but also the aura of suspicion which must have been thrown over the servants and other members of the club." On

[10] *Croker* [1961] Crim.L.R. 842.
[11] *Lewis* [1965] Crim.L.R. 121.
[12] *H.M. Treasury* v. *Harris* [1957] 2 Q.B. 516; [1957] Crim.L.R. 469.
[13] [1957] Crim.L.R. 159.
[14] (1953) 37 Cr.App.R. 125.
[15] [1954] Crim.L.R. 65.

the other hand Morris's sentence was changed to a fine of £10—his was clearly regarded as a technical type of larceny. The cases in juxtaposition are interesting and appear to indicate only that the selection of fine or imprisonment is to be made on the court's assessment of the surrounding gravity of the offence.

An interesting additional point is made in *Markwick* concerning the relationship between a heavy fine and imprisonment. It was said that " when the change was first mooted (*i.e.*, allowing fines for felonies) it was, to my knowledge, opposed by a very high authority on the ground that it would give persons of means an opportunity of buying themselves out of being sent to prison, and therefore one has to take great care that there is not one law for the rich and one for the poor." [16]

It would follow that fines should only be used as alternatives to light sentences of imprisonment where the balance of justice as between the types of punishment is even. Fines should not therefore be exceedingly heavy in such situations. This point is made in the same judgment—" heavy fines are appropriate only where Parliament has particularly provided for them. . . . "

The current tendency is to lay emphasis upon the need for greater uniformity of punishment for like cases. This has led to a movement towards a " tariff " approach to repetitive offences such as the minor road traffic offences. This tendency is bolstered by the manifest injustice of markedly differing amounts of fine in similar cases. And yet a note of caution needs to be injected. A fine can only have meaning in relation to a man's disposable income or, at a more serious level, available savings. Little thought has been given to this problem. It could be argued that the place for a serious means inquiry is before fixing the appropriate fine. It might even be argued that a penalty should be expressed not in terms of a maximum which will inevitably be eroded by inflation but in terms of a weekly wage. There will obviously be many non-wage earners who fall to be fined but it should not be too difficult to evolve a satisfactory formula for dealing with them.

Enforcement

Courts have power to allow time for payment or to order payment by instalments.[17] Where time to pay has been allowed extensions may be sought and granted. Courts sometimes use these powers to lay down special modes of payment—at a police

[16] *Markwick* (1953) 37 Cr.App.R. 125, *per* Lord Goddard C.J.

[17] Magistrates' Courts Act 1952, s. 63 (1).

station on a certain day for example—with a view to reminding the payer of his crime. There appears to be no legal force behind these imaginative gestures.

The Criminal Justice Act 1967 has laid down a new pattern of enforcement with emphasis upon avoiding as far as is possible imprisonment for non-payment. The means inquiry which must precede imprisonment has reluctance to imprison built into it. A warrant for committal to prison may not be issued unless the offence is punishable with imprisonment and the defaulter appears to have sufficient means to pay or all other methods have been considered or tried and have not proved to be or appeared likely to be effective.[18] It is possible for the court inquiring into the defaulter's means to remit the whole or part of the original fine where this appears just because of changes in circumstances since the original fining. Where in such a case a term of imprisonment in default has been fixed, and it must be remembered that this is not now normal procedure, the term of imprisonment has to be reduced proportionately to the reduction in the fine.[19]

Other methods of enforcement are introduced by the Act. Most important, without doubt, is the power to enforce by attachment of earnings.[20] This is a convenient and generally effective method which has been resisted in English law although it has long been used in Scotland, where it is termed arrestment, for a wide number of enforcements. It is true that the drifter who frequently changes his job is hard to follow and there may be employment difficulties for those " in possession of " attachment orders but the administrative advantages in the vast majority of instances outweigh these snags. It is also provided that payment of a fine imposed by the magistrates may be enforced by proceedings in the county court or High Court as if the amount were a civil debt owed to the magistrates' clerk.[21] This enables the civil machinery of enforcement to be deployed.

It may well be that one of the principal motives for these provisions was the desire of the Home Secretary to rid the prisons of the nuisance of short-term offenders imprisoned for non-payment of fines. It is clear that the new system with its emphasis upon flexibility of enforcement and variety of method is far preferable to the old cudgel of the alternative " or seven days " type of enforcement.

18 Criminal Justice Act 1967, s. 44 (5).
19 *Ibid.* s. 44 (10).
20 Criminal Justice Act 1967, s. 46.
21 *Ibid.* s. 45.

Compensation

Most crimes involve actionable torts but it is a basic rule that both types of remedy, the criminal and the civil, cannot be brought in the same proceedings. The victim is always free to bring his civil action although historically it has been the custom until recently to insist upon the criminal proceedings being taken first. Indeed there has been a tendency to keep the two actions strictly separate and the rule in *Hollington* v. *Hewthorne* [22] provides that a criminal conviction (it was careless driving in that case) is not evidence (of negligence) in the subsequent civil trial.

Despite this separation there are some instances where compensation may be awarded in the criminal case. The law is to be found generally in the Forfeiture Act 1870 which provides that a sum of up to £100 may be awarded on conviction of treason or felony.[23] This is to be awarded " by the way of satisfaction or compensation for any loss of property suffered by the applicant." Although this power is not limited to larceny and kindred offences it does not extend to offences against the person.

The Larceny Act [24] and the Sale of Goods Act [25] both have provisions about the revesting of stolen property in the true owner where there has been a prosecution to conviction. One of the peculiarities of the law is found in section 45, Offences Against the Person Act 1861, which provides that if a defendant is convicted of common assault or of aggravated assault on a young female and the charge was made by or on behalf of the victim, then serving of imprisonment imposed or payment of the fine or a certificate by magistrates that they dismissed the charge releases the assailant from all civil liability. This is a tricky point which turns upon who institutes the charge. It might, if the results of the assault subsequently turn out to be serious, be a severe embarrassment to a complainant.

Probation

" We understand by probation the submission of an offender while at liberty to a specified period of supervision by a social caseworker who is an officer of the court." This statement by the Morison Committee [26] is the nearest thing we have to an official definition of probation. The statutes are remarkably silent, and the exact legal nature of probation is hard to define. As it

22 [1943] K.B. 587.

23 s. 4.

24 1916, s. 46 (to be replaced by Theft Act 1968, s. 28).

25 1893, s. 24.

26 Departmental Committee on the Probation Service, Report, Cmnd. 1650, para. 9.

has developed in England, probation is something which is very English: a successful anomaly.

An international definition of probation is that it consists of "the conditional suspension of punishment while the offender is placed under personal supervision and is given individual guidance or 'treatment'."[27] This reflects the legal position in many countries where probation is an adjunct to the older institution of the suspended sentence, or *sursis*.[28] In England, probation originated in the form of voluntary assistance and guidance given to persons bound over to be of good behaviour. Probation was not, and is not, a sentence; it was the implied consequence of, and is now the condition of, a type of binding over. The Morison Committee are wholly right to emphasise the casework by an officer of the court. The legal analysis linking probation and binding over is a matter of history, of little importance to probation officer or client; but it does explain some unusual features of the law relating to probation.

In particular it helps to explain why a probation order is not a "sentence." The courts may make a probation order "instead of sentencing"[29] the offender. Probation is not regarded as being primarily a punishment although there are plainly punitive elements in being under the supervision of a probation officer who has power to bring the probationer before a court if he fails to obey reasonable instructions. Nevertheless probation is regarded as a final way of dealing with an offender. If a probationer offends again during his period of probation, he may be dealt with for the original offence; but this power must be regarded as a safeguard to prevent abuse of the system by a probationer rather than as an indication that probation is conceived as being provisional.

The historical legal background also explains the restricted effect given to a conviction followed by a probation order; and the requirement of the consent of the offender before he is placed on probation.

Legal framework[30]

The basic provision is that in section 3 (1) of the Criminal Justice Act 1948:

[27] *Probation and Related Measures*, UN, 1951; see also the contributions by Pausegrouw and Ancel in the UN European Seminar on Probation, 1952.

[28] See, *e.g.*, Vouin and Léauté, *Droit Pénal et Procédure Pénale* (1960), pp. 137–141.

[29] Criminal Justice Act 1948, s. 3 (1): see below.

[30] For conditions as to residence and mental treatment, see pp. 277–278.

"Where a court by or before which a person is convicted of an offence (not being an offence the sentence for which is fixed by law) is of opinion that having regard to the circumstances, including the nature of the offence and the character of the offender, it is expedient to do so, the court may, instead of sentencing him, make a probation order, that is to say, an order requiring him to be under the supervision of a probation officer for a period to be specified in the order of not less than one year nor more than three years."

Before making a probation order, the court must explain its effect to the offender and, if he is fourteen or over, obtain his consent.[31] Since the alternative to a probation order might well be institutional treatment of some sort, it would be idle to suppose that the often formal question, "Are you willing to be so bound?" receives a fully co-operative affirmative. The Morison Committee considered the possibility of removing the requirement of consent as serving no useful purpose. In the end, the Committee accepted the view of many of their witnesses that "it was valuable for the probationer to have accepted, however grudgingly, obligations about his future conduct, and that such acceptance was a useful sanction during the period of supervision because it emphasised his own responsibility for learning to control his behaviour."[32]

If a probation order is made the conviction has a limited effect. The legal consequences of conviction do not necessarily occur and, in particular, the conviction is ignored in future proceedings, so long as the probation period is successfully concluded.[33]

The generous rule that the conviction will be ignored in later proceedings is not quite as generous as the reader might suppose. The decision in *Harris*[34] must appear odd to a non-lawyer. Harris was charged with an offence under the Vagrancy Act 1824 as being a "suspected person." This is normally proved by reference to previous convictions, but section 12 makes a conviction inadmissible. The Court of Criminal Appeal held that there was no objection to evidence that the accused was heard in court to admit the commission of an offence, and was made the subject of an order as a result.

31 Criminal Justice Act 1948, s. 3 (5).

32 Report, para. 12.

33 Criminal Justice Act 1948, s. 12; *cf.* conditional discharge, where the same rules apply. There are special rules in road traffic cases: Criminal Justice Act 1967, s. 51.

34 [1951] K.B. 107.

"In any future case we think that courts . . . should be careful to see that evidence is given, not that the accused has been convicted . . . but that he was seen doing this, that, or the other, which showed that he is a person of bad character."

The lawyer must respectfully submit that the distinction is a fine one. The non-lawyer will be forgiven if he prefers to say that it is a blatant absurdity.[35]

Breach of probation

Probation is similar to conditional discharge and recognisances in that it may be replaced later, in specified circumstances, by another form of treatment or punishment. The circumstances fall into two categories, a breach of the original order and its terms or requirements; and the commission of a further offence during the probation period.

The first category is dealt with under section 6 of the Criminal Justice Act 1948. A probationer who appears to have broken the requirements of his order can be taken before the court. The appropriate court is either the magistrates' court which made the order, or the magistrates' court which is the supervising court.[36]

The court may decide to continue the existing order (perhaps extending its duration or imposing other conditions), but to punish the probationer for the breach of its requirements. If this course is taken, the only penalties which may be imposed are a fine not exceeding £20 [37] or, where a young offender is involved, an attendance centre order.[38]

Alternatively the court may revoke the original probation order, and deal with the offender in any manner in which the court could deal with him if it had just convicted him of the original offence.[39] This provision can be used to make a fresh probation order for another three-year period, starting from the time of the second appearance.[40]

[35] See also criticisms of s. 12 (1) in *Stobbart* [1951] 2 All E.R. 753.

[36] This is the court for the petty sessional division named in the order; the actual supervisor is an officer of that court. See Criminal Justice Act 1948, s. 3 (2).

[37] Criminal Justice Act 1967, s. 54 (5); previously £10.

[38] See *infra*, p. 203.

[39] Criminal Justice Act 1948, s. 6 (3) (*a*). If the original order was made by a superior court, the offender must be committed to such a court, in custody or on bail, and that court has the same courses of action open to it. *Ibid.* s. 6 (3) (*b*); Criminal Justice Act 1967, s. 54 (4) (5).

[40] *R.* v. *Havant Justices, ex p. Jacobs* [1957] 1 W.L.R. 365.

If the probationer has committed a further offence, he falls into our second category and must be dealt with under section 8 of the 1948 Act. This empowers the appropriate court [41] to deal with the probationer for the original offence, as if it had just convicted him. As before, a second probation order is possible, and if these powers are not exercised the original probation order can be extended or amended.

The courts take breach of probation very seriously. It has been stressed repeatedly that the procedural formalities must be gone through fully. The breach of probation should be put to the offender in the clearest possible terms.

> " The terms in which the matter should be put to him are: first to say where he was convicted and what happened to him, then to tell him how the breach is alleged to have taken place, and, if it be by a further conviction, then to tell him the time of the conviction and the adjudication of the court. He should next be asked to say whether he admits those facts. . . " [42]

When breach is established, a separate sentence should be passed for the original offence; it should not merely be taken into consideration. And where institutional sentences are concerned, the sentence for the first offence should normally run consecutively rather than concurrently.[43] " It is important that offenders should be made to realise that discharge, whether on probation or conditionally, is not a mere formality, and that a subsequent offence committed during the operative period of the order will involve punishment for the crime for which they were originally given the benefit of this lenient treatment." [44]

In practice institutional treatment is ordered in the majority of cases of breach of probation. In 30 to 40 per cent. of cases, on the other hand, the probationer remains on probation, either under the original order, or that order as amended, or under a new order.[45] A court is especially likely to do this when the probation officer expresses the hope that he may be given a further opportunity to influence the client, perhaps because the

41 Determined under the complex rules of Criminal Justice Act 1948, s. 8; note especially s. 8 (7), which empowers the court convicting the probationer of the further offence to act with the consent of the supervising court, or of the court which made the order.

42 *Devine* [1956] 1 W.L.R. 236.

43 *Stuart* [1964] 1 W.L.R. 1381; which provides an exception, for it was undesirable that a prison sentence should be consecutive to Borstal training.

44 *Webb* [1953] 2 Q.B. 390, 393.

45 *Results of Probation* (Cambridge Inst. of Criminology) 1958, pp. 24, 46.

probation period has scarcely begun, so that the supervision has not produced results.

Discharge

A probation order may come to an end in much happier circumstances. The supervising court has power, on the application of the probation officer or probationer, to discharge the order.[46] In practice, this is used to bring the period of probation to a premature end when the officer is satisfied that further supervision is unnecessary. Some 10 per cent. of orders are discharged in this way, and the percentage has increased in recent years.[47]

The Criminal Justice Act 1967 created a new power which may further increase the number of orders discharged in this way. This is a power to substitute a conditional discharge for an existing probation order; the period prescribed in the order of conditional discharge will be the period within which the probation order would otherwise remain in force.[48]

Relationship with other punishments

Probation is a form of treatment selected for the offender by the court " instead of sentencing him." This has raised legal questions of interest when an offender has appeared before the courts on more than one charge. A court may feel, for example, that an offender would benefit from a period on probation, but that some punishment is also called for " to bring him to his senses." Can a penalty be imposed on one charge, and probation on the other?

There is nothing in the statutory provisions dealing expressly with the point, but the courts, rightly it is submitted, have regarded it as improper to combine punishment and probation. The point was discussed in *Evans*,[49] a case in which the court had made a probation order in an attempt to provide a measure of after-care (not then provided by statute) for a detention centre detainee.

Evans was sent to a detention centre on the first count, and a probation order was made on the second. When later charged

[46] Criminal Justice Act 1948, s. 3 and Sched. 1; Criminal Justice Act 1967, s. 54 (1).

[47] See *Trends and Regional Comparisons in Probation*, Table A.

[48] Criminal Justice Act 1967, s. 53.

[49] [1959] 1 W.L.R. 26. The need to change the law, to allow a penal sanction and probation to co-exist was raised by the Royal Commission on the Penal System: see, *e.g.*, R.C.P.S., Vol. 2, p. 25 (Magistrates' Assoc.).

with breach of that order, he argued that the order was an improper one. Lord Parker C.J. said,

> "... if one looks at the express words of the Act, there does not appear to be anything which expressly prevents a probation order being made on the second count instead of a sentence on that second count. . . . Though that may be so, however, the court is clearly of opinion that the making of a probation order in such circumstances is contrary to the spirit and intention of the Act."

He objected to the use of the probation order to provide after-care on other grounds, that after-care was expressly dealt with in other sections of the Act, and that it was wrong in principle to make a probation order which would not come into immediate effect: " One of the things to consider is his character, and it must be his character at the time when the probation order becomes effective." One may question whether the need for probation supervision would really be lessened by the months of detention. Lawyers are not well disposed generally to sentences which do not have immediate effect, and this attitude has helped to lead to restrictions on the possible use of probation.[50]

At one time it was argued that a fine could be combined with probation even if there were only one single count. Reliance was placed on section 13 of the 1948 Act:

> " Any court before which an offender is convicted on indictment of felony (not being a felony the sentence for which is fixed by law) shall have power to fine the offender in lieu of or in addition to dealing with him in any other manner in which the court has power to deal with him."

However, in *Parry*,[51] the Court of Criminal Appeal held that this section did not apply when a probation order was made. This was the policy of the Act, ascertained by reading the various sections together.

One curious possibility is that two probation orders may be in force at the same time. This occurred in the case of *Keeley*.[52] In March 1959, Keeley was placed on probation by the Court of Criminal Appeal in place of a sentence of preventive detention that had been passed at quarter sessions. In September 1959 another probation order was made after a further offence; no action was taken concerning the first order. After yet another

50 The actual point does not now arise, for after-care is now provided for those discharged from detention centres: see p. 131.

51 [1951] 1 K.B. 510.

52 [1960] 1 W.L.R. 749.

conviction, in 1960, Keeley was imprisoned for the offence which had led to the second probation order. He was brought before the court of quarter sessions which was the supervising court for the first order and again sentenced to preventive detention for the original offence.

Keeley argued on appeal that he could no longer be dealt with for breach of the first order; that was ineffective, having been superseded by the second order. The Court of Criminal Appeal would not accept this. For purposes of supervision only one order could be in force; supervision by two officers and two courts was plainly undesirable. But that did not mean that the first order was wholly ineffective; the courts could still deal with the prisoner for the offence which led to it.

The nature of probation

Statutes and legal rules cannot and do not describe probation; they merely give a few clues to its nature. The probationer, for example, is told of the formal requirements of the order, usually

"1. That he shall be of good behaviour and lead an industrious life [53];
2. That he shall inform the probation officer at once of any change of his residence or employment;
3. That he shall keep in touch with the probation officer in accordance with such instructions as may from time to time be given by the probation officer; and, in particular, that he shall, if the probation officer so requires, receive visits from the probation officer at his home."

The probation officer is a little better off. Hidden away in paragraph 3 (5) of the Fifth Schedule to the Criminal Justice Act 1948 is a general statement of his duties:

> "It shall be the duty of probation officers to supervise the probationers and other persons placed under their supervision and to advise, assist and befriend them. . . ."

The phrase "advise, assist and befriend" is a hallowed one, dating from the Probation of Offenders Act 1907. Arguably it is a little out of date, certainly if the order of the words is taken as an

[53] The order used to specify that the offender should lead an honest life; but lawyers found the notion of an honest life extremely vague and unsatisfactory! See Lord Goddard C.J. at (1952) 35 Cr.App.R. 207.

order of priority.[54] What is involved is amplified in the Probation Rules 1965.[55] These provide that a probation officer shall

"... endeavour to ensure that a person under his supervision understands

(a) the effect of the order placing him under his supervision; and

(b) a court's power to amend or discharge the order." [56]

"... keep in close touch with a probationer, meet him frequently, and, unless there is good reason for not doing so, visit his residence from time to time and require him to report to him at stated intervals. The intervals ... shall be determined amongst other circumstances by his behaviour and progress and regard shall be had to the importance of frequent meetings during the early part of the probation period." [57]

"... encourage a person under his supervision ... to make use of any statutory or voluntary agency which might contribute to his welfare, and to take advantage of any available social, recreational or educational facilities suited to his age, ability and temperament." [58]

"... endeavour to ensure that such a person is in suitable and regular employment." [59]

"... from time to time make a confidential report to the case committee concerning the mode of life and progress of persons under his supervision." [60]

The techniques which the probation officer uses in carrying out these duties are those of a trained social worker. He must use his professional skills to create and make use of a relationship between himself and the client. This may be far from easy, and the fact that the relationship is the result of a court order, that the probation officer represents authority, can make for added difficulties.[61]

Different probation officers work in different ways. Research into the types of treatment covered by the term " probation " is being carried out by the Home Office Research Unit.[62] For research purposes a typology of treatment has been developed

54 See King (ed.), *The Probation Service*, 2nd ed., 1964, p. 80.

55 S.I. 1965 No. 723.

56 r. 33.

57 r. 35 (1) (2).

58 r. 36 (1).

59 r. 36 (2).

60 r. 37 (1); for case committees, see p. 169.

61 See King (ed.), *op cit.*, Chaps. 2 and 3; Monger, *Casework in Probation*, 1964.

62 See *Probation Research: A Preliminary Report; Trends and Regional Comparisons in Probation; and A Survey of Group Work in the Probation Service* (all H.M.S.O., 1966).

using the factors of " support " and " control "; of " individual treatment " concentrating on the individual probation and the use of office interviews, and of " situational treatment " concentrating on the social environment and the family of the probationer, relying more on home-visiting.

A pilot study for this research [63] set out to discover the views of a group of officers on factors related to the assessment and treatment of probationers. There was agreement that probation aimed to rehabilitate and achieve emotional adjustment, and not to punish. In assessing the probationer, his family and his own personality and degree of emotional adjustment were all important. In treatment the important factors were classification by discussion, giving the probationer insights, control by discussion, interest in and knowledge of the probationer's behaviour, encouraging him to find his own job, developing sympathetic understanding. Obviously, many of these factors cover the same field.[64]

Perhaps more interesting were the areas of disagreement. Opinions were divided as to the extent to which probation aimed to protect society. In assessing the probationer, there was disagreement as to the importance of the offence, his record and moral standards, his intelligence, school and work records, and his attitude towards probation. Different stress was laid in treatment on discipline and directive help, treatment of the family, the use of the family and of peer groups, and on work as a treatment setting.[65]

The object of such research is to work towards establishing which type of probation treatment is most likely to succeed with which type of probationer. As in so many forms of penal treatment, classification will then assume the greatest importance.

Special conditions of probation

The normal requirements of a probation order have already been set out. The court has power to include in the probation order such other requirements as it considers necessary to secure the good conduct of the probationer and to prevent further offences.[66]

This power is a wide one, and it is a little surprising that courts have not used it to try out idiosyncratic theories, and have not imposed unworkable requirements. It has been necessary to formulate only two restrictions on the power. First, the payment

[63] S.O.M.P.A. (Study of Middlesex Probation Area; part of the first publication in note 62).
[64] Table 1, p. 47.
[65] Table 2, p. 48. See the full discussion in the report, pp. 24 *et seq.*
[66] Criminal Justice Act 1948, s. 3 (3).

of sums by way of damages or compensation cannot be made a requirement of the order [67]; to do so would disturb the delicate relationship between officer and client. Secondly, a requirement which is inconsistent with proper supervision will not be accepted; an example is a condition that a probationer should leave the country, or return to Ireland.[68]

Residence requirements

There are special powers to include requirements as to residence in probation orders. These can only be made after the court has considered the home surroundings of the offender [69]; if they are good, the probationer is usually best left there, for the idea of probation is that institutional treatment is to be avoided.

If a residence requirement is made, any place of residence may be specified. In practice, the order will usually name an approved probation home or hostel.

Approved probation homes and hostels

These are institutions for probationers between the ages of 15 and 21. The homes are institutions in which the probationers both live and work, except towards the end of their stay when some take outside work. In the hostels, the probationers go out to work each day throughout the period of residence. The maximum period of residence is 12 months.[70]

The Morison Committee, which devoted a special report [71] to the hostels, described the training as " training, with mature adult support, and control, in regular habits of work, in the useful employment of leisure, in personal hygiene, and, above all, in living acceptably with contemporaries and older people." There is also training in handling money, for where inmates have outside work they make payments towards the cost of running the institution.

There are some thirty-five hostels with 750 places; and seven homes. Clearly these institutions are available to only a few courts, but more hostels are being provided.[72]

Requirements as to mental treatment

When an offender is mentally ill, a probation order can contain requirements for him to receive treatment as a resident or as an

[67] *Ibid.*, proviso. [68] *McCartan* [1958] 1 W.L.R. 933.
[69] Criminal Justice Act 1948, s. 3 (4) proviso (*a*).
[70] *Ibid.*, s. 3 (4) proviso (*b*).
[71] Cmnd. 1800; for homes, see the Ingleby Report, Cmnd. 1191, para. 530.
[72] See *Report on Probation Dept, 1962–65*, Chap. 7; Cooks, *Home Office Approved Probation Hostels* (1957).

out-patient. These requirements, surrounded by stringent conditions, are examined in Chapter 6. It may be noted that a reasonable refusal to undergo surgical, electrical or other particular types of treatment will not amount to a breach of probation.[73]

Administration

The Probation Service traces its origins to the work of the police court missionaries appointed by the Church of England Temperance Society from 1876 onwards. These men worked amongst those convicted of offences of drunkenness, and for discharged prisoners, but also did what would now be described as rudimentary probation work with the support of the magistrates concerned.

"Probation" is first used in the Probation of First Offenders Act 1887. This did not make any mention of supervision, nor did it refer to probation officers or the agents of the C.E.T.S. But it did authorise the courts, "instead of sentencing" certain offenders to release them on probation, and to bind them over to be of good behaviour. Such probationers had to have a fixed address, so that there was a form of residence requirement, and hostels were operated by the Society. This is plainly the basis of the modern system of probation.

Fresh provisions were made in the Probation of Offenders Act 1907, which led to the appointment of probation officers as officers of the court. After the work and conditions of service of probation officers had been examined by a departmental committee in 1922, all magistrates' courts were required to appoint officers, and the probation service was placed under the control of probation committees of magistrates from one or more petty sessional divisions.[74]

Present administrative structure

The Morison Committee devoted Part III of their principal report to a full examination of the structure and organisation of the service. It is evident from this report that the system is efficient and effective; the Committee had no proposals of a radical nature to make about the organisation. The system involves a balance of power between the central authority of the Home Office and the local control of the magistrates.

[73] Criminal Justice Act 1948, s. 6 (6).

[74] Criminal Justice Act 1925; for the history of the service, see Hinde, *British Penal System 1773–1950*, Chap. 13; King, *op. cit.*, Chap. 1.

The Probation and After-Care Department of the Home Office exercises the wide supervisory powers vested in the Home Secretary.[75] It is under these powers that the Probation Rules are made. The Home Secretary is also assisted by an Advisory Council for Probation and After-Care, which is composed of persons drawn from the magistracy, legal administration, sociology and the probation service itself. The Council has a Training Committee with a specialist sub-committee for recruitment and training. The Home Office Probation and After-Care Inspectorate plays an important part in training.

Much of the success of the system depends on the local administration by committees of magistrates. Probation and After-Care areas consist of a county or county borough for the most part, and each have a committee consisting of magistrates from the petty sessional divisions combined to form the area. The committees are required to co-opt a suitable number of persons who are not justices but have knowledge or experience of the aftercare of discharged offenders.[76]

The committees have the general statutory duty of satisfying themselves that the duties of probation officers in their area are efficiently carried out,[77] and are concerned in practice with the appointment of officers and with accommodation, equipment and finance. The Morison Committee was satisfied that the committees functioned well and considered that administration by magistrates was a natural expression of the relationship between the service and the courts. They rejected the suggestion that probation should become a local authority service, but this matter is still the subject of examination by government.[78]

Each petty sessional division has a probation " case committee " of magistrates which reviews the work of probation officers in particular cases, and advises generally on problems which arise. The existence of these committees has sometimes been criticised on the grounds that the officer is a skilled professional who receives adequate supervision within the service. The Morison Committee recommended that the committees should continue to exist, as they gave the magistrates an insight into the nature of probation and the other work of an officer, and enabled the officer to draw on the wide experience of the magistrates.

75 Criminal Justice Act 1948, 5th Sched. See the periodical reports of the department.

76 Criminal Justice Act 1967, s. 95 (2), which also gives the Home Secretary powers of appointment where the committee fails to act.

77 Probation Rules 1965, r. 16.

78 See the Report of the Committee on Local Authority and Allied Personal Social Services, 1968, Cmnd. 3703, para. 704.

The use of probation

The words of the Morison Committee are perhaps a little fulsome, but they express an attitude to probation which might fairly be attributed to many magistrates:

> " Society must protect itself against the wrongdoer. It must show its disapproval of crime. But we take it as axiomatic that a society whose morality acknowledges the worth and dignity of each of its members must seek, in fulfilling these objects, the minimum interference with life and liberty that is consistent with them.
>
> . . . We see probation as epitomising the principle because, while it seeks to protect society through the supervision to which the offender is required to submit, it both minimises the restriction placed upon him and offers him the help of society in adjusting his conduct to its demand.
>
> . . . Probation exacts from the offender a contribution, within the limits of his capacity, to the well-being of others, whether it be through his useful employment in the community or through his participation in the life of the family or other social group. In so doing it minimises the economic and social disruption caused by the probationer's offences, preserves him from the penal or reformative institution, whose constructive work must inevitably be limited by the delinquent community in which the offender is placed, and seeks to avoid the harm to others that follows, for example, the imprisonment of a breadwinner." [79]

These considerations led the Morison Committee to suggest four conditions for the use of probation in a particular case. The offence must not be so serious that some more severe method of treatment is essential; the risk to society of keeping an offender at liberty must be outweighed by the advantages; the offender must need supervision, for otherwise a fine or discharge would do; and he must be able to respond to such supervision. It is these later factors which are hardest to assess.

Grünhut has pointed out [80] that the assessment involves in the case of juveniles an analysis of both the weaknesses and strengths of the whole family situation. Although there are dangers in using a probation order as a means of coping with a problem family, the weaknesses of the family must be taken into account. If the home surroundings are very bad, the offender may have to be removed. But the adult friendship of a probation officer may

[79] Report, paras. 13, 14.
[80] *Selection of Offenders for Probation* (United Nations).

compensate for lesser weaknesses. In the case of adults, where the nature of the offence may weigh more heavily with the courts, Grünhut suggests that the defects of the situation are more important than its assets.

Some impression of the growth in the use of probation can be gained from these figures:

	Orders made
1938	29,401
1948	32,543
1958	39,623
1960	41,790
1965	49,583

The average length of probation has also increased, as fewer orders are being made for periods of one year, and more for three-year periods.

If the figures are expressed in another way, as a proportion of the number of persons convicted, a slight decline in the use of probation for most groups of offenders becomes clear. This is a small decline, and was delayed in the higher courts as a result of the closer links between those courts and the probation services as a result of the Streatfeild Report.[81] But there is nothing to suggest that probation as a form of treatment does not enjoy the full confidence of the courts.

Some interesting regional variations in the use of probation were discovered during the work on the Home Office Probation Research Project.[82] For example, the greater the amount of indictable crime known to the police in a particular region, the smaller was the proportion of those found guilty who were put on probation. London and the South had a lower proportion of staff who were appointed without training, lower caseloads, and better success rates than the other parts of the country. This work does not in itself establish what may be cause and what effect; but it illustrates the dangers of assuming that there is a single pattern of probation throughout the country.

Bibliography

(a) Imprisonment

The official view is given in:

" Prisons and Borstals," a Home Office descriptive guide.

[81] See pp. 50 and 64.
[82] *Trends and Regional Comparisons in Probation*, Chap. 3.

Report of the Work of the Prison Department (annual, with a supplementary volume of statistical tables published some months after the main report. Previous corresponding publications were Reports of the Prison Commissioners (until 1962) and " Prisoners and Borstals 1963 ").

Report of the Work of the Probation and After-Care Department (triennial).

" Prison and Borstal After-Care," annual report of C.A.C.A.

Other official reports in recent years include:

Alternatives to Short Terms of Imprisonment (A.C.T.O., 1957).

After-Care and Supervision of Discharged Prisoners (A.C.T.O., 1958).

Penal Practice in a Changing Society 1959 (Cmnd. 645).

Work for Prisoners (A.C.E.P., 1961).

Preventive Detention (A.C.T.O., 1963).

Organisation of After-Care (A.C.T.O., 1963).

The War Against Crime in England & Wales, 1959–64 (Cmnd. 2296).

The Adult Offender 1965 (Cmnd. 2852).

Residential Provision for Homeless Discharged Offenders 1966.

Report of the Inquiry into Prison Escapes and Security 1966 (Cmnd. 3175).

The Place of Voluntary Service in After-Care, 1967.

The Régime for Long-term Prisoners in Conditions of Maximum Security (A.C.P.S., 1968).

Other references:

Ancel, M., " The System of Conditional Sentence or *Sursis* " (1964) 80 L.Q.R. 334.

Andry, R. G., The Short-Term Prisoner (Stevens, 1963).

Church Assembly: The Church and the Prisoner (C.A.1332, 1960).

Clemmer, D., The Prison Community (Christopher, 1940).

Conrad, J. F., " The Assistant Governor in the English Prison " (1959–60) 10 B.J.D. 245.

Council of Europe: Status, Selection and Training of Prison Staff, 1963.

——, Status, Selection and Training of Basic Grade Custodial Prison Staff, 1967.

——, Suspended Sentence, Probation and other Alternatives to Prison Sentences, 1966.

Cressey, D., The Prison (Holt, Rinehart, Winston, 1961).

Cross, R., " Indeterminate Prison Sentences " (1962) 67 *The Listener* 289.

Drummond, J. C. and Wilbraham, A., The Englishman's Food (Cape, 1967. pp. 228, 366, 412).

Glaser, D., Effectiveness of a Prison and Parole System (Bobbs-Merrill, 1964).

Hall Williams, J. E., " Alternatives to Definite Sentences," (1964) 80 L.Q.R. 41.

——, " Suspended Sentences at Common Law," [1963] Public Law 449.

Hammond, W. H., and Chayen, E., Persistent Criminals (H.M.S.O., 1963).

Hinde, R. S. E., The British Penal System 1773–1950 (Duckworth, 1951).

Hopper, C. B., " The Conjugal Visit at Mississippi State Penitentiary," (1962) 53 J.C.L.C. and P.S. 340.

Kelley, J., When the Gates Shut (Longmans, 1967).

Klare, H., Anatomy of Prison (Penguin, 1962).

Morris, P., Prisoners and their Families (Allen and Unwin, 1965).

Morris, T., " Research on the Prison Community " in Collected Studies in Criminological Research, Vol. 1, p. 125. (Council of Europe, 1967).

Morris, T. and P., Pentonville, A Sociological Study of an English Prison (Routledge and Kegan Paul, 1963).

O'Higgins, P., " Voluntary Deportation " [1963] Crim. L.R. 680.

Parker, T., The Unknown Citizen (Penguin, 1965).

Smith, A., Women in Prison (Stevens, 1962).

Sykes, G. M., Society of Captives

Taylor, R. S., " The Habitual Criminal " (1960) 1 B.J. Crim. 21.

West, D. J., The Habitual Prisoner (Macmillan, 1963).

(*b*) *Probation and other measures*

Official comment is contained in

Report of the Departmental Committee on the Probation Service 1960 (Cmnd. 1650).

Report of the Probation and After-Care Department (H.M.S.O., triennial).

Other references:

Ancel, M., " The System of Conditional Sentence or *Sursis* " (1964) 80 L.Q.R. 334.

Barr, H., A Survey of Group Work in the Probation Service (H.M.S.O., 1966).
Barr, H., and O'Leary, E., Trends and Regional Comparisons in Probation (H.M.S.O., 1966).
Council of Europe: Suspended Sentence, Probation, and other Alternatives to Prison Sentences, 1966.
Elton-Mayo, P., Probation and After-Care in Certain European Countries, Council of Europe, 1964.
Folkard, S., and others: Probation Research, A Preliminary Report (H.M.S.O., 1966).
Grunhut, M., Probation and Mental Treatment (Tavistock, 1963).
——, Selection of Offenders for Probation (U.N.O., 1959).
King, J. F. S.: The Probation Service (Butterworths 2nd ed., 1964).
Radzinowicz, L., (ed.): The Results of Probation (Macmillan, 1958).
United Nations: European Seminar on Probation, 1952. Report, 1954.
——, Probation and Related Measures.

Chapter 5

YOUNG OFFENDERS

The Treatment of Young Offenders

In this part of the book, we deal with the treatment in the judicial and penal systems of those under the age of 21, dealing first with juvenile courts and then successively with non-institutional and institutional forms of treatment. Although we are primarily concerned with offenders, mention will also be made of cases in which children and young persons who are not convicted of any criminal offence are nonetheless dealt with by the courts and subjected to forms of treatment which are also applied to offenders.

The age of 21 is the traditional age of majority in England. Its legal importance may well be dwindling, for although a person under 21 is an " infant " subject to several legal disqualifications and limits on his contractual capacity, the consequences of infancy are under critical review. From a penological point of view, the age of 21 is of great, and even growing, importance. Most of the special forms of treatment for young offenders cease to be available at that age, and it was at one time government policy to set up young offenders' courts.

Unfortunately, though inevitably, we cannot simply divide offenders into those over and those under 21. For different purposes we have to use differing and at times thoroughly confusing age-groupings.[2] So far as these age-groupings are relevant for treatment purposes, they will be described in connection with each form of treatment; the information is summarised in the Table overleaf; but there are other distinctions of more general importance.

For *judicial* purposes, the most significant age is at present 17. The seventeenth birthday marks the upper limit, for almost all purposes, of the jurisdiction of the juvenile courts discussed in the next section.

Below 17, therefore, we have " juveniles." This is not a term

[1] See *The Child, the Family and the Young Offender* (1965), discussed *infra*, p. 198, later replaced by *Children in Trouble* (1968), see *infra*, p. 317.

[2] *Cf.* the amused exasperation of the Kilbrandon Committee, Cmnd. 2306, paras. 66–67, and the Report on The Age of Majority, Cmnd. 3342.

W.M.—7

AGE AND THE TREATMENT OF YOUNG OFFENDERS

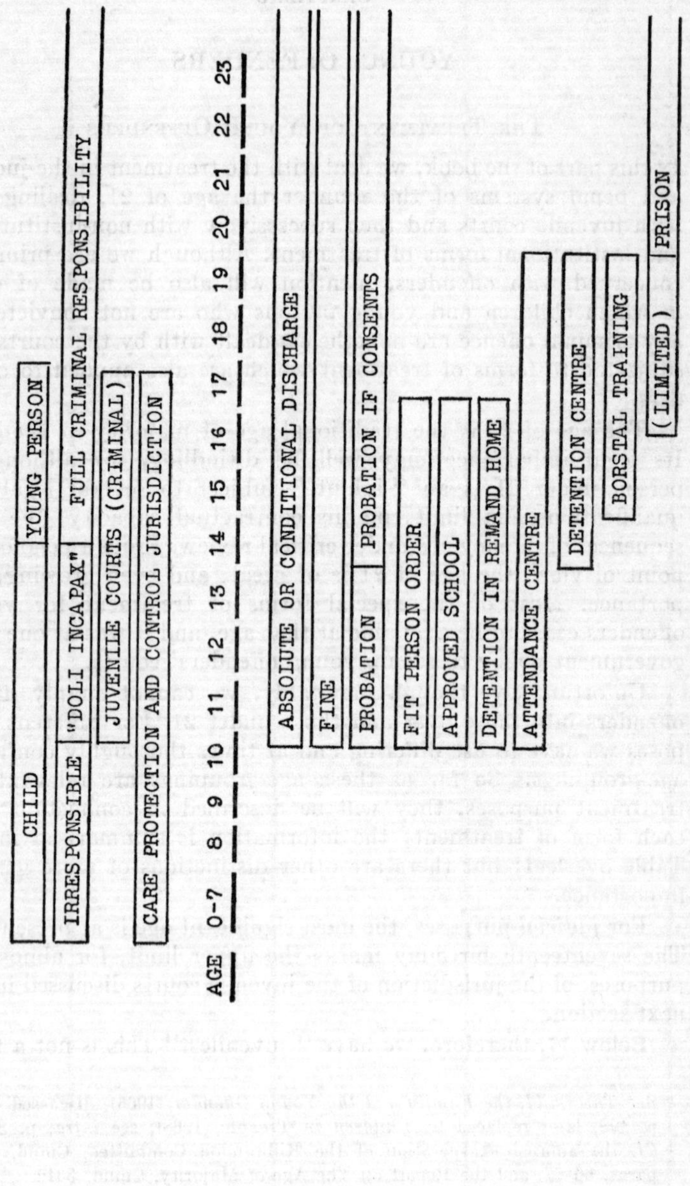

popular with parliamentary draftsmen, who distinguish between "young persons," those in the 14–17 age-group, and "children" who are below the age of 14.[3] Unfortunately even these terms have varying meanings. A "young person" may in some cases be over 17[4]; "child" sometimes means a person under 18.[5] It is hoped that in the present work, the context will make clear the sense in which these terms are used.

The age of criminal responsibility

The treatment of convicted offenders is almost invariably described as "punishment." The idea of punishment in turn involves what Professor Glanville Williams has described as "the mystical theory of moral responsibility."[6] This requires that no person should be punished unless he had the capacity to appreciate that his act was wrongful; and accordingly the mentally ill and young children should be exempt from punishment, and, by extension, from conviction.

It is commonly argued that such thinking is now irrelevant, for the guiding principle in the treatment of children and young persons is to have regard to their welfare[7]; and welfare and punishment may be irreconcilable. This argument may fall short of its target: it may be good for the child that he should be convicted of an offence, so that he may learn that such conduct meets with public disapproval, even if he is not to be punished for it. To remove even conviction, one must rely on further arguments, based largely on the stigma attaching to a finding of guilt.

These matters will be discussed further in connection with proposals for an overhaul in our present methods of dealing with juveniles brought before courts of law.[8] We are concerned here with the present rules as to the age of criminal responsibility.

A child below the age of 10 cannot be convicted of any criminal offence. There is an irrebuttable presumption that he lacks the necessary responsibility. The age has been fixed at 10 since the passing of the Children and Young Persons Act 1963[9]; before that it was eight,[10] and the old common law view fixed the age at

3 Children and Young Persons Act 1933, s. 107 (1).
4 Where he is still subject to juvenile court jurisdiction: see Children and Young Persons Act 1963, s. 23 (8).
5 Children and Young Persons Act 1963, s. 1 (5); Children Act 1948, s. 59 (1).
6 [1954] Crim.L.R. 494.
7 Children and Young Persons Act 1933, s. 44 (1); see *infra*, p. 184.
8 See pp. 198 and 317.
9 s. 16 (1).
10 Children and Young Persons Act 1933, s. 50.

seven, either by holding that a child of such tender years should not be convicted, or that he should be pardoned at once.[11]

Between the ages of 10 and 14, children are in " a twilight zone . . . in which they are morally responsible not as a class, but as individuals, when they know their act to be wrong." [12] The presumption is that a child is *doli incapax*, ignorant of the wrongness of his act, but the presumption is rebuttable, and is more easily displaced as the child nears the age of 14. In practice this rule is unsatisfactory: some courts virtually ignore the presumption, others insist on detailed evidence in rebuttal; there are doubts about the meaning of " wrong," whether it requires knowledge that the act is legally or, more likely, morally wrong [13]; and as to the burden of proof.[14] In effect, the worse the child's home, the less likely is it that the court will be able to interfere, for the less developed will be his moral sense.[15]

Once the magic age of 14 is reached, the child becomes a young person, and has full criminal responsibility.

Treatment of young offenders

Although the law recognised from an early date that children might lack criminal responsibility, it was only in the last century that those children who were convicted could be given forms of treatment expressly designed for them. Indeed the idea that children should not be punished just as were adults is surprisingly modern.

So children of tender years were formerly hanged, transported or imprisoned in the common gaols without any form of " classification " to separate them from older criminals.

The practice of sentencing children to death, or at least recording the death sentence, continued well into the nineteenth century. Actual executions of children were very few, but a 13-year-old boy, John Bell, was hanged for murder as late as 1831.[16] The passing of the death sentence on children and young persons was finally forbidden in the Children Act 1908.[17]

11 The rule dates from at least 1302; see A. W. G. Kean, " The History of the Criminal Liability of Children " (1937) 53 L.Q.R. 364; *Russell on Crime*, pp. 98–99.

12 [1954] Crim.L.R. 494.

13 *Gorrie* (1918) 83 J.P. 136.

14 See G. L. Williams, "*The Criminal Responsibility of Children*" [1954] Crim.L.R. 493.

15 *Cf. F.* v. *Padwick*, *The Times*, April 24, 1959.

16 For an examination of the true number of such executions, see a note by B. E. F. Knell (1965) B.J.Crim. 198–207. See also Radzinowicz, *History of English Criminal Law*, Vol. 1, pp. 11–15.

17 s. 103; see now Children and Young Persons Act 1933, s. 53, as substituted by Murder (Abolition of Death Penalty) Act 1965, s. 1 (5), and *infra*, p. 253.

The passing of sentence of transportation on children and young persons continued until the end of the transportation system; in fact Parkhurst Prison was used to house just this class from 1838.[18]

In practice imprisonment was an almost universal punishment. In the first part of the nineteenth century, informed opinion was moving against its use for children. The Select Committee on Laws relating to Penitentiary Houses, reporting in 1811, after giving a chilling description of Newgate Gaol, observed:

> " It is highly inadvisable . . . to expose young persons of twelve or thirteen years of age to the instructions of those, who can initiate them in all the mysteries of fraud and villainy." [19]

Serjeant Adams giving evidence before another Select Committee, on Juvenile Offenders and Transportation, in 1847, was more positive. He said that so far as children between seven and 12 were concerned, " prison discipline is incompatible with their reform." [20]

The last hundred years have seen the gradual elimination of imprisonment as a form of treatment for children and young persons. The nineteenth century saw the provision of alternatives in reformatory and industrial schools, the predecessors of our modern approved schools.[21] The present century has seen the development of statutory limitations on the use of imprisonment.

The Children Act 1908 forbade the use of imprisonment for children under 14; and a young person could only be sentenced to imprisonment if he was certified as being too unruly or depraved to be detained in a place of detention, the modern remand home.[22] The 1933 Act re-enacted these provisions, but by raising the upper age-limit of the " young persons " class to 17 extended the limitations.

The 1908 legislation by introducing probation and Borstal training also provided further alternatives to imprisonment. The Criminal Justice Act 1948 added two new types of institution, detention centres and attendance centres, and further limited the use of imprisonment. In no circumstances could a magistrates' court impose imprisonment on a person under 17 [23]; the higher

18 Parkhurst Act 1838, s. 3. On the whole topic see Dean Hinde's *British Penal System* 1773–1950, Chap. 7.
19 Sessional Papers (Commons) 1810–11, Vol. 3, col. 571 at 575.
20 Sessional Papers (Commons) 1847, Vol. 7, col. 35, Q. 260.
21 See *infra*, pp. 219 *et seq.*
22 Children Act 1908, s. 102.
23 Magistrates' Courts Act 1952, s. 107 (2).

courts could still impose it on those over 15.[24] No court could pass sentence of imprisonment on a person under 21 unless it decided, after considering full reports, that no other method of dealing with him was appropriate, and magistrates had to state their reasons in writing.[25]

A major step forward was taken in the Criminal Justice Act 1961. This finally prohibited imprisonment for young persons under 17, the special powers of the higher courts being abolished.[26] Restrictions were imposed on the use of imprisonment on those between 17 and 21, as a general rule a court which wishes to pass a sentence of custodial training of between six months and three years must pass a sentence of Borstal training, and may not use imprisonment.[27] Prison sentences of below six months will also be eliminated for this age-group when detention centres are available in sufficient number.[28]

The following table [29] gives some impression of the effect of recent legislation on the pattern of institutional treatment for young offenders. The rise in crime amongst this age-group has effectively prevented any reduction in the absolute numbers of young offenders received into prison; but the proportion so received is falling steadily.

RECEPTIONS OF OFFENDERS UNDER 21

	Imprisonment		*Borstal Training*		*Detention Centres*		*Total*	
	M	F	M	F	M	F	M	F
1948	2,448	255	1,848	132	–	–		
1950	1,374	93	1,852	126	–	–		
1955	1,132	99	1,478	81	586	–	3,196	180
1960	3,099	225	3,476	119	1,295	–	7,870	344
1965	2,957	180	3,923	125	6,740	87	13,620	392

The trends of practice during the present century can be summed up in this way. There has been increasing emphasis on the use of non-institutional forms of treatment, especially probation and, more recently, attendance centres. When institutional treatment has had to be used, the institution has increasingly been one specially designed for children and young persons. After

[24] Criminal Justice Act 1948, s. 17 (1).
[25] *Ibid.* s. 17 (2); Magistrates' Courts Act 1952, s. 107 (3).
[26] Criminal Justice Act 1961, s. 2 (2).
[27] *Ibid.* s. 3: see, for details *infra*, p. 251.
[28] *Ibid.* s. 3 (5).
[29] Source: R.P.D. (Tables), Table C.10.

an examination in the next section of courts which deal with young offenders we shall examine in turn these non-institutional and institutional forms of treatment.

Courts for Young Offenders

Juvenile offenders were once punished as if they were adults; it is now considered obvious that forms of penal treatment designed for adult criminals may be wholly inappropriate for young people. There has been a similar change of approach as regards the judicial system, so that courts for young offenders now differ from the ordinary adult courts in constitution, procedure, and even function.

This change of approach became evident in many countries at the end of the last century. In England and in many other common law countries, the result was the establishment of juvenile courts. Elsewhere, most notably in Scandinavia, cases involving juveniles were largely removed from the courts, and special authorities were established to exercise jurisdiction over juveniles and, in some cases, to supervise treatment.

During the last few years, many have called for a root and branch reformation of the English system involving the disappearance of juvenile courts, and even, perhaps, of the concept of the juvenile offender. These proposals are examined below,[29a] and the present prospects at the end of the book.

Juvenile courts in England

Until the mid-nineteenth century, an English child accused of an offence was tried exactly as if he were an adult.[30] Some cases could be dealt with summarily by magistrates, but many children had to be sent for trial before quarter sessions or assizes. There is no doubt that at the present time many adults are bemused by the ritual and pageantry of assize courts[31]; it is difficult to imagine what the effect would be on a child.

Various nineteenth-century statutes sought to remedy this by extending the jurisdiction of the lower courts, the magistrates' courts, in cases involving juveniles. Cases of larceny were dealt with in this way after the Juvenile Offenders Act 1847. Most other cases were provided for in the Summary Jurisdiction Act 1879.

29a *Infra*, pp. 194 *et seq.*

30 Clearly this applies only to children over the age of criminal responsibility, seven at common law.

31 *Cf.* the description of an assize judge, by an adult offender, as an "old geezer togged up like Father Christmas" (Morris, *Pentonville*, p. 20).

This was only a partial remedy. The procedure in the magistrates' courts was still a procedure designed for adults. The courts were still courts dealing primarily with adult offenders, with whom the juveniles were often free to mingle. The introduction of separate courts with a simplified procedure was still a necessary reform.

Similar considerations led to the passing in 1899 of an Illinois state law establishing a juvenile court for Cook County, Chicago, which is generally regarded as the world's earliest juvenile court.[32] It had jurisdiction over children under the age of 16, who had either committed offences or were " dependent " or neglected. It was not, therefore, solely a criminal court. Its judge was one of regular judiciary who normally sat in the circuit court.

After some experiments by individual magistrates' courts, juvenile courts were established in England by the Children Act 1908. As in the Chicago system, the juvenile courts were special sittings of the ordinary courts, here the ordinary magistrates' court. The constitution and procedure of the courts were not formally changed, though some special provisions did apply. The session had to be held in a different place or at a different time from that of the ordinary sessions [33]; there were limitations on the admission of persons to the courtroom [34]; and the parents of the child or young person could be required to be present.[35]

Dual system of jurisdiction

The principal importance of the Children Act 1908, so far as the courts are concerned, lies in the nature of the jurisdiction it created. The courts retained the power of hearing charges against juveniles, that is " children " under 14 and " young persons " between 14 and 16.[36] They were also given an extended jurisdiction over juveniles in non-criminal cases. This is usually spoken of as the " civil " or " Chancery " jurisdiction. The Sovereign, as *parens patriae*, is said to have the power of protecting infants, in the legal sense of a person under 21; the power is exercised by the Chancery Division of the High Court; whence the name.[37]

[32] For details see Abbott, *The Child and the State*, Vol. 2, pp. 392–401. South Australia and Colorado also made early experiments, and are sometimes claimed as the true originators of juvenile courts. See Caldwell (1961) 51 J.Crim.L.C. & P.S. 493; Nyquist, *Juvenile Justice*, pp. 189–190.

[33] Children Act 1908, s. 111 (1).

[34] *Ibid.* s. 111 (4).

[35] *Ibid.* s. 98.

[36] Defined, *ibid.* s. 131.

[37] It is quite possible that the historical justification for this jurisdiction is spurious. See 3 Blackstone's *Commentaries* (16th ed.), pp. 426–427, especially the editorial note; *Wellesley* v. *Duke of Beaufort* (1827) 2 Russ. 1, 14, 15. As the jurisdiction now rests on a statutory basis, the dispute is of academic interest only; but see *Re H. (G.J.) (An Infant)* [1966] 1 W.L.R. 706.

The Industrial Schools Act 1861 had given magistrates' courts powers for dealing with children who were beyond their parents' control, or who were found without visible means of subsistence. These powers were greatly extended, and given to the new juvenile courts by the Act of 1908.[38] Since 1908, this jurisdiction over children in need of care, protection and control has been still further enlarged.

The result is that juvenile courts in England have two distinct types of jurisdiction. They have their criminal jurisdiction, cases where the juvenile is charged with having committed an offence; and a civil jurisdiction where no offence is alleged, but the juvenile is said to be in need of care, protection or control. Both jurisdictions are exercised in the same court, by the same magistrates. In deciding what should be done with the child or young person, the magistrates are directed to apply the same basic principles, whichever type of jurisdiction is invoked.[39] The forms of treatment available are largely the same in each case. It is a matter which will be considered later whether the survival of the two distinct types of jurisdiction can possibly be justified.

The present juvenile courts

The Act of 1908 contained very few detailed provisions about the juvenile courts which it established. This is probably due to the fact that the special needs of children and young persons finding themselves in court were only appreciated when the juvenile courts had been operating for some time. The first major review of the working of the courts was made by the Departmental Committee on the Treatment of Young Offenders, the Molony Committee, which reported in 1927. Their recommendations as to the constitution, powers and procedure of the courts formed the basis of the Children and Young Persons Act 1933, which is still the principal statute governing juvenile courts.[40] A further review was made in 1960 by the Committee on Children and Young Persons under the chairmanship of Viscount Ingleby, and many of its proposals were incorporated into the Act of 1963.

This section gives an account of the workings of the present juvenile courts. The sections which follow deal with the criminal

[38] Children Act 1908, ss. 58, 59, 60.
[39] Children and Young Persons Act 1933, s. 44; see below.
[40] Its provisions were first enacted as the Children and Young Persons Act 1932; the 1933 Act is a consolidating measure. For the background to the legislation, see Rose, *The Struggle for Penal Reform*, Chap. 12.

and civil jurisdiction of the courts, and this is followed in turn by a discussion of some alternatives to the present system.

Guiding principle

In cases involving the custody or guardianship of infants, the courts have always regarded the welfare of the child as " the first and paramount consideration." [41] the Molony Committee stressed that this principle of guardianship lay at the root of all juvenile court procedure,[42] and the principle is now given statutory recognition in the Children and Young Persons Act 1933.[43]

> " Every court in dealing with a child or young person who is brought before it, either as being in need of care or protection or as an offender or otherwise, shall have regard to the welfare of the child or young person and shall in a proper case take steps for removing him from undesirable surroundings, and for securing that proper provision is made for his education and training."

Although this is presented as a principle governing the treatment of the juvenile, it is also basic to the procedure adopted by the courts.

Constitution

At first, no special arrangements were made for selecting the magistrates to sit in the juvenile courts; the juvenile court sittings were in many areas treated as just another court to be fitted into the existing rota arrangements.

Some courts did take considerable care in selecting magistrates for juvenile court duty, but no special statutory requirements existed. The Juvenile Courts (Metropolis) Act 1920 established a special panel of magistrates with special qualifications for dealing with young offenders, and provided for a woman magistrate to be a member of each juvenile court. The Molony Committee hoped to see similar rules in force throughout the country.

This position has now been achieved, although the prejudice against women magistrates in some parts of the country delayed the introduction of the rule that a woman should be a member of each court until 1955. Under the present rules,[44] each petty

41 Guardianship of Infants Act 1925, s. 1; *Re McGrath* [1893] 1 Ch. 143.
42 Report, Cmd. 2831, p. 20.
43 Children and Young Persons Act 1933, s. 44 (1).
44 Juvenile Courts (Constitution) Rules 1954; Children and Young Persons Act 1933, Sched. 2, as substituted by Children and Young Persons Act 1963. On the need for a woman justice, see *Re J. S.* (*An Infant*) [1959] 3 All E.R. 856.

sessions area must have a panel of juvenile court magistrates, who must be below the age of 65,[45] elected by their fellow justices every three years as being specially qualified for dealing with juvenile cases. Where there is a shortage of qualified people, magistrates acting for neighbouring areas may be included in the panel,[46] or a single panel may be established for two or more petty sessions areas.[47]

The courtroom

The importance of the physical separation of juveniles from adult offenders is still recognised. A juvenile court cannot be held in an adult courtroom unless there is an interval of at least an hour between the sittings of the juvenile and the adult court.[48]

This is a necessary rule; but its existence reveals a situation which is far from satisfactory. In many areas, the juvenile court has to meet in the room used for ordinary sittings of the magistrates' court. The furnishing and design of this room makes it, in many cases, quite unsuitable for use as a juvenile court. To a child, the average courtroom must seem a huge place, filled with a veritable jungle of woodwork. It will have an impressive bench, far above eye-level; a lesser throne at eye-level occupied not by a presiding officer but by a clerk; one or two docks; witness boxes; pews for counsel and solicitors; and in the older courts a general air of forbidding dignity. As the Molony Committee put it, for a juvenile court

> "No dock or witness box or lofty bench is required; ordinary tables and chairs are suitable, and they should be so arranged that the child or young person can stand as near the presiding Magistrate as is convenient, and understand clearly who are the persons adjudicating on his case." [49]

The important thing is that the child, and his parents, should not be so intimidated that they cannot express themselves as well

[45] The Lord Chancellor may waive this rule in particular cases where there is a shortage of qualified justices: 1954 Rules, r. 5; see Home Office Circular No. 96/1958.

[46] 1954 Rules, r. 1 (4).

[47] Children and Young Persons Act 1933, Sched. 2 (as substituted by Children and Young Persons Act 1963, s. 17 (2)). See also Children and Young Persons Cmnd. 1191, paras. 163–166; and also the Report of the Royal Commission on Justices of the Peace 1948, Cmd. 7463. See also Juvenile Courts (London) Order 1965, S.I. 1965 No. 584.

[48] Children and Young Persons Act 1933, s. 47 (2), as amended by Children and Young Persons Act 1963, s. 17 (2). See also Children and Young Persons Act 1933, s. 31, and Home Office Letter 208/1964.

[49] Cmd. 2831, p. 36; cited with approval by the Ingleby Committee, Cmnd. 1191, para. 194.

as possible; that they should not be confused as to the functions of those present; that the setting should be as natural as possible without detracting from the minimum of dignity which the court should possess. Wherever possible, this means that the courtroom and the ancillary waiting rooms should be specially designed for the use of the juvenile court.[50]

Privacy

The Ingleby Committee expressed the view that proceedings in a juvenile court should be as private as possible.[51] This is the policy of the legislation, although in practice juvenile courts seem to contain a large number of people.

Apart from the magistrates and their staff, there are some people who must be present. Most important are the parents of the child before the court. Not only do the magistrates wish to see the parents and hear their views, but the order must be explained to the parents and their co-operation sought. The court has the power to enforce the attendance of both parents at all stages of the proceedings.[52]

In addition any legal advisers of the parties, probation and children's officers, witnesses and others may be present. The general public, however, are excluded. No one who is not directly concerned with the case may be admitted except with the special permission of the court, which will be given to such people as students and newly-appointed magistrates wishing to observe the workings of the court.[53]

This exclusion does not apply to " bona fide representatives of newspapers and news agencies." [54] Reporters may be present, but in the interests of the child or young person, there are restrictions on the matters which they may report. They may not publish the name, address or school of the child or young person, nor a photograph or other identifying particulars. The court may waive these restrictions, and courts sometimes do so in serious cases involving older children.[54]

50 For a full discussion see Watson, *The Child and the Magistrate*, pp. 60–69, and the illustrated report of the Working Party on Accommodation for London Juvenile Courts, 1961 (Home Office).

51 Cmnd. 1191, para. 188.

52 Children and Young Persons Act 1933, s. 34, as substituted by Children and Young Persons Act 1963, s. 25; see Ingleby Report, Cmnd. 1191, paras. 199–203. Attendance can be enforced by summons or warrant: Summary Jurisdiction (Children and Young Persons) Rules 1933, r. 30.

53 Children and Young Persons Act 1933, s. 47 (2).

54 *Ibid.* s. 49, as amended and extended to broadcasting by Children and Young Persons Act 1963, s. 57; see also Children and Young Persons Act 1933, s. 39, similarly amended.

Procedure

The language of the law is not the language of children. It is clear that if a child is to understand the proceedings in a court before which he appears, the procedure must be greatly simplified.

The simplification of juvenile court procedure was one of the main recommendations of the Molony Committee. Their report led to the publication of statutory rules of procedure.[55] Since then further minor improvements have been made, such as the introduction of a simplified form of oath for use by juveniles.[56]

The problem, however, is not one which can be solved by statutory provisions or rules of procedure. The children who appear before the court come from a wide range of ages and backgrounds. The needs of a backward 10-year-old are wholly different from those of a 16-year-old making his sixth appearance before the court. The success with which the court's procedure is adjusted to suit the offender depends almost entirely on the qualities of the chairman.[57]

For example, there are still problems of terminology. The juvenile courts no longer ask a child or young person " to plead guilty or not guilty," nor do they use the term " conviction " [58]; instead the child is asked whether the statement of the offence is true or not, and if the court finds the case proved it makes a " finding of guilt." But there are many other terms, such as " remand," which have to be used and must be explained to the child and his parents.

The rules as to the examination of witnesses are meant to apply in juvenile courts, but here again the chairman must use his discretion. It is absurd to expect a young child, invited to ask questions of a policeman, to formulate his questions—or, more likely, his statement—in a form which avoids the numerous pitfalls of the law of evidence.

One matter which has been much discussed, and which illustrates these procedural problems very clearly, concerns the use made of reports prepared for the assistance of the court. The relevant statutory rules [59] require the court to obtain and consider

[55] Summary Jurisdiction (Children and Young Persons) Rules 1933; amending Rules were made in 1938, 1950 and 1963. See Molony Report, Cmd. 2831, pp. 29–34.

[56] Children and Young Persons Act 1963, s. 28.

[57] On this whole topic see Watson, *The Child and the Magistrate*; Cavenagh, *Juvenile Courts, The Child and the Law*. Both authors are magistrates of great experience.

[58] Children and Young Persons Act 1933, s. 59 (1).

[59] *Ibid.* s. 35, as amended by Children and Young Persons Act 1963; Summary Jurisdiction (Children and Young Persons) Rules 1933, r. 11.

information about the child's general behaviour, home and surroundings, school or work record, and medical condition, and reports may be received from probation officers, doctors or the local Children's Department.

The Rules provide that these reports *may* be considered by the court without being read aloud, but that

"(a) the child or young person shall be told the substance of any part of the report bearing on his character or conduct which the court considers to be material to the manner in which he should be dealt with;

(b) the parent or guardian, if present, shall be told the substance of any part of the report which the court considers to be material as aforesaid and which has reference to his character or conduct, or the character, conduct, home surroundings, or health of the child, or the young person." [60]

The task of the chairman can be an extremely difficult one. Without any chance to consider the report in advance, and without taking much time to read it through in silence, he has to decide how much should be read out, and whether the child should be sent out for a part of the time. When it is realised that these reports will deal with the state of the parent's marriage, and with matters like illegitimacy and drunkenness, and that the court must at all times seek to obtain the full co-operation of the parents, the chairman's problems will be appreciated. There is no easy solution; all must depend on the chairman's tact.[61]

Appeals

Courts of quarter sessions deal with some appeals from juvenile courts, and are also called upon to pass sentence on young persons committed to them with a view to a sentence of Borstal training being passed. There are no special appeal courts for juvenile cases, but provisions now exist for ensuring that members of quarter sessions hearing such cases have sufficient knowledge of juvenile court work.[62] In borough courts, where the recorder

[60] *Ibid.* r. 11 (iv), proviso; it is further provided that evidence may be called in rebuttal.

[61] See Ingleby Report, paras 207–217; Watson, *op. cit.*, pp. 147–150.

[62] Criminal Justice Administration Act 1962, s. 4 (7) as amended by Children and Young Persons Act 1963, and the Administration of Justice Act 1964.

usually sits alone, he is now assisted by juvenile court magistrates acting as assessors.[63]

Criminal jurisdiction

As a general rule, all criminal charges made against children and young persons are tried summarily by juvenile courts [64]; as a result of the Molony Committee's report, the definition of "young person" was extended to include those under 17 years of age.[65] To this general rule there are a number of exceptions:

1. In some cases a young person over 14 may claim trial by jury. Where the offence is indictable, the court must obtain the consent of the young person before proceeding summarily; and in certain summary offences, the young person can opt for trial by jury.[66] The young person is told that he may consult his parents before exercising any such choice.[67]

   In practice, the right to opt for trial by jury is hardly ever exercised, and it is often said that neither the young person nor his parents appreciate the significance of the choice. The Molony Committee's recommendations led to the right of a child to trial by jury being removed [68]; the Ingleby Committee resisted suggestions to remove the right from young persons.[69] This is a part of the larger problem of juvenile court procedure considered below.

2. Where a child or young person is charged jointly with an adult, the hearing is in the adult court.[70] It is thought better that some children should be tried in the adult court than that any adult offender should be admitted to the precincts of a juvenile court. Similar provisions apply where an adult is charged with "aiding, abetting, counselling, procuring, allowing or permitting" an offence with which a juvenile is charged, or vice versa; and where an adult and a juvenile are charged with

63 Children and Young Persons Act 1963, s. 19; Borough Quarter Sessions (Assessors) Rules 1964. Note that the provisions described in this section apply to Crown Courts. In this and other matters, special rules apply to courts in Greater London.

64 C. and Y.P.A. 1933, s. 46 (1); M.C.A. 1952, ss. 20, 21.

65 Report, Cmd. 2831, p. 25; Children and Young Persons Act 1933, s. 107 (1).

66 Magistrates Courts' Act 1952, s. 20 (4) and s. 25, as amended by Sexual Offences Act 1956.

67 Summary Jurisdiction (Children and Young Persons) Rules 1933, r. 8; strictly, this applies only to the case of consent to summary trial.

68 Report, Cmd. 2831, pp. 30–31.

69 Report, Cmnd. 1191, paras. 237–239.

70 Children and Young Persons Act 1933, s. 46 (1) (*a*).

offences arising out of the same set of circumstances.[71] But for these provisions, the witnesses involved, and the juvenile, would have to appear twice before different courts.

3. Any charge of homicide against a child or young person must be tried in the usual way, by an assize court after preliminary investigation before magistrates. The justification for this exception is presumably the gravity of the charge; opinions may differ as to the adequacy of the justification.
4. In some cases, a child or young person may be brought before an adult court by mistake. If his age is then discovered, the adult court may decide to continue the proceedings.[72]

The main objection to the trial of juveniles by adult court arises at the sentencing stage; the juvenile court magistrates alone have the necessary experience and special knowledge to select the appropriate sentence, and they alone are accustomed to dealing with the procedural difficulties which arise at this stage in connection with probation reports. To meet this objection, a court other than a juvenile court which has found a juvenile guilty of an offence may, and in the usual case must, send him to a juvenile court for sentence. The provisions on this subject were strengthened as a result of the Ingleby Report.[73]

Civil jurisdiction

Quite apart from its criminal jurisdiction, every magistrates' court has a wide jurisdiction in civil matters. Many cases heard within this jurisdiction raise issues which affect the welfare of children or young persons; this is true of many matrimonial cases, and of affiliation and guardianship proceedings. Some cases are reserved to the juvenile court. These include adoption cases and certain proceedings under the Children and Young Persons Acts and the Education Act. It is with these latter proceedings that we are concerned, for they can lead to the making of orders, such as approved school orders, which are the same as, or very similar to, orders made in criminal cases.

Much of what has been said about cases within the criminal jurisdiction applies here. The rules governing the constitution

[71] *Ibid.* s. 46 (1) (*b*); Children and Young Persons Act 1963, s. 18.
[72] Children and Young Persons Act 1933, s. 46 (1) (*c*).
[73] *Ibid.* s. 56, amended by Children and Young Persons Act 1963, Sched. 3, para. 14. See Ingleby Report, Cmnd. 1191, para. 176.

and sittings of the court are the same. The same problem of devising a form of procedure fitting the needs of the court and the child arises. Most important, the same guiding principle, that the welfare of the child is the paramount consideration, applies in these as in criminal cases.[74] To carry out this principle, the court needs adequate information; as in criminal cases, the authority initiating proceedings, be it the police, the local authority Children's Department, or the educational authorities, must ensure that full reports are obtained and placed before the court.[75]

Care, protection and control cases

A juvenile court can take action if it is satisfied that a child or young person is " in need of care, protection or control." The statutory definition of this state is an unhappy piece of draftsmanship, but it can be summarised as follows:

It must be proved that the child " is not receiving such care, protection and guidance as a good parent may reasonably be expected to give "[76]

and either that the child is " falling into bad associations "[77] or is " exposed to moral danger,"[77]

or that " the lack of care, protection or guidance is likely to cause him unnecessary suffering or seriously to affect his health or proper development,"[78]

or that he had been the victim of certain specified offences, or lived in the same household as a victim or offender.[79]

Finally, a child will also be in need of care, protection or control if he is found to be " beyond the control of his parent or guardian."[80]

Quite apart from its complexity, this definition has some unsatisfactory features. The home situation may be intolerable as

74 Children and Young Persons Act 1933, s. 44 (1); see above, p. 184.

75 *Ibid.* s. 35.

76 Children and Young Persons Act 1963, s. 2 (1) (*a*).

77 *Ibid.* s. 2 (2) (*a*).

78 *Ibid.* s. 2 (2) (*b*).

79 Ibid. s. 2 (2) (*c*) (*d*) (*e*). The offences are offences against the person, especially sexual offences, or offences involving cruelty to children, etc. See Children and Young Persons Act 1933, Sched. 1 (as amended by the Sexual Offences Act 1956; the Indecency with Children Act 1960; and the Suicide Act 1961) for the list. For procedure, see Home Office Circulars 22/1964, 90/1965. In cases where these offenders appear before adult courts, those courts may make an order affecting the child: Children and Young Persons Act 1933, s. 63 (1).

80 Children and Young Persons Act 1963, s. 2 (1) (*b*). These are especially distressing cases; the situation is better than it was, for it is now provided that the parents may no longer themselves initiate proceedings, so that a direct conflict in court between parent and child is avoided; the child is absent from these proceedings today: *ibid.* s. 3.

a result, for example, of sexual offences by a member of the household. In this situation, the court can only intervene if the parents can be shown to have failed to behave as good parents would in the circumstances; and this may be impossible.

In effect, the legislation is attempting the impossible. Provisions of this sort are designed, in part, to protect parental rights. Yet the whole of this jurisdiction is based on the paramountcy of the child's welfare. In some cases, the interests of the child and those of the parents will conflict; it is impossible to satisfy the claims of both parties, and legislative attempts to do so are bound to fail.

Education Act cases

The reader may be surprised to find school attendance dealt with in a work of this kind. It is relevant in two ways: first, a truant can be brought before a juvenile court and dealt with as if he were in need of care, protection and control; and, second, there seems to be a close connection between truancy and juvenile delinquency, both reflecting a malaise in the home situation.

Persistent absence from school of a child below school-leaving age is investigated on behalf of the local education authority by a school welfare officer. If there seems no good reason for the child's absence (such as illness), various steps will be taken, including the service of a school attendance order on the parents. Ultimately the parents may be charged with an offence, and brought before the magistrates' court.[81]

The magistrates may direct that the child concerned shall be brought before the juvenile court. The local education authority may also, of its own motion, bring the child before that court, whether or not the parents have been proceeded against.[82] Similar provisions apply to vagrant children who are not receiving proper education.[83]

In all these cases, the juvenile court can make any order which it could make if the child were in need of care, protection and control.

Forms of treatment available [84]

In all these cases, the primary decision before the court is whether or not the child or young person should be removed

[81] Education Act 1944, s. 39.
[82] *Ibid.* s. 40, as amended by the Education Acts 1948 and 1953, and Children and Young Persons Act 1963.
[83] Education Act 1944, s. 40, added by Children and Young Persons Act 1963.
[84] Children and Young Persons Act 1933, s. 62, as amended by Children and Young Persons (Amendment) Act 1952, Magistrates' Courts Act 1952, and Children and Young Persons Act 1963.

from his home. If it decides that this is unnecessary, the court can order the parents to enter into recognisances to exercise proper care and guardianship in future. In addition, or as an alternative, the court may place the child under supervision.[85]

If the court feels that a child must be taken away from home, it may send him to an approved school,[86] or make a fit person order,[87] which may be coupled with a supervision order.

Supervision orders

Supervision is the only form of treatment which is peculiar to the civil jurisdiction of the juvenile court. In fact it is very similar to probation, and the statutory provisions have been assimilated to those governing probation as far as possible.

Although the supervisor need not be a probation officer, he will be in the usual case, and he will be under the duty, as in a probation case, to " visit, advise and befriend " the person under supervision.[88] As in the case of probation, a supervision order can contain special requirements, including requirements as to medical treatment or as to residence in an approved probation home or hostel.[89]

Supervision is not a punitive measure, so there is no equivalent in the strict sense to " breach of probation." However, the supervisor has the power to bring the person under supervision before the courts " in his interests," and the court can then substitute any other form of treatment, including for example an approved school order, which it thinks appropriate.[90]

A supervision order is for a stated term of not more than three years, but may not extend beyond the eighteenth birthday of the person under supervision.[91] A total of 3,417 orders were made in 1964, as follows:

	M	F	Total
Care, protection and control cases	436	1,313	1,749
Education Act cases	920	694	1,614
Others [92]	19	35	54
			3,417

85 See below.
86 See pp. 219 *et seq.*
87 See pp. 217–219.
88 Children and Young Persons Act 1933, s. 66.
89 Children and Young Persons Act 1963, s. 5 and Sched. 1, paras. 7–10.
90 Children and Young Persons Act 1933, s. 66 as amended by Children and Young Persons Act 1938, Criminal Justice Act 1948, Children and Young Persons Act 1963. See also Children and Young Persons Act 1963, s. 6.
91 Children and Young Persons Act 1963, s. 5 and Sched. 1, para. 2
92 Cases under Children and Young Persons Act 1933, s. 84; orders made on the application of the fit person or authority having the care of the child.

Local authority powers

It would be quite misleading to end this section without a reference to the work of local authority Children's Departments for children who might otherwise appear before the juvenile court. This work has increased enormously in importance and scope in recent years, the latest extension being encouraged by the Children and Young Persons Act 1963, which provides as follows:

> "It shall be the duty of every local authority to make available such advice, guidance and assistance as may promote the welfare of children by diminishing the need to receive children into or keep them in care under the Children Act 1948 . . . or to bring children before a juvenile court . . ." [93]

This makes quite clear the preventive role of the Children's Department in connection with delinquency. It also refers to the procedure of taking a child into the care of a local authority as an alternative to juvenile court procedure; this very important procedure needs some explanation.

The Children Act 1948 empowers local authorities to take children into care where such action is necessary in the interests of the welfare of the child, and the child has lost his parents or been abandoned by them, or the parents are prevented from providing for his proper accommodation, maintenance and upbringing.[94] On March 31, 1967, 69,405 children were in the care of local authorities, including those subject to a Fit Person Order. It is clear that many of these might have been brought before the juvenile courts, which in fact deal in their care, protection and control jurisdiction with some 9,000 cases a year.[95]

Reform of the juvenile courts

During the recent controversy, it seemed very probable that English juvenile courts in their present form would disappear. Before discussing possible alternatives, it is necessary to consider precisely what role a juvenile court can and should play, and what objections are raised to the present system.

[93] s. 1 (1); "child" here means a person under 18.

[94] s. 1; confusingly, "child" here means a person under 17!

[95] For a fuller account of these local authority powers, see the *Report on the Work of the Children's Department*, 1961–63, chaps. 1 and 2, and see the Seebohm Report, Cmnd 3703, pp. 252 *et seq.*

The Ingleby Committee went to the root of the issue [96]:

"The weakness of the present system is that a juvenile court often appears to be trying a case on one particular ground and then to be dealing with the child on some quite different ground. This is inherent in combining the requirement for proof of a specified event or condition with a general direction to have regard to the child's welfare. It results, for example, in a child being charged with a petty theft or other wrongful act for which most people would say that no great penalty should be imposed, and the case apparently ending in a disproportionate sentence. For when the court causes enquiries to be made, if those enquiries show seriously disturbed home conditions, or one or more of many other circumstances, the court may determine that the welfare of the child requires some very substantial interference which may amount to taking the child away from his home for a prolonged period. It is common to come across bitter complaints that a child has been sent away from home because he has committed some particular offence which in itself was not at all serious."

In this passage, the Committee were discussing the criminal jurisdiction of the juvenile courts. As we have seen, the courts also have a civil jurisdiction, in which they can impose similar types of treatment, but for rather different reasons—or with different precipitating events, for the principles underlying the selection of treatment are the same.

In all cases, criminal or civil, the courts have two duties to discharge. They have first to act as judges of facts, to establish either that an offence has been committed, or that a child *is* in need of care, protection or control. Having made this decision, the courts must next consider which form of treatment is to be selected.

Those who believe that the juvenile courts need radical reform would change almost every statement made in the last two paragraphs. They would argue that the criminal jurisdiction should be abolished, and that the court's function as a tribunal of fact (if that is a necessary function at all) and as a sentencing body should be removed, in whole or part.

The criminal jurisdiction

There is a growing body of opinion which favours the abolition

[96] *Report of the Committee on Children and Young Persons*, Cmnd. 1191, para. 66.

of criminal jurisdiction over children of school age; in other words, the raising of the age of criminal responsibility to 15, or shortly 16.[97] Two main arguments are usually advanced in support of this proposal.

The first is that " children should be spared the stigma of criminality." [98] This statement is taken from Government proposals contained in a White Paper, *The Child, the Family and the Young Offender*, which sets out former proposals for reform. It is astonishing that the paper nowhere indicated whether the Government accepted what many would assume to be the logical result of the proposition, that the age of criminal responsibility should be raised.[99] It is even more surprising that no reference was made to the view of the Ingleby Committee, in a very similar context [1]:

> " We doubt whether there is any force in the argument, used by those who favour substituting a non-judicial tribunal for the juvenile court, that the change would avoid the stigma of a court appearance and the stigma of a finding of guilt. We think it likely that any stigma there may be would come to attach to appearance, as a result of bad behaviour, before any tribunal."

The second argument is more fundamental. It is the argument that the retention of the notion of criminal liability in the case of juveniles is a needless obstacle to the thorough application of the " welfare " principle which is meant to guide the courts. So, Baroness Wootton argues [2] that we need to substitute an educational for a penal setting. If our own children get into trouble, they are full of mischief, and any problem is an educational one. If other people's children get into trouble they are delinquent, and the courts must apply penal sanctions. If criminal responsibility can be removed from the picture, this contrast will also go.

The reader may well feel that these two arguments rest on the same assumption: that the sending of a child to a special residential institution for educational purposes found to be necessary

[97] For the age of criminal responsibility, see also pp. 177–178.

[98] *The Child, the Family and the Young Offender*, Cmnd. 2742, para. 10.

[99] As will appear, the latest Government proposals in effect raise the age of criminal responsibility to 14; see *infra*, p. 317.

[1] Report, Cmnd. 1191, para. 71; note that a finding of guilt against a child under 14 is disregarded in any proceedings brought when the offender is over 21: Children and Young Persons Act 1963, s. 16 (2).

[2] [1961] Crim.L.R. 675–677. See also, on the whole topic, Nigel Walker, " The Age of Criminal Responsibilty," *The Times*, June 11, 1965; and an article under the same title by " a medical correspondent," *The Times*, February 11, 1963.

because of his behaviour leads to markedly different social reactions than the sending of a child to an approved school for an offence. The validity of the assumption may be doubted.

The function of the courts

Criminal courts developed as fact-finding bodies; their sentencing role is more recent. Many assume that the two functions are inseparable, from each other and from the court; in fact either or both could be removed from the courts and handed to some other tribunal, committee or council.

One extreme view should be mentioned; some would argue that the establishment of certain specifically alleged facts is unnecessary. As Lady Wootton puts it, " if the welfare, not the punishment, of the child is the governing consideration, the safeguards of the criminal trial become irrelevant." [3] This argument usually rests on some analogy with decisions made within the family; can decisions by public bodies ever be truly analogous to such decisions?

The Ingleby Committee had no doubts on this issue. In the passage immediately following that quoted earlier, they say [4]:

> " Despite this very real difficulty, we are in favour of retaining the present basic principle that specific and definable matters must be alleged and that there should be no power to intervene until those allegations have been adequately proved. We think that the maintenance of this basis is essential if State intervention is to be fitted into our general system of government and be acceptable to the community."

This is not to decide that the fact-finding function should be carried out by a court. It can be handed over, as in many countries especially the Scandinavian states, to a Child Welfare Board or Council; this can be a more expert body than a normal court, and is free from the need to maintain a dignity which may be proper to a court but may equally hinder justice in juvenile cases.[5] In practice, of course, these bodies, like our juvenile courts may spend a small amount of time on fact-finding; in most juvenile cases the facts are not disputed.

Similarly, the sentencing function can be handed to a

[3] [1961] Crim.L.R. at p. 673.

[4] Report, Cmnd. 1191, para. 66.

[5] The Swedish Child Welfare Board System is described in Nyquist, *Juvenile Justice*. See the discussion on question IV [2] at the 12th International Penal and Penitentiary Congress, 1950; *Proceedings*, Vol. 6. It may be that the differences *in practice* between Board and court is very slight: see Nyquist, *op. cit.*, p. 199.

sentencing tribunal, or, where a custodial sentence has been chosen, its detailed application can be left in the hands of an authority within the correctional system.[6]

Against this background can be considered the proposals made by the Government in 1965 in the White Paper "*The Child, the Family and the Young Offender.*"[7]

Proposals for reform

At present, the seventeenth birthday marks the division between juvenile and adult status. It is proposed to substitute two dividing lines, one drawn at school-leaving age, the other at the age of 21. Between these ages, an offender would be subject to the jurisdiction of a young offenders' Court. This would resemble in constitution the present juvenile courts, being composed of lay magistrates selected for their special knowledge of the age-group. In some circumstances, a legally qualified chairman would sit, and the sentencing powers of the court would be greater when he was present.[8]

Much more radical changes are proposed for dealing with children under 16. In the White Paper, only the outlines of the proposed system are given; but as the proposals are based to a large extent on the thinking of Lord Kilbrandon's Committee on the Law relating to Children and Young Persons in Scotland,[9] and on Lord Longford's Labour Party study-group,[10] it seems reasonable to suppose that the detailed proposals will also follow their suggestions.

The main object of the proposals is to involve the parents more clearly in the consideration of the case: "the present arrangements do not provide the best means of getting parents to assume more personal responsibility for their children's behaviour."[11] It is therefore proposed to deal with as many cases as possible through the local Children's Departments. The departments would appoint Family Councils "consisting of social workers of the children's service and other persons selected for

6 *e.g.*, the Californian Youth Authority, also described by Nyquist. *Cf.* the provisions of the U.S. Federal Youth Corrections Act, and Juvenile Delinquency Act. 18 U.S.C. 5005, 5031; see *Deskbook for Sentencing* (Judicial Conference of the U.S.).

7 Cmnd. 2742. The following section should be read with the recent proposals set out at pp. 317 *et seq.*

8 Perhaps even legally qualified authors may be allowed to question, in a footnote, the relevance of legal qualifications in sentencing. Predictably, the Magistrates' Association makes the same point: Paper 65/228.

9 Cmnd. 2306; see paras. 72–76 and Chaps. IV, V and VI.

10 *Crime, A Challenge to us All* (Labour Party, 1964); see pp. 23–26.

11 *The Child, the Family and the Young Offender*, Cmnd. 2742, para. 10 (3).

their understanding and experience of children and, in particular, for their awareness of the problems facing the children and adults likely to come before them." [12] If the majority of members are to be trained social workers, the strain on the few qualified workers would be intolerable; there are not enough for present caseloads. If social workers are in the minority, the composition of the Family Councils may well be very similar to that of juvenile courts.

The major change is in the method of working of this body. Each council would meet away from court buildings, in the locality in which the family lives; it would enter into unhurried discussions with the parents of the child; and, most important, would take no action without the full agreement of the parents. The council might decide that the parents themselves could take any necessary action, or might order the payment of compensation (but not a fine [13]), supervision by the children's service,[14] or training at an attendance centre or detention centre, or commitment to the local authority for longer-term training, which could include attendance at what would now be called an approved school.

The main objection to this proposal is put by the Magistrates' Association: " Parental agreement would often prove illusory, and in some cases appear to the child as a betrayal." The doubts as to the reality of the parents' consent are intensified when it is realised that there is what might appear to be a sanction applied in cases where they refuse to agree. In this case, the matter goes to court—to a family court, akin to the present juvenile court. This reference may even be made twice, if there is disagreement at both the fact-finding and treatment stages.[15]

There are a large numer of other points of difficulty in the present proposals, caused principally by their " outline " nature. It is not clear, for example, how proceedings would be initiated. The circumstances are to be reported to the Family Council. This appears to exclude the present system of police cautioning—and, incidentally, police juvenile liaison schemes.[16] What is not clear is whether any other sifting procedure would be introduced. Lord Kilbrandon's committee proposed that the juvenile panels

12 *Ibid.* para. 12.

13 Presumably, because this might seem to be equivalent to the parents " buying out " the child; *cf.* the present practice of some juvenile courts, which impose fines in 60 per cent. of all cases.

14 *Not* the probation service, as at present; the consequences for the service are not discussed.

15 For details of the procedure, see paras 13–15 of the White Paper.

16 See *infra*, pp. 201–202.

to be established in Scotland should have a "Reporter" who would initiate proceedings; and also a "Director" to act as the executive officer for each panel: no similar proposals are made in the English White Paper.[17]

Finally, it is not clear what effect the proposals have on criminal responsibility. It is to be a ground for proceedings that the child "had committed what would in an older person be an offence." [18] Speaking of a similar proposal by the Ingleby Committee, Baroness Wootton said that it "could fairly be described as a device for putting the age of criminal responsibility up with one hand, and putting it down, at least in fact, if not technically in law, with the other." [19]

New proposals involving the retention and reform of the juvenile courts were published in 1968. They are discussed at the end of this book.

NON-CUSTODIAL MEASURES

As we have seen, courts will always try to deal with a young offender without resorting to custodial measures; subject always to the welfare principle,[20] which may sometimes dictate removal from home. The range of non-custodial measures available in a juvenile court is broadly similar to that in the adult court, with the addition of attendance centre orders discussed in the next section.[21] So, a juvenile can be given an absolute or conditional discharge, be fined, or be put on probation. Only in some small particulars are the legal rules different: an example is the fact that an offender under 14 can be put on probation without his consent.[22]

Almost more important are methods of dealing with young offenders which involve action by the police rather than any use of the machinery of the courts. This can consist of cautioning, or of police supervision.

Cautioning

It is common practice, especially where a minor offence is involved, for the police to use their discretion in prosecution policy and issue a caution rather than initiate proceedings. The

[17] For some implications of the proposals at the treatment stage, see K. W. Patchett and J. D. McClean, "Decision-making in Juvenile Cases" [1965] Crim.L.R. 699.

[18] para. 13.

[19] [1961] Crim.L.R. at p. 674.

[20] Children and Young Persons Act 1933, s. 44 (1).

[21] Fit person orders are a form of custodial measure, even if they only lead the offender to a substitute home: see Chap. 217.

[22] Criminal Justice Act 1948, s. 3 (5).

caution is issued by a senior officer, and may be in writing (*e.g.*, to an adult motoring offender) or be given orally, which is perhaps more usual where young offenders are concerned. The caution is recorded, and it is hoped that the warning will be an effective deterrent measure on its own.

This procedure is used a great deal for the younger age-groups, as the Table, which relates to 1966, makes clear.[23]

CAUTIONS AND CONVICTIONS FOR INDICTABLE OFFENCES, 1966

Age-group	*Males* *Cautions*	*Males* *Convictions*	*Females* *Cautions*	*Females* *Convictions*
Under 14	11,222	21,648	2,385	2,469
14 and under 17	6,459	32,948	1,942	5,068
17 and under 21	2,554	45,243	392	4,771
Over 21	2,966	101,619	2,089	19,088

It will be seen from this table that in the youngest age-group, one-third of the boys and one-half of the girls known to have committed indictable offences are cautioned and not prosecuted.

What is a little disturbing is that there is evidence that the criteria on which police decisions are based vary considerably from one part of the country to another. For a young offender, the decision whether or not he should appear before the court is too important to be influenced overmuch by the accidents of police geography.[24]

Police supervision

In a number of towns, a caution for a juvenile offender is accompanied by the offer of some supervision of the offender by a "juvenile liaison officer." The first of these schemes—juvenile liaison schemes—was introduced in Liverpool in 1949 and they have spread fairly rapidly to other towns, especially after receiving publicity in a Home Office Circular in 1954.

The arrangements vary a great deal from one force to another.[25] Often the liaison officer, a selected police officer who has volunteered for this work, will call at the child's home for "a chat" from time to time, maintaining this contact as long

23 Source: *Criminal Statistics* 1966, Chaps. V and IX.

24 See K. W. Patchett and J. D. McClean [1965] Crim.L.R. 699; and L. Sebba [1967] Crim.L.R. 347.

25 The Liverpool scheme is described in a booklet *The Police and Children* (2nd ed., 1962); see Appendix C to the Kilbrandon Report (Cmnd. 2306), which reproduces an outline of the scheme.

as he thinks necessary. In other places, the offenders report to the officer, much as a probationer does at the probation offices.

Although the Liverpool scheme is closely linked to cautions, this need not be so. In West Ham, for example, children known to be frequenting low-class cafés, or to be associating with undesirables, or who have been reported as missing may all be brought within the scheme, which then assumes a more clearly preventive aspect.[26]

From the point of view of the police, juvenile liaison schemes are a rational part of their crime prevention programme. The analogy of the " friendly, village bobby " is often used. But there are objections to the schemes, seen in the conclusions of the Ingleby Committee who examined them in 1960:

> " We were impressed with what we heard of the results obtained by juvenile liaison schemes in Liverpool and elsewhere, and of the way in which juvenile liaison officers had devoted themselves unsparingly to their work. It seems clear, however, that the process of ' following up ' the caution by a period of supervision, help and guidance for the child and his family involves the juvenile liaison officer in work that nowadays is recognised as a skill to be acquired by special training in case-work which the juvenile liaison officer has no opportunity to receive. It is work that should be done by other social agencies. While, therefore, we have nothing but commendation for the aims and achievements of those who have instituted and worked police juvenile liaison schemes, we are unable to recommend that the Government should encourage their general adoption." [27]

The " other social agencies " will obviously include the Children's Department of the local authority, whose preventive functions have already been noted.[28]

Binding over [29]

If the young offender is taken to court, there is no reason why he should not be bound over in the same way as an adult; in practice, this is very rare. Rather more use is made of the power to order the parents to give security by way of recognisances for the good behaviour of their child.[30] This provides

[26] R.C.P.S., Vol. 4, pp. 53-57 (Simpson).
[27] Cmnd. 1191, para. 147.
[28] See *supra*, p. 194.
[29] See *supra*, pp. 150–152.
[30] Children and Young Persons Act 1933, s. 55 (2).

some encouragement for the parents to exercise proper supervision, but the relatively low numbers of orders suggest that magistrates doubt parental will or ability: in 1966, only 600 orders were made.

Fines

There are obvious difficulties in fining young offenders, and some special rules apply. Young offenders are unlikely to have much money, and for those at school it will be in the form of pocket-money perhaps variable in amount. A fine of any size must amount to a fine imposed on the parents. This is recognised by provisions limiting the size of fines, and making them payable by the parents in certain cases.

In the case of a child under 14, the maximum fine is £10,[31] and the court must order the parents to pay it, unless the parents cannot be found or have " not conduced to the commission of the offence by neglecting to exercise due care." [32] In practice a surprisingly small number of orders are made against parents: in 1966, 8,366 fines were imposed on persons under 14; 332 orders were made against parents.

In the case of young persons between 14 and 17, the maximum is £50,[33] and the court may order that the parents should pay. In 1966, over 50,000 young persons were fined, but in only 275 cases were parents ordered to make payments.

Although a court may order that the parents be liable in law for the payment of the fine, this is often qualified by a magisterial homily suggesting that payments of pocket-money should be reduced for an appropriate period so that the child feels the effect of the order.

Where the young offender is ordered to pay a fine himself, and fails to do so, he can ultimately be sent to an attendance centre, detention centre or remand home. In practice default is rare in juvenile courts.[34]

ATTENDANCE CENTRES

An attendance centre order requires a young offender to attend a centre, usually in police or school buildings, for certain periods

31 Magistrates' Courts Act 1952, s. 32, as amended by Criminal Justice Act 1961, s. 8.

32 Children and Young Persons Act 1933, s. 55 (1). The same applies to costs (which may not exceed the amount of the fine) and compensation ordered to be paid.

33 Magistrates' Courts Act 1952, s. 20 (5); Criminal Justice Act 1961, s. 8 (2) (3).

34 See Criminal Justice Act 1948, s. 19, as amended; Criminal Justice Act 1961, s. 15; and Criminal Justice Act 1967, s. 44.

in his leisure time. In a typical case, he will be ordered to attend for a total of twelve hours, two hours on each of six Saturday afternoons, and will spend his time on physical training, craft-work and "fatigues."

The purpose of the order is usually seen as being punishment through the deprivation of leisure. There is no doubt that the regular loss of leisure time at the weekend is irksome, perhaps more so than the imposition of a small fine, or the supervision of a probation officer. This "punitive" view is probably correct historically: the centres were introduced in the Criminal Justice Act 1948 and with detention centres were seen as penal measures replacing such former possibilities as corporal punishment and short-term imprisonment.[35]

On the other hand, there are other explanations of the function of attendance centres. Some see them as giving a fore-taste of institutional life, and as acting as a strong deterrent to those who might be tempted to continue in crime. Some courts use attendance centre orders expressly as a last chance before approved school.[36]

Yet another view emphasises the educational, reformative effects of the centre. An attendance centre order can be viewed as a more economical method, for some offenders, of obtaining the improvement in behaviour which a probation officer would encourage. It is this view which leads to requests for more positive character training in the centres; the "punitive" view usually leads to the suggestion that some form of supervision could usefully be made available to be coupled with an attendance centre order. It is a measure of the ambiguity about the centres that these two suggestions can be made at the same time, and urged in the same memorandum to the Royal Commission on the Penal System.[37]

The regime and operation of the centres

Attendance centres are the responsibility of the Home Office: the Home Secretary decides where they are to be opened, and makes rules for their management.[38] The actual running of the centres is carrried out in a variety of ways. Senior centres for youths over 17 are staffed by prison officers; centres for boys under 17 are run by the police or, exceptionally, by school staff or Children's Department officers. There are no centres for girls.

[35] See 156 Parliamentary Debates (Lords), col. 296; McClintock, *Attendance Centres* (1961), Chap. 1.
[36] McClintock, *op. cit.*, 17.
[37] R.C.P.S., Vol. 2, pp. 9–10 (Magistrates' Assoc.).
[38] Attendance Centre Rules 1958.

Centres are not available to all courts. It has been found impracticable to open them away from main centres of population; it is only in large towns that sufficient use would be made of the facilities on a regular basis. There were sixty-one centres at the end of 1966, only two catering for the senior group, in Greenwich and Manchester.[39]

The actual programme of activity varies from centre to centre. An outline programme has to be approved by the Home Office, which maintains some informal inspection. There is a general direction that training should be "conducive to health of mind and body"; in practice it has been described as tending, in some cases, "to be spasmodic and not particularly constructive."[40]

A session begins with a roll-call and inspection for cleanliness of hands, feet and shoes. Between a half and three-quarters of an hour will be spent in some form of physical training. If the centre has a gymnasium this may involve the use of gymnastic equipment; otherwise it will be more akin to foot-drill.

In most centres a period of craft-work is included. Lack of facilities, and of instructors willing to attend on Saturdays, may limit this. In any case the purpose of the work is often unclear: making purses out of leather is an interesting way of passing the time, but its value as instruction in the constructive use of leisure[41] must be limited by the extreme improbability of those attending taking up leatherwork as a hobby during the long winter evenings.

"Fatigues," varying from scrubbing floors to washing cars, form part of the programme at most centres. Instructional talks on road safety or first-aid are given at some others.

It is clearly possible within this general framework to produce widely differing types of programme. What is not clear is whether there is any link between the regime of a centre and the sentencing policy of the local court.

Legal framework

Attendance centres are available for offenders aged between 10 and 21, although, as we have seen, the great majority of

[39] The sources of the statistics in this chapter are the annual Statistics Relating to Approved Schools, etc. (a House of Commons paper), and Attendance Centre Index Statistics (Home Office).

[40] R.C.P.S., Vol. 2, p. 9. (Magistrates' Assoc.). For a description of a senior centre, see N. Goodman, "Manchester Senior Attendance Centre" (1965) 5 B.J.Crim. 275.

[41] *cf. The Sentence of the Court*, p.8.

centres cater only for those under 17; not all cover the full junior age-range.

There are certain limitations on the power of the courts to make attendance centre orders:

1. The power is normally only available to magistrates' courts.[42] With the development of centres for offenders over juvenile court age, the higher courts might feel the need for such a power.

2. An order can only be made as a result of a conviction for an offence punishable, in the case of an adult, with imprisonment. This prevents the centres being used to punish mere infringements of, for example, road traffic regulations for which a fine is appropriate. Where an offender has failed to comply with the terms of a previous probation order, the court can order attendance at a centre even if the original offence could not have been punished with imprisonment.[43] This is a useful provision, for considerable use is made of attendance centres in the case of probationers who are tempted to disregard the terms of their probation; attendance can be ordered without any interruption in the probation order.[44]

3. There are important limitations on the classes of offender who may be sent to an attendance centre, designed to exclude all those with experience of institutional treatment. These are partly to reduce the risk of " contamination " which was felt to exist in the short prison sentences formerly used, but are also a recognition of the nature of the discipline in the centres. This depends on the influence of a few instructors, and could easily be undermined by determined boys with experience of institutional treatment.

Accordingly the proviso to section 19 of the Criminal Justice Act 1948 excludes all persons who have been previously sentenced to imprisonment, Borstal training, or detention in a detention centre, or who have been sent to an approved school. Those who have been detained in a remand home[45] are not excluded, but to send them to an attendance centre would seem to be against the spirit, if not the letter, of the Act.[46]

[42] Quarter sessions can make an order as respects a person committed with a view to a sentence of Borstal training, or on appeal from a magistrates' court.

[43] Criminal Justice Act 1948, s. 19 (1).

[44] *Ibid.* s. 6 (3).

[45] Under s. 54 Children and Young Persons Act 1933.

[46] The statistics for 1964 show that in 59 cases the boy had previously been to a remand home. There were also, inexplicably, 10 boys who had been in an approved school, and one to a detention centre.

4. A further limitation was given statutory force in 1961. Section 10 (3) of the Criminal Justice Act 1961 forbids the making of an order " unless the court is satisfied that the attendance centre to be specified in the order is reasonably accessible to the person concerned, having regard to his age, the means of access available to him and any other circumstances." " Other circumstances " would include, for example, unusual or unpredictable hours of work which might prevent regular and prompt attendance at the centre. An attendance centre order which is made contrary to these rules or which changed circumstances, such as the offender's change of address, have made inappropriate can be revoked by the court.[47]

The original statutory provisions limited the duration of attendance to a maximum of 12 hours.[48] There was considerable feeling amongst those with experience of the centres that this was the minimum time for effective work, and that a much higher maximum should be fixed. This feeling was partially satisfied by the enactment of section 10 (2) of the 1961 Act which provides that the aggregate number of hours

" (a) shall not be less than twelve except where [the offender] is under fourteen years of age and the court is of opinion, having regard to his age or any other circumstances, that twelve hours would be excessive; and

(b) shall not exceed twelve except where the court is of opinion, having regard to all the circumstances, that twelve hours would be inadequate, and in that case shall not exceed twenty-four hours."

The following Table of orders made during 1966 shows how these rules operate in practice.

Age	*Number of hours specified in order*								*Total*
	6	8	12	14	16	18	20	24	*orders*
10 or 11	13	—	457	—	2	38	—	191	701
12 or 13	24	1	1,475	1	2	109	—	747	2,359
14, 15 or 16	—	—	1,877	—	7	187	1	1,545	3,617
17, 18, 19 or 20	—	—	62	—	—	—	—	51	113
All Ages	37	1	3,871	1	11	334	1	2,534	6,790

[47] Criminal Justice Act 1948, s. 19 (3).
[48] *i.e. ibid.* s. 19 (1).

This makes it clear that while nearly 60 per cent. of orders are for a 12-hour period, many courts have taken advantage of the new maximum, especially for the older offenders.

The making of orders for periods other than of 12 or 24 hours is often due to the offence having been committed by a group of boys, the court wishing to distinguish degrees of guilt. Of the 6,161 offenders under 17 in 1964, 1,882 were known to have been with one companion at the time of the offence, and 2,415 with two or more.

The hours of attendance are not served in one session. The only statutory rules are that the times of attendance should avoid, so far as practicable, interference with school or working hours [49] (which has the effect of limiting sessions to Saturdays) and that no offender should be required to attend twice in one day, nor for more than three hours at a time.[50] In practice a session usually lasts for two hours, and at the end of the session each offender is told when next to report. This flexibility enables centres to hold sessions on alternate weeks for different age-groups, to close periodically to give the staff a free Saturday, and is also useful for disciplinary purposes: attendance on two Saturday afternoons for an hour on each occasion is more irksome than one attendance of two hours.

General rules as to discipline are contained in the Attendance Centre Rules 1958.[51] Punishments are limited to the separation of the offender from others attending the centre, giving him less attractive work, and sending the offender away from the centre before the end of the session; this will mean that he must make an extra attendance to complete the prescribed number of hours.

In an extreme case of misbehaviour, or for non-attendance without reasonable excuse, application may be made to the court for the revocation of the order, in which case the court may impose such sentence as would have been available to them if they had originally decided not to make an attendance centre order.[52] In 1966, sixty-eight persons were dealt with in this way, sixty-five for non-attendance and three for other breaches. Half received a sentence involving institutional treatment, most of the rest being fined.

[49] Criminal Justice Act 1948, s. 19 (2). Conflict with working times is a ground on which an order can be discharged under s. 19 (3).

[50] *Ibid.*, proviso.

[51] S.I. 1958 No. 1990, made under Criminal Justice Act 1948, s. 52.

[52] Criminal Justice Act 1948, s. 19 (7) (8).

Sentencing policy

Magistrates' courts are making increasing use of attendance centres. In 1966, 6,790 orders were made compared with 6,288 in 1964, 4,600 in 1962; and 754 in 1953. This increase is only partially explained by the increase in the number of juvenile offenders and in the number of available centres.[53] It is unfortunate that practical considerations are likely to prevent the opening of many more centres; most magistrates' courts which at present lack a centre are most anxious to have one.

These practical considerations are mainly concerned with the number of persons attending. The efficient functioning of the centres requires a minimum attendance of about half-a-dozen and this can only be guaranteed in large urban areas. This means that the present type of attendance centre will never be available in much of the country; some other form of deprivation of leisure could perhaps be introduced in those areas.

As far as the use of the existing centres is concerned, one of the most remarkable facts is the large number of cases in which an offender subject to an attendance centre order is also on probation. In 1964, of boys under 17 ordered to attend, 15 per cent. were placed on probation at the same time as the attendance centre order was made, having been convicted of two or more offences; 17 per cent. were already on probation when they were convicted of a further offence for which the attendance centre order was made; and 2 per cent. were ordered to attend for breach of probation. Although these figures are lower than those found by the Cambridge study, where the corresponding percentages of a sample taken between 1950 and 1955 were 21, 22 and 3 per cent.,[54] they are still large enough to suggest that many courts use attendance centres as a form of reinforcement for probation.

On the other hand there are a number of orders made in cases where the boy concerned has several previous convictions. In 1964, 8 per cent. of orders affected boys with four or more previous convictions; one boy had 14. 359 boys (6 per cent.) served a second period of attendance. This is a further illustration of the uncertainty which exists as to the function of the centres.

[53] In 1966 there were 61 centres, in 1964, 57; 1962, 48; 1953, 22.
[54] McClintock, *op. cit.*, p. 21; the sample contained 1,499 cases.

Detention in Remand Homes

The Children Act 1908 forbade the use of imprisonment for children under the age of 14 years. Children who would otherwise have been sent to prison, and suitable young persons under 16, were to be sent instead to " places of detention " provided by the police.[55] In practice, these places of detention proved unsatisfactory, and fell into disuse.

But no one doubted the importance of keeping young offenders out of the prison environment, and the Children and Young Persons Act 1933 introduced the present system of " remand homes " for persons under 17, provided by local authorities and serving the same sort of purposes as the earlier places of detention.

The main purpose for which remand homes are used is the observation of juveniles who are to appear before the courts. The 1965 White Paper, *The Child, the Family and the Young Offender*,[56] proposed that they be renamed " observation centres." They are at present also used for the detention of offenders, and this is the group with which we are primarily concerned.

Detention cases

Detention in a remand home as a sentence is governed by section 54 of the Children and Young Persons Act 1933. This provides that where the child or young person is found guilty of an offence punishable in the case of an adult with imprisonment, he may be detained in a remand home for a maximum period of one month. It is expressly provided that the period of detention in a remand home may not exceed the maximum period of imprisonment laid down for the offence.[57]

A further and very important proviso prevents the making of an order for detention in a remand home when a detention centre is available for offenders of the relevant age and sex.[58] As more detention centres become available, fewer and fewer courts will have the power to send juveniles to remand homes.

Even if a detention centre has been declared to be available, it may be full to capacity. In that case the court can order no

[55] Children Act 1908, s. 106. For a fuller account of the history of remand homes, see *Detention in Remand Homes*, prepared by the Cambridge Dept. of Criminal Science (Macmillan, 1952), pp. 1–5.

[56] Cmnd. 2742, para. 16.

[57] Children and Young Persons Act 1933, s. 54 (2), as substituted by Criminal Justice Act, 1961.

[58] *Ibid.* s. 54 (1) proviso.

form of short-term institutional treatment, and may be tempted to order detention in a remand home under cover of a remand for inquiries. This has been repeatedly declared to be improper, but allegations that the practice continues are still to be heard.[59]

The régime within a remand home depends very much on the facilities available. A large home may have a gymnasium, and rooms for craft-work. A smaller home may have to house the inmates during the day in one large room, which serves as class-room, recreation-room, and exercise area. In all, a full day's schooling is provided for those of school age, but the range of age and ability and the short duration of most inmates' residence place severe restrictions on the content of teaching. In almost all homes it is impossible to provide separate facilities for different classes of child; in a small community it would be undesirable, as being likely to cause friction and ill-feeling, even if it were physically and financially possible. In any case, children under detention form a very small proportion of the total as the following Table shows:

ADMISSIONS TO REMAND HOMES 1966 [60]

	Under 14		14 *to* 17	
	Total Admissions	s. 54 Detention	Total Admissions	s. 54 Detention
Boys	4,882	322	10,258	92
Girls	498	2	3,597	10
Total	5,380	324	13,855	102

The numbers of those sent for detention has remained fairly constant for several years. Nearly 85 per cent. of those punished in this way have committed offences in the larceny or housebreaking groups.

There is really little to be said in favour of the continued use of remand homes for the detention of offenders. The homes are geared to their main work of observing and reporting on juveniles before the courts. In a period of three weeks, this task can be usefully discharged with the aid of reports on the home background. But it can scarcely be argued that a period of four weeks' detention can do much for a boy. He may leave

[59] *e.g., Toynbee Hall Juvenile Court Justices, ex p. Joseph* [1939] 3 All E.R. 16; see the report of a conference call by "Justice" in November 1965.

[60] Sources: *Criminal Statistics* and *Statistics Relating to Approved Schools, etc.*, 1966.

the remand home cleaner and perhaps healthier than when he was admitted; his knowledge of table manners will certainly be improved. For the majority, little more can be done.

There is no provision for after-care for remand home detainees. It would appear to be impossible to use a probation order to provide such after-care, unless the offender is convicted of a second offence.[61]

Other uses of remand homes

Although we are primarily concerned with detention as a penal measure, it is necessary to put this into its context by dealing with the other uses of remand homes, and with their administration.

In dealing with the use of remand homes it will be necessary to refer to other institutions, "remand centres" and "special reception centres." These are designed to relieve the remand homes of certain cases; a major criticism of the remand home system is that the staff have in their charge children and young persons of widely differing ages, who are in the homes for a whole variety of reasons.

Remand centres were provided for in the Criminal Justice Act 1948; they are officially defined as "places for the detention of persons not less than 14 but under 21 years of age who are remanded or committed in custody for trial or sentence."[62] Remand centres were given a low priority in the government's building programme. The first centre was not opened until 1961, thirteen years after the passing of the enabling legislation. There are now nine centres, one of which, at Risley, is also used for adult prisoners on remand, or sent for observation after sentence.

The main reason for the introduction of remand centres was the desire to keep those aged between 17 and 21 out of prison as far as possible. The centres serve this purpose by housing persons on remand,[63] or committed by a magistrates' court to quarter sessions with a view to a sentence of Borstal training.[64] Where no centres exist, local prisons have to be used.

Some young persons who would otherwise go to remand homes may be considered too "unruly or depraved" to be sent

61 This seems to follow from *Evans* [1959] 1 W.L.R. 26 (detention centre case); H.O. Letter 48/1959.
62 Prison Act 1952, s. 43 (1) (*a*).
63 Criminal Justice Act 1948, s. 27 (1).
64 Magistrates' Courts Act 1952, s. 28 (4).

there. In the past they had to go to prison, but they are now sent to "remand centres" where such centres are available.

Similarly, it was thought desirable to separate some of the younger children from the ordinary remand home inmates. These children can be sent to "special reception centres." These are local authorities' children's homes provided for the temporary accommodation of children under the Children Act 1948. About half of these homes have been made available to the courts for use as special reception centres.[65] The uses to which these centres are put will be made clear in the course of the discussion which follows; the important point is that they are *not* used to accommodate children sentenced to detention there, but only those who would otherwise be in a remand home for some other reason.

1. There are a number of cases in which a child or young person who has not yet been brought before the juvenile court can be placed in a remand home.

The clearest case is where he has been arrested for an offence. When a person under 17 is arrested, the police are under a duty to consider the grant of bail, and in the great majority of cases it will be granted.[66] In the few cases in which bail is refused, the short period before the court hearing [67] will normally be spent in a remand home. If the child concerned is under the age of 12, he may be placed in a special reception centre if one is available.[68]

Children and young persons who are not offenders but who are to appear before the juvenile court in its civil jurisdiction may also be taken to a remand home to await the court hearing. In this type of case, remand homes are one of a number of "places of safety" to which the child may be taken.[69]

2. The second group of cases, numerically the most important, are those in which the court has met but has not yet made a final order; the child or young person may be sent or returned to the remand home as an interim measure.

When the case involves criminal charges, this will be by way of remand, from which the homes take their name. The remand may be due to some delay in the court hearing, in

65 Under the Children and Young Persons (Amendment) Act 1952, s. 3, following the recommendations of the Curtis Committee (Cmd. 6922).

66 Children and Young Persons Act 1933, s. 32 (1).

67 Which cannot exceed 72 hours: Children and Young Persons Act 1963, s. 22.

68 Children and Young Persons Act 1933, s. 32 (2) as amended by Children and Young Persons (Amendment) Act 1952.

69 Children and Young Persons Act 1933, s. 67 (1). "Place of safety" is defined in s. 107 (1).

which case the maximum period is eight days, but is more usually for inquiries or for a medical report after a finding of guilt. In this case, the maximum period is three weeks.[70]

Remand homes are used for persons under 17 remanded in custody in this way, with certain exceptions.[71] If he is under 15 and is considered " suitable," the person on remand may be detained in a special reception centre. As far as possible, the court must seek the views of the local authority concerned, through its Children's Department, before sending a child over the age of 12 to a special reception centre, and the courts have been advised to consult with the local authority to establish general criteria of " suitability " for particular centres.[72]

In certain cases, a young person between 14 and 17 may be remanded in custody to a remand centre or prison.

Remand centres may be used for the medical examination of persons in this age-group if facilities are not available elsewhere.[73] Similarly, one who is " of so unruly a character that he cannot safely be detained in a remand home, or . . . of so depraved a character that he is not fit to be so detained " [74] will be sent to a remand centre or, if none is available, to prison.

Some anxiety was felt, when remand centres first became available, at the prospect of boys or girls of 14 and 15, even if they were " unruly or depraved," being housed with much older and more criminally sophisticated youths. A number of remand homes will now accept these cases, housing them in special secure accommodation.[75]

Where the juvenile court is acting in its civil jurisdiction, the equivalent of a remand in custody is an " interim order " under section 67 (2) of the Children and Young Persons Act 1933. This may specify detention in a remand home as a " place of safety." In the case of a person aged between 14 and 18 who is too unruly or depraved for a remand home, or who has been sent for a medical examination for which facilities do not exist in the remand home, a remand centre may be used.[76]

[70] Magistrates' Courts Act 1952, s. 105.
[71] Criminal Justice Act 1948, s. 27.
[72] *Ibid.*, as amended by Children and Young Persons (Amendment) Act 1952; Children and Young Persons Act 1963, s. 24; Home Office Circular 207/1952 (July 19 1952). The maximum age for special reception centres may be raised to 16 when the school-leaving age is similarly raised: Children and Young Persons Act 1963, s. 24 (2).
[73] Magistrates' Courts Act 1952, s. 26.
[74] Criminal Justice Act 1948, s. 27 (5).
[75] Home Office Circular 118/1961 (July 13 1961).
[76] Criminal Justice Act 1948, s. 75 as amended by Children and Young Persons Act 1963.

3. Remand homes may also be used for the detention of persons who are the subject of final orders of the court. This includes the cases already discussed in which detention in a remand home is the form of treatment selected by the court for an offender. There are three other groups to be mentioned.

It is possible for remand homes to be used for those in default of fines.[77] The remaining groups comprise persons awaiting a place in an approved school,[78] or in some specially designated homes undergoing approved school classification.[79]

4. Finally, there are two very different groups of persons who may be accommodated in a remand home.

A child who has been taken into care of the local authority or committed to its care as a fit person may be housed in a remand home in certain cases.[80] In these cases no court order need exist or be contemplated.

In sharp contrast are the very small number of young persons over 15 who have been committed to an approved school and have proved to be " so seriously unruly or subversive " that they have to be removed to maintain the discipline of the school. They may be sent to a remand home on a justice's warrant as a temporary measure.[81]

Administration

The arrangements for the provision of remand homes are not altogether satisfactory. Although there is a measure of central government control, the primary responsibility rests with local authorities; county and county borough councils have a duty to provide adequate facilities.[82] The multiplicity of local authorities which is such a strong feature of English local government immediately causes problems in the development of a coherent policy for the provision of homes. To some extent co-operation between neighbouring authorities can help to overcome these problems, but there is a case for stronger central government control.

The Home Secretary has certain powers. He can make general provision for the administration of the homes by making

77 See p. 203.
78 Children and Young Persons Act 1963, s. 9.
79 *Ibid.* s. 11; three homes had been so designated by the end of 1965.
80 Children Act 1948, s. 13 (6).
81 Criminal Justice Act 1961, s. 15.
82 Children and Young Persons Act 1933, s. 77 as amended by Criminal Justice Act 1948. They co-operate in some cases with voluntary organisations, or even with private householders.

Remand Home Rules[83]; inspectors from the Home Office Children's Department visit the homes and inquire into the general standards of accommodation and staff; and superintendents of local authority homes are appointed subject to Home Office approval.[84]

Under the Criminal Justice Act 1948, the Home Secretary may take further powers. He is authorised to introduce, by statutory instrument, a system of certificates of approval without which no premises could be used for remand home purposes.[85] These powers have not yet been taken.

The central exchequer bears one-half of the local authority's expenditure on homes. Here, too, some changes are possible under recent legislation, in cases where several authorities use one home.[86]

On December 31, 1966, there were fifty-eight remand homes, of which two were provided by voluntary organisations. They had places for 1,187 boys and 397 girls.

Future of remand homes

The White Paper *The Child, the Family and the Young Offender*[87] proposed the replacement of remand homes by observation centres. These would continue to be provided by the local authorities, which means that so far as physical plant is concerned, the remand homes would continue under a new name.

Their functions would change. Detention in remand homes as a penal measure would disappear, and the other work of the homes would be extended. In particular, facilities would be provided for the examination of children still living at home; and the homes would take over the functions of classifying approved schools, in advising on the selection of appropriate residential treatment.

In many respects, these proposals seem to have the support of remand home staffs as represented by the National Association of Remand Home Superintendents and Matrons.[88]

83 The current rules are the Remand Homes Rules 1939, S.R. & O. 1939 No. 12.

84 Criminal Justice Act 1948, s. 49 (3).

85 *Ibid.* s. 49 (1).

86 Children and Young Persons Act 1933, s. 104 (1) (*a*). For possible changes in the financial arrangements see Children and Young Persons Act 1963, s. 59, and the 9th report of the Children's Dept. (1964).

87 Cmnd. 2742.

88 R.C.P.S., Vol. 3, p. 184.

Fit Person Orders

Courts are always reluctant to take children away from their homes, but sometimes it is essential. A court is under a statutory duty to take steps, in a proper case, to remove a child or young person from undesirable surroundings and to make provision for his education and training.[89] Sometimes the desired result can be achieved by making a probation or supervision order with a condition as to residence, but the period of residence cannot then exceed 12 months.[90] The more usual methods are fit person and approved school orders.

Both types of order can be made whether the child or young person concerned is an offender or comes within the civil jurisdiction of the juvenile court. Both remove the child from his undesirable surroundings, but an approved school also provides residential education and training and is more likely to be used in the case of the older child, especially offenders.

Legal framework

A fit person order is an order committing a child to the care of a fit person, who may be a relative or friend of the child but is usually a local authority, a person only in a technical legal sense.[91] So long as the order remains in force, the fit person takes over all parental rights and duties to the exclusion of the natural parents. The parents remain under a duty to contribute to the child's maintenance, but the sums actually collected are very small.[92]

No special qualifications are required of individual fit persons, but they should normally be of the same religious persuasion as the child and are required to bring the child up in accordance with that persuasion. It may, of course, be difficult to discover the religious views, if any, of the child, or of the natural parents, but the court must make the attempt and declare the persuasion of the child.[93]

Where the fit person is an individual, the fit person order may be coupled with a probation or supervision order, which allows the court to maintain some oversight of the child's case, and may provide a valuable source of help and advice for the

[89] Children and Young Persons Act 1933, s. 44 (1).
[90] See p. 167.
[91] Children and Young Persons Act 1933, s. 76.
[92] *Ibid.* s. 86.
[93] *Ibid.* ss. 75, 84 (7).

fit person. Where the fit person is a local authority, probation or supervision orders in force are usually revoked.[94]

A fit person order remains in force until the child attains the age of 18, but the court may revoke it before then, and the Home Secretary also has power to discharge a child from the care of a fit person.[95] In either case the child is returned to the parents, and a supervision order or equivalent arrangements can be made.

The power to make a fit person order exists in a number of types of case; in all cases, an approved school order is an alternative. An order may be made in respect of a child found guilty of an offence, either immediately or after an unsuccessful probation order or conditional discharge. In the civil jurisdiction, children in need of care, protection or control, including the victims of certain offences; truants, children already under supervision or in the care of the local authority and brought by their supervisor or the authority before the court; in each case an order can be made.[96] The use of the orders for each category is set out in the Table below.

FIT PERSON ORDERS 1966 [97]

Grounds for order	*Number of Orders* Boys	Girls	Total
Offenders			
on finding of guilt	898	226	1,124
breach of probation, etc.	122	53	175
Total	1,020	279	1,299
Non-Offenders			
care protection or control	779	1,025	1,804
truancy cases	232	166	398
supervision cases	36	67	103
in care of local authority	1	4	5
Total	1,048	1,262	2,310
Total	2,068	1,541	3,609

In practice

The great majority of fit person orders name a local authority as the fit person. In 1966, of the 3,609 orders made, 3,531

[94] *Ibid.* s. 76 (1). [95] *Ibid.* ss. 75 (3), 84 (4) (6).

[96] In every case, the relevant statutory provision is the same as that giving power to make an approved school order. For full references, see *infra*, p. 220.

[97] Source: *Criminal Statistics* 1965, Table VI.

named the local authority. In these cases, the local authority can make use of a wide range of facilities including special schools, schools and homes for maladjusted children (if available) and children's homes. But the majority of children committed to the care of local authorities do not remain in institutions; the authority is under a duty to board out children in its care unless it is impracticable or undesirable to do so in a particular case. Some 50 per cent. of children in the care of local authorities now live with foster parents.[98] Elaborate provisions govern the inspection of the homes of prospective foster parents, and for regular visits to be paid by the authority's officials during the period of boarding out.[99] In some cases the local authority may send the child to its own parents, usually for a trial period with a view to revocation of the fit person order.

The Table below indicates the age and sex of children subject to fit person orders in 1966. The differences in use of fit person orders as between boys and girls revealed by this and the preceding Table are also found in approved school cases.[1]

FIT PERSON ORDERS 1966

Age	*Boys*	*Girls*
Under 10	498	399
10–14	992	408
14–18	578	734
	2,068	1,541

APPROVED SCHOOLS

Approved schools are institutions providing residential education and training for children and young persons, offenders and non-offenders, sent to the school under a court order. Many of the children sent to approved schools could have been dealt with in other ways, by a fit person order, a probation or supervision order with a condition as to residence, or by a sentence of Borstal training. All would have removed the child from his

[98] See the annual paper *Children in Care in England and Wales*, which gives figures for the period ending March 31 each year. In some areas no children are boarded out, for others 70 or 80 per cent. are.

[99] Boarding-Out of Children Regulations 1955; the Home Office published a convenient memorandum giving the effect of these regulations in rather less intractable language. For the effectiveness of the authority's supervision, see the Dorset case, the subject of much discussion and a Home Office report in early 1966.

[1] See *infra*, p. 222.

home; but a fit person order would not provide residential training, a condition of residence in a probation or supervision order lasts only for twelve months, and Borstal training is intended for the offender who has some degree of criminal sophistication.

Legal framework

Children and young persons may be sent to approved schools for many reasons. Although the majority are sent as offenders, this statement obscures a number of variations: in girls' schools, for example, offenders are in a minority; and there are children in approved schools who are below the age of criminal responsibility. The cases in which an approved school order may be made are these:

1. Where a child or young person is found guilty of an offence. The offence must be one punishable in the case of an adult with imprisonment.[2]
2. Where a child or young person is in need of " care, protection or control." [3]
3. Truancy cases under the Education Acts.[4]
4. Cases in which a child or young person under supervision is brought before the court " in his interests." [5]
5. Where a child or young person in the care of a local authority is brought before the court as refractory, or with a view to the substitution of another order for one committing the child to the care of the authority.[6]
6. Where a child or young person runs away from the person named in a Fit Person Order.[7]

The following Table [8] gives an impression of the relative importance of these categories.

An approved school order is indeterminate; the maximum length of training is fixed by statute, but the actual length varies with the needs of the individual. The maximum period of detention varies with the age of the child or young person concerned. If he is a child, in the legal sense of being under 14, at the date of

[2] Children and Young Persons Act 1933, s. 57.
[3] *Ibid.* s. 62; for " care, protection and control," see *supra*, pp. 191–192.
[4] See *supra*, p. 192.
[5] Children and Young Persons Act 1933, s. 66; see *supra*, p. 193.
[6] Children and Young Persons Act 1933, ss. 65 and 84 (8), both as substituted by Children and Young Persons Act 1963, s. 7.
[7] Children and Young Persons Act 1933, s. 85 (1).
[8] Adapted from *Statistics relating to Approved Schools, etc.*, 1966, Table 2.

APPROVED SCHOOL ADMISSIONS 1966

Ground for committal	*Number of admissions*		
	Boys	Girls	Total
Offenders guilty of			
larceny or receiving	1,596	265	1,861
breaking and entering	2,100	64	2,164
all other offences	659	31	690
Total	4,355	360	4,715
Non-offenders			
Care, protection or control cases [9]	67	203	270
Truancy cases	75	48	123
Supervision cases	58	114	172
In care of local authority	44	103	147
Escape from fit person	0	8	8
Total	244	476	720
Total (offenders and non-offenders)	4,599	836	5,435

the order, he may be detained for three years, or until four months have elapsed since he ceased to be of compulsory school age,[10] whichever is the *longer* period. If he is a young person, over 14, he may be detained for three years or until he is 19, whichever is the *shorter* period.[11] In practice, the average period of detention is about 18 months.

The schools

At the end of 1966 there were 123 different schools, some very small. The average size of a boys' school is just under a hundred, but most girls' schools are only one-third of that size. The following Table [12] shows the formal classification of the schools.

Although the Home Office Children's Department has considerable powers of control, exercised through an inspectorate, and the schools are all in receipt of a certificate of approval issued by the Home Office, approved schools are established and

[9] Including cases of children beyond their parents' control, which formed a separate category until February 1, 1964, when the relevant part of Children and Young Persons Act 1963 was brought into force.

[10] At present, therefore, until he reaches the age of 15 years 4 months.

[11] Children and Young Persons Act 1933, s. 71, as amended by Criminal Justice Act 1948.

[12] Source: *Statistics relating to Approved Schools, etc.*, 1966.

NUMBER AND CATEGORY OF APPROVED SCHOOLS ON DECEMBER 31, 1966

Category	*Normal age on admission*	*Number of schools*	*Number of places*
Boys' schools			
Classifying	Up to 17th birthday	4	338
Senior	Between 15th & 17th birthdays	27	2,538
Intermediate	Between 13th & 15th birthdays	29[13]	3,147
Junior	Up to 13th birthday	30[14]	2,324
	Total	90	8,365
Girls' schools			
Senior	Between 15th & 17th birthdays	19	720
Intermediate	Between 14th & 16th birthdays	9[15]	87
Junior	Up to 15th birthdays	5	72
	Total	33	1,379

run by local voluntary bodies, religious or charitable organisations, or, in a few cases, by local authorities. It may seem extraordinary that such an important part of the penal system should remain under essentially amateur control, and the anomaly is almost certain to disappear, but it reflects the schools' history, which is one of private charitable initiative.

History

One of the best-known examples is the Royal Philanthropic Society, which still maintains one of the leading approved schools, at Redhill in Surrey. It can trace its origins back to the work of Robert Young in 1788, although the Society itself dates from 1806, and its work at Redhill, led by the Revd. Sydney Turner, from 1849.

During the first half of the nineteenth century many schools and institutions were established, usually on a firm Christian basis, as part of a wider movement which also led to better educational standards and restrictions on child labour. The early experiments in England had parallels on the Continent. Wichern's Rauhes Haus near Hamburg and Demetz's institution at Mettrai were especially influential; many of the English workers visited them, and they were constantly cited as examples in evidence to the various parliamentary Committees of the period. Their particular contribution was the practice

[13] Including three schools that admitted both intermediate and junior boys.

[14] Comprising 14 secondary schools and 16 combined primary and secondary schools.

[15] Including one school that admitted both intermediate and junior girls.

of dividing the inmates into small family groups, so making individual treatment a possibility.[16]

In England, the institutions gradually fell into two groups which came to be known as industrial schools and reformatory schools. Both dealt with "children of the perishing and dangerous classes," but reformatories were for convicted offenders, whilst industrial schools had a preventive role.

Industrial schools trace their origins to institutions such as the ragged schools, the earliest dating from 1818, and the Juvenile Vagrant and Industrial School, Aberdeen. Legislation in 1857 and 1861 gave the courts power for the first time to send children to industrial schools up to the age of 16. Those who could be sent included vagrant children, children beyond their parents' control, and offenders under the age of 12. Later the schools came within the scope of the Education Acts.

The history of reformatory schools took a rather different turn, largely through the passing of the Parkhurst Act 1838. To Parkhurst Prison were sent children and young persons sentenced to transportation, and many were ultimately released to the care of institutions such as the Redhill Reformatory. This established the pattern of release to a reformatory from some other penal institution which was to continue until 1899.

The position of reformatory schools was greatly changed by an Act of 1854. This provided that where a court had sentenced a person under 16 to imprisonment for at least 14 days, it could also order that after completing the sentence of imprisonment he should attend a reformatory school for between two and five years. Some provision was made for contributions from parents and the Exchequer towards the expenses of the schools, and every school had to receive a certificate of approval from the Home Secretary, who had powers of inspection.

The name "approved schools" and the bringing together under that name of the old industrial and reformatory schools came with the 1933 legislation, which remains as the basis of the present system.

16 See Sydney Turner on Family Division, cited Hinde, *British Penal System 1773–1950*, pp. 106–107; for the general history of the early developments see Grünhut, *Penal Reform* (1948), pp. 365 *et seq.* The principal parliamentary Committees were the Lords' Committee on Juvenile Offenders and Transportation (1847) Sessional Papers (Commons), Vol. 7, p. 1, and the Commons' Committee on Criminal and Destitute Children (1852) Sessional Papers (Commons), Vol. 23, p. 3.

Present system

In theory, control over each approved school is vested in its "managers"; a committee set up by the organisation owning the school, or, where the school was established by a group formed for that purpose, a self-perpetuating committee of local people. The managers apply for a certificate of approval, granted by the Home Office after inspection and other inquiries.[17] The certificate can be withdrawn, and this possibility is the sanction behind the Home Secretary's considerable powers over the schools.[18] There is a nice balancing of powers between the local managers and the central government authority.

In particular, the Home Secretary can and does limit the number of children who may be admitted; this is referred to as the school's "certified number."[19] Although the managers have full responsibility for the day-to-day running of their school, they must carry out the directions of the Home Secretary on any subject concerning the school's activities,[20] and the Home Secretary has powers to regulate the constitution and proceedings of the managers,[21] and the appointment of a headmaster needs his approval.[22] All schools are regularly visited by Home Office inspectors, and alterations to approved school premises need Home Office permission.[23]

Although there is no statutory bar to the creation of new voluntary schools, local authorities now have a duty to take the initiative in remedying any deficiency in approved school accommodation, and can make grants to other bodies to help in establishing approved schools; ultimately the Exchequer bears much of the cost.[24] The normal running expenses of approved schools are also met almost entirely from public funds, one half being contributed by the Exchequer and one half by the local authorities using the school. The parents of children sent to the schools can also be ordered to make contributions, but the total of these contributions amounts in practice to only one-fortieth of the total cost.[25]

17 Children and Young Persons Act 1933, s. 79.
18 Demonstrated in the troubles of the Court Lees School in 1967.
19 Approved School Rules 1933, r. 13.
20 Criminal Justice Act 1961, s. 18.
21 *Ibid.* s. 19. The additional powers conferred in 1961 were recommended by the Ingleby Committee or by Mr. Durand in his report on *Disturbances at the Carlton Approved School*, 1960, Cmnd. 937.
22 Approved School Rules 1933, r. 14.
23 Children and Young Persons Act 1933, Sched. IV, para. 2.
24 *Ibid.*, ss. 80 and 104.
25 The rules governing approved school finances are extremely complicated. See *ibid.* ss. 86, 87, 90 as amended; the Children and Young Persons (Collection of Parental Contributions) Regulations 1933, the Approved Schools

The system of balancing national and local interests is a common one in English administration. In many contexts it is an ingenious and satisfactory arrangement. So far as approved schools are concerned, a critical examination soon reveals serious weaknesses.

The managers

The position of the school managers is a major target for criticism.[26] They form a Board which has a position similar to that of governors of an ordinary school.

In any ordinary school, the position of the governors is a difficult one. Their powers, even in theory, are extremely limited. In practice, it is unusual for governors to know the staff or pupils of the school. Their contact with the school, apart from its being their meeting-place, is entirely through the headmaster. On most issues, the governors, with no knowledge of their own, must act merely as a sounding-board for the headmaster's views.

Approved school managers are under the same handicap, though their position is slightly different. The Rules give them, in theory, control over the day-to-day running of the school, and decisions affecting individual pupils, such as the date of release, have to be made by the managers, and by no-one else.[27] Managers have greater responsibilities than governors; the Rules provide that some managers must live sufficiently close to the school to exercise effective supervision, but it is doubtful if this means overmuch in practice.

Another criticism is directed at the composition of boards of managers. An approved school teacher, writing in *The Guardian* in a correspondence which ultimately led to the Court Lees inquiry,[28] expressed this criticism with some force:

> "The school managers are (so far as my experience goes) from a single class; persons with some money, no work, and a desire to salve their consciences by devoting an hour or two a month to 'good works.' Thus at my school we number retired army officers, retired members of branches of the legal professions, unemployed country gentlemen, and various middle-class wives.

(Contributions by Local Authorities) Regulations 1962 and 1966; and for statistics, Annex 1 to the annual paper *Statistics relating to Approved Schools, etc.*

26 See, *e.g.*, Rose, *Schools for Young Offenders*, pp. 220–230.

27 Report of the Carlton School Disturbances, Cmnd. 937, esp. para. 149.

28 *The Guardian*, March 2, 1967.

"With very few exceptions the boys come from working-class families, always with a long history of social difficulties that result not only in child delinquency but also in homes that are socially and materially defective. The managers do not understand the boys or their parents, and have no idea at all of what living on a low working-class income may involve."

On the other hand, managers can give very real assistance and encouragement to the school staff; good managers can help the headmaster to launch valuable experiments in attempts to improve his school.

Administration generally

Approved schools are in a distinctly anomalous position. Most penal establishments, including Borstals and detention centres, are run directly by the Prison Service, under the Home Office Prison Department. On the other hand, remand homes (from which approved school children come), and the educational establishments, special schools and residential schools for many types of child, are provided by local authorities, with guidance from the Home Office Children's Department. Approved schools fit neither pattern.

The White Paper, *The Child, the Family and the Young Offender*,[29] published in 1965, contained proposals which would end the present system. Most schools would become part of the range of educational facilities of local authorities; the powers of the existing managers would, presumably, disappear or become advisory only.

From one point of view, there is much to be said for these proposals. The existence in separate compartments of "fit person" and approved school orders is difficult to justify. On the other hand, the case for maintaining a system of specialist schools and a regional classifying system is strong,[30] but the earlier proposals were repeated in the 1968 White Paper, *Children in Trouble.*

The 1965 proposals also envisaged the merging of senior approved schools with the Borstal system. This met strong opposition, for the two types of institution are very different, the schools, but not Borstals, containing non-offenders. This proposal was dropped in 1968.

29 Cmnd. 2742, paras. 22–23.

30 Rose, *op. cit.*, Chap. 11; two articles by M. Wall, *The Guardian*, March 21 and 22, 1967.

Approved school training

It is always dangerous to generalise about a group of institutions. No one institution is the same as another. It is physically different, its inmates are different, and so, most important of all, is its staff. All this is particularly true of approved schools.

They cater for a wide range of children, and, more than some other types of institution, seem to lack an agreed approach. Detention centres have a basis of brisk régime, disciplined and ordered; Borstals, though full of experiments, have a traditional philosophy based on the house system and expounded in the classics of Borstal literature. But what about approved schools? A headmaster writes:

> " Basic to everything in approved schools today is that we sit squarely in a grave conflict. Either we hold centres that protect society by penning its misfits, or else we are agents of rehabilitation. Time and again this contradiction comes up. We have to be resilient, to some extent permissive, and to absorb bizarre behaviour from boys acting out their problems. Yet notwithstanding, the school is always part of a wider environment that is bound to react if boys run away or steal in the locality. When this does happen, there is very little understanding or sympathy and we are forced into a defensive posture. Misbehaviour by boys implies that we are incompetent. Often we have to put public relations before the individual wellbeing of boys." [31]

Each school has to resolve this problem in its own way. It must create a stable environment, and within that environment educate and train children who may be the victims of tragic circumstances, may be verging on mental disorder, or may, at least on the surface, be plain wicked.

A wide variety of methods can be used. The school may aim to work as much like an ordinary school as possible, emphasising formal education, obedience to school rules, healthy sport. Or it may concentrate training through small groups in a house system, with house-parents presiding over a sort of family. Generalisation is quite impossible.[32]

Classification and admission

When an approved school order is made, the boy or girl

[31] " Approved schools troubled by conflict of aims," *The Times*, August 24, 1967.

[32] For a useful review of possible systems, see Rose, *op cit.*, pp. 183 *et seq.*

usually goes to a remand home, and then to the approved school. Because approved schools differ one from another a classifying process, selecting the right school for each child, so far as vacancies permit, is essential. Sometimes this is carried out at the remand home, where the particular home has been designated for that purpose.[33] Otherwise, the first approved school entered is the "classifying school."

The classifying schools themselves are subject to the control of managers in the usual way. This explains, in part, the exclusion until recently of Roman Catholic boys from the usual classifying procedure, and the closure of the only classifying school for girls in 1966.

In practice a regional classifying system is in operation for boys, with four classifying areas. The classifying schools in each area have larger staff numbers than normal schools, and greater security. The classifying process is complicated by geography. It is obviously an advantage for a boy to be sent to the school best suited to his needs; but equally, he should not be removed too far from his home. This is desirable not only to ease visiting by the parents, but also home visiting by the social workers of the school. In recent years this consideration has been given much greater weight in the process; classification within individual local schools has become more important as a result.

Inevitably, this process leads to some delays. Rather more than 10 per cent. of cases involve a delay of six weeks or more between the making of the order and admission to the first school.[34] Sometimes, of course, this will be due to special problems, *e.g.*, medical problems, discovered on remand.

In the training schools

The institutions are all "schools" and formal education has a place in all of them. Children of compulsory school age spend a normal school day in class, and older children spend some time in the class-room. Although the available evidence suggests that approved school-children are not far behind their peers in intelligence the majority are well behind in educational attainment. Teaching them presents problems not dissimilar from those found in special schools. It follows that schoolwork for the older children, those above compulsory school age, may

[33] Stamford House (boys) and Cumberlow Lodge (girls), in London; and The Moss (girls) in Sheffield.

[34] *Statistics relating to Approved Schools, etc.*, Table 3.

still be concentrated on the basic skills of reading, writing and arithmetic.

Those not in school spend the bulk of the day at work. As in most institutions the maintenance of the fabric, the construction of extensions and the feeding of the inmates absorb much of the labour force. Others are trained in joinery, or in farming, or for the merchant navy. The great majority of those discharged from approved schools take up work classed as " operative, unskilled "; very few take up clerical or technical work.[35] In most schools work is done within the school limits; in a few, outside work is encouraged.

For most of the day, the pupils are in school or at work, directed by their teachers or instructors. In the evening and at weekends there is a wide range of sport and general recreational activities, despite the problems of adequate supervision at these times.

It is probably the time spent away from the school-room or the workshop which reveals most clearly the problems of approved schools. In a normal boarding-school, which is not of course a fair analogy, activities out of school are based on a house presided over by a house-master who is one of the teaching staff. Whatever its disadvantages, that system does give each boy a secure base in a small group with a person to whom he can turn; and the traditional Borstal follows a similar system.

Some approved schools have a house system, but the house staff, house-masters or house-fathers, have " social " duties, and are distinct from the teachers and instructors. Others have a house system similar to that of normal day-schools, unconnected with physical buildings, a division merely for competitive purposes.

Whatever the system, there are obvious difficulties in co-ordinating the training received by a particular child, and some friction between the teachers, the instructors and the house-parents. The teaching staff may resent the children being in the care of others whose qualifications they suspect; or there may be problems in compiling proper records, or in the relationship between the headmaster and his staff. These problems were much aired during 1967, when the approved schools suffered from some unwelcome publicity surrounding the Court Lees affair; they exist, but must not be exaggerated.[36]

35 *Ibid.*, Table 11.
36 On the attitudes of approved school staff, see Rose, *op. cit.*, pp. 192 *et seq.*

Discipline and misfits

Discipline in the schools is strictly governed by the Approved School Rules 1933.[37] Punishments must be recorded in specified ways, and the records inspected; but the statistics are not published as they are for Home Office institutions. Available forms of punishment include loss of marks for a house in a competitive scheme, loss of privileges, limits on food,[38] separation from other inmates, and corporal punishment.

Corporal punishment is always controversial,[39] and its use is severely limited by the Rules which provide that [40]:

> "Every effort shall be made to enforce discipline without resort to corporal punishment."

From time to time allegations are made concerning the excessive use of corporal punishment. Reports of inquiries confirm that some members of approved school staff do rely on caning more than others, and that the rules are by no means always observed.[41]

Approved school children are much more "difficult" and have many more problems than the average boarding-school pupil. There are some special problem cases—pregnant girls, enuretics, persistent absconders. In extreme cases a pupil must be removed from a particular school; secure accommodation is available at some classifying schools to receive such cases.[42]

In some cases, a pupil may be removed after court proceedings. If a further offence has been committed, the normal procedure is followed. In cases where there is no offence, the managers, with the consent of the Home Secretary, may start proceedings in a juvenile court on the ground of serious misconduct in the approved school. This may lead to a new approved school order, an extension by up to six months of the existing order, or committal for Borstal training where the

[37] rr. 34 to 37.

[38] Subject to special rules; there is nothing approaching a "bread and water diet."

[39] See Chap. 7.

[40] r. 34 (iv).

[41] See the Carlton House report, Cmnd. 937, and the report on *Administration of Punishment at Court Lees Approved School*, Cmnd. 3367.

[42] See Children and Young Persons Act 1963, s. 8 (1); Children and Young Persons Act 1933, Sched. IV, para. 9, as amended by Children and Young Persons Act 1963.

young person is 15 or over.[43] Similar provisions apply to absconders.

Where a young person is 15 or over and is considered to be so seriously unruly or subversive that he must be removed to maintain the discipline of the school, any justice of the peace, acting on sworn information from the managers, may order his temporary removal to a remand centre, remand home, or to another approved school for a maximum of 28 days. In an emergency, a justice can authorise detention in a police station for 48 hours.[44]

These are temporary measures. A permanent end to detention in an approved school may come after proceedings under section 16 of the Criminal Justice Act 1961. Under that section, the managers (with the Home Secretary's approval) may ask a magistrates' court to remove a young person of 15 or over to a Borstal institution. The court can take this action when it is satisfied, having regard to the young person's conduct, that "his continued detention in an approved school would be ineffective for the purposes of his own reformation or would be detrimental to the training or welfare of other persons therein" and that he needs Borstal training.[45]

Most of these provisions were introduced after the disturbances at Carlton School, which attracted much attention, and the publication of the Ingleby Report. They may only be used in a dozen cases in any year, but experience has shown that prompt action in an emergency can avert disaster.

A final group consists of those who are mentally disturbed or in need of psychiatric treatment, and who should never have gone to an approved school. In 1966, twenty-two pupils were transferred to hospitals under the Home Secretary's transfer powers,[46] and a further forty-five were admitted to hospital informally.[47]

Release and after-care

The decision to release a child from an approved school must be taken by the managers who usually accept the advice of the

43 Children and Young Persons Act 1933, Sched. IV, para. 8; Criminal Justice Act 1948, s. 72. Note that in this case, magistrates may themselves pass a sentence of Borstal training without the delay of committal to quarter sessions.

44 Criminal Justice Act 1961, s. 15.

45 The consequences are set out in *ibid.* ss. 16, 17.

46 Mental Health Act 1959, s. 72; see *infra*, Chap. 6.

47 Children and Young Persons Act 1933, Sched. IV, para. 4. See also R.C.P.S., Vol. 2, pp. 161–162 (Nat.Assoc. for Mental Health).

headmaster. The Home Secretary may, however, order a release, and his consent is needed before anyone can be released within the first six months of his detention in a particular school.[48] After release, there is a period of supervision which is normally two years. During this period, the managers remain responsible and have the sanction of recall, subject only to the need to obtain the Home Secretary's consent to the recall of a person over 19; a person over 21 cannot be recalled. Recall is for a maximum of six months in the usual case, unless less than that time is left of the original period of detention.[49] The managers must provide further advice and assistance at the request of a former inmate for a longer period [50]; although this is imposed as a statutory duty, it is an unnecessary provision, for the staff of approved schools are always willing to help old pupils.

The managers must decide which agency will provide after-care and supervision. The choice is usually between the probation and after-care service and the Children's Departments. The nature of a particular case will determine which is selected. Some schools have their own social workers who devote some of their time to after-care work; this is only practicable when the school's " catchment area " is small.[51]

Detention Centres

Detention centres are, as they have been since their introduction, one of the most controversial features of the English penal system. The controversy has been encouraged by the unusually memorable nature of the officially-encouraged description of the training they provide: the " short, sharp, shock." [52] It is a label of which those who work in the centres are heartily tired and, as Dr. Grünhut pointed out,[53] from the outset it aroused the suspicion that this was a reactionary and repressive device. Nonetheless, it is a reasonably accurate description.

The centres are designed to provide short-term residential training for offenders between the ages of 14 and 21 who have not yet developed a definitely anti-social attitude, and do not

48 Criminal Justice Act 1961, s. 14 (1).

49 For details see *ibid.* 2nd Sched., Part I; and see also Children and Young Persons Act 1933, Sched. IV, para. 7.

50 Criminal Justice Act 1961, 2nd Sched., Part II.

51 The former Approved School Welfare Service, an after-care organisation for boys, finally disappeared in April 1967.

52 Used, *e.g.*, in the first Prison Commission report after the opening of the pioneer centre: R.P.C. 1952, p. 91.

53 (1959–60) 10 B.J.Crim. 178.

need to be removed from their homes for prolonged training, but who need to be taught that the law cannot be defied with impunity.[54] The centres are intended to be deterrent, to be penal; this accounts for their unpopularity with many social workers, who find this approach inconsistent with the modern stress on education and reform.

But equally, the existence of this sort of institution fills a need, at least from the point of view of the courts. Detention centres were introduced in the Criminal Justice Act 1948. That Act abolished corporal punishment and discouraged the use of remand homes for the detention of convicted offenders. At the same time, opinion was running strongly against short prison terms, especially for young offenders.[55] Detention centres provide an alternative form of treatment, suitable for *some* of those previously dealt with by one of the other methods. The Home Office has faced an up-hill task in persuading some courts that the centres were not suitable for all those cases; that their proper use required careful selection.

In the public mind, detention centres have become associated with a particular type of case, one which excites public alarm. The activities of noisy vandals, of the "Teddy-boys" of the 1950s, and their successors the "Mods" and "Rockers," are thought to deserve the short sharp shock. These types are found in detention centres; but they form a minor element. As is usual, most inmates were sentenced for offences of dishonesty.

Many courts would explain their use of detention by saying that the individual concerned had not responded to more lenient, and usually non-institutional, treatment, but was not in need of prolonged training in a Borstal. Even this is a generalisation; over a quarter of those sent to junior centres in 1964 had received no previous treatments.[56]

Legal framework

Offenders aged between 14 and 21 may be sent to detention centres. To this general statement, there are a number of important exceptions.

1. The offence for which the offender is being sentenced must be one which is punishable in the case of adults by

54 R.P.C. 1952, p. 91; Home Office Circular 167/1952, paras. 6–7.

55 See Dunlop and McCabe, *Young Men in Detention Centres*, Chap. 1. See also the critical comments of Hood in *Collected Studies in Criminology Research* (Council of Europe), Vol. 1 at p. 103.

56 R.P.D. (Tables), 1964.

imprisonment.[57] This rule is laid down for all types of institution available for young offenders, and is designed to prevent the use of institutional treatment for petty offences.

2. In the usual case, a sentence of detention may not be passed on an offender who is serving or has already served a sentence of imprisonment for a term of not less than six months or a sentence of Borstal training.[58] This prohibition is accounted for by the fact that such persons would be both criminally sophisticated and accustomed to institutional life, and so unlikely to benefit from the short term training of the detention centre. As we shall see, there is considerable evidence that the institutionalisation of a period in an approved school is enough to make a person a bad prospect for detention; but the prohibition does not extend that far.

The prohibition is no longer absolute as it was in the 1948 Act. Where there are " special circumstances (whether relating to the offence or to the offender) " exceptions may be made, provided that the court considers any report on the offender laid before it, and (if it is a magistrates' court) adjourns the hearing until such a report is produced.[59]

3. The final limitation is a severely practical one. Despite great efforts to provide sufficient centres to meet the demand for places, there are still an inadequate number. No court may order detention unless it has been informed that a centre is available to it for persons of the age and sex concerned.[60] It will be remembered that the ultimate aim is to provide sufficient detention centres for all short-term institutional sentences to be served there; then, prison sentences of under six months, which may still be passed on those over 17, will be prohibited.[61]

In addition to offenders, detention centres may also receive on committal for default of payment of a fine young persons between 14 and 17, and, exceptionally, persons over that age.[62]

Length of sentence

The 1948 legislation allowed courts a certain amount of freedom in deciding the length of a detention centre sentence; it could vary between one and six months.[63] The normal period

57 Criminal Justice Act 1961, s. 4 (1).
58 *Ibid.* s. 4 (4).
59 *Ibid.* See Home Office Circular 138/63/C4, and *Cairns* [1965] Crim.L.R. 616.
60 Criminal Justice Act 1961, s. 4 (3).
61 See p. 251 and Criminal Justice Act 1961, s. 3.
62 *Ibid.* ss. 5, 6.
63 Criminal Justice Act 1948, s. 18 (1), sets out the, rather complex, rules.

was three months, and as the training programme was geared to this period, detention centre wardens found it difficult to deal satisfactorily with inmates sent for other lengths of time.[64]

A detention centre order must now be for three months whenever the offender is under 17, or is sentenced by a magistrates' court. Offenders over 17, appearing before assizes or quarter sessions, may be sentenced to terms between three and six months in length.[65] Consecutive terms in detention are possible for offenders over 17, but not more than six months' detention can be ordered on any one occasion, and the total term for which any person can be detained under any circumstances must not exceed nine months.[66]

In practice, the courts are discouraged from making use of sentences of more than three months. As Lord Parker C.J. pointed out in *Moreby and King*,[67] after the first three months little further benefit can be gained. The Court of Criminal Appeal was prepared to recognise that some longer sentences might be sentences of mercy imposed instead of Borstal training.

Remission is granted of one-sixth of the term, up to a maximum of one month.[68]

After-care

For many years, it was a major criticism of the detention centre system that no provision existed for compulsory after-care. Although after-care was available on a voluntary basis, very few took advantage of it. The need for after-care was recognised in the very first Warden's Report,[69] and by the authorities in the provision of women social workers in some centres. Dr. Grünhut's study of the first hundred inmates led him to conclude that the period of detention seemed "to be followed by a time of grace which should be used for every possible effort to help the boy to a lasting social adjustment" [70]; for "time of grace," he later substituted "danger-zone." [71]

Many courts tried to overcome the problem through probation orders. Where an offender was convicted on two counts, a detention centre order could be coupled with a probation

64 See, *e.g.*, R.P.C. 1955, p. 111.
65 Criminal Justice Act 1961, s. 4 (2). For special provisions for defaulters, see s. 5 (2).
66 *Ibid.* s. 7. A second sentence of detention is rarely appropriate: *Moore* [1968] 1 W.L.R. 397.
67 (1965) 109 S.J. 472.
68 Detention Centre Rules 1952, r. 26.
69 R.P.C. 1952, p. 96.
70 (1954–55) 5 B.J.D. 191, 208.
71 See R.P.C. 1957, p. 87.

order, which would provide the equivalent of after-care. The objection to this was that the probation order could not take effect immediately; it could only be justified as being based on a guess at the offender's needs in three months' time. On these grounds the practice was held to be illegal in 1958 by the Court of Criminal Appeal.[72]

This decision led to renewed pressure from interested persons for the introduction of compulsory after-care. Both the Advisory Council on the Treatment of Offenders [73] and the Ingleby Committee [74] supported the proposal. Legislation followed in 1961. The Criminal Justice Act provided for supervision for one year for all those released from detention centres; the sanction is recall to the centre for the period of remission, or for 14 days, whichever is the longer.[75]

Detention centres in practice

The centres are provided by the Prison Department of the Home Office, which has faced an almost impossible task in keeping pace with the demand from the courts for detention centre places.[76] The first centre, Campsfield House, had a waiting list within a few months of its opening in 1952. There are now eighteen centres, which received nearly 6,000 inmates in 1964. A special survey by the Prison Department in 1966 led to the preparation of plans for the provision of many more places, but financial and other difficulties may well delay their realisation.

Of the centres, the majority are for the senior age-group—between 17 and 21; one is an " open " centre. Four are junior centres, and one (Moor Court, opened in 1962) is for girls. In addition the psychiatric prison at Crendon receives some detention cases.

The régime is strict and brisk. The day begins with physical training before 7 a.m., and the inmates are kept active until the day ends about 9 p.m. Smoking is forbidden, there is great emphasis on physical fitness, and an almost obsessional concern with cleanliness; visitors to one centre are told repeatedly that the inmates have " eight baths and thirty-five washes " a week, and an alarming number of changes of clothing.

[72] *Evans* [1959] 1 W.L.R. 26.
[73] Report on the Treatment of Young Offenders, 1959.
[74] Report, Cmnd. 1191, paras. 326–330.
[75] Criminal Justice Act 1961, s. 13 and First Sched.
[76] See Home Office Circular 86/1962 for a prohibition of the practice of reserving places in advance.

Some controversy surrounds the emphasis on physical training, and what seemed to some observers a rather military form of discipline. The Prison Commissioners went to the lengths of publishing a defence of physical education in their report for 1956,[77] asserting that while for many boys in their first fortnight physical education was the least popular part of the day, opinion rapidly changed as they got fitter until it could be regarded as enjoyable recreation. This is borne out by Dunlop and McCabe who found a notable change in attitude on this point during the period of training.[78] The arrival of circuit-training, and more emphasis on team games have also helped.

On the general question of discipline, too, there have been changes since the early days of detention centres when the approach was over-militaristic. A conference of wardens held in 1963 discussed the matter:

> "The general feeling of the wardens was that it was necessary to have high standards of formal behaviour in the centre. The wardens agreed that exaggerated forms of behaviour, e.g., shoulder-high arm swinging and marching in Indian file were unnecessary. Some wardens also queried the necessity for the constant clothes changing that occurred during the day at the centre. On the other hand the majority of wardens said that time was not on their side and that simple practical lessons of personal behaviour had to be learned quickly and thoroughly, and that the strict discipline required for this and the high standards laid down were the only means of getting across the teaching of good habits in a short time." [79]

The real dispute is as to the importance of the particular good habits that are taught. Cleanliness and table manners matter; but do manners make the non-delinquent man? There has certainly been a much greater emphasis on more personal training in recent years, with experiments with discussion groups in some centres. It is also true that discipline problems tend to disappear as a particular centre becomes established.[80]

The normal three-month term is too short for trade training courses to be run. Vocational training is only available at

[77] R.P.C. 1956, p. 111.

[78] *Young Men in Detention Centres.*

[79] *Prisons and Borstals 1963*, p. 38. For details concerning disciplinary penalties, etc., see Detention Centre Rules 1952, S.I. 1952 No. 1432.

[80] See Dunlop and McCabe, *op cit.*, p. 19; and a warden quoted at R.P.C. 1961, p. 47.

Swinfen Hall where many of those serving six-month terms are sent. For the ordinary inmate, most of his time is spent on domestic work, on keeping the centre clean, and on work in the grounds. Only a few enter anything approaching a "prison industry," usually mat-making. Throughout the important thing is thought to be the standard of work; it does not matter that the work itself may be routine and unexciting.

The evidence of the Fabian Society to the Royal Commission on the Penal System is fair comment:

> "If one of the purposes of detention was to keep young people out of prison establishments was it ever intended that they should find themselves in an institution whose tone is more that of a prison than a school? . . . Detention is a restricting environment. Young people live under orders, and failure to obey brings immediate consequences. Except in so far as it aims to build a boy up physically detention does not set out to develop his potential as a person. Conformity is easy, and inmates can often give the right answers. But the system does nothing or little to develop young people's confidence in themselves or to turn them into more self-assured, self-reliant individuals." [81]

Sentencing practice

The effectiveness of detention centres was studied by Dr. Grünhut, whose views have been influential in forming sentencing policy.[82] He was convinced of the value of the centres, even for those with some considerable criminal experience, where they provided the first experience of institutional life. The results of detention where the person concerned had experience of approved schools were a good deal less satisfactory.

This led to an official attempt to guide the sentencing policy of the courts. A Home Office Circular [83] advised the courts:

> "For certain classes of boy, notably those who have already undergone long-term institutional training, have appeared many times in juvenile courts, show symptoms of maladjustment or more serious mental disturbance, are dull and backward, or are physically unfit for strenuous exercise,

[81] R.C.P.S., Vol. 2, pp. 102–103; but *quaere* whether the teaching of self-assurance is all that important.

[82] "Juvenile Delinquents under Punitive Detention" (1954–55) 5 B.J.D. 191; "After-Effects of Punitive Detention" (1959–60) 10 B.J.D. 178.

[83] Circular No. 37/1956. (March 15, 1956).

> detention centre treatment is generally found to be unsuitable. The most hopeful category is perhaps that of the well-developed, undisciplined young "rough" who has hitherto come off best in his conflicts with authority, and without having developed a bent for crime, requires to be taught a lesson, through an unpleasant experience and enforced discipline, that interference with other people and their property will be dealt with firmly and inescapably by society."

In one respect, this advice needs underlining. Offenders who are physically unfit are too often sent to detention centres. They have included boys with club feet, diabetics, epileptics, and one youth who had been under treatment for tuberculosis of the spine for thirteen years.[84] None of these should ever have received sentences of detention.

Many hold the view that *girls* should never be sent to detention centres. Clearly some girls may need short-term residential training, but there are doubts as to the suitability of the regime at Moor Court.[85]

Borstal Training

Borstal training is now the standard form of treatment for offenders aged between 15 and 21 in those cases "where the court is of opinion having regard to the circumstances of the offence and after taking into account the offender's character and previous conduct, that it is expedient that he should be detained for training for not less than six months."[86] As we have seen, detention centres provide short-term institutional treatment for this age-group; Borstals provide longer-term training, short of actual imprisonment. For the younger members of the age-group, approved schools provide an alternative form of longer-term training.

Borstal training is not wholly institutional. It involves both a period of institutional training and a further period of two years on licence under the supervision of a probation officer. The institutional period is indeterminate within the statutory limits of six months and two years. How long an individual offender remains in a Borstal depends upon the assessment of

84 *Jobes* [1962] Crim.L.R. 715; R.C.P.S., Vol. 3, p. 95 (Prison Officers' Assoc.).

85 See R.C.P.S., Vol. 2, pp. 11–12 (Magistrates' Assoc.); and *infra*, p. 264.

86 Criminal Justice Act 1948, s. 1 (2).

his needs, which determines the particular institution which receives him, and on his own response to training.

Borstals are now found in many parts of the world, but in origin they are wholly English, taking their name from the village in Kent where the first institution was established. They represent the English contribution to the solution of the problem of the young adult offender. The thinking behind their introduction can be seen with unusual clarity in the report of the Gladstone Committee (1895).[87]

Answering their own question " Where are the headsprings of recidivism? " the Committee said,[88]

> " It is certain that the ages when the majority of habitual criminals are made lies between 16 and 21. . . . It appears to us that the most determined effort should be made to lay hold of these incipient criminals and to prevent them by strong restraint and rational treatment from recruiting the habitual class. . . . The habitual criminals can only be effectually put down in one way, and that is by cutting off the supply."

This idea, that the 16–21-year-old age-group required separate and special treatment, now universally accepted, was then quite novel. It seems to have come from within the Committee and was received with some surprise by witnesses.[89] The Committee went on to develop its proposal for the treatment of these offenders.

> " We are of opinion that the experiment of establishing a penal reformatory under Government management should be tried. . . . The courts should have power to commit to these establishments offenders under the age of 23, for periods of not less than one year and up to three years, with a system of licences graduated according to sentence, which should be freely exercised. . . .
>
> The penal reformatory should be a half-way house between the prison and the reformatory [*i.e.*, the modern approved school]. It should be situated in the country with ample space for agricultural and land reclamation work. It would have penal and coercive sides which could be applied according to the merits of particular cases. But

87 A full account of the development of the Borstal system is to be found in Hood, *Borstal Re-assessed*.

88 Report, p. 11, para. 29.

89 See *e.g.*, the evidence of Capt. Stopford, representing the Prison Commissioners; *Minutes of Evidence*, especially questions 445–448.

it should be amply provided with a staff capable of giving sound education, training the inmates in various kinds of industrial work, and qualified generally to exercise the best and healthiest kind of moral influence." [90]

After a period of experiment, the Borstal system was given legal effect in the Prevention of Crime Act 1908, since modified in many particulars but similar in principle to the present legislation.

Legal framework

Before a sentence of Borstal training can be passed, the court must satisfy itself on a number of points:

1. The offence committed must be one punishable with imprisonment, in the case of an adult.[91]
2. The offender must be between 15 and 21 at the time of his conviction.[92]
3. The court must consider it expedient in all the circumstances for the offender to be detained for training for not less than six months.[93]
4. If the offender is under 17, the court must be satisfied that no other method of dealing with him is appropriate.[94]
5. In any case, the court must consider any report on the offender prepared by the Prison Department.[95]

Some of these points need further discussion.

Offence punishable with imprisonment

The statutory requirements are satisfied if the offence is punishable with a term of imprisonment, however short. There may seem to be a certain injustice in sending an offender, convicted of an offence carrying a maximum penalty of, say, three months' imprisonment, for a period of Borstal training which could involve his detention for two years. This difficulty has received attention from the courts.

In a number of cases, sentences of Borstal training were set aside when the maximum prison term was shorter.[96] But in

90 Report, pp. 30–31, para. 84 (b).
91 Criminal Justice Act 1948, s. 20 (1).
92 *Ibid.*, as amended by Criminal Justice Act 1961, s. 1 (1).
93 Criminal Justice Act 1961, s. 1 (2), cited above.
94 *Ibid.*, proviso.
95 *Ibid.* s. 1 (3).
96 *Longstreeth* (1952) [1960] 1 W.L.R. 812n.; *James* [1960] 1 W.L.R. 812. Both involved vagrancy offences, maximum term three months.

1961, a Full Court of Criminal Appeal held that these cases went too far if they suggested that Borstal was an impossible sentence in these circumstances: it was a factor to be weighed with others.[97]

General criteria for selecting Borstal training

The present position, that Borstal institutions cater for all offenders of this age-group needing more than short-term training, dates only from the coming into force of the Criminal Justice Act 1961. Before that time, the courts were required to go through a further, ill-defined, process before selecting a Borstal sentence. In the words of the 1948 Act, they had to be satisfied, " having regard to [the offender's] character and previous conduct, and to the circumstances of the offence, that it [was] expedient for his reformation and the prevention of crime that he should undergo a period of training in a Borstal institution."

As one would expect, a quantity of case-law grew up to explain these words. For example, in a number of cases the Court of Criminal Appeal set aside sentences of Borstal training on the ground that, while the offence was serious, the offender's " previous conduct " was not such as to justify a Borstal sentence.[98] In most of these cases, a medium term of imprisonment was substituted, a course not permissible since 1961. Generally, the policy was to use Borstal as a measure of reform, and other forms of treatment (often imprisonment) for punishment and deterrence.

The 1961 Act, and especially its further limitation on the use of imprisonment,[99] have changed this policy. Where imprisonment is not available the court must pass a Borstal sentence even where it feels that the offender is not in need of training but is in need of punishment. This was made clear by Lord Parker C.J. in *Lowe* [1]; he suggested that in these cases the judge should make his view known for the benefit of those deciding which Borstal should receive the offender. As he put it in a later case, Borstal training nowadays ranges from schooling to near imprisonment and the courts may indicate the kind of treatment they consider defendants should receive.[2]

97 *Amos* [1961] 1 W.L.R. 308; see *Appleyard* [1963] Crim.L.R. 62.

98 See, *e.g.*, *Smith* [1959] Crim.L.R. 868; *Gall* [1960] Crim.L.R. 640 is an illustration on the other side of the line.

99 See p. 251.

1 [1964] 1 W.L.R. 609.

2 *Angell* [1964] Crim.L.R. 553. On this and the next following section, see Hall Williams and Thomas [1965] Crim.L.R. 273–280.

Offenders under 17 years of age

If the offender is of juvenile court age, no court may impose a sentence of Borstal training unless it is satisfied that no other method of treatment is appropriate. For these offenders approved schools are available as an obvious alternative, but the court must consider all alternatives. A survey of the practice of the Court of Criminal Appeal in the first year of operation of the relevant parts of the 1961 Act [3] revealed that the cases in which sentences of Borstal training were upheld for offenders under 17 involved offenders who had already had experience of several institutions. If approved schools have been tried and failed, and the discipline of a detention centre had been equally unsuccessful there is really no alternative to Borstal training.

Reports and procedural matters

The court passing sentence of Borstal training must consider a report from the remand centre or prison in which the offender has been detained, if one is available.[4] The absence of a report does not prevent the passing of a sentence of Borstal training [5]; in most cases a report will be available.

When a report is presented, the court is not strictly speaking bound by the recommendation it contains, but it is a very strong thing for the court to act against the advice in the report.[6]

On the other hand, the Court of Criminal Appeal has sometimes approved such action. The report has been described as "one of the factors to be weighed up." [7] If the report is evidently based on incomplete information,[8] or if, despite the report, the court is unable to find another form of treatment which is suitable,[9] Borstal training may be upheld.

Under the present system of courts for offenders under 21, Borstal training is in a special position, for a magistrates' court cannot pass the sentence. If the magistrates consider the case

[3] The period August 1, 1963, to August 1, 1964; Hall Williams and Thomas [1965] Crim.L.R. 146, 193 and 273.

[4] Criminal Justice Act 1961, s. 1 (3); for procedural details see Practice Note [1959] 1 W.L.R. 849, and Home Office Circular 107/57 (May 29, 1957).

[5] *Lowe* [1964] 1 W.L.R. 609, 613.

[6] *Cf. Murray* [1951] 1 K.B. 391, a corrective training case where similar principles applied.

[7] *Tilton* [1957] Crim.L.R. 456.

[8] *Taylor* (1956) 40 Cr.App.R. 170.

[9] *Cox* [1954] Crim.L.R. 63. This situation will be more frequent since the coming into force of the Criminal Justice Act 1961. See also Mannheim and Wilkins, *Prediction Methods in Relation to Borstal Training*, pp. 105–106: in 1946–47, 25 per cent. of Borstal boys were there despite their having been reported as unsuitable.

suitable for Borstal training, they must commit the offender to quarter sessions for sentence of Borstal training.[10] In the usual case the offender is committed in custody to a remand centre, if one is available, or a prison, and there reports can be prepared for quarter sessions.

Quarter sessions, having considered all the circumstances of the case and the reports may either pass the Borstal sentence or pass any other sentence available to the lower court at the date of committal.[11]

Mention may be made here of the power of the Home Secretary, after consultation with the court which passed the original sentence, to transfer to a Borstal institution a prisoner who is under 21.[12] Magistrates' courts may also order transfers to Borstal, of persons detained in approved schools on the application of the approved school managers.[13]

The form of Borstal training

We have already seen that the period of detention in a Borstal institution must be between six months and two years.[14] Until 1961 the limits were *nine* months and *three* years; now, the lower limit may well be changed again, for " experience with Borstal training has shown that the present minimum period of six months is too short to enable good results to be achieved." [15] The average length of training is at present about 16 months, but this is not a particularly significant figure, as each Borstal inmate has his needs assessed quite separately.

Allocation

As soon as possible after sentence, the allocation process begins at one of the Borstal Allocation Centres, Wormwood Scrubs and Manchester for boys and Bulwood for girls. It is unfortunate that the southern allocation centre for boys should still be housed in a prison, especially as there was formerly

10 Magistrates' Courts Act 1952, s. 28, as amended. On the arguments for and against the present procedure see Samuels [1961] Crim.L.R. 755.

11 Criminal Justice Act 1948, s. 20 (5); *Hammond* [1963] 2 Q.B. 450. For the alternative method of committal under s. 29 see *Dangerfield* [1960] 1 W.L.R. 269, and for a snag which this may cause, *Robinson* [1963] Crim.L.R. 206.

12 Prison Act 1952, s. 44 (1), as amended.

13 Criminal Justice Act 1961, s. 16 (1). It is government policy to abolish the use of Borstals for offenders under 17 when other facilities are available: *Children in Trouble*, para. 23.

14 Prison Act 1952, s. 45 (2) as amended by Criminal Justice Act 1961.

15 *The Child, the Family and the Young Offender*, para. 39.

a separate centre at Latchmere House, converted into a detention centre in 1964.

The actual process of allocation has been the subject of some criticism. The few weeks spent in the allocation centre are intended to be used in telling the inmate what will be expected of him in Borstal, gathering full information as to his needs and capabilities, and selecting the particular training Borstal which meets those needs and capabilities. With this in view, he receives medical and psychological examinations, his educational standard is tested, and his interests, both in terms of hobbies and possible vocational training, are inquired into. All this information is passed to the selected institution when the allocation decision has been made.

The Borstal Rules expressly provide that "methods of training may vary as between one Borstal and another,"[16] and it is this which requires and justifies the allocation procedure. As in prisons, the most obvious and important distinctions are those between closed and open institutions. Others are concerned with the age of the inmates, location, facilities for particular trades and vocational training, educational opportunities, and, perhaps most important, in general atmosphere. Some institutions have an authoritarian regime, others are more permissive, giving the maximum possible responsibility to the boys themselves.

Allocation should balance all these factors. In practice, there are periods during which most of the closed institutions are full. Allocation may deteriorate into finding a vacancy in some institution not wholly unsuited to the needs of the offender. Finer points, such as the availability of particular trades, may be neglected. In times of great pressure, too much attention may be paid to the Mannheim-Wilkins predictive device.[17]

It may also be that criticism of the allocation procedure is one aspect of the growing concern amongst Borstal governors at the quality of their intake.

"*Quality*"

There is evidence that Borstal boys received in recent years are of poorer "quality" than was the case in the past. "The

16 Borstal Rules 1964, r. 2 (1).

17 H. Mannheim and L. T. Wilkins, *Prediction Methods in Relation to Borstal Training* (H.M.S.O., 1955). For an analysis of the method of reaching allocation decisions, see Morrison, "Borstal Allocation," (1957–58) 8 B.J.D. 95–105. For criticisms see Hood, *op. cit.*, pp. 159 *et seq.*, 213–215.

bulk of the population has now become more resistant to training than was the case two years ago. The receptions which we are getting are more suspicious and shut-in, less ready to respond to a friendly approach, more ready to exploit trust and abuse privileges than they were previously." [18] A Governor has described the average Borstal boy as "eighteen years of age, dull in mind, having a bad record, a poor home and an uncertain future." [19] In recent years, drug addiction has been more frequent.

Perhaps more important is the evidence that the present Borstal population is producing lower scores than earlier samples on the Mannheim-Wilkins equation. Although that equation is sufficiently old to need revision, the number of high scores being obtained does seem to be declining. To some extent this can be explained as a result of the abandonment of selectivity in the 1961 legislation, but other factors are probably at work.[20] Whatever the explanation for these changes, they have obvious implications for training policies.

Some indication of the criminal sophistication of the Borstal population can be obtained from the following table, which relates to Borstal boys received in 1965.[21]

	Previous offences	*Previous institutional sentences* [22]
0	124	1,337
1	259	1,563
2	439	645
3	612	249
4	684	95
5	605	19
6–10	1,131	14
11–20	68	1
20+	1	–
	3,923	3,923

[18] Quoted, R.P.D. 1965, p. 20.

[19] R.P.C. 1962, p. 32.

[20] See Little, "The 'Quality' of Borstal Receptions" (1965) 5 B.J.Crim. 190–196, and his earlier Note at (1962) 2 B.J.Crim. 266.

[21] Source: R.P.D. (Tables) 1965, Table D.9.

[22] Includes 224 previous Borstal sentences.

Training

The Borstal Rules set out some general principles of Borstal training:

"The purpose of Borstal training requires that every inmate, while conforming to the rules necessary for well-ordered community life, shall be able to develop his individuality on right lines with a proper sense of personal responsibility. Accordingly officers shall, while firmly maintaining order and discipline, seek to do so by influencing the inmates through their own example and leadership and enlisting their willing co-operation.

"The objects of Borstal training shall be to bring to bear every influence which may establish in the inmates the will to lead a good and useful life on release, and to fit them to do so by the fullest possible development of their character, capabilities and sense of personal responsibility." [23]

These principles lay great stress on the role of the staff of the institution. Traditionally the staff of Borstals have exercised their influence principally through the "house system." [24] Each boy is a member of a house, a small community which is expected to command his loyalty. More important than the house itself is the housemaster who has special responsibility for the training of the boys in his house and who has the greatest opportunities for exerting his influence.

Experiments within the Borstal system aimed at improving the training given have weakened the house system in recent years. For example, at one Borstal the basic unit became a group of twelve boys within, in turn, an induction unit, a junior wing, a senior wing, and a discharge hostel.[25]

At another Borstal, experiments with different programmes for inmates who have committed different types of offence were reported to have aroused "great resistance from the entrenched house system." [26]

Another technique relatively recently introduced into Borstals is group counselling. This was first tried in 1957 at Pollington Borstal, an institution which catered especially for boys with good prediction scores. Similar methods, either group counselling in a strict sense or discussion groups run on similar lines, are now found in most Borstals. They appear equally

[23] Borstal Rules 1964, r. 1.
[24] *Ibid.* r. 4.
[25] R.P.C. 1962, p. 30.
[26] R.P.D. 1964, p. 24.

successful with boys with only an average prediction score, and early anxieties as to the effect of counselling on the traditional role of the housemaster have abated.[27]

Work and education in Borstals

The routine of a Borstal institution is built around a full working day. The Borstal Rules stipulate a normal working week of 44 hours[28]; in sharp contrast with the situation in prison there is no shortage of work or of workshop facilities.

Equally important for the Borstal age-group are opportunities for vocational training. The whole question of work and vocational training in Borstals was examined in a report published in 1962[29]; the picture is a favourable one. About a third of Borstal inmates receive vocational training. This has in the past usually been in a skilled trade, the course leading to an examination set by the prison authorities; since the 1962 report, efforts have been made to provide training courses for those boys who will never make skilled craftsmen, to familiarise them with the tools and procedures of, for example, building site work.

In several cases, inmates undergoing vocational training may attend courses at local technical colleges, and obtain practical experience in local industry. Some take the examinations of outside examining bodies, and some pass with high honours.

All Borstals have education classes in addition to vocational training. For a few, these provide opportunities for continued formal education leading to G.C.E. examination. At the other extreme, classes for illiterates or semi-illiterates are necessary. For the majority any suggestion of formal schooling is anathema, and instead attempts are made to encourage the inmates to think about and express themselves on current problems of more general interest.

Physical education is popular, and an enormous range of activities can be found in the various institutions. Athletics, gymnastics, weight-lifting and swimming can all take place within Borstals; canoeing, fell-walking and camping (sometimes with groups of university students) provide opportunities for travel outside the institution.

27 See Bishop, "Group Work at Pollington Borstal," (1960) 10 *Howard Journal* 185–193.

28 Borstal Rules 1964, s. 29.

29 Advisory Council on the Employment of Prisoners (2nd Report), "Work and Vocational Training in Borstals," 1962.

Discipline

The Borstal Rules prescribe in detail punishments available to the Governor, or in serious cases the Board of Visitors or the Home Secretary for breaches of discipline.[30] The most frequently used punishments are removal from House for a period, confinement to room, restricted diet, stoppage of earnings, and reduction in grade or delayed promotion to a higher grade; the effect of this latter punishment does, of course, depend on the system of grades adopted by the Governor of the particular Borstal. In some Borstals, experiments have been made in giving some disciplinary powers to a committee of inmates.

There are some inmates who cannot be adequately disciplined in their training Borstal. They can be transferred to the correction centre at Reading, which, as its name suggests has a regime of strict discipline.

Reading also receives some absconders. Absconding—the word "escape" is not part of the Borstal vocabulary—is a serious problem, growing in recent years. In 1965, when the daily population was nearing 5,000, there were 1,129 absconders. If they are sent to the correction centre, they usually return to their "own" Borstal to complete their normal training.

In extreme cases, the Home Secretary, on the advice of a Board of Visitors, may transfer an incorrigible Borstal boy to prison.[31]

Release and after-care

At some stage in his training, usually towards the end, an inmate is allowed the highly-prized privilege of home leave. This was originally designed to give him a chance to meet his future supervisor and to inquire about a job to which he might go on release. It still serves these functions, but it is also recognised as providing a break from institutional routine, and the chance to strengthen relationships with family and friends at home. Inevitably some abscond; but never more than 3 or 4 per cent.

The date of actual release is fixed by the Board of Visitors on the advice of the Governor, and his Institution Board composed of members of the staff. It is followed by supervision for two years, with the sanction of recall, either to Reading or to

30 Borstal Rules 1964, rr. 46 *et seq.* The Board of Visitors, at least two of whom must be J.P.s, have duties similar to those of prison Boards of Visitors. See Prison Act 1952, s. 6.

31 Prison Act 1952, s. 44 (2) as amended.

Portsmouth where experiments are being made with a "more relaxed, almost permissive atmosphere." [32]

After-care arrangements were formerly made by Borstal After-Care, the Borstal Division of the Central After-Care Association. As that organisation runs down, more of the work is being handled by the staff of the Borstals, the housemasters dealing directly with the Probation and After-Care Service.[33]

One of the most difficult problems is the provision of suitable after-care for homeless boys, who may be too institutionalised to settle in lodgings; to place them in a hostel is merely to substitute one institution for another. An experimental home for some of these cases has been established in London: it aims to be "home," not "a home," and has a very supportive regime, with considerable help from a psychiatrist.[34]

What if a Borstal trainee offends again? In 1958, the Court of Criminal Appeal considered the merits of second and third sentences of Borstal training. In some cases a second sentence may be desirable, but cases where a third period of training could be appropriate must be rare.[35] For such cases, imprisonment may be the only sentence, and the rules governing the availability of imprisonment for young offenders recognise this fact.[36]

IMPRISONMENT

The introduction to this Part traced the growth of limitations on the imprisonment of young offenders. This section examines briefly the present position. As the Table on page 180 shows, this is not unimportant; despite the Criminal Justice Act 1961 there are nearly 3,000 prison sentences each year on offenders under 21; and this figure is well over half the corresponding figure for Borstal training. In 1965, the figures were 3,137 prison and 4,048 Borstal receptions.

Legal framework

The prohibition of the imprisonment of young persons under the age of 17 is now absolute; it applies to all courts of what-

32 R.P.D. 1964, p. 29.

33 See *Probation and Borstal After-Care*, 1964, pp. 11–12.

34 Hood, *Homeless Borstal Boys*; Miller, *Growth to Freedom*.

35 *Noseda* [1958] 1 W.L.R. 793; much of the detail in this judgment does not survive the Criminal Justice Act 1961. A case in which a third period of Borstal training was upheld is *Roderick* (1966) 51 Cr.App.R. 70.

36 Criminal Justice Act 1961, s. 3 (3), see p. 251.

ever rank.[37] Imprisonment of those between 17 and 21 is subject to a number of safeguards.

1. A sentence of imprisonment is only available if the court is of opinion that no other method of dealing with the offender is appropriate. Before the court forms this opinion it must obtain and consider information about the circumstances of the case, and consider any available information about the character and mental and physical condition of the offender.[38] Quarter sessions and magistrates' courts which form such an opinion must state their reasons in open court, and in the case of magistrates, must record them in both the warrant of commitment and in the court register.[39]

2. Since the coming into force of the Criminal Justice Act 1961 there have been further limitations designed to prevent the passing of medium term, and ultimately of short term sentences of imprisonment.

As a general rule, the sentence can only be for a term *either* not exceeding six months *or* not less than three years.[40] As soon as sufficient detention centre accommodation is available for all those sentenced to short-term training, the power to pass sentences of imprisonment for six months or less will be removed by Order in Council.[41] The position will then be that only sentences of three years and over will be available in the usual case.

There are certain exceptions to these rules. An offender who has served a previous prison sentence of six months or more, or who has completed the institutional part of Borstal training, and is then reconvicted may be sentenced to imprisonment for any term of not less than 18 months.[42]

Finally, there are no limitations on the length of sentence which may be imposed on an offender who, at the time of sentence, is already detained in prison under sentence or on recall from release on supervision or licence.[43]

37 Magistrates' Courts Act 1952, s. 107 (2); Criminal Justice Act 1948, s. 17 (1) as amended by Criminal Justice Act 1961.

38 Criminal Justice Act 1948, s. 17 (2).

39 Criminal Justice Act 1948, s. 17 (3); Magistrates' Courts Act 1952, s. 107 (3); *Frew* [1964] Crim.L.R. 220.

40 Criminal Justice Act 1961, s. 3 (1); magistrates' courts will not, of course, be able themselves to pass sentences for the longer term.

41 *Ibid.* s. 3 (5).

42 Criminal Justice Act 1961, s. 3 (3).

43 *Ibid.* s. 3 (2).

Sentencing practice

The introduction of the limitations on medium-term prison sentences for young offenders caused some little difficulty in the courts.

One difficulty was essentially a transitional one. In a number of cases, the judge felt that the appropriate sentence was one of imprisonment rather than Borstal training, and that a medium-term sentence, of perhaps two years' duration, was required. Faced with the provisions of the 1961 Act, the judge imposed the minimum possible prison sentence for such a case, that is one of three years. In fact the scheme of the 1961 Act is that all medium-term training is to take place in Borstals. The correct procedure therefore, having determined the length of training required, is to commit for Borstal training and not to increase the sentence so that a prison sentence is possible.[44]

The major difficulty is caused by the importance in the new scheme of the period of three years. If the appropriate sentence is one of three years or more, there is no question of Borstal training, and imprisonment is legally possible.

The practice of the Court of Appeal on this point places great emphasis on the nature of the offence. Serious crimes of violence, sexual or otherwise, and property offences involving especially valuable property have been treated as justifying the three-year sentence. If the offence is of this degree of seriousness, the youth or good record of the offender will rarely help him.[45] Put crudely, the point has been reached at which rehabilitative thinking is rejected in favour of "old-fashioned deterrence." The reasonableness of this policy was accepted without discussion when the proposals which led up to the 1961 Act were before the Advisory Council on the Treatment of Offenders: one may well question its validity.[46]

Treatment

Generalisations are difficult about this group of young prisoners. Some may be serving very short terms, and may spend the whole time in the local prison to which they were originally committed. Where possible, these short-term prisoners will be transferred to special centres in other prisons, and

[44] *Lowe* [1964] 1 W.L.R. 609; *Brown* [1964] Crim.L.R. 418; *Angell* [1964] Crim.L.R. 553; *Cronin* [1964] Crim.L.R. 331 is a similar case under s. 3 (3).

[45] See the elaborate survey by Hall Williams and Thomas in [1965] Crim.L.R. 193–206.

[46] *The Treatment of Young Offenders*, 1959; see, *e.g.*, para. 60.

attempts have been made to introduce as far as possible a regime akin to that of detention centres.

In all the centres for young prisoners physical exercise and vocational training are stressed. The latter is especially important for the long-term prisoners who are allocated partly on a regional basis, and partly in accordance with the length of their sentence.[47] In some young prisoners' centres housing the long-term prisoners, attempts have been made to institute a regime similar to that found in a closed Borstal. The determinate nature of the sentences being served, and the criminal sophistication of many of the young prisoners make it very difficult to establish any satisfactory regime for a group whose prospects are singularly unpromising.

Special forms of detention

Mention must be made of two types of case in which a young offender can be detained which fall into none of the categories already considered. In each case the offender is " liable to be detained in such place and on such conditions as the Secretary of State may direct "; the language is deliberately imprecise, for these cases are exceptional and of special difficulty. A scheme of treatment has to be designed individually in each case.

The first type of case is one in which the offender has committed murder, or technically any of the offences which remain capital.[48] In such a case, no offender under the age of 18 may be sentenced to death or to life imprisonment, but is instead ordered " to be detained during Her Majesty's pleasure,"[49] an indeterminate sentence amounting to life sentence except that it may be served elsewhere than in an adult prison.

The second type of case leads to a determinate sentence. The relevant provision is as follows:

> " Where a child or young person is convicted on indictment of any offence punishable in the case of an adult with imprisonment for 14 years or more, not being an offence the sentence for which is fixed by law, and the court is of opinion that none of the other methods in which the case

[47] Details of the centres available are given in the annual Reports of the Prison Department.

[48] Treason, piracy, arson of H.M. dockyards; the contingency is about as remote as may be.

[49] Children and Young Persons Act 1933, s. 53 (1), substituted by Murder (Abolition of Death Penalty) Act 1965, s. 1 (5).

may legally be dealt with is suitable, the court may sentence the offender to be detained for such period, not exceeding the maximum term of imprisonment with which the offence is punishable in the case of an adult, as may be specified in the sentence. . . ." [50]

This represents what American writers describe as "a give-it-up formula" to cover extreme cases where prolonged detention is thought necessary, but cannot be ordered in any of the normal legal guises. If the court cannot even fix an appropriate period it can order detention for life, leaving the Home Office to sort out what should be done.[51]

Bibliography

Official publications and reports include:

Reports on the Work of the Children's Department (H.M.S.O. triennial).

Statistics relating to Approved Schools, Remand Homes and Attendance Centres (H.M.S.O. annual).

Directory of Approved Schools, Remand Homes and Special Reception Centres in England and Wales (H.M.S.O.).

Children in Care in England and Wales (H.M.S.O. annual).

Report on the Work of the Prison Department (H.M.S.O. annual).

Report of the Departmental Committees on the Treatment of Young Offenders 1927—the Molony Report (Cmnd. 2831).

Report of the Committee on Children and Young Persons 1960—the Ingleby Report (Cmnd. 1191).

Report of the Committee on Children and Young Persons (Scotland) 1964—the Kilbrandon Report (Cmnd. 2306).

The Child, the Family and the Young Offender 1965 (Cmnd. 2742).

Report of the Committee on the Age of Majority 1967 (Cmnd. 3342).

Children in Trouble (Cmnd. 3601).

Other references:

(1) *General and juvenile courts*

AUBREY, M., "The Future of Juvenile Courts" [1965] Crim.L.R. 641.

[50] Children and Young Persons Act 1933, s. 53 (2), as amended by Criminal Justice Act 1961, ss. 2 and 41; see Hall Williams and Thomas [1965] Crim.L.R. at 279–280, and *Knowles* [1966] Crim.L.R. 57.

[51] *Abbott* [1964] 1 Q.B. 489.

BARRETT, BROWN, and CRAMER, " Juvenile Delinquents, The Police, State Courts, and Individualised Justice " (1966) 79 *Harvard Law Review* 775.

CALDWELL, R. G., " The Juvenile Court: its development and some major problems " (1961) 51 J.C.L.C. & P.S. 493.

CAVENAGH, W. E., Juvenile Courts, The Child and the Law (Penguin, 1967).

GRÜNHUT, M., Juvenile Offenders before the Courts (O.U.P., 1948).

Liverpool City Police: The Police and Children (2nd ed., 1962).

LORD LONGFORD'S group: Crime—a Challenge to us all (Labour Party, 1964).

NYQUIST, O., Juvenile Justice (Macmillan, 1960).

PATCHETT, K. W., and MCCLEAN, J. D., " Decision-Making in Juvenile Cases " [1965] Crim.L.R. 699.

SCOTT, P. D., " Juvenile Courts, the Juvenile's Point of View " (1958–59) 9 B.J.D. 200.

Twelfth International Penal and Penitentiary Congress, Proceedings, vol. 6.

VOELCKER, P. M. V., " Juvenile Courts: the Parents' Point of View " (1960–61) 1 B.J.Crim. 154.

WATSON, J. A. F., The Child and the Magistrate (3rd ed., Jonathan Cape, 1965).

WEST, D. J., The Young Offender (Penguin, 1964).

WILLIAMS, G. L., " The Criminal Responsibility of Children " [1954] Crim.L.R. 493.

WOOTTON, B., " The Juvenile Courts " [1961] Crim.L.R. 669.

(2) *Attendance centres*

GOODMAN, N., " Manchester Senior Attendance Centre " (1965) 5 B.J.Crim. 275.

MCCUNTOCK, F. H., Attendance Centres (Macmillan, 1961).

(3) *Remand homes*

RADZINOWICZ, L. (ed.): Detention in Remand Homes (Macmillan, 1952).

(4) *Approved schools*

GITTENS, J., Approved School Boys (H.M.S.O., 1952).

SCOTT, P. D., " Approved School Success Rates " (1964) 4 B.J.Crim. 525.

Rose, A. G., Schools for Young Offenders (Tavistock, 1967).

See also a series of monographs issued by the Association of Headmasters, Headmistresses and Matrons of Approved Schools; and the following:

Disturbances at the Carlton Approved School 1960 (Cmnd. 937).

Administration of Punishment at Court Lees Approved School 1967 (Cmnd. 3367).

(5) *Detention centres*

Council of Europe: Short-Term Methods of Treatment for Young Offenders, 1967.

Dunlop, A. B., and McCabe, S., Young Men in Detention Centres (Kegan Paul, 1965).

Grünhut, M., "Juvenile Delinquents under Preventive Detention" (1954–55) 5 B.J.D. 191.

—— "After-effects of Punitive Detention" (1959–60) 10 B.J.D. 178.

(6) *Borstal training*

The classic statement of the aims of Borstal training is to be found in

Paterson, A., The Principles of the Borstal System (Prison Commission, 1932).

For a more recent view, see

Hood, R., Borstal Re-assessed (Heinemann, 1965).

Other references:

Bishop, N., "Group Work at Pollington Borstal" (1960) 10 *Howard Journal* 185.

Epps, P. Two articles on Borstal girls (1950–51) 1 B.J.D. 187 and (1953–54) 3 B.J.D. 265.

Gibbens, T. C. N., Psychiatric Studies of Borstal Lads (Oxford, 1963).

Hood, R., Homeless Borstal Boys (Bell, 1966).

Little, A., "Penal Theory, Penal Reform and Borstal Practice" (1963) 3 B.J.Crim. 257.

—— "The 'Quality' of Borstal Receptions" (1965) 5 B.J.Crim. 190.

Mannheim, H., and Wilkins, L. T., Prediction Methods in relation to Borstal Training (H.M.S.O., 1955).

MILLER D.: Growth to Freedom (Tavistock, 1964).
MORRISON, R. L., "Borstal Allocation" (1957–58) 8 B.J.D. 95.
ROSE, A. G., 500 Borstal Boys (Blackwell, 1954).
THOMAS, D. A., "Sentencing Young Offenders" [1963] Crim.L.R. 536.
—— and HALL WILLIAMS, J. E., "Use of Imprisonment and Borstal Training" [1965] Crim.L.R. 146, 193 and especially 273.
Work and Vocational Training in Borstals (A.C.E.P., 1962).

Chapter 6

SPECIAL GROUPS

Women and Girls

Crime is overwhelmingly a masculine affair. Women offenders are few in number, their offences differ from men's, and their treatment presents special problems. Clearly, even if the criminal law seldom distinguishes between the sexes, the penologist must.

Crime amongst women

In 1966, 86·5 per cent. of those found guilty of indictable offences were men. There were more women than men in the population at risk; allowing for this, criminality amongst men is more than six times as great as amongst women.[1] It has been estimated that 29 per cent. of all men in England and Wales will be convicted of an indictable offence at some time during their lives; for women the figure is only 7 per cent.[2]

Lady Wootton's comment would seem a fair one: ". . . it would seem that the overwhelming dominance of the male in this, as in many other fields, although clearly subject to challenge more particularly by the younger generation, cannot yet be said to be seriously threatened." [3]

The figures must, of course, be treated with caution, for the *Criminal Statistics* may well be at their least accurate on this point. There is a reluctance to initiate proceedings against women, and their crimes include many which most often pass undetected.

There are a few offences committed more often by women than by men. They include some offences which only women can commit, such as infanticide; a group of offences involving childbirth or the upbringing of children, such as concealment of birth, abortion, child-stealing or cruelty to children; offences connected with prostitution; and some forms of larceny, an offence which dominates the calendar of women's crime even more than that of men. In particular, the larceny takes the

[1] *Criminal Statistics* 1965, Introductory Note, Appendix II.
[2] Radzinowicz, *Ideology and Crime*, pp. 62 and 129.
[3] *Crime and the Criminal Law*, p. 5.

form of shoplifting. Women offenders easily outnumber men in this category, so far as adults are concerned though not in the younger age-groups.

This is not the place for a discussion of the causes of crime amongst women, and there is in fact very little known about the subject.[4] It will be noticed, though, that many of the offences listed in the last paragraph are related to a woman's traditional functions, keeping house, doing the shopping, bringing up the children. Certainly some women offend because they cannot make ends meet, they really need more money to clothe and feed the family. This may be due to the woman's inability to plan a budget, to her husband's meanness, to illness, or just to a state of mind in which the wife feels unable either to cope or to ask for help or advice.

There is a wide agreement that " the forces which influence the delinquency of young women are generally far more complex, deep-seated and difficult to eradicate than in the case of young men." [5] There is evidence, too, of a link between some offences by women and physical conditions associated with menstruation, pregnancy and the menopause. A small group of women offenders are unusually disturbed, violent and aggressive.[6]

In the circumstances, the courts might be expected to require fuller social and medical information on women offenders before reaching sentencing decisions. There is no evidence that this information is in fact obtained. On the contrary, Dr. Grünhut expressed surprise at the small proportion of women shoplifters who receive medical treatment, citing one particular case of a married woman of 69, of good social position, living apart from her husband, who had had twelve convictions, and six prison sentences in fifteen years. Only on her thirteenth conviction did medical evidence lead to a probation order with a condition as to medical treatment.[7]

Sentencing policy

Because women's crimes are different from those of men it is difficult to make any meaningful comparisons between the sentences passed on the two groups. It is possible to make a

4 For a good review of the literature, see Ann Smith, *Women in Prison*, Part I, and see McCabe, " *Studies of Female offenders* " [1968] Crim.L.R. 207.

5 Smith, *op. cit.*, pp. 193, 100 *et seq.*

6 See R.C.P.S., Vol. 2, p. 322 (Visiting Committee, Holloway).

7 Grünhut, *Probation and Mental Treatment*, p. 13.

number of assertions based on the statistics and on observation in the courts.

It is clear that the courts are very reluctant to pass sentences of imprisonment on women. The small number of prison sentences can be explained in part as reflecting the pettiness of many of their offences, but even in cases serious enough to go to quarter sessions or assizes imprisonment is used with marked restraint. The courts are understandably influenced by the position a woman occupies in the home, by the effect on any children of her removal. Imprisonment of a husband and father is disturbing enough to any family; imprisonment of the mother even more so. Mothers whose husbands are in prison can usually keep the children, with the aid of Non-Contributory Benefit (formerly National Assistance). When the mother is removed, the children must almost always be cared for by someone other than their father.

For young girls the same argument applies in reverse. Where the home is not wholly unsatisfactory, the courts are most reluctant to take a girl away from her parents. 7·5 per cent. of boys aged between 14 and 17 convicted of indictable offences are sent to approved schools; only 3 per cent. of the girls. The result is that girls' approved schools contain more girls committed by juvenile courts under their "civil" jurisdiction, that is mainly care and protection cases, than actual offenders.

There are very few *long* prison sentences passed on women. In a single year, over 2,000 men received sentences of two years or more; the corresponding number of women would be between thirty and forty. This means a very large proportion of women prisoners are received under short sentences, which are open to all the objections directed against short sentences for men.[8]

On the other hand, probation orders [9] are made more readily in cases involving women offenders than men. This is true for all age-groups, but especially where the offender is aged between 17 and 30, significantly the ages at which the woman is most likely to be caring for young children. The high use of probation would seem to reflect not only this factor, but also a belief that a woman's offence is often a symptom of some emotional problem which a sympathetic probation officer can resolve. Women probationers are more likely to complete their period of probation successfully than men, but the power to terminate a probation

[8] See above, pp. 124 *et seq.*

[9] For statistics, see *Criminal Statistics*, Introductory Note, Chap. VII; *Trends and Regional Comparisons in Probation* (H.M.S.O., 1966), esp. Chap. 2.

order before the end of its normal term is used marginally less frequently where women are concerned. This last fact may simply be the result of the smaller case-load carried by women probation officers, who may be under less pressure to have orders discharged as soon as it becomes possible. Or it may reflect the desire of the officer to continue her supportive role as long as possible.

The treatment of women and girls

To an appalling degree, the history of the penal treatment of women is the same as that of men. Dr. Ann Smith's admirable historical survey, *Women in Prison,* contains very little about women as a separate category until her account reaches the present century. The prison service has always been run by men—Holloway's first woman Governor was appointed in 1945—and with the needs of the male prisoners in mind.

In earlier centuries, there was no segregation of the sexes in penal institutions. Even in the nineteenth century, when this was of course established, women were sent to the hulks and transported to what was often a life of domestic slavery or prostitution in the colonies.[10] Women's prisons had the same plank beds as men's. On the other hand, the work in women's prisons of women like Elizabeth Fry is one of the brighter parts of English penal history.[11]

We are, however, more concerned with the modern situation, and some comment will be made on treatment in prison, Borstals and the detention centre in turn. Two general points may be made. The first is that the smallness of the number of women and girls in custody makes it very difficult to provide an adequate range of treatment. Different categories of prisoner—Borstal recall girls and preventive detainees—must be housed in the same institution, though in separate divisions. Vocational training and other forms of activity are more difficult to arrange when numbers are small; for example, the number of women with the interest or ability to take a particular course may be too small for the class to be viable.

The second point concerns staff. It is arguable that women prisoners' officers have a more difficult task than their male counterparts. Recruitment is extremely difficult, and wastage high, so that staffing problems are a constant anxiety.

10 Smith, *op. cit.*, Chap. 7.
11 *Ibid.* Chap. 8.

In prison

The annual reports of the Prison Department seldom provide material for satirists and cartoonists; one remark in the 1965 Report turned out to be an exception. "The old type of reliable, hardworking woman prisoner seems no longer to exist."[12]

The decreasing population, some 700 in all, is becoming a more difficult group. It includes drug addicts, women who are mentally or emotionally disturbed, others who are apathetic or socially inadequate, pregnant women (who almost always have their babies in outside hospitals, and may keep their babies with them until the child is nine months old, and sometimes longer), and even some with husbands also in prison.

There are two special groups who present special problems, the alcoholics and the prostitutes. Many return to prison frequently and for short sentences. For the majority, little can be done. The alcoholic can be cleaned up, the prostitute given medical treatment; both are soon released, to resume their old habits—the prostitute may well be fitter and bonnier than on reception, and so leaves prison with her trade prospects enhanced! For a few of the younger prostitutes, group counselling sessions seem to offer some hope.[13]

Generally speaking, the organisation of women's prisons is similar to men's, but there are points of difference. Women are more concerned about their surroundings, and may need training in domestic management. Wherever possible, for example at Styal, the main women's prison in the North, once "cottage-homes," a house-system operates, the women decorating the house and preparing the food to a fixed budget. There are some prisoners for whom this responsibility is too great, and more conventional secure provision is made for them.

A large number of women prisoners need medical treatment; even more demand it. Medical facilities are well developed both at Styal and in Holloway,[14] the depressing, obsolescent London prison. (It was decided in 1937 that Holloway should be replaced; it is not unreasonable to expect that the decision will be implemented within the next ten years.)

Another aspect of the prison service under particular strain in a women's prison is that concerning welfare and after-care.

[12] R.P.D. 1965, p. 34.

[13] See Joanna Kelley, *When the Gates Shut*, pp. 42, 114. For alcoholics, see Woodside, "Women Drinkers admitted to Holloway" (1960–61) 1 B.J.Crim. 221.

[14] A full and fascinating account of Holloway prison, as seen by a former Governor, is contained in Joanna Kelley's book; see last note.

A woman's links with her family outside need to be maintained, especially where there are children, who may well be in the care of a local authority. The location of accommodation for discharged prisoners, especially those with illegitimate children, is an acute problem.

In Borstals

Once again, this is a difficult and unhappy group of offenders. A sad illustration is the case of A, discharged from Borstal at the age of 18.

> " She had previously been placed in the care of a Children's Department when her father was convicted of incest against her, and later, because of her unsatisfactory behaviour, committed to an approved school where she could receive psychiatric treatment; this in itself will indicate that she is of above average intelligence. She absconded from the school so many times (twenty-two successful and eight abortive attempts, according to the headmistress's report) that she was ' unavailable ' for psychiatric treatment. On discharge from Borstal, she could not, for various reasons, return home, and she was found a residential job with an understanding employer and an equally understanding supervisor. She disappeared after ten days, and so began a saga which included multiple journeyings up and down the country on lorries, an uncountable number of unsuccessful attempts to resettle her in lodgings, hostels and/or jobs, and five appearances before the court, leading to two recalls to Borstal and lastly to a prison sentence, which she is now serving. A gave birth to an illegitimate daughter while on her second recall; she also had at least one miscarriage (on one of her lorry trips to Scotland)." [15]

In the circumstances, it is scarcely surprising that a large amount of staff time and effort goes into listening to and trying to solve the personal problems of the girls, some of whom have high intelligence and potential. Inevitably some of the girls are rebellious; attempts are made to deflect their energies into hard work, wherever possible outdoors. There is a growing emphasis on "normality" in training conditions: male instructors are used, some girls on recall wear civilian clothes, and girls with babies have them with them during training.[16]

15 " Prison and Borstal After-Care " (C.A.C.A. Annual Report, 1964), p. 22.
16 There is a special mother-and-child unit at Exeter.

Girls of Borstal age who have been sentenced to imprisonment —" young prisoners "—are not separated from the older women but are detained with them at Styal. An attempt was made in 1964 to create a separate " house " for them, but it was soon abandoned. Without the steadying influence of older women, the group became unhappy and showed fresh signs of immaturity.[17]

In a detention centre

There is one girls' detention centre, Moor Court, serving the North and catering for both junior and senior age-groups. Its opening in 1962 created a certain amount of anxiety, if not hostility. It was difficult to see how very short-term training with very strict discipline could help immature " problem " girls. This view was most valid when the discipline in boys' centres was at its most militaristic, but is still widely held.

The regime has been described as one " of hard work, austerity and good manners." [17a] Work is either domestic, or heavier work outside; there is a dismantling workshop. It is reported that many girls received are found to bear tattoo marks, a finding which would delight the followers of Lombroso.

Offenders who are Mentally Disordered

For centuries, the common law of England has recognised the special position of the mentally ill. " *Furiosus furore solo punitur* . . . A total idiocy, or absolute insanity, excuses from the guilt, and of course from the punishment, of any criminal action committed under such deprivation of the senses." [18]

No modern lawyer would write with Blackstone's assurance; he would be too well aware of the uncertainties which in this context surround even familiar words like " guilt " and " punishment." All would agree that some of the mentally ill must be exempted from criminal responsibility; to go beyond that statement needs caution and courage.

The legal notion of responsibility rests on certain assumptions about an individual's freedom of will. Professor Glueck has suggested that this be defined as a " capacity for conscious, purposive controlled action when confronted with a series of

[17] See R.P.D. 1964, p. 42. For the history of Borstal training for girls, see Ann Smith, *op. cit.*, Chap. 16.

[17a] See Taylor in 8 B.J.C. 170.

[18] Blackstone, 4 *Commentaries*, pp. 24–25 (16th ed.).

alternatives." He comments, " as soon as ' freedom of will ' is so defined, it becomes evident that individuals differ in their capacity to make necessary choices and to manage the manipulation of means to achieve ends with reference to the prohibitions of the penal code. They differ in this respect just as they vary in intelligence, in physique, in health, or in any other human quality." [19]

When an individual's capacity, in this sense, is reduced to a certain level, he is clearly in need of medical treatment rather than punishment. His actions in contravening the criminal law should be regarded as providing the occasion for ordering medical treatment, rather than the basis of a conviction. In other words, he should be regarded as lacking criminal responsibility, and exempt from conviction and punishment.

Public attitudes to mental illness are notoriously ungenerous and lacking in understanding. The law has tended to reflect this by limiting strictly the class of persons exempt from responsibility, and by insisting on a conviction, a declaration of guilt, even where the need for medical treatment is recognised. In a Utopian legal system, the demands of the law would be fitted to the capacity of each individual, and the sanctions for misbehaviour would be similarly tailored to meet his needs. In practice, this level of individualisation is impossible. The law must use broad categories; as indeed must psychiatry, although a psychiatrist may use a different system of classification designed to suit his particular clinical function. English law has been open to criticism over the form of its system of categorisation.

Until the present century, our criminal law was content with two categories; the legally normal and the legally insane. The division was inevitably crude; and the insane category was a limited one, for it was felt that " the mere existence of madness ought not to be an excuse for crime " [20]; there had to be some clear causal relationship between the insanity and the offence. The test for this relationship was contained in the McNaghten Rules, laid down in 1843 and reflecting the state of knowledge as to mental illness of the time.

The law did make two further concessions, from an early date. It forbade the trial of an accused person whose insanity prevented him from making a defence; and the execution of

[19] S. Glueck, *Law and Psychiatry*, p. 12.

[20] Stephen, 2 *History of the Criminal Law of England*, p. 125; see Chap. 19 generally.

offenders who became insane before the sentence could be carried out.[21]

In all these cases, a finding of insanity would lead to prolonged detention for treatment; the detention could be permanent. This meant that pleas of insanity were virtually restricted to cases involving capital charges, especially murder. This had the unfortunate result of linking in the public mind two issues, capital punishment and legal insanity, both of which excite extreme and often prejudiced views.

This unfortunate state of affairs was responsible for the unhappy outcome of fresh efforts after the Second World War to secure changes in the McNaghten Rules, or even the abandonment of the attempt to distinguish sharply between the insane, lacking all responsibility, and the legally normal, subject to the full rigour of the law. Against the advice of a Royal Commission,[22] English law accepted the " precious absurdity "[23] of diminished responsibility. Under this doctrine, certain mental states—it is difficult to say which—take a killing out of the category of murder, for which crime the punishment is fixed by law, and into the category of manslaughter, for which any punishment up to life imprisonment can be imposed.[24] Nothing is said in the statutory provisions about medical treatment.

Much more important was the reform of the whole of the law relating to the mentally ill affected by the Mental Health Act 1959. This greatly extended the powers of the courts to order mental treatment, residential or non-residential, instead of punishment; before 1959 their powers were limited and unsatisfactory.[25] It is under the provisions of this Act that most mentally ill offenders are dealt with, and the various measures available are reviewed in this section. One point may be noted here: lower courts are enabled to make orders under the Act without convicting; they have a discretion whether to record a conviction or not. This discretion, and its absence when a higher court is involved, may point to a continuing ambivalence in the attitude of the law towards the mentally ill offender.

21 Coke, 3 *Institutes*, p. 6.

22 Royal Commission on Capital Punishment, 1949–53. See its Report (Cmd. 8932), and *infra*, pp. 287 *et seq.*

23 The phrase is James L.J.'s: (1881) 17 Ch.D. 299.

24 Homicide Act 1957, s. 2.

25 See J. D. J. Havard [1961] Crim.L.R. 296, for the immediate background to the Mental Health Act. See also Jones, *Mental Health and Social Policy 1845–1959*.

The framework: the Mental Health Act 1959

The Mental Health Act 1959 is the basic piece of legislation on this whole subject of the care and treatment of the mentally ill. It governs the provisions of hospitals and welfare services for mental patients,[26] regulates private nursing homes and residential homes accepting mental patients,[27] provides safeguards for patients especially the Mental Health Review Tribunals to which patients may apply for a discharge,[28] and sets out the powers and functions of the Court of Protection, the body responsible for managing the property and affairs of patients.[29]

Most important of all, it establishes the basic grammar of the subject by defining and classifying mental illness. The essential provision is section 4, which deserves to be set out in full:

> " (1) In this Act ' mental disorder ' means mental illness, arrested or incomplete development of mind, psychopathic disorder, and any other disorder or disability of mind; and ' mentally disordered ' shall be construed accordingly.
>
> (2) In this Act ' severe subnormality ' means a state of arrested or incomplete development of mind which includes subnormality of intelligence and is of such a nature or degree that the patient is incapable of living an independent life or of guarding himself against serious exploitation, or will be so incapable when of age to do so.
>
> (3) In this Act, ' subnormality ' means a state of arrested or incomplete development of mind (not amounting to severe subnormality) which includes subnormality of intelligence and is of a nature or degree which requires or is susceptible to medical treatment or other special care or training of the patient.
>
> (4) In this Act, ' psychopathic disorder ' means a persistent disorder or disability of mind (whether or not including subnormality of intelligence) which results in abnormally aggressive or seriously irresponsible conduct on the part of the patient, and requires or is susceptible to medical treatment.
>
> (5) Nothing in this section shall be construed as implying that a person may be dealt with under this Act as suffering from mental disorder, or from any form of mental disorder

26 Part II.
27 Part III.
28 s. 3 and Part IX; see Fleming, " The Tribunal in Action " (1964) J.Ment. Subnormality 118.
29 Part VIII.

described in this section, by reason only of promiscuity or other immoral conduct."

The last two subsections are perhaps the most significant; they recognise the existence of psychopathy, a matter of considerable controversy because of the difficulty of distinguishing the psychopath from the normal offender.[30]

The Mental Health Act makes elaborate provision for the treatment of patients suffering from one or other of these types of disorder. Inevitably, the larger part of the Act is concerned with compulsory admissions; it is in those circumstances that considerations of the liberty of the individual arise with the need for adequate safeguards. Nonetheless the policy of the Act is to encourage the use of informal procedures wherever possible.[31]

The procedure for compulsory admission to hospital is set out in Part IV of the Act. There are various procedures, admission for observation, admission for treatment, and emergency admissions: the common features are explicit time limits on the authorised detention, and the need for medical recommendations from two practitioners (one approved by the local health authority as having special experience in the diagnosis or treatment of mental disorder [32]) at each stage. In addition to procedures for admission to hospital, there are also procedures for guardianship, which gives to the named guardian powers in relation to the patient corresponding to those of a father in relation to a child under 14; there are also special rules in guardianship as to medical attention.[33]

An important feature of the legislation is the scope of the powers given to the nearest relative of the patient,[34] especially as to discharge. A patient can be discharged either by the appropriate medical or health authorities or by the nearest relative. The only qualifications concern patients certified as being dangerous; the nearest relative cannot have the patient discharged while such a certificate is in force.[35]

In addition there is a procedure whereby a patient can, in effect, discharge himself by absconding and staying away from the hospital for 28 days. This is really a form of discharge by

[30] Walker, *Crime and Punishment in Britain*, pp. 82–88; Wootton, *Crime and the Criminal Law*, p. 73.
[31] Mental Health Act 1959, s. 5.
[32] *Ibid.* s. 28.
[33] See *ibid.* ss. 34–36, and Regulations of the Minister of Health.
[34] Defined, Mental Health Act 1959, ss. 49–53.
[35] *Ibid.* s. 48; note the right of appeal to the Mental Health Review Tribunal: s. 48 (3).

operation of law, for the effect of absence for 28 days is to make arrest and return to the institution illegal.[36]

These provisions are not of course specially designed for offenders. We must now examine the position of offenders, or those involved in criminal proceedings, who are or become mentally ill.

The offender who is mentally ill

Several varieties of criminal procedure lead to accused or convicted persons, or certain other persons brought before a court, receiving medical treatment for mental illness. The most frequent type of case involves the making of hospital guardianship or restriction orders under the Mental Health Act; in cases of insanity under the McNaghten Rules or of unfitness to plead, the verdict of the jury leads automatically to an order with a similar effect to one under the Mental Health Act; a probation order may contain a requirement as to treatment; or a court may consent to informal procedures for admission to hospital being used. Finally, a person in legal custody may be transferred for treatment by administrative procedures. All these must be considered in turn.

Hospital and guardianship orders

A hospital order directs that a person be admitted to a named mental hospital within the following 28 days. In the meantime he is detained in a place of safety.[37] Once admitted to hospital, he is in approximately the same legal position as a patient admitted under the compulsory admission procedures already described, with the important proviso that in these cases the nearest relative cannot order his discharge; application must be made to a Mental Health Review Tribunal.[38]

A number of conditions have to be satisfied before a hospital order can be made.

The offence which the accused has committed must not be one for which the sentence is fixed by law (that is, it must not be murder or treason); it must be an offence which has led to his appearing before assizes or quarter sessions or, if the trial

36 *Ibid.* s. 40. The period is six months in the case of adult patients classified as psychopathic or subnormal.

37 Mental Health Act 1959, ss. 60 (3), 63 (1), 64 (1): the Minister of Health may in "special circumstances" order the patient's admission to a hospital other than that specified.

38 *Ibid.* s. 63 (3) (4).

is in a magistrates' court, it must be punishable with imprisonment.[39] The higher courts must actually convict; magistrates have the power, which they seldom use, of making a hospital order without recording a conviction—they must be " satisfied that the accused did the act or made the omission charged." [40] It is not necessary for there to be any causal connection between the offence and the mental disorder.[41]

There must be evidence from two medical practitioners that the accused is suffering from one of the types of mental disorder defined in the Mental Health Act,[42] of such a nature as warrants his detention for treatment [43]; the court must decide which type of mental disorder exists, and state their finding in the order.[44] They must also be satisfied that arrangements have been made for the admission of the accused as a patient if an order is to be made.[45]

Finally, the court must decide " having regard to all the circumstances including the nature of the offence and the character and antecedents of the offender, and to the other available methods of dealing with him, that the most suitable method of disposing of the case " is by means of a hospital order.[46] This raises some questions of sentencing policy which must be considered later.

A guardianship order can be made as an alternative to and in the same circumstances as a hospital order. It confers the same powers on the named guardian as guardianship created in the usual way, subject to the same restrictions on discharge as apply in the case of a hospital order.[47]

Both hospital and guardianship orders may be made in the case of juveniles brought before a juvenile court as being in need of care, protection or control, where no offence need be involved.[48]

[39] *Ibid.* s. 60 (1).

[40] *Ibid.* s. 60 (2). Convictions were recorded in over 90 per cent. of hospital order cases before magistrates' courts in 1966. *Quaere* whether the passage quoted in the text is intended to affect the normal rules of burden of proof; *i.e.*, must the magistrates be satisfied beyond all reasonable doubt?

[41] *Hatt* [1962] Crim.L.R. 647.

[42] *i.e.*, by s. 4, set out *supra*.

[43] s. 60 (1) (*a*); s. 62 sets out detailed rules as to the evidence.

[44] *Ibid.* s. 60 (5).

[45] *Ibid.* s. 60 (3).

[46] *Ibid.* s. 60 (1) (*b*). Note that no other sentence can be passed when a hospital order is made; but orders for costs or restitution orders are possible. See s. 60 (6).

[47] *Ibid.* ss. 60, 63 (2) to (5).

[48] *Ibid.* s. 61, as amended by Children and Young Persons Act 1963. Note the special restrictions in the " beyond control " cases. For " care, protection and control " cases generally, see *supra*, pp. 191 *et seq.*

Restriction orders

Where a hospital order is made by assizes or quarter sessions, and not by an ordinary magistrates' court, a further order may be made restricting the patient's discharge from hospital for a stated period. This is usually called a " restriction order " and may be made whenever " it appears to the court, having regard to the nature of the offence, the antecedents of the offender and the risk of his committing further offences if set at large, that it is necessary for the protection of the public so to do." [49] Although magistrates cannot make a restriction order themselves they can commit to quarter sessions with a view to that court making hospital and restriction orders.[50]

The effect of a restriction order is that the time of discharge is entirely in the hands of the Home Secretary. The independent powers of the hospital authorities, the nearest relative and the Mental Health Review Tribunal are all excluded. The Home Secretary can order discharge, imposing conditions if he thinks fit, the sanction being recall to hospital, or he may terminate the restriction order, so that the discharge procedures applicable to a normal hospital order can operate.[51]

The advantages of making a restriction order were summarised by Lord Parker C.J. in *Gardiner* [52]:

> " It must be borne in mind that when only a hospital order is made; (1) it is only authority for the patient's detention for one year in the first instance. This authority can be renewed if the medical practitioner in charge of the treatment of the patient (whom I will call the ' responsible medical officer ') reports to the hospital managers that it appears to him that further detention is necessary in the interests of the patient's health or safety or for the protection of others. The hospital managers, however, are not bound to act on such a report and may refuse to extend the period and accordingly discharge the patient. Further, if the patient is 16 or over he or his nearest relative can apply at certain intervals to a Mental Health Review Tribunal who may in any case direct the patient's discharge and must do so if satisfied that he is no longer suffering from a mental disorder or that his further detention is not necessary. (2) The patient can be discharged at any time

[49] Mental Health Act 1959, s. 65.
[50] *Ibid.* ss. 67, 68.
[51] *Ibid.* ss. 65, 66.
[52] [1967] 1 W.L.R. 464, 468–469.

by the hospital managers, whose power is unlimited, or by the responsible medical officer, whose power is also unlimited, or by a Mental Health Tribunal as already stated. (3) Once discharged the patient is no longer liable to recall. (4) A patient who is absent without leave cannot be retaken into custody and indeed ceases to be liable to be detained (a) if he is over 21 and is classified as psychopathic or subnormal, after six months' absence; (b) in any other case, after 28 days' absence.[53]

If, however, a restriction order is made in addition to a hospital order, (i) there is authority to detain the patient for at any rate the duration of that order, though the Secretary of State may terminate it at any time if satisfied that it is no longer required for the protection of the public; (ii) the patient can only be discharged with the consent of the Secretary of State or by the Secretary of State himself; (iii) the Secretary of State has power in discharging the patient himself to make the discharge conditional, in which case the patient remains liable to recall during the period up to the expiration of the restriction order. This power is particularly useful as a means of keeping a discharged patient under the supervision of a probation officer or mental welfare officer for a longer period than would be possible if there were no restriction order; lastly a patient who is absent without leave may be taken into custody again at any time.

Accordingly it will be seen from the above that a restriction order enables the Secretary of State to exercise the function (as recommended by the Royal Commission on the Law relating to Mental Illness and Mental Deficiency) of a central authority which pays special regard to the protection of the public in controlling the discharge of dangerous patients. Apart from a restriction order it is inevitable that the hospital's first concern is the welfare of the patient and this does result in some cases in a patient who is subject to a hospital order alone securing his discharge earlier than he would do if he were also subject to a restriction order. The Secretary of State might well feel that although the patient was apparently no longer in need of medical treatment a further period in hospital under observation was advisable and was required to guard against the possibility of relapse leading to further crime."

[53] See Woolf, "The Back Door" (1966) 6 B.J.Crim. 59.

Lord Parker C.J. suggested that the courts were making restriction orders in too few cases. They should be made in all cases where the protection of the public was required, especially where the illness had led to violent or serious sexual offences. In the usual case, the restriction order should be unlimited in point of time. This is required because of the importance of protecting the public,[54] and the only exception would be where the doctors could assert confidently that recovery would take place within a stated period.

This summary of the Court of Appeal's attitude was the more welcome as it replaces some very obscure rulings of the Court of Criminal Appeal, some denying and some stressing the importance of the security arrangements at the hospital named in the order.[55]

It is clear that security considerations are important. Most hospitals for mental patients are not secure; locks and bars have largely disappeared. Only certain hospitals, designated as "special hospitals" are secure institutions. These hospitals are designed for persons of "dangerous, violent, or criminal propensities" [56] and include Broadmoor (the original "Criminal Lunatic Asylum"), Rampton and Moss Side. One way of ensuring that security is observed is to specify one of these hospitals in a hospital order.[57] Where no place is available at a special hospital, and the accused needs secure conditions, the courts should use their ordinary penal jurisdiction, sending the accused to prison [58]; he may then be transferred to a special hospital when a place becomes available, under administrative powers to be discussed below.

It is probably true to say that restriction orders are unpopular with the medical staff of the hospitals, who feel that the control of the Home Office may be so close as to limit their powers of granting short leaves as an experiment.

Sentencing practice

The use made by the courts of their powers under the Mental Health Act are set out in the following Table,[59] which also gives

54 *Rose* [1963] Crim.L.R. 653.

55 *Davie* [1962] Crim.L.R. 258; *Collett* [1962] Crim.L.R. 640.

56 Mental Health Act 1959, s. 97.

57 Thomas (at [1965] Crim.L.R. 691) points out that a restriction order prevents a patient being transferred from a special hospital to some other hospital without the Home Secretary's consent: Mental Health Act 1959, s. 65 (3) (*c*) (*ii*). But consider also the powers of the Minister of Health: *ibid.* s. 99 (2).

58 *Morris* [1961] 2 Q.B. 237; *Higginbotham* [1961] 1 W.L.R. 1277.

59 Sources: *Criminal Statistics*, Tables XIII and XV; Prison Department Reports.

details of the incidence of some of the other procedures still to be discussed.

	1962	1964	1966
Hospital orders	1,173	1,358	1,439
Guardianship orders	14	14	9
Restriction orders	138	185	180
Transfer directions	134	144	141 [60]
Unfit to plead	43	21	22
Special verdict of insanity	11	6	2

The sentencing problem with which the courts are most frequently faced is whether or not to make a hospital order. The alternative is usually a sentence of imprisonment. The courts are aware that a prison sentence does not necessarily exclude the possibility of the accused receiving hospital treatment; in particular they are aware of the Home Secretary's transfer powers under section 72 of the Act. It would clearly be wrong for the court to pass a sentence on the assumption that these powers would be exercised; they cannot " pass the buck " in this way.[61]

Lord Parker C.J. has made the point in more formal language: " . . . although the discretion [given by s. 60] is very wide indeed, the basic principle must be that in the ordinary case where punishment as such is not intended, and where the sole object of the sentence is that a man should receive mental treatment and be at large as soon as he can safely be discharged, a proper exercise of the discretion demands that steps should be taken to exercise the powers under section 60, and that the matter should not be left to be dealt with by the Secretary of State under section 72."[62]

Lord Parker went on to refer to exceptional cases where, although his responsibility was substantially impaired, the prisoner was to some extent responsible and had to be punished, even though medical treatment was also needed; a sentence of imprisonment was then proper.[63] It is not very easy to see what this means; it seems to add little to the general principle which is well expressed by Mr. Thomas's dictum that " treatability has replaced responsibility as the basis for the court's decision."[64]

60 1965 figure.
61 See *infra*, p. 278.
62 *Morris* [1961] 2 Q.B. 237 at 243.
63 *Ibid.*, see also *James* [1961] Crim.L.R. 842; *Edglington* (1961) unreported cited by Walker (1965) 5 *Medicine Science and the Law* 17.
64 [1965] Crim.L.R. 685.

This means in practice that where a case is brought within the terms of section 60, and the accused's condition and his attitude towards treatment are such that there is a reasonable chance of benefit resulting from treatment, a hospital order will be made.[65]

Special verdict of insanity

"Where in any indictment or information any act or omission is charged against any person as an offence, and it is given in evidence on the trial of such person for that offence that he was insane, so as not to be responsible, according to law, for his actions at the time when the act was done or omission made, then, if it appears to the jury before whom such person is tried that he did the act or made the omission charged, but was insane as aforesaid at the time when he did or made the same, the jury shall return a special verdict that the accused is not guilty by reason of insanity."[66] When this verdict is returned, the court must make an order that the accused be admitted to a hospital named by the Home Secretary[67]; in practice, one of the special hospitals. This order has the effect of a hospital order coupled with a restriction order for an indefinite period.[68]

Before bringing in this special verdict, the jury have to be satisfied not only that the accused person was insane, but also that he did the act charged; in other words, so far as the external facts of the offence are concerned the verdict is equivalent to one of "guilty." It is possible for the accused to appeal on the ground that he did not do the act. His appeal may succeed; but he remains a person who has been found insane by a jury. In such a case the Court of Appeal makes an order which has the effect of placing the accused in a hospital selected by the Home Secretary as if he had been admitted for observation under the Mental Health Act 1959.[69]

The number of cases in which the defence seek to obtain a special verdict is very small; partly this is a reaction against the prospect of prolonged, even life-long, detention in Broadmoor, but it also reflects the very strict test of irresponsibility,

65 See, *e.g.*, *Norman* [1961] Crim.L.R. 846; *Wallbank* [1962] Crim.L.R. 120; *Harrison* [1963] Crim.L.R. 709.
66 Trial of Lunatics Act 1883, s. 2 (1) as amended by Criminal Procedure (Insanity) Act 1964.
67 Criminal Procedure (Insanity) Act 1964, s. 5 (1).
68 *Ibid.* Sched. 1, para. 2 (1).
69 *Ibid.* ss. 2, 3, 5 and Sched. 1, para. 3.

that contained in the McNaghten Rules. Despite the use of this convenient name, the rules were not laid down in the case of Daniel M'Naghten, acquitted of murder on the ground of insanity in 1843.[70] They are taken from the answers given by the judges to a set of questions put to them by the House of Lords after a debate on the whole issue. The most important answer was to the effect that

> "to establish a defence on the ground of insanity, it must be clearly proved that, at the time of the committing of the act, the party accused was labouring under such a defect of reason, from disease of the mind, as not to know the nature and quality of the act he was doing; or, if he did know it, that he did not know he was doing what was wrong." [71]

This test has received enormous criticism in recent years, and has been rejected in a number of common law jurisdictions.[72] In particular the test is criticised as being limited to cognitive factors, excluding all matters concerning volition, or the emotions. All that can be said here is that the number of cases in which the defence relies on the McNaghten Rules is now small.

Unfitness to plead

It would be unjust to permit an accused person to be tried if at the time of the trial he is so mentally disturbed as to be unable to conduct his defence, instruct counsel, or exercise the other rights of an accused person. A person who is grossly disturbed will not in fact be taken for trial; he will be transferred to a hospital before the trial is due.[73] In less clear-cut cases, the issue may be raised at the trial, by the defence, the prosecution or the court itself, and will be determined by a jury specially sworn for the purpose. If the jury find the accused

[70] (1843) 4 St.Tr.(N.S.) 847. The spelling of McNaghten's name is a study in itself. See [1957] 1 W.L.R. 1122n.: "The Real McNaughton," 74 L.Q.R. 1; and "The Real Mhicneachdain," *ibid.* 321.

[71] 10 C. & F. 200, 210. Maule J. gave a separate, and in part dissenting, opinion.

[72] See *e.g.*, Williams, *Criminal Law: The General Part*, Chap. 10; the Report of the Royal Commission on Capital Punishment, 1953; Donnelly, Goldstein and Schwartz, *Criminal Law*, Part 6; *Durham* v. *U.S.*, 214 F. 2d. 862 (1954); *U.S.* v. *Freeman*, 357 F. 2d. 606 (1966), applying the A.L.I. Model Penal Code, art. 4.01; Parker, "The Decline of Daniel McNaghten" [1967] Crim.L.R. 327.

[73] Under the Home Secretary's administrative powers: see *infra*, p. 278.

unfit to plead, they return a verdict that he is "under disability"; the court then makes an order that the accused be admitted to a hospital specified by the Home Secretary.[74]

It is thought inappropriate that an accused should be committed to hospital in this way unless there is a case for him to answer; in other words, unless it is probable that he did the act which forms the basis of the charge. Accordingly, the judge may postpone consideration of the question of fitness to plead until the prosecution case has been closed; he may do this when it is "in the interests of the accused" and is expedient "having regard to the nature of the supposed disability."[75]

Probation

In some circumstances a probation order can include a condition requiring treatment for mental illness. Section 4 (1) of the Criminal Justice Act 1948[76] provides

> "Where the court is satisfied, on the evidence of a duly qualified medical practitioner, approved for the purposes of section 28 of the Mental Health Act 1959, that the mental condition of an offender is such as requires and may be susceptible to treatment but is not such as to warrant his detention in pursuance of a hospital order . . . , the court may, if it makes a probation order, include therein a requirement that the offender shall submit, for such period not extending beyond twelve months from the date of the order as may be specified therein, to treatment by or under the direction of a duly qualified medical practitioner with a view to the improvement of the offender's mental condition."

The order may specify whether the treatment shall be as an out-patient or as a resident in-patient, in which case any hospital or mental nursing home within the Mental Health Act may be used, but not a special hospital.

As in the case of hospital orders, treatability is an important factor influencing the court's decision.[77] The court must also balance the possible risks to the public as a result of making an order for out-patient treatment, or treatment in a hospital

[74] The effect of this is the same as in a case of McNaghten insanity; for details of the procedure, see Criminal Procedure (Insanity) Act 1964, ss. 4, 5 and Sched. 1.
[75] Criminal Procedure (Insanity) Act 1964, s. 4 (2).
[76] As amended by Mental Health Act 1959.
[77] *Docherty* [1962] Crim.L.R. 851.

from which the offender can discharge himself at will, with the dangers of harming the offender by sending him to a penal institution.[78]

A full analysis of the practice of the courts in these cases was undertaken by Grünhut, who concluded that there was "a large untouched territory where the traditional punishments of fines and imprisonment prevail but where probation with mental treatment might be tried with success."[79] Courts outside London seem particularly reluctant to make such orders, and a number of hospitals will not accept patients whose treatment is a condition of probation.[80]

Transfer directions

A number of references have already been made to the powers of the Home Secretary to order the removal to hospital of a person in legal custody. These powers are exercised by the making of a transfer direction which has the same effect as a hospital order. The medical grounds for the order, and the requirements as to medical reports, are similar to those which apply in the case of hospital orders.[81]

The powers apply not only to prisoners serving a sentence of imprisonment, or other institutional sentence, but also to those committed in default of payment of fine, or for refusing to enter into recognisances, to persons committed in custody for trial or sentence, remanded in custody or detained as civil prisoners.[82]

The Home Secretary can also give a direction restricting discharge, which corresponds to a court's restriction order,[83] and may order the reception into guardianship of children in approved schools.[84]

There is some evidence that the transfer direction system is not working satisfactorily. The Royal Commission on the Penal System were told that the division of responsibility between the Home Office and the Ministry of Health, which is responsible for the hospitals and so must be consulted, was leading

78 *Ascher* [1965] Crim.L.R. 564; *Hough* [1965] Crim.L.R. 665.
79 Grünhut, *Probation and Mental Treatment* (1963).
80 See also Sparks, "The Decision to Remand for a Mental Examination" (1966) 6 B.J.Crim. 6.
81 Mental Health Act 1959, ss. 72, 76, 77, 78, as amended by Children and Young Persons Act 1963, and Criminal Procedure (Insanity) Act 1964.
82 Mental Health Act 1959, ss. 72 (6), 73 as amended by Criminal Justice Act 1961, Children and Young Persons Act 1963, Criminal Appeal Act 1964 and Criminal Procedure (Insanity) Act 1964.
83 Mental Health Act 1959, s. 74.
84 *Ibid.* s. 79.

to inordinate delays in transfers. As some witnesses pointed out, " nobody really wants convicted psychopaths." [85]

Treatment within the prison service

There are many prisoners who do not need to be sent to a mental hospital under any of the procedures already described, but who are in need of psychiatric help. To discover these offenders, and to assist the courts, psychologists and testers within the prison medical service are attached to a large number of institutions: they have increasing functions as advisers to the prison staff.[86] Psychiatric treatment units exist at the prisons in London and at some of the larger provincial institutions; but since 1962 the most important centre for this work has been Grendon Prison.

This is a prison for men, women and boys who do not require detention in a mental hospital but who are selected as needing psychiatric treatment and who volunteer for it. It is headed by a medical superintendent who has a carefully selected staff, who in addition to their treatment functions are expected to make a contribution to research, especially into the nature and treatment of psychopathy.[87]

The state of the law

Looked at as a whole, this part of the law lacks coherence. In cases under the McNaghten Rules, the mental state of the offender at the time of his criminal act is examined, the object being to determine his responsibility. A finding of irresponsibility leads to treatment. In most other cases where mental disorder is suspected in an offender, the object of his examination is the determination of his mental state and his susceptibility to treatment. A finding of treatability will usually lead to treatment.

There remains a horrible anomaly which further complicates the picture. This is the defence of " diminished responsibility," which if successful reduces murder to manslaughter. Here the question in issue is one of responsibility; a finding that responsibility is *reduced*, but not removed, *may* lead to treatment but can lead to punishment.

[85] R.C.P.S., Vol. 4, p. 97 (Drs. Coats, Prewer and Knox); see also Vol. 2, p. 22 (Magistrates' Assoc.).
[86] See *Prisons and Borstals 1963*, p. 9.
[87] See Tollington, " Grendon Prison " (1966) 6 B.J.Crim. 39; and a critical report at R.C.P.S., Vol. 2, p. 173 (National Association for Mental Health).

This notion of diminished responsibility was introduced in section 2 of the Homicide Act 1957 and is there stated to be

> " such abnormality of mind (whether arising from a condition of arrested or retarded development of mind or any inherent causes or induced by disease or injury) as substantially impaired [the accused's] mental responsibility for his acts and omissions in doing or being a party to the killing."

The interpretation of this section has occupied an inordinate amount of judicial time.[88]

More important, the whole principle has been criticised by many writers, notably Baroness Wootton.[89] Apart from the difficulties it presents in practice, especially as regards psychopaths, the defence is unnecessary. It is in effect a cumbersome way of enabling the provisions of the Mental Health Act to be applied to homicide; the same result could be achieved by removing a few words from that Act.[90]

One might go further, and suggest that not only diminished responsibility but the special defence of insanity also should be abolished, leaving the code contained in the Mental Health Act to apply generally.

Bibliography

(a) *Women and Girls*

The various official reports, and many other publications dealing with penal methods, contain sections concerning the treatment of women and girls. The following may also be consulted:

Kelley, J., When the Gates Shut (Longmans, 1967).
Parker, T., Five Women (Hutchinson, 1965).
Smith, A. D., Women in Prison (Stevens, 1962).

(b) *Mentally disordered*

The literature is enormous. There follows a selection of recent references:

[88] For the case-law, see Smith and Hogan, *Criminal Law*, pp. 112–114.

[89] See (1960) 76 L.Q.R. 224; *Crime and the Criminal Law*, Chap. 3 and Appendix; see also Walker, " Psychopathy in Law and Logic " (1965) 5 *Medicine Science and the Law* 3.

[90] It might be objected that the notion of diminished responsibility also allows *punishments* less than life imprisonment to be imposed in cases of homicide. It is rarely so used, and life imprisonment can mean a few months' detention in extreme cases.

American Law Institute: Model Penal Code, Tent. Draft No. 4 (1955).

DONNELLY, R. C., GOLDSTEIN, J. and SCHWARTZ, R. D., Criminal Law (Part 6) (Free Press, 1962).

GLUECK, S., Law and Psychiatry (Tavistock, 1963).

GRÜNHUT, M., Probation and Mental Treatment (Tavistock, 1963).

HAVARD, J. D. J., "The Mental Health Act and the Criminal Offender" [1961] Crim.L.R. 296.

JONES, K., Mental Health and Social Policy 1845–1959 (Routledge and Kegan Paul, 1960).

PARKER, G., "The Decline of Daniel McNaghten" [1967] Crim.L.R. 327.

Royal Commission on Capital Punishment: Report, 1953 (Cmd. 8932).

SPARKS, R. F., "The Decision to Remand for a Mental Examination" (1966) 6 B.J.Crim. 6.

THOMAS, D. A., "Sentencing the Mentally Disturbed Offender" [1965] Crim.L.R. 685.

WALKER, N., "Psychopathy in Law and Logic" (1965) 5 *Medicine Science and the Law* 3.

——, "Crime and Insanity in England," Vol. 1 (Edinburgh U.P., 1968).

WHITLOCK, F. A., Criminal Responsibility and Mental Illness (Butterworths, 1963).

WOOTTON, B., "Diminished Responsibility—A Layman's View" (1966) 76 L.Q.R. 224.

——, Crime and the Criminal Law (Stevens, 1963).

Chapter 7

OBSOLETE PENALTIES

Capital Punishment

The most severe penalty available to any penal system is the ending of the life of the convicted offender. In England, the death sentence is now available only in cases of treason, when it must be pronounced, and of obsolete offences under the Dockyards Protection Act 1772, and the Piracy Act, 1837. Should such a case ever occur, the judge could direct that the sentence of death be recorded but refrain from pronouncing it, a procedure amounting to a remission of the penalty.[1]

From the middle of the nineteenth century onwards, capital punishment was reserved during peacetime for cases of murder. Some types of murder became non-capital as a result of the Infanticide Act 1922 [2] and the unsatisfactory Homicide Act, 1957. In 1965, capital punishment was abolished for all types of murder, but the statute making the change, the Murder (Abolition of Death Penalty) Act, expires at the end of July 1970. Unless both Houses of Parliament resolve otherwise, the earlier law will then revive.[3] In no event can sentences of death be passed on a young person under 18,[4] or on a woman found to be pregnant.[5]

Forms of execution

In England, sentence of death is carried out by hanging. In practice, this means that the offender is taken to an execution chamber within the prison and is dropped, bound, through a trap-door. The rope around his neck is of such a length and is so knotted that the force of the drop causes the chin to be thrown back, producing a fracture dislocation of cervical vertebrae and immediate death.[6] Since 1965, there have been no

1 Judgment of Death Act 1823.
2 Now re-enacted as the Infanticide Act 1938.
3 Murder (Abolition of Death Penalty) Act 1965, s. 4.
4 Children and Young Persons Act 1933, s. 53 (1) as substituted by the Murder (Abolition of Death Penalty) Act 1965, s. 1 (5).
5 Sentence of Death (Expectant Mothers) Act 1931.
6 Chap. 13 of the Report of the Royal Commission on Capital Punishment, Cmd. 8932, discusses methods of execution in detail sufficient to satisfy the most ghoulish taste.

statutory provisions governing executions, except for a curious provision allowing the Queen to order that traitors be beheaded rather than hanged.[7]

Abroad, a number of different methods are used. They include the firing squad, used especially for military offences; electrocution; the gas chamber; the guillotine, to which France remains faithful; and the garotte, a Spanish method which can best be described as a refined form of mechanical strangulation. In some countries, executions are in public; in England they have been held within prisons since 1868.[8]

A great number of countries, especially in Europe, have wholly discontinued the use of capital punishment. They include Austria, Belgium, Denmark, the German Federal Republic, Finland, Iceland, Italy, Luxembourg, Norway, Portugal, Sweden and Switzerland.

Capital punishment in England

During the last ten years of capital punishment in England, 1955–64, thirty-eight persons were executed. During the corresponding period two centuries earlier, 191 persons were executed in London and Middlesex alone. This in turn is less than a quarter of the number of executions a century earlier.[9] This historical perspective is essential for a proper consideration of the subject.

Before the nineteenth century

By 1800, some two hundred separate offences were capital. Many had been created in the eighteenth century. The offences included some offences of burglary and housebreaking, some sexual offences, the theft of cattle, sheep or horses, and even several types of larceny: stealing from the person, and stealing goods from a shop to the value of five shillings are examples.[10]

In practice only a small proportion of those suspected of such offences were executed. There might be no prosecution, the grand jury might reject the bill of indictment, the trial jury

[7] Treason Act 1814, s. 2.

[8] Capital Punishment Amendment Act 1868, repealed in 1965. See *Capital Punishment* (United Nations, 1962), pp. 57–67.

[9] A comprehensive examination of the history of capital punishment down to the early nineteenth century is to be found in Radzinowicz, *History of English Criminal Law*, Vol. 1.

[10] In theory, all felonies were capital until 1827. In practice, capital offences were those where benefit of clergy was withheld. The abolition of benefit of clergy in 1827 rationalised matters a little.

might acquit, or the goods stolen might be undervalued. All these were devices involving perjury, or at least a breach of duty; the criminal law was being distorted and abused to make it tolerably humane. This clearly indicated the need for reform. In the meantime, the administration of justice was uncertain and unpredictable; to that extent criminal justice was not administered.

One further humanising element which survived throughout the period during which capital punishment was used was the royal prerogative of mercy. This is the system of "reprieve," which means, strictly, a temporary stay of execution, but is generally used to refer to the commutation of the death penalty to some other form of punishment. In the modern system, the last few weeks of the convict's life were used by the Home Office to gather all available information about possible mitigating circumstances including further inquiries into the convict's mental state. A few days before the date of the execution, the Home Secretary decided whether or not to recommend a reprieve, royal approval being virtually automatic.

Under the Hanoverians, the outcome depended much more upon the whim of the sovereign who would periodically review death sentences passed in London, and selected cases referred to him by judges on circuit. The king would be surrounded by his Privy Council, but the decision was his alone.[11] This was true despotism: the king had at his disposal the lives of some hundreds of his subjects each year.[12]

Nineteenth century [13]

The nineteenth century saw the end of public executions. Until 1868, hangings were public spectacles and attracted huge crowds. The crowd which assembled to see the death of Fauntleroy in 1824 was said to number 100,000; enough to fill the largest public stadium in present-day England, but in fact all jostling for position in the streets around Newgate prison. So great was the press, so enthralling the spectacle, that pick-pockets had a field-day; so much for the deterrent effect of public executions.[14]

Although held in private, executions continued to receive a

[11] See, *e.g.*, the anecdote of Lord Eldon, noted Radzinowicz, *op. cit.*, p. 166, n. 35.

[12] See Bresler, *Reprieve, A Study of a System*, Parts 1 and 2.

[13] For this period and later developments, see Tuttle, *The Crusade against Capital Punishment in Great Britain.*

[14] At least two public executioners were themselves executed for capital crimes.

great deal of publicity. This at least served to excite public opinion when executions were bungled, and that led in turn to the Lords' Select Committee of 1886, whose recommendations did much to ensure the efficiency of modern executions.

These improvements were the end of a long process of civilising capital punishment. Until the eighteenth century, executions followed a long public procession during which the condemned man would be acclaimed or abused according to the taste of the crowd. Hanging was a slow process, and so inefficient that the "dead" man could sometimes be revived by solicitous friends. Still earlier, there was greater scope for horror: traitors were sometimes half-hanged, then disembowelled while still conscious. Beheadings, by the use of an axe, were sometimes terribly botched. Women were burned at the stake. All these atrocities had passed away; the nineteenth century was able to consider whether capital punishment was necessary at all.

Sir Samuel Romilly entered the House of Commons in 1806. He was convinced that the severe penalties imposed by the English criminal law had proved ineffectual [15]; he was determined to have the death penalty removed so far as lesser crimes such as larceny were concerned. In the twelve years before his death in 1818, Romilly made little progress in terms of legislation. Pickpockets, some vagrants, and those who stole from clothmakers were exempted from the threat of capital punishment. Nothing else was accomplished; but much was put in hand.

In particular, Romilly won over important sections of opinion to his views; including the House of Commons, for in his last years he repeatedly had Bills passed by that House, only to be defeated by the Lords. Romilly was not an abolitionist; he would keep capital punishment for some offences. But abolitionist movements began as a result of the public debate he stirred up.

In the year after Romilly's death, a Commons Select Committee recommended the repeal of a large number of obsolete statutes imposing the death penalty, and a relaxation in the severity of the larceny statutes. There was strong resistance to the direct implementation of these proposals, but during the following decade Peel's revision of the criminal law, aimed more at consolidation and modernisation than penal reform, carried

[15] See the original preamble to his first Bill, quoted Radzinowicz, *op. cit.*, p. 499.

through a number of changes and greatly reduced the number of capital offences. From this point onwards, murder was in practice the only capital offence.

William Ewart and John Bright were now the leaders of the movement for the complete abolition of capital punishment. They introduced Bills into the Commons, without success, but secured the appointment of a Royal Commission in 1864. The main recommendations of the majority were the division of murder into two degrees, only first-degree murder to be capital [16]; and that executions should be in private, a proposal from which Ewart and Bright dissented. The former proposal was never put into effect.

The twentieth century

The next major developments followed the First World War. In 1922, the Infanticide Act took the killing of a newly-born child by its mother out of the category of murder; a partial recognition of the long-standing practice that precluded the execution of a mother for killing her child, and, incidentally, an implementation of one of the proposals of the 1864 Commission.

By this period, new forces were on the scene. The Howard League for Penal Reform took its new form in 1921. Four years later Roy Calvert founded the National Council for the Abolition of the Death Penalty. In 1924 and again in 1929 the Labour Party, more sympathetic to penal reform than its opponents, formed the Government.

In 1930, a Select Committee of the House of Commons recommended the abolition of capital punishment; murderers were to receive life imprisonment instead. As an alternative, an experimental suspension of the death penalty for five years was suggested. The Conservative members of committee boycotted the final stages of its work, and within a year the Labour Government had resigned. Apart from a Commons vote in favour of suspension on a private member's motion in 1938,[17] no progress was made before the Second World War. The element of party politics which had by now entered the issue was to cause greater trouble in the future.

In April 1948, the Commons debated the issue once again. Sidney Silverman moved a new clause to the Criminal Justice

[16] Defined as murder either found by the jury to be with express malice aforethought, or committed in or with a view to the perpetration of arson, rape, burglary, robbery or piracy.

[17] 341 Commons Debates (5th series), cols. 954 *et seq.*

Bill removing the death penalty for murder, and the clause was carried by 245 votes to 222.[18] The House of Lords rejected the clause by 181 votes to 28.[19] After the Lords had also rejected a compromise formula, the Bill was passed without the clause to save it from becoming a total loss.

The whole subject was referred to a Royal Commission presided over by Sir Ernest Gowers. This Commission deliberated for four years, during which time its chairman was converted to the abolitionist position; he explained why in a book published in 1956.[20] The Report is an exhaustive examination of the whole issue, but contains no direct recommendation, for abolition was not within the terms of reference. On the question of the punishment for murder, the Commission said that the quest for a solution by the division of murder into "degrees" was chimerical, and must be abandoned. They considered the possibility of allowing the jury to decide whether there were mitigating circumstances which might exclude the death penalty, but felt that the disadvantages of such a procedure might outweigh its merits. They concluded:

> "If this view were to prevail, the conclusion would be inescapable that in this country a stage has been reached where little more can be done effectively to limit the liability to suffer the death penalty, and that the real issue is now whether capital punishment should be retained or abolished." [21]

When the Commons debated the report, a move to suspend the death penalty was defeated by 245 to 214.[22]

In the next Parliament, Silverman again introduced a Bill to abolish the death penalty. It was finally passed by the Commons in July 1956. Once again, the House of Lords threw out the Bill. The Government's reaction to this was to introduce what became the Homicide Act 1957, which created degrees of murder flatly against the advice of the Royal Commission. The Bill was passed into law after voting which followed party divisions almost throughout. Capital murders included murders by shooting or by causing an explosion, murders "in the course or furtherance of" theft, and murders of police or prison officers. Second murders were also capital.

18 449 Commons Debates (5th series), cols. 979 *et seq.*
19 156 Lords Debates (5th series), col. 176.
20 *A Life for a Life?* (Chatto and Windus).
21 Report (Cmd. 8932), para. 611.
22 536 Commons Debates (5th series), col. 2180.

The proportion of murders which fell within the capital class was 14·4 per cent. for the five years before the passing of the Act. The figure for the next ten years was 14·2 per cent.[23]

After a few years there was a wide measure of agreement that the Homicide Act was unsatisfactory. Silverman and his supporters made further attempts to secure complete abolition. They succeeded in the Parliament elected in 1964. Silverman's Murder (Abolition of Death Penalty) Bill had an exciting passage through the Commons. The Committee stage was begun twice after the House reversed a previous decision to commit the Bill to a Standing Committee; at one stage the vital clause ordered convicted murderers to be sentenced to "imprisonment for," an unhelpful directive to the judges; there were dark hints that the division bells were not ringing as they should. But the Bill finally passed the Commons and the Lords, to receive the Royal Assent on November 8, 1965.

The merits of capital punishment

The argument about capital punishment is scarcely over. It broke out with renewed vigour in the summer of 1966 after the murder of three London policemen. The issue must come before Parliament before the expiry of the 1965 Act in July 1970. A brief review of the main arguments for and against capital punishment is therefore not out of place.

Arguments for capital punishment

(1) *Arguments associated with retribution*

Lord Denning, giving evidence to the Royal Commission of 1949, said that the ultimate justification of any punishment is not that it is a deterrent but that it is the emphatic denunciation by the community of a crime; and that from this point of view, there were some murders which, in the then state of public opinion, demanded the most emphatic denunciation of all, namely, the death penalty.

This is one form which can be taken by the feeling shared by most supporters of capital punishment. During the debates on the 1965 Bill, the League for Justice and Liberty presented a petition with 50,000 signatures to the Commons, declaring that "penalties should be imposed . . . in the first place to restore the violated moral and legal order of God's universe by giving the convicted criminal his just deserts."[24]

[23] 731 Commons Debates (5th series), col. *251* (Written Answer).
[24] 714 Commons Debates (5th series), col. 213.

This approach includes elements of vengeance, of atonement, of indignation. It is clearly the basis of the popular support which capital punishment enjoys.

(2) *Arguments based on deterrence*

An alternative basis for capital punishment, relied on especially when the death penalty is suggested for certain categories of murder (*e.g.*, killing police officers) is its unique deterrent value. The police, prison officers and judges are convinced that capital punishment has this deterrent effect, although, of course, their experience is limited to those whom, for one reason or another, it has failed to deter.

Statistical evidence is available in quantity on this point, but its interpretation is extraordinarily difficult. The statistics usually compare the murder rate in a state for the years before and the years after the abolition or introduction of the death penalty. Such statistics are frequently objected to, as referring to foreign states and therefore inapplicable to English conditions; as lacking any " control group," so that it is impossible to decide whether there is any causal relationship between the change in penalty and any change in the rate of crime; and the statistics are in any case complicated by changes in legal definitions which accompany the change in penalty, and by a suspension of the death penalty which accompanies the debate on the proposed changes.[25]

Some evidence survives these attacks.[26] The fairest summary seems to be that of the Royal Commission:

> " Prima facie the death sentence is likely to have a stronger effect as a deterrent to normal human beings than any other form of punishment. There is some evidence (though no convincing statistical evidence) that this is in fact so; and also that abolition may be followed for a short time by an increase in homicides and crimes of violence. But there is no clear evidence of any lasting increase, and there are many offenders on whom the deterrent effect is limited and may often be negligible. It is therefore important to view the question in a just perspective and not to base a penal policy in relation to murder on exaggerated

25 Both these last points applied in 1956–57, at the time of the Homicide Act debates.

26 See Appendix 6 of the Royal Commission's report (Cmd. 8932), or Gowers, *A Life for a Life?*, Appendix; Sellin, *The Death Penalty* (American Law Institute, 1959).

estimates of the uniquely deterrent force of the death penalty." [27]

(3) *Arguments concerning alternative punishments*

Where capital punishment has been abandoned, it is almost invariable practice to use "life" (*i.e.*, indeterminate) imprisonment as the alternative. It is argued that this involves great expense, is less humane than execution, and that difficulties are caused to prison authorities. There are also fears that released murderers will repeat their offences. It is only on the last two points that evidence is available.

The Royal Commission concluded that murderers were no more likely than other prisoners to commit acts of violence, or to attempt to escape. Evidence received from other countries suggested that murderers were, on the whole, better behaved than most prisoners.[28]

This is mainly because many murderers are first offenders, basically law-abiding men and women who have killed when under quite exceptional pressure. An examination of murder cases is to be found in a Home Office Research Unit study,[29] published in 1961, and supplemented by parliamentary answers on a number of more recent occasions. Three pieces of information seem relevant.

First, a small proportion of murder suspects are actually convicted of murder. Many more are mentally disturbed, or commit suicide. The following Table relates to the period 1955–64 [30]:

Number of suspects	1,408
Committed suicide	367
Acquitted	182
Found to be insane	213
Diminished responsibility cases	242
Convicted of murder	387

Of men convicted of murder, over 40 per cent. killed during quarrels or rages; 20 per cent. for financial gain; 10 per cent.

[27] Report, para. 68. In 1965, when the Abolition Bill was under debate, the number of victims of murder rose by 11 over the 1964 figures if account is taken of cases subsequently reduced to manslaughter because of diminished responsibility. Cases of murder excluding such cases were two fewer than in 1964.

[28] Report, para. 617.

[29] Gibson and Klein, *Murder* (H.M.S.O.).

[30] See 731 Commons Debates (5th series), col. *258*.

from sexual motives.[31] As many as one-half have no previous convictions.[32]

Finally, at least half of all murders take place within the family, involving for example the murder by one spouse of another, or of a child by a parent.[33]

In other words, there is a large group of sane murderers who are essentially law-abiding, but who kill after a violent argument, often within their own family. There is, of course, another, but smaller group, of hardened criminals, killing deliberately or recklessly.

(4) *Argument based on public opinion*

It is undoubtedly true that a large proportion, probably a majority, of the public favour capital punishment. Some regard this as being in itself an argument to be weighed, but strictly it is rather a measure of the impact of the earlier arguments.

Arguments against capital punishment

(1) *The ethical argument*

The ethical argument is that it is wrong, or unjustifiable, to take human life, even when the life is that of a convicted murderer. This argument rejects the " life for a life " equation, and emphasises the value of each and every human being. In Christian terms, the argument is that hanging a man is no way of showing love to one's neighbour.

Most branches of the Christian Church are now ranged against capital punishment. The Church of England, in this as in other fields, is embarrassed by its Articles of Religion, one of which declares that " the Laws of the Realm may punish Christian men with death for heinous and grievous offences." [34] This has not prevented very clear statements by the Convocations which have both voted in favour of the abolition or at least suspension of capital punishment.[35]

A variant of this argument puts it in slightly weaker terms, that killing to be permissible needs very clear justification, and continues that the evidence does not provide adequate justification.[36]

[31] See Gibson and Klein, Table 35. [32] *Ibid.*, Table 41.
[33] *Ibid.*, Tables 32 and 33.
[34] Article XXXVII.
[35] Canterbury, January 18, 1962; York, May 16, 1962.
[36] This seems to be Sir Ernest Gowers' position; see his comments on Archbishop Temple's views, *op. cit.*, p. 77, and his conclusions in Chap. 8.

(2) *Arguments based on the frailty of criminal justice*

There are two related points here. It is said that on several occasions innocent men have been hanged. The courts can make mistakes, but a hanged man cannot be unhanged.

The other point is that any legal system which uses capital punishment, whether the death sentence is mandatory or optional, needs some machinery of review corresponding to our "reprieve" system. It is said that no satisfactory system is available.

There seems little doubt that innocent men have been executed. In recent years in England there have been two cases which have aroused a good deal of anxiety, those of Graham Rowland and Timothy Evans,[37] and some others where no reprieve was given despite the existence of at least a scintilla of doubt.[38]

The Royal Commission on Capital Punishment examined the system of granting reprieves in England. At that time, 45 per cent. of those sentenced to death were granted reprieves.[39] The Home Office practice had developed its own case-law, although reasons for a reprieve in an individual case were never discussed. The Royal Commission listed three classes which attracted almost automatic reprieves; suicide-pact cases, the killing by a mother of her child, and mercy-killings. None were likely to come within the "capital" class after 1957. Reprieves were also granted in cases where drunkenness, provocation or mental instability, though falling short of a legal defence, was recognised as a mitigating circumstance. Factors of age and sex, local public opinion, or a scintilla of doubt about the conviction were further grounds.

Criticism of the system is usually directed against its secrecy; the Home Secretary is acting as a form of additional, private Court of Appeal. The answer would seem to be that, at least in the murder cases where it was used, there was an urgent need for just such a tribunal. Nuances of doubt, comprehensive and up-to-date medical examinations, these are difficult to provide for in a normal court system.

A more potent criticism is that, as operated in England, the

[37] See the Report of the Inquiry by Brabin J., who concluded that it was more probable than not that Evans did not kill his daughter Geraldine, for whose murder he was executed: Cmnd. 3101.

[38] See Sellin, *The Death Penalty*, pp. 63–65; Hale, *Hanged in Error*; Bresler, *Reprieve*, Part 3.

[39] After the Homicide Act, the reprieve rate for capital murder fell to 25 per cent.; this for the period 1957–63.

results were sometimes very surprising. The case of George Riley, hanged in 1961 when he was 21, is in point.[40] His conviction rested almost entirely on his own confession. In particular, his conviction for *capital* murder in the course or furtherance of theft rests on his statement that he went to his victim's home because he knew she had some money; he was in no need of money, and took none. He was also drunk, but his previous record was bad. Many feel that a reprieve should have been given, and a fierce debate took place in the Commons after the execution. At least, the decision to hang must have been a nice one, and the critics of the reprieve system think it wrong that a Home Secretary and his advisers should have to take such a decision.

(3) *Other arguments*

It is said that the morbid interest shown in executions is an unhealthy feature of any society; that hangings have a brutalising effect on prison staff, and other prisoners in the building; and that the consequences of the sentence for the convicted man's family are unjust. These are not matters on which much evidence can be given; they are matters for the individual to judge.[41]

Corporal Punishment

Corporal punishment raises similar emotions, and some of the same arguments as does capital punishment. On the level of dogma, there is the same opposition between the argument that violence must be met by violence and the objection that it is nonsensical that when a savage offence has taken place those responsible for enforcing respect for the law should resort to savage punishment.[42] On the level of statistics, there is the same conflict of interpretation over the statistics of deterrence.

In England, all corporal punishment other than as part of prison discipline[43] was abolished in the Criminal Justice Act 1948. That it is scarcely a live issue at the present time is largely due to the masterly report of the Advisory Council on the Treatment of Offenders published in 1960.[44]

40 Bresler, *op. cit.*, Chap. 24 contains a good summary of the case.

41 Capital punishment excites such strong passions that it should perhaps be said that this section of the book was written by a convinced opponent of the death penalty.

42 See the Report of the Departmental Committee on Corporal Punishment, Cmd. 5684 (The "Cadogan Report"), para. 61.

43 Abolished by the Criminal Justice Act 1967.

44 Corporal Punishment, Cmnd. 1213 (The "Barry Report").

Form of the punishment

Corporal punishment was administered through " the birch " or " the cat." The birch was used for all young offenders and some adults; in adult cases, the court could specify the implement. The birch itself was " a bundle of birch twigs—somewhat similar in appearance to the broom or besom used by a gardener for sweeping up leaves, but less bulky and not having a wooden handle." [45] The cat-o'-nine-tails consisted of a short handle with nine " tails " of whipcord, each 33 inches long. The birch was applied to the bare buttocks, the cat across the back. The procedure used is described in the reports of the two committees on the subject.[46]

Its history in England

As capital punishment was once a standard punishment for felonies, so flogging was a standard for misdemeanours. It took place in public, and some old whipping-posts can still be seen. Women were liable to this punishment until 1820.

In 1861, the use of corporal punishment for adults, meaning here persons over 16, was virtually abolished. The abolition Act left a number of exceptions, a catalogue of curios: pointing a firearm at the sovereign, contrary to the Treason Act 1842; some vagrancy offences; and some offences under the Diplomatic Privileges Act 1708 and the Knackers Act 1786. After 1861, corporal punishment was again extended to be available to punish garrotters (those who resort to attempted strangulation to commit offences), certain offenders connected with prostitution, and robbery with violence. Much of this legislation was passed in response to the outcry at " waves " of particular crimes, " panic legislation after the panic had subsided."

These powers of ordering flogging of adults were only exercisable by the superior courts. In practice, the penalty was imposed almost entirely for robbery with violence, and by the Second World War there were some two dozen sentences a year.[47]

Corporal punishment for juveniles survived for a longer period, possibly because of the absence of alternative forms of treatment in the nineteenth century. The major power was that of juvenile courts to order the whipping of boys under 14

[45] Cadogan Report, para. 10.
[46] *Ibid.* paras. 10, 11 and 33; Barry Report, para. 75 (same text).
[47] About 15 per cent. of convictions for that offence group.

convicted summarily of any indictable offence.[48] Its use declined sharply in the early part of this century, from around 3,000 at the turn of the century to below 200 for most of the 1930s. By 1944 its use had almost ceased; and it seems to have been only those courts with inadequate alternative forms of treatment which retained it all.

The House of Commons voted to abolish corporal punishment for juveniles in 1932 and 1933, but the relevant clause in the Children and Young Persons Bill was defeated in the Lords. In 1937, the whole question was referred to a departmental committee, which reported that corporal punishment for all age-groups should be abolished. After delays due to the war, this was accomplished in the Criminal Justice Act 1948.

In 1959, there was growing public demand for the introduction (or, as was generally but quite wrongly thought, reintroduction) of flogging for all crimes of violence, and sexual offences. This applied especially to "young thugs," presumably the 17–21 age-group. Despite evidence that three-quarters of the population would support such a change, the Advisory Council reaffirmed the views of the 1938 Committee.

The case as seen by the Advisory Council

The Council rejected a return to corporal punishment for six reasons.[49] First, that acceptance of the public demands would mean putting the clock back a hundred years. Secondly, that this was quite against the trend in other countries; the proposal to reintroduce flogging here excited adverse comment abroad, and reintroduction would damage this country's reputation as a pioneer in the use of enlightened methods of penal treatment.

The third point deals with deterrence:

> "We consider that, in these circumstances, the reintroduction of judicial corporal punishment could be justified only if there was a reasonable assurance that it would substantially reduce crime and afford real protection to potential victims. We think that there cannot be any such assurance. There is no evidence that corporal punishment is an especially effective deterrent either to those who have received it or to others."[50]

[48] Summary Jurisdiction Act 1879, s. 10 (2).
[49] Barry Report, Part VII.
[50] Barry Report, para. 87.

So far as general deterrence was concerned, it had often been claimed that the introduction, or heavy use, of corporal punishment had been effective in stamping out local outbreaks of certain types of crime, such as the outbreak of offences of robbery against drunken sailors in Cardiff in 1908. Many of these cases were examined by the 1938 Committee, and no conclusive evidence of any causal link between the floggings and the end of the outbreaks was found.[51]

As regards those who are themselves flogged, the evidence is unhelpful. It seems that offenders who were flogged were more often reconvicted than those who were not flogged.[52] Since those selected for corporal punishment were likely to have worse records than other offenders, this is not surprising. In fact it is not possible from the available statistics to isolate the effect of corporal punishment from that of other factors.

The Advisory Council's argument continued that judicial corporal punishment was out of line with modern penal methods, and in practice would militate against the success of reformative treatment. This conclusion seems to have been based largely on the medical evidence.[53] This was to the effect that corporal punishment, while it would not harm those with stable personalities (who would in any case respond well to other forms of treatment), might cause psychological harm to some offenders, making them bitter and resentful. In addition these offenders were least likely to be deterred by flogging. The new forms of treatment, such as detention centres, which were just being introduced at the time of the 1960 report, seemed less open to objection.

Finally, there were a number of practical difficulties over the administration of corporal punishment. The normal procedures of criminal justice are relatively slow; adequate medical examination of offenders is a lengthy process. Together they introduce a serious delay between the offence and the punishment. Those who support flogging often draw parallels with corporal punishment in the home or in school; in that situation, not only is there a continuing relationship of respect between punisher and punished, but the punishment is swift, and clearly related to the offence. Punishment two months later, by a policeman who has never been seen before, is a totally different matter.

[51] Cadogan Report, para. 56.
[52] See, for example, Barry Report, Statistical Tables, Table VII.
[53] Barry Report, paras. 34–38; Cadogan Report, para. 21.

It is significant that no group of persons is willing to take on the task of administering corporal punishment; not the police, prison or probation officers. We should need a special Brigade of Whipping Boys if flogging were ever reintroduced in England.

Bibliography

(*a*) *Capital punishment*

Official publications of government or international agencies include:

Capital Punishment 1948 (Cmd. 7419).

Capital Punishment (United Nations, 1962).

Report of the Royal Commission on Capital Punishment 1953 (Cmd. 8932).

Other references:

Ancel, M., The Death Penalty in European Countries (Council of Europe, 1962).

Calvert, R., Capital Punishment in the Twentieth Century, 1936.

Gardiner, G., Capital Punishment as a Deterrent (Gollancz, 1956).

Gowers, Sir E., A Life for a Life? (Chatto and Windus, 1956).

Koestler, A. and Rolph, C. H., Hanged by the Neck (Penguin, 1961).

Radzinowicz, L., History of English Criminal Law, Vol. 1 (Stevens, 1948).

Sellin, T., Capital Punishment (Harper and Row, 1967).

Tuttle, E., The Crusade against Capital Punishment in Great Britain (Stevens, 1961).

and see the ingenious:

" Is there such a thing as capital punishment?"—Zelmanowits (1961–62) 2 B.J.Crim. 78.

(*b*) *Corporal punishment*

A very full survey is contained in the two Government publications referred to in the text:

Report of the Departmental Committee on Corporal Punishment 1938 (Cmd. 5684).

Corporal Punishment (A.C.T.O.) 1960 (Cmnd. 1213).

Chapter 8

FINANCIAL ASPECTS

Costs in Criminal Cases

The usual legal rule, like that of the games player, is loser pays. This gives rise to twin expectations. The convicted criminal must expect to pay at least some of the costs of his prosecution; the accused who secures a dismissal of the charges laid against him might expect to be recompensed for his expenses. Despite this apparent simplicity of the basic rule there is considerable misunderstanding and confusion about costs.

The award of costs against the convicted criminal is fairly usual—it is particularly so in summary offences and in indictable offences which are based on fraudulent monetary gain. The powers to award costs are set out in the Costs in Criminal Cases Act 1952. The chief problem of costs against a convicted criminal is that of fixing an appropriate amount. The court must fix a sum—it cannot just order that costs be paid.[1] It would seem normal practice for a court to have in mind the total commitment it desires a criminal to undertake. It can then think in terms of fine and costs, or of course imprisonment and costs, within the global figure.

Of far greater interest is the problem of the award of costs to the defendant whose defence has been successful or against whom no case has been presented. The best place to begin a discussion of this problem is perhaps the practice direction given by the Lord Chief Justice in 1959.[2] He pointed out that there were two opposing views. One felt that costs should only be awarded where the prosecution had done something wrong. On the other hand it is sometimes maintained that acquittal should carry with it the expectation of costs. Adoption of either of these extreme views was said to be a fetter on the discretion of courts in whose power costs lie. This is not a very convincing argument, there could still be a wide discretion to depart from whatever principle was established. The practice note left the matter somewhat vague, ruling that the matter was one for the discretion of the court. Costs should certainly

1 *Pwllheli Justices, ex p. Soane* [1948] 2 All E.R. 815.
2 [1959] 3 All E.R. 471.

be awarded if the prosecution was unreasonable, either in being started or continued. On the other hand the fact that a judge felt that a jury's verdict was perverse or unduly lenient should not prejudice against the award of costs. The earlier emphasis that costs should only be awarded in exceptional cases, particularly where the prosecution was at fault, was certainly corrected but in the interests of flexibility certainty of rule had not been achieved. Indeed in a case decided very soon afterwards the judge had to make it very clear that the award of costs was not a reflection upon the conduct or propriety of the prosecution.[3]

The position remains roughly the same. There is still a lingering feeling that the award of costs is in the nature of a penalty against one side. We have seen that it is certainly, and perhaps usefully, so regarded when fixing penalties against a person who has been convicted. Unfortunately the same feeling may inhibit the compensation of a person who has been acquitted. Thus in a more recent case the magistrates fixed a penalty on a charge saying that they were taking into account another charge on which the accused was not guilty because of a technicality. This was clearly improper and the fine was reduced on appeal. The question of costs was raised and the court having sympathy for the defendant awarded him costs but expressed some doubt as to their powers. The Divisional Court ruled that costs should not have been awarded and said that the police were only doing their duty in appearing as respondents at the appeal. In view of this an order that they should pay costs was inappropriate.[4] This case clearly continues the " fault " principle as at least one of the bases for the award of costs.

Where the appeal is by way of certiorari, that is for review of the lower court's action, fault seems clearly to be the test. Thus where an appellant claimed that he had been wrongly disqualified in his absence the Divisional Court ruled that an order for costs would only be made if the lower court had " behaved badly, either flouting decisions of the court or having been guilty of some outrageous conduct."[5] Again the matter is looked at as " punitive " rather than " compensatory."

The reluctance of the courts to regard costs as a method

[3] *Sansbury* [1959] 1 W.L.R. 1091.
[4] *David* v. *Commissioners of Police for the Metropolis* [1962] 2 Q.B. 135.
[5] *Amersham Justices, ex p. Fanthorne* [1964] Crim.L.R. 825. It is an annoying technicality that a withdrawal of a summons precludes an order for costs against the prosecution, *Phipps, ex p. Alton* [1964] 2 Q.B. 420.

of compensating an innocent man put to trouble and expense seems well established. It is not merely confined to those cases where the court is virtually expressing its doubts about the "innocent" label and it would seem that if costs are to be regarded as compensatory then it will have to be achieved by legislation. Once the Criminal Justice Act 1967 puts legal aid in criminal cases on the footing of contributions by the accused then the case for a change in practice on costs will be made stronger.

Compensation for Victims of Crimes

It is said all too often that penologists are only interested in the offender, and ignore the victim of criminal behaviour. In one, rather academic, sense this used to be true: criminological research was directed almost entirely at the offender. More recently, research workers have realised that the victim, and his relationship to the offenders, repays study; the deplorable term "victimology" has been coined to describe it.

The complaint is, of course, much more concerned with interest in a material sense. Opponents of penal reform can paint a pathetic picture. The criminal, newly convicted of a foul offence, is taken to a warm and well-equipped building, perhaps without locks or bars and situated in attractive rural surroundings. He has fine athletic and gymnastic facilities, prompt medical attention, television, a library within easy walking distance, and food which may be better than anything he had outside. The victim is patched up by the Health Service, and then quite neglected apart from a day or two spent waiting in the corridors of a draughty court building waiting for an ordeal by cross-examination in the witness-box.

The defects in this argument are obvious and need not be spelt out. Their existence must not be allowed to distract attention from the fact that legal provision for victims of crimes is inadequate if it is accepted that a victim should receive full compensation for damage to his property and, so far as it can be expressed in monetary terms, for injury to himself.

Legal remedies

Almost any crime which results in injury to person or property is also a tort, a civil wrong for which the victim can obtain damages from the wrongdoer. Someone who is attacked, whose property is stolen or damaged, or whose house is broken into, can recover damages in a civil action, subject to the various rules of the law of torts.

In theory this is an answer to the complaint that victims of crimes receive no compensation. The law offers them a remedy, available on request. In practice, the remedy is almost always useless; the law of torts is hardly ever invoked by the victim of crime.[6]

There are several reasons for this. The majority of crimes known to the police are never cleared up; without an identified defendant a civil action is impossible. Even if the offender is identified there are problems of evidence. In any event, civil proceedings based on tort cannot be combined with criminal proceedings, as they can in some other countries,[7] so the trouble and expense of separate proceedings have to be faced. Most important of all, proceedings are unavailing if the defendant has no money or other means; a judgment which cannot be enforced is cold comfort.

To meet some of these difficulties there are a number of legal provisions allowing compensation to be ordered by the criminal trial court. Their scope is limited, and the identification and conviction of the offender is a condition precedent for the award of compensation.

The most general provision derives from the Forfeiture Act 1870.[8] In its present form this authorises compensation to the amount of £400 for loss of or damage to property as a result of an indictable offence. It does not apply to loss or damage arising out of "the presence of a motor vehicle on a road."[9]

Where an offender is put on probation, or an order conditionally discharging him is made, he can be ordered to pay compensation to the victim. This covers "injury" as well as "loss," but is usually only available in minor cases (far more serious offences would attract a greater penalty) and in magistrates' courts the maximum award is £100.[10]

6 But see *Barclays Bank Ltd.* v. *Cole* [1967] 2 Q.B. 738 in which the bank obtained judgment for £52,250 against a robber; the action was based on the count for money had and received and on the tort of trespass.

7 *e.g.*, the German *Adhäsionprozess*; see the comparative study in Schafer, *Restitution to Victims of Crime.*

8 s. 4, as amended by the Criminal Law Act 1967, Sched. 2, para. 9, and applied by Magistrates' Courts Act 1952, s. 34.

9 *Quaere* as to the effect of this when the car swerves off the road, damaging property.

10 Criminal Justice Act 1948, s. 11 (2); compensation payments cannot be made conditions in the court order itself, but must be enforced as an order for costs: *ibid.* s. 11 (3).

Special powers exist where the damage is caused by particular offences or in special ways. Under the Riot (Damages) Act 1886,[11] compensation is payable out of the local police rate for damage to buildings, or property within buildings, by persons " riotously and tumultuously assembled together." Before compensation is payable the elements of a riot must be established: at least three persons assembled for a common purpose and resolved to help one another meet opposition, by force if necessary, must carry out their purpose, and use such force or violence as alarms at least one person of reasonable firmness and courage.[12] Many gangs of robbers must satisfy those requirements but their assembly must also be " tumultuous," [13] and that requirement greatly narrows the scope of the Act: few robbers attract public attention to themselves.

Where the offence is larceny or malicious damage, other statutory provisions may help. The Larceny Act 1916 provides for the making of restitution orders, revesting the property in the original owner after the offender has been convicted.[14] It also provides for compensation to be payable to an innocent purchaser forced to surrender the goods out of money found on the thief at the time of his arrest.[15] In malicious damage cases, compensation may be ordered after a summary conviction for causing damage of a sum of not more than £100.[16]

Finally, the higher courts can reward individuals who have been " active in or towards the apprehension of " persons charged with certain offences, to compensate them for their expenses, exertions, and loss of time.[17] In the most recent reported case, a girl was rewarded after she went to the aid of a policeman who had been knocked unconscious and was surrounded by a hostile crowd; she summoned help by blowing his whistle.[18]

11 s. 2.

12 *Field* v. *Metropolitan Police Receiver* [1907] 2 K.B. 853.

13 *J. W. Dwyer Ltd.* v. *Metropolitan Police District Receiver* [1967] 2 Q.B. 970.

14 Larceny Act 1916, s. 45 (1) (2). This applies when the prosecution is " by or on behalf of the owner "; and restitution orders will not be made when there is any doubt as to the owner's identity: see *Stamp* v. *U.D.T.* [1967] 1 All E.R. 251. The section will be replaced in 1969 by the Theft Act 1968, s. 28.

15 *Ibid.* s. 45 (3). The whole of s. 45 applies in magistrates' courts: Magistrates' Courts Act 1952, s. 33.

16 Criminal Justice Administration Act 1914, s. 14, as amended by Malicious Damage Act 1964.

17 Criminal Law Act 1826, s. 28 (assizes); Criminal Justice Administration Act 1851, s. 8 (quarter sessions: maximum £5).

18 *Platt and Sines* (1905) 69 J.P. 424.

None of these legal remedies covers the field adequately. Victims of crimes of violence who sustain personal injuries are often left with no effective legal remedy, and their plight often excites public sympathy and support. This state of affairs led to a demand for some form of state compensation for such victims.

Compensation by the state

Leading proponents of the idea of a state compensation scheme were the late Margery Fry, who wrote an unusually influential newspaper article on the subject which stimulated great interest,[19] and Mr. Reginald Prentice, M.P., who introduced a Private Member's Bill on several occasions.

One problem which faced the advocates of state compensation was finding a sound justification for state action. Why should the state do more than provide the possibility of redress through the civil law? A number of arguments were relied on [20]:

1. It was said that there existed a duty resting upon the state to prevent criminal offences, and a duty to compensate citizens who suffered through its failure to prevent them. The Riot (Damages) Act 1886 was seen as a partial application of the principle. Governments do maintain police forces, and do endeavour to maintain law and order; but this does not establish a duty to compensate for every criminal act. Governments sometimes operate a Health Service; they do not compensate those whom medicine cannot help. In undertaking compensation in cases of riotous and tumultuous assemblies, where it is impossible to identify an individual offender, the state is making special provision to meet special hardship.

2. It was said that citizens were discouraged by the state from safeguarding their own interests; the law of firearms discourages the carrying of weapons for possible use in self-defence. The same law discourages the carrying of weapons for possible use in the commission of crimes of violence; the argument cuts both ways with equal vigour.

3. It was said that imprisonment as the result of state actions prevented the offender earning the money with which to satisfy a judgment obtained in a civil action. The state should provide the money directly. There is some truth in this argument, but

[19] *The Observer*, July 7, 1957.

[20] See the Report of "Justice": *Compensation for Victims of Crimes of Violence*, 1962, p. 3 *et seq.*, and the White Paper of the same title, Cmnd. 1406 (1961). *Cf.* Cross, *The Listener*, May 16, 1963.

it greatly underestimates the other difficulties in obtaining and enforcing a judgment; and few victims would be happy if punishment were *not* imposed.

The Working Party which reported in the 1961 White Paper rejected these arguments as " fallacious and dangerous." They advanced a " more practical " ground:

> " that although the Welfare State helps the victims of many kinds of misfortune, it does nothing for the victims of crimes of violence as such, notwithstanding that they are largely deprived of the means of self-protection and in most cases have no effective remedy at law. There is an argument for filling this gap, based mainly on considerations of sympathy for the innocent victim, but falling short of the acceptance of any bounden duty to mitigate the victim's hardship." [21]

This argument was ultimately accepted as the basis for a compensation scheme,[22] but the ambiguity of " considerations of sympathy " has caused some practical difficulties.[23]

Criminal Injuries Compensation Scheme

The acceptance of the principle of state compensation was by no means the end of all controversy. The scope of the Scheme, the nature of the awards to be made, and the administrative machinery to be used, all presented problems and gave rise to disagreements. These can be followed in the official papers and debates leading up to the introduction of the Scheme.[24]

The Criminal Injuries Compensation Scheme came into force in August 1964. Under it, a Criminal Injuries Compensation Board is empowered to make *ex gratia* payments to applicants whose cases fall within the scope of the Scheme.

The Scheme is experimental, and on a most unusual non-statutory basis. The Scheme was debated by both Houses of Parliament, and its funds have to be voted in the usual way; but there is no legislation, the Scheme has been amended by

21 Cmnd. 1406, para. 18.

22 See *per* Lord Dilhorne L.C., 257 Parliamentary Debates (Lords), col. 1353.

23 See under " Applicant's responsibility " *infra*, pp. 310–311.

24 In addition to those already cited see the report of a Conservative Party committee published in 1962; the White Paper containing the draft scheme, Compensation for Victims of Crimes of Violence (Cmnd. 2323); and debates at 694 Parliamentary Debates (Commons), col. 1127, and 257 Parliamentary Debates (Lords), col. 1351.

ministerial announcement, and the whole thing can only be explained as a rather unusual exercise of the royal prerogative.[25] This may intrigue, and perhaps alarm, students of the constitution, but the practical effects have been beneficial.

Amendment of the Scheme has been easy, and the detailed rules have been worked out by the Board in the light of their experience. The rules have grown up in a case-law fashion, rather than as a result of the interpretation of the draftsman's handiwork. Allocations can be made to " deserving cases by sympathetic administrators, without all the paraphernalia to entitlement, rights at law, and tribunals " [26]; though, as will be seen, the courts can intervene in some cases—a possibility not foreseen in 1964.

The scope of the Scheme

This type of case within the Scheme is described in paragraphs 5 to 8 reproduced here:

> 5. The Board will entertain applications for *ex gratia* payment of compensation in those cases where:
>
> (a) the applicant, or, in the case of an application by a spouse or dependant (see para. 11 below), the deceased, suffered personal injury directly attributable either to a criminal offence or to an arrest or attempted arrest of an offender or suspected offender or to the prevention or attempted prevention of an offence or to the giving of help to any constable who is engaged in arresting or attempting to arrest an offender or suspected offender or preventing or attempting to prevent an offence, where such injury occurs in Great Britain or on a British vessel or aircraft;
>
> (b) the injury was incurred after the commencement of the Scheme; and
>
> (c) the injury gave rise to at least three weeks' loss of earnings or is an injury for which compensation of not less than £50 would be awarded; and
>
> (d) the circumstances of the injury have been reported to the police without delay or have been the subject of criminal proceedings in the courts; and
>
> (e) the applicant is prepared to submit to such medical examination as the Board may require.

25 *Criminal Injuries Compensation Board, ex p. Lain* [1967] 2 Q.B. 864.
26 Lord Denning, 245 Parliamentary Debates (Lords), col. 274.

6. The Board will scrutinise with particular care all applications in respect of sexual offences or other offences arising out of a sexual relationship, in order to determine whether there was any responsibility, either because of provocation or otherwise, on the part of the victim (see para. 12 below), and they will especially have regard to any delay that has occurred in submitting the application. Provided, however, that the circumstances have been immediately reported to the police, the Board will consider applications for compensation arising out of rape and sexual assaults, both in respect of pain, suffering, and shock and in respect of loss of earnings due to pregnancy resulting from rape and, where the victim is ineligible for a maternity grant under the National Insurance Scheme, in respect of the expenses of childbirth. Compensation will not be payable for the maintenance of any child born as a result of a sexual offence.

7. Offences committed against a member of the offender's family living with him at the time will be excluded altogether.

8. Motoring offences will also be excluded from the Scheme, except where the motor-vehicle has been used as a weapon—*i.e.*, in a deliberate attempt to run the victim down.

Personal injury

The Scheme is limited to compensation for personal injuries; there is no compensation for crimes against property. To extend the Scheme to property cases would be prodigiously expensive, and would invite fraudulent claims. Those cases do not excite the same "considerations of sympathy," and are generally covered, or at least coverable, by insurance. Insurance is possible where personal injury is concerned, but few people seek to guard against the remote possibility of their being the victims of some criminal attack.

Directly attributable . . . to a criminal offence

The Scheme contains no list of offences to which it applies. It is possible that some future legislation will contain a schedule of offences, as does the New Zealand scheme, and as suggested by many before the English Scheme was introduced.[27] The

[27] Criminal Injuries Compensation Act (N.Z.) 1963, s. 17 and Sched.; see Harris, in *The A. G. Davis Essays in Law*, pp. 45 *et seq.* *Cf.* the "Justice" and Conservative Party proposals.

Board is compiling a list of offences which occur in its cases.

The first draft of the English Scheme spoke of offences "involving the use of force." These words are not in the final Scheme, and this has enabled the Board to make an award where the offence was arson.[28] Despite the unqualified terms of the Scheme, it does not extend to offences involving breach of some duty under the Factories Acts or similar legislation.[29]

The phrase "directly attributable" has given the Board some difficulty. In one case,[30] an underground installation of the R.A.F. was set on fire by an arsonist. Three firemen died while fighting the fire; they lost their way in the underground passages and died from exposure to heat, or in one case, the exhaustion of the oxygen supply. An award was made. The Board decided that their task was to discover the effective or immediate cause of the injury, the *causa causans*, or the proximate cause. In the case before them, there was an unbroken chain of causation from the arson to the injury and death.

In a case on the other side of the line,[31] the death of a girl passenger in an accident to a stolen car was held not to be directly attributable to the offence.

In every case, the applicant must prove, on the balance of probabilities that his injuries were caused by a criminal offence.[32]

Reported to the police without delay

Whether there has been unreasonable delay is obviously a question of fact, which will vary with the nature of the offence and other circumstances. From the start the Board interpreted this rule liberally, holding that a hospital patient could not be expected to report the case while ill.[33] Similar difficulties in other cases led to instructions from the Home Secretary that the strict requirement of prompt reporting to the police could be waived where the Board was satisfied of the bona fides of

[28] Case H.62, discussed below.
[29] Case H.3 [1965] Crim.L.R. 184. See also the Board's Second Report, p. 10 (negligent control of dog outside Scheme). Short reports of the Board's decisions are published in duplicated form monthly and are obtainable from the Board's offices; in 1965 and 1966, some of these reports were reproduced in the *Criminal Law Review*. The case number when prefixed by the letter H indicates a hearing before three members.
[30] Case H.62, July 1967.
[31] Case H.60, June 1967.
[32] Case H.12, November 1965 [1966] Crim.L.R. 121.
[33] Case H.1 [1965] Crim.L.R. 183.

the applicant [34]; the rule was intended to provide a test of good faith, not to be an absolute bar.

Sexual cases

In the discussion leading to the introduction of the Scheme, sexual offences received much attention. It was suggested that fraudulent claims might be numerous, and that provocation considerations would give difficulty. This anxiety is reflected in the terms of paragraph 6. In practice, there have been few claims, and almost all have been cases where the offence had resulted in a conviction.[35]

Family cases

"Family" has a very flexible meaning. It includes a "common law wife" or mistress,[36] but apparently not an illegitimate child.[37] The whole rule excluding offences committed against a member of the offender's family has been sharply criticised [38]: anxiety about fraudulent claims, difficulties in assessing blame, and the fear that the offender himself might benefit from the award are arguments for the present rule.

Motoring offences

Injuries arising out of motoring offences will usually be covered in insurance or will be compensated by the Motor Insurers' Bureau Scheme. This justifies the rule in paragraph 8, but its interpretation has proved difficult. An applicant injured in an incident involving a "get-away" car being chased by the police received an award under the Criminal Injuries Scheme: his injuries were directly attributable to the original robbery from the site of which the offenders were fleeing.[39] A very similar case had earlier led to a quite different conclusion.[40]

The Scheme talks of "motoring" not "road traffic" offences; dangerous riding of a bicycle is within the scheme! [41]

[34] 733 Parliamentary Debates (Commons), col. 154; see Case H.59, June 1967 (a prisoner need only report case to prison authorities), and Board's second report, para. 21.

[35] Board's second report, para. 39.

[36] Case H.19 [1966] Crim.L.R. 351.

[37] Case A.33 (before a single member) [1965] Crim.L.R. 505.

[38] Samuels, 17 Univ.Toronto L.J. 31–33.

[39] Case H.28 [1966] Crim.L.R. 461.

[40] Case B.77 (before a single member) [1966] Crim.L.R. 237.

[41] Case A.430, June 1967.

Offender not criminally responsible

In a number of cases presented to the Board in its first 18 months, the injury was caused by conduct which would have been an offence were it not that the actor was mentally disturbed or a child below the age of 10. After these cases had been referred to him, the Home Secretary announced that they were to be treated as within the Scheme.[42]

Nature of compensation payments

The basis of compensation and the type of award made is governed by paragraphs 9 to 14 of the Scheme:

"9. Subject to what is said in the following two paragraphs, compensation will be assessed on the basis of common law damages[43] and will take the form of a lump sum payment, rather than a periodical pension. More than one payment may, however, sometimes be made—for example, where only a provisional medical assessment can be given in the first instance.[44]

10. Where the victim is alive the amount of compensation will be limited as follows:

(a) the rate of loss of earnings (and, where appropriate, of earning capacity) to be taken into account will not exceed twice the average of industrial earnings at the time that the injury was sustained[45];

(b) there will be no element comparable to exemplary or punitive damages.[46]

11. Where the victim had died, no compensation will be payable for the benefit of his estate,[47] but the Board will be able to entertain claims from his spouse and dependants. For this purpose, compensation will be payable to any person entitled to claim under the Fatal Accidents Acts 1846 to 1959. . . . The amounts of compensation will be

[42] 733 Parliamentary Debates (Commons), col. 154.

[43] Damages at common law seek to take all possible circumstances into account. Included are, *e.g.*, damages for pain and suffering, loss of the amenities of life, loss of expectation of life.

[44] In the first two years of the Scheme, interim awards were made in 6 per cent. of cases.

[45] *Cf.* para. 5 (c) above.

[46] *i.e.*, payments ordered not as compensation but to demonstrate the court's displeasure: they are now strictly limited at common law: *Rookes* v. *Barnard* [1964] A.C. 1129.

[47] This is possible in an ordinary civil action: Law Reform (Miscellaneous Provisions) Act 1934.

governed by the same principles as under those provisions. . . .

12. The Board will consider whether because of provocation or otherwise, the victim of the crime bears any responsibility for it, and in accordance with its assessment of the degree of responsibility, will reduce the amount of compensation or reject the claim altogether.

13. Where applicable, the compensation will also be reduced by the amount of any payments from public funds accruing, as a result of the injury or death, to the benefit of the person to whom the award is made.

14. The Board will have a discretion to make special arrangements for the administration of any sum payable to an infant." [48]

Two matters dealt with in these paragraphs require special attention.

Payments from other public funds

The provisions of paragraph 13 are, at first sight, highly desirable. Without them, an applicant might receive benefits from two sources, receiving public funds in each case. The argument is that once compensated from public funds, the applicant is to that extent not deserving of further sympathy, not expressed in money at least.

As the Board themselves pointed out in their second report,[49] this rule has odd effects in practice. If a policeman and an employee of a private security organisation were both killed on duty, the claim by the policeman's widow would be affected by the gratuity and pension she would receive from police funds. The widow of the other man, who might receive a larger sum from the private firm, would receive compensation in full from the Board. A Board ruling to this effect has been upheld by the courts; but the situation is so anomalous that reconsideration is clearly needed.[50]

Applicant's responsibility

The interpretation of paragraph 12 has proved extremely

48 Awards up to £500 are paid into a Post Office Savings Bank account controlled by the Board; greater sums are administered by the Public Trustee. Board's First Report, para. 13. In cases of adults incapable of managing their affairs arrangements are made through the Court of Protection.

49 para. 23.

50 *Criminal Injuries Compensation Board, ex p. Lain* [1967] 2 Q.B. 864.

controversial. The paragraph is very widely drawn, and the Board can take note of any element of responsibility on the victim's part.

Two positions can be taken on this issue. If the purpose of the Scheme is to provide a substitute for common law actions, then any victim can come to the Board for full compensation less any element of causal responsibility borne by him. But if the Scheme is intended for "deserving cases,"[51] then a wider range of factors become relevant. For example, if a prostitute is the victim of an assault, her profession is no bar to a civil action against her assailant. But, granted that prostitution is an occupation with known risks, which she voluntarily undertook, is she a "deserving case"?

In practice, the cases have largely concerned fights: no award will be given for injuries sustained in a fight arranged to settle a dispute, unless the offender used some unexpected weapon—a knife in a fist fight—when a reduced award can be made.[52]

Where there is some responsibility on the victim's part, the award is given as a percentage of full compensation. This does not, of course mean that where both parties are equally to blame the applicant will receive 50 per cent. of his claim: both parties will then be 100 per cent. to blame, and no award will be made.

Administration of the Scheme

The Scheme established a body known as the Criminal Injuries Compensation Board, of a Chairman and five other members, all legally qualified.[53] The Board is independent of all government control, though the Home Secretary and the Secretary of State for Scotland can vary the terms of the Scheme, and have done so.

The Scheme provides that the Board's decisions "will not be subject to appeal"[54]; this needs some considerable qualification. Applications are considered, after a preliminary sifting procedure by the Board's staff, by a single member of the Board. Paragraph 17 of the Scheme provides that

> "if the applicant is not satisfied with that decision, whether because no compensation is offered or because he considers

51 *Cf.* Lord Denning, cited *supra*, p. 305.

52 *Cf.* Case N.B.181 (July 1967) (firework thrown in retaliation for similar act earlier same evening: 50 per cent. award).

53 Scheme, para. 1; the first Chairman is His Honour Sir Walker Carter Q.C.

54 Scheme, para. 4.

the amount offered to be inadequate, he will be entitled to a hearing before three other members of the Board, excluding the one who made the initial decision. It will, however, also be open to the single member, when he considers that he cannot reach a just and proper decision, himself to refer the application to three other members of the Board for a hearing." [55]

This hearing by three members is not strictly an appeal, but a new application.[56] Despite the apparent intention of the Scheme, the decisions of the Board are subject to review by the courts, for it is possible to seek certiorari, an order quashing a decision on the ground of an error of law by the Board.[56]

The actual procedure for dealing with an application begins with inquiries by the Board's staff of police and medical witnesses, and of other relevant parties. Their reports are sent to a single member, together with a note of the injuries sustained. The staff maintain an index of injuries, with a record of compensation ordered for each type. The single member is thus provided with full information on which to base a decision.

The index provides a form of precedent system which is especially valuable for the Board as most of their cases involve small amounts of compensation; had they been court cases, they would fall within the county court jurisdiction, and decisions of these courts are seldom reported.

Every case and decision is recorded on punched cards for future reference.[57]

Compensation and other legal remedies

Because of the *ex gratia* nature of the Board's awards, a successful applicant is in no way debarred from bringing a civil action. For the reasons already given, this will rarely assist him. To avoid double benefits, a successful applicant to the Board is required to give an undertaking to repay the sum received by way of compensation so far as he recovers damages as a result of a civil action.[58] One case has occurred, the applicant repaying £338 to the Board having recovered £548 from a court action.[59] The difference in the level of awards is striking, but too much must not be based on a single case.

[55] This later power was added in 1965 at the Board's request: see its first report, para. 14, and 717 Parliamentary Debates (Commons), col. 300.

[56] *Criminal Injuries Compensation Board, ex p. Lain* [1967] 2 Q.B. 864.

[57] Board's second report, para. 4.

[58] Scheme, para. 20.

[59] Case A.264 [1966] Crim.L.R. 405; Board's second report, para. 34.

The working of the Scheme

By the end of August 1967, over £1,900,000 had been paid in compensation; the Scheme had then been in force for just over three years. After a very slow start, during which the Board were concerned at the problem of publicising the Scheme, compensation payments began to average £100,000 a month. This is in line with early estimates of the annual cost of a scheme; the 1961 Working Party Report estimated annual costs of £955,500 or £1,517,000, depending on the machinery adopted.[60]

BIBLIOGRAPHY

The official papers leading up to the introduction of the Compensation Scheme include:

Compensation for Victims of Crimes of Violence 1961 (Cmnd. 1406)

Compensation for Victims of Crimes of Violence 1964 (Cmnd. 2323).

See also the " Justice " report of the same name (Stevens, 1962) and the Conservative Party report (1962).

The Board publishes an Annual Report and Accounts. See also:

HARRIS, D. J., in The A. G. Davis Essays in Law, ed. J. F. Northey (Butterworths, 1965).

SAMUELS, A., " Compensation for Criminal Injuries in Britain " (1967) 17 Univ. of Toronto L.J. 20.

SCHAFER, S., Restitution to Victims of Crime (Stevens, 1960) and a " Round Table " on the subject in (1959) 8 *Journal of Public Law* 193.

[60] Cmnd. 1406, Appendix C.

Chapter 9

THE FUTURE

The legal system in prospect

This book has been prepared at a time when the reform of the legal system is under wide review. Changes have already been made but it could well be that the next few years will see a fundamental recasting of a system of courts which still owes overmuch to the medieval system of assizes. The Royal Commission on Assizes and Quarter Sessions chaired by Lord Beeching is expected to report at any time and it is bound to suggest far-reaching changes. It can confidently be expected that there will be both consolidation of the higher criminal courts and greater regionalisation. Current trends in the organisation of the police forces of the country have already set this pattern and it is one which the Maude Commission on Local Government is also expected to encourage.

The law itself is also in the process of thorough overhaul. Here the existing Criminal Law Revision Committee will continue its work—its mammoth recasting of the law of larceny and kindred offences has become law from the beginning of 1969. The Law Commission will also have an important part to play, they are already proposing to undertake the codification of the criminal law.

The Criminal Justice Act 1967 is openly spoken of as a beginning in the process of change. It is fairly obvious that its changes in the procedure of magistrates' courts as courts of committal for trial are only a half-way house to a simpler structure. It may well be that the civil summons for directions, by which the parties can settle their procedural difficulties simply before an officer of the court, may be a suitable model for the future role of committal magistrates.

It would, however, be idle to suggest that this movement for reform will be as fast as some would like or in the ultimate as comprehensive. There is obviously a great deal in our present system that must be preserved; there is only a certain amount of change that can be acceptable in practice at any one time. Nonetheless the atmosphere of reform is present and it is to be hoped that when the inevitable reaction against continual change finally sets in there will have emerged an efficient legal framework in which the necessary regard for the rights and freedom of the individual is combined with the opportunity to use the growing expertise on the problems of treatment of offenders.

Crime and the treatment of offenders

We can expect no revolution in the penal system. Despite the best endeavours of research workers, we know relatively little about crime and about the operation of the penal system on offenders. Although available information will be more readily accessible when the recommendations of the Perks Committee [1] are put into effect, the problems are not such that they can be "solved" by some sensational breakthrough in research. Future changes in the penal system will continue to be made on the basis of intelligent guesswork,[2] the collection of informed opinion.

Another limiting factor is cost. Most measures of penal reform involve expenditure, which is not popular. The pessimist may enjoy speculating which will survive the longer, the clouds of ignorance or the chill economic climate.

A good deal of attention is likely to be concentrated on the fundamental problems of using institutions for penal treatment. It has become fashionable to doubt whether the constructive aspects of institutional treatment justify the social dislocation caused by imprisonment. Although these arguments may sometimes do less than justice to the work of the prison service, and the successes which are achieved, they have stimulated an examination of some special problems of imprisonment and of the possibilities of developing alternative, non-custodial measures.

Despite the check to the increase in crime revealed in the 1967 statistics, inevitably hailed in various parts of the country as the result of the local experiments carried out in different police areas, there is no clear sign of a reduction in organised crime, leading to serious offences and long prison sentences.

A sub-committee of the Advisory Council on the Penal System has examined the special difficulties inherent in designing a prison regime for the very long-term prisoner. Its report published in mid-1968 contains important recommendations, not

1 Report of the Departmental Committee on Criminal Statistics (Cmnd. 3448).

2 *Cf.* Cross [1966] Crim.L.R. 184, cited *supra*, p. 85.

only for the special group which was its prime concern, but for imprisonment in general

Another special group are prisoners in need of psychiatric help. The Home Office is considering the establishment of a second psychiatric prison on the lines of Grendon.[3] Financial difficulties may well delay this, and perhaps Alvington Prison too.

Another sub-committee of the Advisory Council is examining the possibilities for the development of non-custodial methods. This follows the interest taken in this matter by the abortive Royal Commission on the Penal System. The Commission received evidence advocating various forms of day or weekend centres for adults, ranging from weekend imprisonment (designed to avoid interference with normal employment and to minimise dislocation of the family) to supportive centres akin to day hospitals.[4] The Commission also explored the possibility of extending the system of approved probation hostels to adults.

Similar proposals have been made for young offenders, usually by way of extension of the attendance centre idea. Evening or weekend centres, and day schools for children who might otherwise go to a residential approved school have all been suggested.[5] Sadly, the administrative changes in the management of approved schools, their integration into a comprehensive system of residential establishments for children, may take priority.[6] It is to be hoped that administrative wrangling will not absorb too much precious energy.

There have been many changes in the penal system in the last decade. Those who work within it will be grateful if the pace of change slows for a few years. There will even be an opportunity for reactionary changes when the Murder (Abolition of Death Penalty) Act 1965 has to face renewal.

Any who feel that penal reform has scarcely begun should consider the state of the penal system two or even one hundred years ago. Even the Gladstone Committee of 1895 spoke in terms which alarm the modern reader. Great progress has been

[3] 753 Parliamentary Debates (Commons), col. 150 (November 9, 1968).

[4] R.C.P.S., Vol. 2, pp. 19 and 25 (Magistrates' Assoc.); pp. 214–215 (Free Church Federal Council); Vol. 3, p. 167 (Nat. Assoc. of Probation Officers). See generally, R. H. Maudsley, "The Advantages of Semi-Liberty," *The Times*, April 12, 1965.

[5] R.C.P.S., Vol. 2, p. 10 (Magistrates' Assoc.); pp. 296–297 (Assoc. of Workers for Maladjusted Children); p. 351 (Rainer Foundation). *Cf.* Rose, *Schools for Young Offenders*; and 287 Parliamentary Debates (Lords), col. 1266.

[6] See now *Children in Trouble* considered below.

made since then; even if decisions have been based on intelligent guesswork, the progress seems to have been made in roughly the right direction.

Children in trouble

At the last moment in the preparation of this book has appeared the Home Office White Paper on Children in Trouble.[7] This has replaced the earlier proposals contained in the White Paper published in August 1965 entitled *The Child, the Family and the Young Offender*.[8] As has been noted earlier the proposals in this document to establish family courts met with widespread criticism. The proposals blurred the distinctions between the legal and social aspects of the problem and understandably, as a consequence, were welcomed neither by lawyers nor social workers.

The aims of the earlier White Paper were nonetheless sound. It is clear that the problem of juvenile delinquency is to a large extent a family problem and that wherever possible the family is the right place to tackle it. It was perhaps unrealistic to expect the family unit always to be stable enough to provide a firm basis for this in a fair proportion of the cases which at present come before the courts. The new White Paper may therefore in one sense be regarded as a compromise and perhaps unsatisfactory on that account. This should not be used to prevent advances being made in this area and the success of partial reform may be preferable to attempts to establish a more idealist but impracticable solution.

The basis of the new proposals involves the division of juveniles into three groups—under 10, 10 to under 14, and 14 to under 17. The only type of proceedings possible in the first group who are below the age of criminal responsibility will be the in-need-of-care-and-protection type of case. This will be extended into the next age-group and will form the usual type of dealing with this age of offender. The present criminal juvenile court type of situation will be integrated into the care-and-protection type of proceeding by providing that the commission of an offence shall be a ground for initiating such proceedings parallel with existing grounds such as exposed to moral danger or falling into bad associations. It is provided that the police and Children's Department concerned must

[7] Cmnd. 3601.
[8] Cmnd. 2742.

consult together before deciding whether such proceedings should be brought.

The changes will lead to a variety of reactions to an offence by a child. The police might decide to warn verbally or by formal caution. After discussion with the Children's Department it might be decided that some informal action is all that is required. Finally it might be decided to bring a care-and-protection case. This flexibility is welcome and any criticism must be directed to the somewhat top-heavy double trial that the care-and-protection case may involve. It will, of course, be necessary to establish the offence in the usual way. Once this has been done it is then presumably incumbent upon those taking proceedings, and it may be either the police or the Children's Department, to establish lack of care, protection and guidance such as may be expected from a good parent. If the present nature of care cases is a guide, there will be a marked disparity between the standards and approach required for the two aspects of the new procedure. If the result is to temper in some way the rigidity and formality of the criminal part and to tighten up and give some semblance of shape to the care-and-protection part then there may be a general benefit. But to achieve this there must be considerable modification of present attitudes.

Where the child is 14 and under 17 the normal procedure will remain prosecution. This is to be modified, except in cases of homicide, by providing that it may only be initiated by summons or warrant given by a juvenile court magistrate. There must in this age-group be prior consultation between police and the Children's Department and the magistrate must be told of the views that have been formed.

Perhaps the most fundamental feature of these provisions is the encouragement it gives to co-operation between the various agencies concerned in child welfare and control. It is an obvious opportunity for the police to develop their participation in the social work aspects of crime prevention. The White Paper goes further and envisages that magistrates, the police, probation officers and social workers generally will arrange periodic meetings to review the working of the new procedures. This is a means of integration of effort which could have welcome results.

The White Paper also outlines changes affecting treatment. These are fairly drastic. The approved school order will be abolished and the method for removal of a child from its home will be committal to the care of the local authority. The courts will not lose all their power to provide for specific treatment. New forms of intermediate treatment are proposed falling between the child remaining at home and its being placed in the care of the local authority. This treatment will be of two sorts. The court will be able to fix a period of up to one month of temporary residence, attendance or participation away from the child's home. It will be for the supervisor, the local authority or probation officer to select the most appropriate form of treatment. The second category will involve residence of up to three months away from home. Again the position will be that the court fixes the period and the supervisor chooses the institution.

To meet the new concepts of training the old approved schools, local children's homes, remand homes and centres, reception centres and some voluntary children's homes will be replaced by an integrated system of " community homes." The aim is to provide centres for observation and assessment followed by a wide variety of differing residential establishments to achieve a choice of suitable treatment. Similarly the existing detention and attendance centres for these age-groups will disappear and only the integrated community home system will remain.

Success here depends upon how much real change can be achieved. If all that happens is that existing institutions remain with a different name nothing significant will be achieved except perhaps a measure of disillusionment.

INDEX